Love Letters from World War 2

The letters of Alan & Sheila Stevenson

1941 to 1945

transcribed by Robert Stevenson

Love Letters from World War 2

The letters of Alan & Sheila Stevenson

1941 - 1945

ISBN: 978-0-9955749-0-8

Published by Robert Stevenson Publishing in conjunction with Writersworld, this book is produced entirely in the UK, is available to order from most book shops in the United Kingdom, and is globally available via UK-based Internet book retailers.

Cover Design by Jag Lal

Copy edited by Sue Croft

WRITERSWORLD
2 Bear Close, Woodstock,
Oxfordshire
OX20 1JX
UK
www.writersworld.co.uk

The text pages of this book are produced via an independent certification process that ensures the trees from which the paper is produced comes from well managed sources that exclude the risk of using illegally logged timber while leaving options to use post-consumer recycled paper as well.

This book is dedicated with love and gratitude
to the memory of

Alan Carruth Stevenson
and
Annie Gordon Sheila Steven

Mum & Dad

PREFACE

Fifteen years after my father's death in 1995, at the age of 86, I found a cardboard box in my loft containing 524 letters. I know this is a 'device' used by authors to introduce fictional characters, but in this case it's true!

They were personal letters written during World War 2 between my father, Alan Stevenson, and my mother Sheila. Periodically I looked at this formidable heap of dusty paper, then I read a few random letters and was surprised by the passion and longing that shone through them, in spite of wartime censorship. I wondered if reading such private material was not intrusive, let alone transcribing them. But there they were, neatly packaged and sorted by year; they must surely have wanted their children to read them later. Alan confirms this in a diary, writing as being -

". . . one who hopes to himself that someone - sometime - without bribery - will publish something that I write."

Many letters written by Sheila had no dates on them, but not long before his death (Sheila had died in 1989) Alan had sorted through them and written the year on those lacking it. I concluded he wanted these very personal letters, some day, to be read by his family.

I like to think that as a social commentary and a story this book, intended for family, may have a wider appeal. Other sources include military records and periodic diaries unofficially kept by Alan.

Some letters are missing, some have pages missing. Alan burnt a number of letters and papers after Sheila's death; it is possible some were very personal and he destroyed them.

I began to transcribe the letters in April 2014 with the encouragement of my family. It was a terribly slow process. My mother's writing was not bad but my father's was just awful. However, as I progressed I was rewarded. A new and unsuspected father and mother emerged - vibrant, passionate people who were 'doing their duty' but longed for the end of the war and to be together again with their children.

How much they read! I had never realised how widely read they both were. Alan wanting to be a poet! Sheila fretting to travel and agonising over her first grey hair. Would she be 'an old hag' by the time he got back? They both had a strong sense of their life passing by apart as the war dragged on. I felt privileged, all these years later, to get to know my parents as young people, not only as 'Mum' and 'Dad'.

They are not heroic letters. They are not of awful suffering or fighting - after all, he was a doctor. He went to France when war broke out, retreated to Dunkirk and was taken off by a destroyer. In October 1943 he was sent to Africa to battle mosquitos and disease in the Gold Coast (Ghana) and did not return until June 1945. These letters are just the story of two ordinary people, separated for six years by the Second World War.

So this book is all about Alan Carruth Stevenson, a doctor of medicine, and Annie Gordon Sheila Stevenson (née Steven) known as Sheila, and is dedicated to their memory.

There are 442 letters written between 1941 and 1945. There are a further 82 letters written 1935-1936 before they were married, which cover Alan's struggle for employment in London. I intend to publish them in a separate booklet.

I have resisted the temptation to censor references to my behaviour, or comments that might be considered politically incorrect today.

I want to let the letters speak for themselves and tell their story. The reader may dip in anywhere and they will come alive. I have provided footnotes, introductions to the events of each year, an epilogue and appendices, but they can be ignored - the letters stand on their own.

Where words in a letter are unclear and I could only guess at them, they are printed in *italics*. Where I cannot even guess, they are shown as [*illegible*]. Sheila frequently missed dates out completely, or wrote the day with no month or year. I have tried to work out where her undated letters fit in to the timeline. To show where I have done this, I have in the letter headings made clear that the date is my estimate by showing it *in italics*.

Robert Stevenson
Lymington, Hampshire 2016

TABLE OF CONTENTS

INTRODUCTION

Alan Stevenson married Sheila Steven in 1937. He was a doctor and in 1939 was Deputy Medical Officer of Health in Wakefield, Yorkshire.

He had joined the Territorial Army in 1927 at age 18 as a 2nd Lieutenant in the Highland Light Infantry. As war loomed with Germany, the British army began mobilisation. I was born on 4th June 1939. On 19th July 1939 Alan was transferred to the Royal Army Medical Corps (RAMC) as a Lieutenant. On 30th August 1939 Alan commenced mobilisation at the Royal Victoria Hospital, Netley, Southampton.

In September 1939, when I was three months old, Britain and France declared war on Germany. Alan embarked and sailed to Cherbourg with the BEF (British Expeditionary Force) on 29th September 1939. It was to be six years before he could live with Sheila again. He took with him one of their two Dalmatian dogs, Morlich. The other, Larig, stayed with Sheila. He made it back from Dunkirk (Appendix 2) in

Alan as Major in 1940

June 1940 though Morlich had to be shot and was left in the sand at Bray Dunes.

All Alan's letters right up till May 1945 were censored, which must have cramped his style, though I doubt any censor could read his writing. When the war started, Sheila had been left behind on her own in their rented house in Wakefield, with me. Wakefield then was a drab and dirty industrial town. There was food and clothing rationing, and coal for heating was very hard to get. Petrol rationing was introduced in 1939 and most cars, including Alan's old Alvis, were immediately laid up on bricks.

Rationing was introduced early in 1940 and food rationing finally ended 9 years after the war ended, on 4th July 1954, when restrictions on the sale and purchase of meat and bacon were lifted. I remember vividly my first-ever ice cream in 1953. I was 14 and ate so much of it I was ill.

Hitler shot himself on 30th April 1945 (having poisoned his new wife and his dog), and Germany surrendered unconditionally on 8th May 1945.

Japan, however, remained, with the real possibility of Alan being sent east to Burma (now Myanmar) for a five-year tour straight from Africa. The grim belief was that the Japanese would fight to the death in defence of their home islands as they had done in the Pacific. The atom bomb brought a blessed - to the Allies - end to the Pacific war. It is controversial now but then few of the Allies saw it as anything but a universal saviour. It undoubtedly saved tens of thousands of Allied and Japanese lives.

Sheila was lucky - she got her husband back - and uninjured. He had had a 'good war' ending up as full Colonel.

Alan loved Africa and matured. He had been sent there to work primarily on mosquito control. Many allied soldiers, British and American, transited through West Africa, and in World War 1 troops had suffered high casualties from malaria. This time the Army were determined not to lose men that way, and were successful!

His work in Africa became the foundation of a career in Tropical Medicine, Genetics and Research. The letters about this land of warmth, no rationing, servants, exciting new experiences, flying, swimming and canoeing, must have been hard to bear for Sheila in dirty Wakefield, freezing cold with two demanding small boys - by this time my brother David had been born - who seemed to be ill much of the time.

Robert Stevenson 2016

Timeline: Key Dates

1909 Jan 27th	Alan Carruth Stevenson is born
1913 Aug 2nd	Sheila (Annie Gordon Sheila) Steven is born
1930	Alan & Sheila meet for first time
1933 Jan	Hitler becomes German Chancellor
1936	Alan & Sheila become formally engaged
1937 Mar 25th	Sheila & Alan get married and go to Wakefield
1939 Mar 15th	Germany occupies Czechoslovakia
1939 Apr 27th	Conscription introduced in UK
1939 Jun 4th	Robert is born
1939 Aug 30th	Alan commences mobilisation at Royal Victoria Hospital, Netley, Southampton
1939 Sep 1st	Germany invades Poland
1939 Sep 3rd	Britain declares war on Germany
1939 Sep 29th.	Alan sails from Southampton and arrives Cherbourg, France, with BEF
1940 Jun 1st	Alan evacuated from beach at Dunkirk
1940 Jun 10th	Italy declares war on Great Britain & France
1941 Jun 22nd	Germany invades Russia
1941 Dec 7th	Japan bombs USA naval base at Pearl Harbour
1941 Dec 8th	Japan declares war on the USA & Britain
1941 Dec 11th	Germany declares war on the USA
1942 Apr 30th	David is born
1943 Oct 13th	Alan leaves Sheila and sails for Africa
1943 Nov 2nd	Alan arrives in at Accra, Gold Coast, Africa
1944 Jun 6th	D-Day. The Allies invade France
1945 Apr 30th	Hitler commits suicide
1945 May 8th	Germany unconditionally surrenders
1945 Jun 24th	Alan returns from Africa. Posted to Chester
1945 Jul 27th	Last letter, from Chester
1945 Aug 6th	The 1st atom bomb is dropped on Hiroshima
1945 Aug 9th	A 2nd atom bomb is dropped on Nagasaki
1945 Sep 2nd	Japan unconditionally surrenders
1945 Dec 27th	Army releases Alan from active military duty

DRAMATIS PERSONÆ

Alan Carruth Stevenson born 1909 in Glasgow, son of Allan Stevenson, CBE, and Christine Kennedy Lawson. Sisters Moira and Doreen. Attended Glasgow Academy and Glasgow University. BSc 1930, MB, ChB 1933, MD 1946. Captained Glasgow University Rugby team, Shot 3 times for the Territorial Army at Bisley.

Sheila (Annie Gordon Sheila) Steven born 1913 daughter of James (Jimmy) Steven, Bronze-founder and Managing Director of Steven & Struthers. An only child, educated at home. Married Alan in 1937. She had three children, Robert born 1939, David born 1942 and Gill (Aileen Gillian) born1947.

Sheila was a keen member of Scottish Flying Club. Her cousin, Robert Faulds, after whom I was named, was a pilot.

The Stevensons

The Stevensons were a farming family at Balgray Farm near Beith in Ayrshire (now sadly demolished). They had been there for over 100 years. Allan Stevenson (Alan's father) left the farm at about 16 and walked into Glasgow where he got an apprenticeship in the booming shipbuilding business. He worked his way up to be a director of David Rowan & Co. He became President of the Institute of Engineers and Shipbuilding in Scotland, and Deputy Director Merchant Shipbuilding and Repairs during WW2. He was awarded the CBE (Commander of the British Empire) in 1948 for his services to ship repair during the war. Alan's mother, Christina Lawson, was a Glasgow girl. Alan went to Glasgow Academy and then to Glasgow University to study medicine.

The Stevens

Sheila's father, James Steven, known as Jimmy, inherited a Bronze Founding company, Steven & Struthers, from his father. Her mother was Jessie Helen Hodge, known as Mamie.

James Steven (Jimmy), Sheila's father
Jessie Steven (Mamie), Sheila's mother
Christina Stevenson, Alan's mother
Allan Stevenson, Alan's father

OTHER PLAYERS

Aunt Aggie: Agnes Steven born 1878, James (Jimmy) Steven's sister and Sheila's aunt. Married William Stephens (Uncle Willie) born 1876, Jimmy's brother in law. They had a son William (Bill) born 1910 and a daughter Alice (Bunty). This William married Aileen. They had a son, William, known as Young Bill, born 1942.

Aileen (or Eileen) Winifred **Stephens, nee Davis:** lived in London and suffered from the air raids. She stayed with Sheila in Wakefield at one time. Born 1916, died Eastbourne May 2005. Married Williams Stephens in Taunton, Somerset, in January 1941.

Dr Frank (Frankie) Allardine: Medical Officer of Health (MOH) in Wakefield and consequently Alan's boss before Alan left to join the army.

Aunt Bet: Bethia Campbell Hodge, Mamie's sister and Sheila's aunt.

Aunt Daisy: Margaret Connell Hodge, sister to Jessie (Mamie) Hodge and Sheila's maternal aunt. The name Daisy was often short for Margaret, the French for Margaret - Marguerite - being French for a daisy. She married Alexander Crawford and lived at Crawford Lodge, Ardrossan not far from Seamill. They were apparently childless and appear to have kept Sheila's dog Tilda. (see Appendix 3 on Dogs about Tilda.)

Doreen Stevenson: Alan's younger sister, born 1915, died 2008. Doreen qualified as a doctor in Glasgow and served in the Royal Navy. She claimed to be the first woman ever to go to sea in a Royal Navy ship as an officer. She married Dr Thomas Colver and had four children - my cousins Allan, Graham, Hilary and Christine. All followed the parents into the medical profession, Christine becoming a nurse and the others doctors.

Downe - Richard Dawnay: 10th Viscount Downe (1913-1965) Page of Honour to King George V. OBE 1945. Assembled a notable collection of Rembrandt etchings.

Steven Faulds: son of Archibald Galbraith Faulds and Janet Boyd Steven, another of Jimmy's sisters and cousin by marriage to Shelia. Doctor in Carlisle, married to May Morrison.

John Fergie, John: long-time friend of Alan's and was at Glasgow University with him.

Frankie: see Dr Frank Allardine

Sheila Hipson: sub-let 66 Manygates Lane, Wakefield, to Hipson when she was in Scotland.

James Duncan Hodge: Elder brother to Mamie and Sheila's maternal uncle. Married Violet née Hollebone.

Kenny MacLennan: see Appendix 5

Lannie MacLennan: see Appendix 5

Mamie: Jessie Helen Steven née Hodge, Sheila's mother, always known as Mamie.

Moira Stevenson: Alan's elder sister, born 1903, died 1951 at age 48. She graduated as a doctor from Glasgow University but suffered from poor health and never married. She was loved and much mourned by her siblings.

Muriel Moyes: wife of Andy McKie

Andrew (Andy) McKie: a Glasgow dentist married to Muriel and friend of Alan & Sheila

Moira Stevenson

Monica & Jim McVicars: friends of Alan and Sheila in Wakefield. Monica was good company for Sheila as both husbands were away at the war. Apparently their son Anthony and I did not get on well.

Nancy (Actually Agnes) Faulds & May Faulds: Sheila's cousins, daughters of Janet Steven and Archibald Faulds

Aunt Nettie: I can only think this was another nickname for Margaret Hodge, or Aunt Daisy. See under Daisy.

Nonie Andrew Julian Norman Brown: one of Sheila's 13 Brown cousins. His mother was Sarah Armour Steven, Jimmy's sister.

Nonie married in 1954 at the age of 47.

James Peebles: another old University medical friend of Alan's.

Aunt Sadie Brown: cousin of Sheila's. Later known as 'Sadie the Axe' after she assaulted her husband with one.

Aunt Sara: Sarah Helen Brown, born 1903, daughter of Agnes Henderson & John Steven, sister of James (Jimmy) Steven.

Sibbald: owner of 'Barona', 30 Greenock Road in Largs, where David was born. Sheila had rented the house, presumably to be near her family, and Sibbald complained of damage.

Sister Brown: the mysterious 'Sister', apparently a nurse cum help cum babysitter who was often called on until she was dismissed by Sheila in distressing circumstances.

William (Bill) Stephens: born 1910, son of Aunt Aggie & Uncle Willie. Bill was Sheila's first cousin by marriage. He married Aileen and they had a son, William Stephens, known as 'Young Bill', in 1942.

Violet Hodge: married to James Duncan Hodge, Sheila's uncle. Lived in Belfast. She had no children.

Brigadier Wigmore: James Buckley Aquilla Wigmore, born 1887, died 1962. Entered Gonville & Caius College, Cambridge, 1905. Captain 1916. Brigadier 1941. District Director of Medical Services, West Africa. Variously referred to as Wiggy, Wiggie, the Wig, Col Wig. Wigmore was Alan's superior officer in Tunbridge Wells and seems to have been a keen supporter. Wigmore also turns up in the Gold Coast and certainly did all he could to help Alan. See testimonial Appendix 4. He recommended Alan for an OBE.

William Stephens: see Aunt Aggie.

Uncle Willie, William Stephens: see Aunt Aggie for the various Stephens.

Charlie Whittaker and his sister: she is always referred to as "Miss Whittaker" - a couple in Wakefield, friendly with Sheila.

1941

Notes On 1941

There was just the one letter. Britain's early sweeping victories against the Italians in North Africa were countered in February 1941 by Hitler's dispatch of the Africa Corp, under General Erwin Rommel, to Libya where they inflicted a series of defeats on British forces. In April 1941 Germany invaded Russia (with whom they had a 'pact of friendship') with an army of 3 million men.

On 7th December 1941 Japan attacked Pearl Harbour, the great American naval base in Hawaii, and declared war on the United States of America and Britain. On December 11th 1941 Germany and Italy[1] also declared war on America. The number of our enemies was growing.

Since Dunkirk in May 1940 and the French surrender, Britain had stood alone with her Empire against Germany and the news had all been of failure and defeat. But by the end of 1941 Britain had powerful new allies in the USA and Russia. 'Our' war had become a World War.

In 1941 Alan was based at HQ 5th Corps, Home Forces. This was variously in Boyce Barracks, Crookham (HQ of RAMC), or Aldershot. Certainly Alan & Sheila rented the Malt House at Crookham nearby.

Addresses

The only full addresses that matter in 1941 were:

The Malt House, Gally Hill Road, Church Crookham, Hampshire. Sheila stayed there and Alan joined her from HQ in Aldershot whenever possible.

HQ 5th Corps, Home Forces. Aldershot, Hampshire. He was DADH. (Deputy Assistant Director of Hygiene)

66 Manygates Lane, Wakefield, Yorkshire. This is the house Alan rented when he moved to Wakefield to take up his job as Deputy Officer of Health (DOH) in December 1936.

---

[1] Italy had declared war on Britain in January 1940.

Pictures taken at The Malt House, Crookham, Fleet, late 1940

3rd Sep 1941, Alan, HQ 5th Corps, Aldershot, to Sheila
My Dear,[1]

I got in here for lunch after a good journey. It's a bit of a heat-wave here & I hope it's the same with you. I'm not going to *Newtarbet* meanwhile. It's been cancelled in view of the other thing I spoke about but I won't need to be away at that for more than a day at a time.

There is exceedingly good news about my work for it looks as if a big reorganisation would take place with me as Lieut. Col[2] and five Majors under me over a big area. I would have a lot of work and an exceedingly interesting job. Things have been moving since I was away and the Brigadier has recommended this. So I'm vastly cheered by that. Oh I hope you and my wee Robert are enjoying the sun and having a nice time. I'll come and see you early on Monday evening.

There is still no word of the camera but I'm not worried as it's not my responsibility.

So Dear, till Monday. It will not be any good my writing after this. I'll try to phone tonight. I've been praying every night as I did on Sunday night. Love to the twibe[3] & tell them we shall soon have family times again.

Your loving husband, Alan

---

[1] There is no clue as to where this letter was addressed - maybe Wakefield, but could be anywhere.

[2] Quick promotion in war. He was only a Lieutenant in 1939.

[3] 'twibe' is not a mistype.

1942

Notes On 1942

My brother David was born 30th April 1942. We were still living in the rented house in Wakefield, but had gone with Sheila to another rented house, 'Barona', 30 Greenock Road, Largs, in Ayrshire, Scotland, for David's birth. Presumably this was to be near her family and get some support. None of her children were born in a hospital. Alan was there for David's birth so he must have got leave.

In November 1942 at last there was a victory when the Germans and Italians under Rommel were defeated at El Alamein on the Egyptian border and started their long retreat towards Tunisia.

Alan is now 33 and Sheila is 29.

Alan is still at General Headquarters (GHQ), Home Forces. His postal address is the same as before but it's now 12 Corps. Alan has been promoted to Lt Colonel in the Royal Army Medical Corp (RAMC) and is now in Tunbridge Wells. I cannot be sure when this move from Crookham took place. I am presuming he was moved when he joined 12 Corps and he is there, more or less, until October 1943.

It seems Sheila was in Wakefield for most of 1942 but was in Glasgow for Christmas, although Alan could not get leave to be with her.

TW means Tunbridge Wells.

3rd Jun 1942, Alan, HQ 12 Corps, TW, to Sheila

I enjoyed 'Sweet Aloes' at the Repertory Theatre last night but not as much as 'Tony Drowns a Horse' the previous week.

Well my own one the time is nearer every day when we can be together & I exist and live for that time. After being married so happily as I have, any life apart is not complete however busy it is or interesting.

I shall phone tomorrow if I can to wish Robert 'many happy returns'. The infinite joy and thankfulness of the time when I came in to see you when Robert was born often came to my thoughts & always my eyes fill with tears which are echoes of the tenderness which I felt then. Surely no-one could ever have felt like that and then ceased to love their wife in good times or bad.

It's curious what a different significance a birthday will always have for Robert & David & for us.[1] My dear I love you and you must always love me & forgive me when I'm selfish & unkind. Alan.

19th Sep 1942, Alan, HQ 12 Corps, TW, to Sheila

My Very Dear,

Just a short note to greet another day for you before the leave. It's a glorious sunny morning but last night I was at the club in a party given by Col & Mrs Collingwood. I was extremely bored - it was hot and stuffy & everyone was drinking too much. Oh my dear I compare every girl with you & they don't make the grade at all. There is nothing in all the world like your expression & at the oddest times I suddenly catch a look when I'm with you & fall in love all over again.

I've just been writing to John Fergie, he must have had a most interesting time.

I sent you some Balkan Sobranie this morning. Think of me when you smoke them.

Oh my very own Dear, I love you, Alan

---

[1] I would be three and David 1 month & 3 days.

24th Sep 1942, Alan, HQ 12 Corps, TW, to Sheila

My Dear,

I have your letter about your visit to the Radiologist and I'm so sorry you had such an exhausting time. I'm longing to see my boy David because he must be shooting up. I'm going to try to phone you and I'll stop now until you have been through.

25.9.42

Dear it was grand to talk to you last night. Don't worry about David, it will be alright. I expect to get word from Sloan Robertson tomorrow. I won't post this today for it won't reach you in any case until Monday. I've also had your letter written on Tuesday this morning. Beloved I don't expect you to write long screeds & I get many more letters than I expect for I know how busy you must be.

I'm enclosing a cutting from B.M.J. on baby rearing which confirms some ideas of my own which have never been clearly formulated. Also a cutting from "the Mother" with a mark against the note on the *course* we attended on our Honeymoon. Beloved it was a wonderful Honeymoon. I always remember you saying that you had never been so happy before and could never be so happy again.

reminiscing on happier times

26.9.42

No special news except that it's jolly cold & I've had to put on my winter woollies!

I'm enclosing yet another cutting! This time it's an advert for the book.[1] I hope that the "Fast Selling Out" as alleged at the top has some basis in fact but I doubt it.

Well My Own One it will soon be October and then soon be leave. It can't be too soon. Love to my boys. Alan

---

[1] The book referred to is *Build Your Own Enlarger*, first published by Fountain Press September 1942. Reprinted April 1945. Second Edition January 1946. I still have a copy with some press cuttings in it. Still available on Amazon today!

3rd Oct 1942, Alan, HQ 12 Corps, TW, to Sheila

My Dear,

I have your letter on 30th this morning. I'm so glad you had a good day at Bearsden[1] and I'm longing to know whether the new help turned up. It's a very short time now until I see you and I am as excited as any bridegroom at the prospect.

I enclose press cuttings about the book which you will perhaps keep for me, it would be fun to place them into a copy of the book. The publishers, when sending on the letter, seem rather bucked by the way it is selling.

I'm sorry to hear about Ruth. It's a rotten time for her. I fancy that they are nearly as fond of each other as we are and it does not make it any easier.

Yesterday in Maidstone, I met James Peebles who was in the Intelligence Corps and I last saw him in 1930. He has just married a wife aged 22 and I have promised to go out and visit them next week as they are in a cottage about 3 miles from here.

I hope the apples and pears arrived all right. Dawson assures me that he packed them well, but the P. O. are expert wreckers these days. When you get to Wakefield, I'll try to get a case of good eating apples and send it up.

It's been like summer again for a few days even though it's cold at nights. Last night, after a lovely warm day, when I, dressed up in breeches, was cursing the heat, there was a sharp frost and I woke up half frozen at 5 P. M.

There is a dance at one of the other messes tonight and I am going up to prop up the bar for a while. Beloved do you remember when we used to go off to the Plaza all by ourselves for an evening and sit and talk and talk and have coffee and sandwiches and dance and have a lovely evening? And do you remember how puzzled your Dad used to be at us going off by ourselves? I think we shall have a night on the loose when I'm up in Glasgow. What do you say?

Give my boys my love and whisper to them the Old Man will be home soon. I love you dear, Alan

---

[1] Bearsden is a district of Glasgow, so Sheila had been there recently.

4th Oct 1942, Alan, HQ 12 Corps, TW, to Sheila

My Dear,

I'm hoping to get through to you by phone tonight and I won't be able to write for the next two days because we are off on a short exercise. By the time that is over it will be time to think of railway warrants & train times and all the exciting details necessary for me to get back to my Beloved.

I went up to the dance at the other mess last night & drank gin & tonic and danced several times but oh my one I could have enjoyed myself so much if you had been there. There is a quality about you, a fineness that is so crisp, a friendliness that makes people want to be friendly & at their best.

For me there is the thrill to know that this person, whom I fall in love with again and again whenever I see her, loves me and wants to be loved by me.

Oh My Dear you have made me so critical that no second best has ever or will ever have any place in my way of living. I felt sort of detached last night and kept picturing you there and the effect was to make all the girls seem dowdy or withered or harsh voice and noisy.

I hope I get a word with Robert tonight. It's grand to hear him speak on the phone and I always am amazed at how well he understands what I say and how sensibly he answers.

I'm annoyed with Sloan Robertson for not writing to me. There is no possible excuse. But I'm not worried about David and I should not let it worry you. I hope the new help turned up, My Poor One must be very busy if she hasn't. Well Beloved six days and I'll be with you. Kiss my Boys. I love you my beloved, Alan

6th Nov 1942, **Sheila, Wakefield, to Alan**

Friday 8.45 am

My Dear,

I can't think exactly when I wrote you last. Beloved thanks for yesterday's letter and please don't stop writing immature letters. I do like them.

It's fine to have next Wednesday to look forward to. Lannie

arrives sometime tomorrow. I am a bit sorry not to have the place to ourselves when you come, but I will not be sorry to be done with lonely evenings. I don't mind for a few weeks but it would be distinctly depressing for the whole winter.

David and Robert are recovered except that they are still "bunged up".

I have the painter doing David's wee room and it's going to look sweet. I have a painful swollen finger this a.m. but am hoping it won't come to anything

I haven't had breakfast yet so excuse hasty letter. You'll soon be with us beloved and I'm aching for you. Sheila

9th Nov 1942, Alan, HQ 12 Corps, TW, to Sheila

Dear,

Sorry to write a hurried note again but I want to get the post and I'm very busy today. I've no particular news except that I love you more than yesterday & as far as I see on all tomorrows I'll be loving you more. It's an awful thought isn't it? But then I've always thought I could not possibly love you more. Oh my Dear I can still hear you speaking to me last night.

Hug my dear boys. Alan

12th Nov 1942, **Sheila, Wakefield, to Alan**

Thursday

Dear One,

Thanks for your letter received this afternoon. Am sorry you had such a rotten return journey but glad you had a little nap in the afternoon

Robert has spent today also in bed and if he has another night like last night am going to get back Dr Smith tomorrow. He seemed to spend the whole night coughing and I'll swear whooping and weeping about it all. I was miserable as sin in the night watches because David had coughed several times yesterday as well and I just can't bear to think of David with that. He (Robert) doesn't cough a lot during the day but seems to get really bad when he lies down. However, I think he is a little better today so will see what the night brings forth. I'd quite decided about four AM that I would wire for Sister[1] first thing this morning. However, when I woke the sun was shining and nothing seems so desperate in the morning. I'm going to try to concoct a mixture of honey and lavender and possibly butter to give him in the night. Mrs Grimshaw sent me a candidate for the post this morning but she was quite definitely half witted and I was thankful to get her out of the house. Monica is collecting my meat tomorrow so that's a help.

I am greatly enjoying "The South Sea Man" and can just imagine how much you did. Excuse more tonight but for some unearthly reason I have a confounded stiff neck and I don't think writing helps.

I'll add a few things tomorrow and give the latest about Robert.

Friday

No coughs all night and have got him up today. My neck much better. Great haste. Love Sheila

14th Nov 1942, Sheila, Wakefield, to Alan

Saturday

Beloved,

Thanks for another call tonight. I'm afraid I didn't hear all you said, our sons kept getting in the way, but I got most of it. I had an extraordinary dream the other night, you came in the door to announce that you were no longer in the army, it was the realness of it that made it so odd. I woke up with a terrific surge of joy and was awake quite a few moments before I realized there was a snag somewhere! It's dreadful I have a lot of sewing I should be doing these evenings when I'm alone I never seem to be able to settle to anything.

David is being a terribly good baby and simply couldn't be less trouble and Robert is very wicked and very sweet! Monica's legs were too stiff to walk up tonight.

---

[1] "Sister" will be a recurring character in the letters.

Ah well it means I'll get to bed at my usual early hour and you know I get a great kick out of getting into bed!

I've found several more pure white hairs, you'll probably be taken for my son soon! Joking apart though it's a bit early to go grey and I admit I'm considerably depressed about it.

My advice to you about Sibbald[1] is - send him the money for his radiator and intimate to him that a kettle will be sent when obtained and that so far as you are concerned the matter is closed. In the absence of agreement and inventory he couldn't do a thing about anything. I'd dearly love to write to him myself and a real rude letter, remarking amongst many other things that on the occasion last April when his wife visited us she felt she had so little control over herself that she preferred not to see me, that my time is much too valuable to waste in a farcical day going over a house to check things which I have no inventory of, and that no possible benefit could have been derived from opening a new correspondence with such rude and reasonless people.

I trust he found his bracket in good order! I was not aware that the cover of the other radiator was damaged and I do think he ought to have returned the india rubber!

Sunday 8.15 PM

I hope you are not too dreadfully sore and stiff today. I've been thinking of you such a lot. Robert has invented a song about you falling off a horse into the water, your hat comes into it somewhere but it's rather hard to follow! I'm rather hoping this will be my last Sunday completely alone. I'm probably only half the woman I ought to be but I find it rather complicated and get very bad tempered as evening comes on and then suffer agonies of remorse when the Wob is gone to sleep! I'm having the sweep[2] at 7.00 in the morning and plan to have a bath and go to bed almost fully clothed in order to be in a fit state to receive him!

David is positively the most adorable baby in the world and so

---

[1] Sibbald is the Landlord of 'Barona', the house in Largs where David was born.
[2] Sounds Dickensian today! Sweep would come, complete with brushes on poles, and clean the chimneys. Soot everywhere.

good nowadays. He doesn't seem to have gained anything at all this week, which startled me a bit, but it would be worse if he went on at his ½ pound a week rate!

I'm a bit shaky tonight due to taking Ephedrine for the "sneezes" - funny I had an attack last Saturday too before which I haven't had it for months. I've taken Ephedrine[1] both days about lunchtime and they certainly are a certain cure in one way, but my goodness they shake me! Heard any more of the ultimate possibility of getting Edna? I don't expect you have or will do for a long time.

Well beloved I'm counting the hours till Friday but oh dear it will be so quickly over! I'll arrange somehow that you miss the Sunday night train anyway! For pity's sake take care of yourself and come home all in one piece.

I'm sorry I didn't get this off today but even with the letter box so near it just wasn't possible. Anyway although there isn't much in it, it is a long letter isn't it? Your wife, Sheila

15th Nov 1942, Alan, HQ 12 Corps, TW, to Sheila
Beloved,

It was good to speak to you and to Robert on the phone last night. I can't say that your reception of the news of my hunting was very complimentary to my horsemanship! Still even if not elegant I enjoyed myself. I probably added to the gaiety *of the field.* by my style; but people were polite enough not to smile too broadly when I was looking.

Dear, you would have enjoyed yourself. My mount was "Lonsdale" which is evidently a well-known point-to-point winner and which completed all the jumps and finished in the Grand National in 1938. When the groom gave me this news and led out the enormous beast, you in perfect truth, could have "knocked me down with a feather".

When we first went off in a canter along slippery paths in the woods, I was terrified. No other words would do justice to my emotions, but I gradually realised that this beast knew its job if left

---

[1] Ephedrine - Sheila presumably taking this for asthma. Common side effects: anxiety, fast heart rate, high blood pressure

alone and by the end of the day apart from being so tired that I could hardly sit upright, we had an understanding. He was only really troublesome when I was trying to prevent him going off to the front with his Master and Huntsman. My modesty prevented me from wishing to show them a clean pair of heels or rather from casting lumps of mud in their faces - "Lonsdale" had no such modesty.

We parted company once, before I really understood him. There was a muddy ditch about seven feet wide with its muddy banks about 2 ft 6" ins deep. We cantered up to it in great style, but my horror at seeing it get closer so rapidly caused me to check him as he was about to jump with the result that he stopped rather like [*illegible*], I went over his head into the ditch and he, free from all encumbrances, jumped over like a cat. After that I just closed my eyes and held on tight and we actually crossed the same ditch twice again with superb aplomb.

I occasionally embraced his neck after that but we did what all the others did (I could not prevent it) and were up with the field all the time.

At checks people kept turning round to view this muddy officer. The phrase to use is apparently "Oh, bad luck, you've been on the ground". I did not enter into arguments as to whether it was earth, air, fire or water I'd been "on" but merely grunted or said to strangers "so you noticed did you" and to brother officers I tended to be sarcastic. In other words a high state of dignity was upheld through all misfortune.

There were lots of low brush hedges and two or three two-bar gates and we had one real gallop over open fields.

The hounds killed in a wood after an hour and a half and a little girl of 12 riding a small pony was "bloodied" by having each cheek touched with the brush. I rode back with her afterwards and I've never seen a child so happy. She was just wild with excitement to get home and tell her father all about it and with her velvet cap on the back of her head, her eyes shining and the blood on her cheeks, she looked like a child possessed. She left saying "I've never, never had a day like this".

The pack seemed to be good, so far as I knew, with the exception of two half bloodhounds half foxhounds. That couple I met often sitting on their haunches looking very tired and depressed while the pack was hunting a line half a mile ahead.

The biggest thrill to me was when we were standing spaced out on a slope above a spinney to prevent the fox from breaking that way. Suddenly the hounds started to cry and the horns went and we saw them stream out of the other side of the spinney away along a sunlit hillside. The horses knew perfectly well - they were off. Away we went round the spinney and after the pack which by then was out of sight.

Oh beloved, why were you not there? Heaven knows I enjoyed it plenty but you would have enjoyed it more, and with you there my pleasure would have doubled.

Well beloved, my leave is off until Saturday next but, by leaving it until then, I won't need to travel back until Tuesday morning, so it's worth leaving it for another day. I could not get off until about 6 o'clock on Friday and would have had to be here at 9 o'clock on Monday.   NEXT PAGE MISSING

25th Dec 1942, Alan, HQ 12 Corps, TW, to Sheila

My Dear,

I wish I could be with the tribe this above all mornings for I want to play with you all. Perhaps future Christmases will all be good and happy with no wars to worry us. We have just been to church and are now going down to the sergeant's mess to drink beer with them. (at 11.30 AM)!

James Peebles phoned up yesterday and invited me to dine with his wife and self and his wife's sister in the Spa Hotel.[1] The place was full of aged people rather like the hotel at Hindhead. After dinner there was a concert of carols & then a short dance. It was pretty grim going. Tonight we are all going up to dine with Brigadier Wigmore and that should be more cheerful as Wiggie is a cheery old boy.

---

[1] I think this is the Spa Hotel, Tunbridge Wells, Kent.

I'll try to phone at 6 tonight but there may be so much delay that I won't be able to.

Oh beloved, it's not long till 5th Jan. In fact it's a week on Tuesday & I <u>might</u> slip away on Jan 4th.

Give my boys all my love. I love you dear one. What happiness I've had with you you'll never know but perhaps you can guess.

Your loving husband, Alan[1]

---

[1] Alan had leave on 5th January 1942.

1943

Notes on 1943

Robert & Sheila approx mid 1943
I was about 4.

David circa late 1943,
about 18 months

At the beginning of 1943 Alan is still at GHQ 12 Corps, Home Forces, at Tunbridge Wells in Kent (TW). He does not think he is doing anything useful and yet it is hard for him to get leave to see his family. Later in Africa he refers to his work there as being the first useful thing he has done since '1st Army' in Tunbridge Wells.

In 1943 the tide of war is turning. In May, the German Africa Corp and Italian forces in North Africa surrendered. In July, the Germans were defeated at Kursk by the Russians in a gigantic tank battle.

In September, the Italians surrendered and imprisoned Mussolini, the Italian dictator, on a mountain top. Germany seized control of Italy. Mussolini was rescued in an amazing raid and re-installed as a German puppet. The Allies landed at Salerno, where Sheila lost two cousins in the fighting.

There were great changes for Alan and Sheila as well. In his diary, he writes in July 1943 that "after a good deal of uncertainty I am now not going to West Africa as had been expected but am staying at this Corps".

It was generally accepted that Germany could only be finally defeated by a seaborne invasion of the European mainland from Britain. Now that Russia, previously hostile to Britian, had been invaded by Germany she demanded help and pressed strongly for the allied invasion to take some pressure off her armies.

Alan was sent to a camp near Tenby in South Wales which was apparently training for the "Second Front", the invasion of the Continent. It was known that this would happen in conjunction with the Americans and a huge build up was under way. Substantial casualties were inevitable and Sheila dreaded it. We now call this invasion D-Day, or sometimes 'The Normandy Landings'.

The Western Allies, mindful of past disasters such as Gallipoli in WW1 and a failed assault on Dieppe, wanted to make sure that they assembled sufficient force and shipping before undertaking the huge landing on a strongly defended shore. As is evident in the 1943 letters, Sheila, while wanting the Second Front and the defeat of Germany as soon as possible, was terrified of Alan being part of the invasion force.

But in October 1943 Alan learnt he was going to Africa after all. His departure to a part of Africa where there was no fighting was a huge relief to Sheila even though it meant them being totally apart for at least another 18 months.

Alan spent his last night with Sheila on 12th October 1943 at the Lismoyne Hotel, Crookham, Fleet, Hampshire. We know he parted from her on October 13th to catch his train ("The last glimpse I had of her was walking - looking straight ahead, into the gates of the Lismoyne Hotel").

The gates of the Lismoyne Hotel

Robert, Alan and Sheila, about June 1943

Alan was on his ship on the 14th and sailed for Africa on 15th October.[1]

Censorship meant that Alan could not say where he was or where he'd been right up to 31st July 1944. Then he was able to advise that his new address was "GHQ Accra, Gold Coast, West African Forces". Due to his unofficial diary, we know something of his movements and we know he was in Accra most of the time. Where I have put his location in Square Brackets [ ] it indicates that his letters did not give his location though we know it from his diaries.

Sheila: addresses

Sheila is variously at 6 Crown Mansions and 6 North Gardner Street in Glasgow. They are the same place. I have settled on 6 Crown Mansions in letter headings for the sake of clarity. The full address is, I suppose: 6 Crown Mansions, North Gardner Street, Glasgow W1.

6 Crown Mansions was a flat and the home of Sheila's parents, James (Jimmy) Steven and Jessie (Mamie) née Hodge. It is just off the Hyndland Road and only about ¼ mile from 1 Kingsborough Gardens where Alan's parents lived. Apparently, Allan Stevenson, Alan's father, used to tease him back in 1930 saying as he stood looking out of the window from where he could see the Hyndland Road, "There's that Steven girl walking her dog again. Why don't you go down and talk to her, Alan?"

Sheila spends some time at Seamills. The full address is: Wayside, Summerlea Road, Seamill, West Kilbride.

On 27th May 1943 Sheila rented 66 Manygates Lane to the Hipsons and moved to Wayside for June, July and August. Anything to get away from Wakefield and have some friends and family around.

---

[1] Alan boarded ship at Southampton. The ship moved out to anchor for the night in Spithead, then sailed for Africa.

1 Jan 1943, Sheila, Wakefield, to Alan

Another letter! Anyhow it seems a good thing to do on the first day of the year. It's a wild day. This morning the rain was torrential and I got out my old oilskin and cycled into Wakefield - you know, I thoroughly enjoyed it! I arrived at the butchers with rain streaming down my face and running in rivers off the oilskin and bumped into Monica all very smart with her hat at the correct angle and under a large umbrella. Her eyes nearly popped out of her head when she saw the weird apparition approaching. I couldn't imagine Monica at our country cottage![1] Then I had to dodge Mrs Stott, because I was far too wet for polite conversation but I got home feeling very fresh and fit, much better than sitting in a steamy house with sneezing all round.

I was thinking a lot about the house and the boat[2] on the way home. I'd have gone anywhere in the boat today, spring must be in the air I think! It's high time we learned to sail, the years are slipping by so quickly.

I found Lannie baking when I got home and took Miss Whittaker round a bundle of hot scones and pancakes. Bless you beloved I'm gasping for Tuesday. The boys flourish exceedingly. I love you, Sheila

25 Jan 1943, Alan HQ 12 Corps, TW, to Sheila

My Very Dear,

It's only 4½ days until I see you now and I hope that nothing comes in the way of your getting down.[3]

I've fixed up two horses for 10 o'clock on Sunday morning and a room in the hotel from Friday until Wednesday morning. They think they could fix you up after Wednesday if necessary but not in the same room.

I'll try to meet you and go up to the hotel with you on Friday. I expect I'll get my day off and a good deal of extra time but I'm not

---

[1] The 'country cottage' is, I think, Camusglashlan (see Appendix 6)
[2] The boat refers to the ex lifeboat Alan purchased in Achiltibuie in, I think, 1942. (see Appendix 10)
[3] Sheila is joining Alan in 4 days at an hotel - in or near Tunbridge Wells, I think.

sure how many nights I shall be able to stay with you.

Sam *Glessow's* wife is coming down on Monday and we shall dine together on Monday night. I'm hoping James Peebles and wife will dine with us on Saturday night.

Oh beloved. I'm so looking forward to seeing you and showing you off to my friends for I've got a very lovely wife and I'm very proud to be married to her.

I'm just off now and I think I'm going to have a pretty strenuous week for there is going to be a lot of night work. Bless you beloved and kiss my boys for me. Your loving husband, Alan.

3ʳᵈ Feb 1943, Sheila, Wakefield, to Alan

Wednesday 1 pm

Dear,

The photos are marvellous and what splendid paper. I think they are some of the best you've ever taken. The home front has been very shaky but still holds. Robert is out and about again as usual. David hasn't been out yet because he is still coughing and has such a trying wee wheeze that it's almost funny, but I'm taking no risks altho the weather is perfect and have been keeping him warm and as much in the same temperature as possible.

As for me I've had the filthiest cold which has ranged through almost everything a cold can, so I presume must be getting better. I've been very, very disgustingly sorry for myself. And tonight will see an end of the "whisky" so I will have no option and will have to be cured tomorrow!

A final notice about the telephone account came fluttering through the letter box today, I'd clean forgotten the account had come in! You know beloved it cheers me up so much to write to you. Oh! I wonder so when your next 48 hrs will be.

Robert has been good again today or perhaps it is that during the last few days I've been too dazed to notice! Anyhow I love the wee blighter an awful lot and he swears he wouldn't change me for a non-cross Mummy, so perhaps we don't do so badly. Yours always. Sheila

4th Feb 1943, Alan, HQ 12 Corps, TW, to Sheila

Dear,

I'm missing you badly. It was so nice to have you that I feel at a loose end when I'm not actually working. But ten days only and I'll be with you again.

I was on the run this morning and while a bit out of condition I enjoyed it and feel better for the exercise. It was a lovely running day but with rather a cold wind.

I started off with Sam and Tony *Amerigo-Jones* but left them and managed to be first officer in. Beloved it's a wee weakness and vanity of mine but I love being first officer in.

I'm going down to 'The Castle' tonight at 7.15 to have a drink with Sam and his wife and Jim and I may go to the Swan for a snack and then go to the flicks. The title 'Twin Beds' is rather discouraging!

Dear I'm always thinking about the boat. It has become symbolic of freedom and being alone with you after the war. Oh Sheila I do so thrill to you and love your wee black cape with the red carnations in it.

I love all my family. Alan

Feb 5th 1943, Alan, 12 Corps, TW, to Sheila

My Dear,

Surely very few husbands and wives who have been married for six years and have a family of two write to each other as we do.

Today I received your letter written on Wednesday night and I read it at least six times. The more I see of you Sheila the more I admire you and love you and the more I see of you and other people the more I know that there is one woman in all the world I could love and admire for any time or to whom I would remain faithful. I may be wrong in all this for I never have known any girl but you at all well and I can't imagine that anyone else seeing you or even knowing you slightly would imagine how deeply you could love or the single-mindedness with which you would plot and plan for one man and your boys.

As I say there may be other women like you but I don't know and

I don't care, and I never shall know nor care.

What I do know is that the one woman to whom I can give all and show my weaknesses and my love and passion, loves me and needs me. I am content.

Dear Sheila there are good and happy days coming for us when we shall not be separated and when we shall play together as we used to play with no fear hanging over us. We shall make two new men and two good ones who in their home have seen love and faithfulness and joy. And in the happy times that they will have will be recompense for all this.

Dear there is no more to be said except again that I love you. Alan

7th Feb 1943, Sheila, Wakefield, to Alan

Sunday

Dear One,

You're not due a letter but it's really been so absurd you not being here today that I feel I must have a wee chat with you. Firstly I'm terrifically pleased with my son Robert! The McVicars were up this afternoon and Jim played with the two boys all afternoon and was wonderfully good with them. He read them stories to calm them down for a spell between constant rough houses. Robert is definitely as advanced as Anthony, to be honest more so. He's an odd child Robert - as sharp as a needle. But you know beloved he is appallingly wild and in every sort of mischief but touch wood he has a good temper and holds on to it and Anthony alas hasn't. Much, I may say, to the McVicars' distress! He has blind spasms of rage and slaps them and grinds his teeth and I'm sitting thanking my stars for my own wild boy who is I think too balanced and humorous ever to be like that. He and I spend most of the day at daggers drawn but at intervals we fall on each other's necks and state out mutual affection and he says in a pawky way "you couldn't possibly do without your wee boy", and assured of the impossibility of my existing without my wee boy he goes gaily off to some new and dreadful wickedness! Elsie, the daily, says "you know it's right queer but I look forward to seeing Robert in't morning." He accompanies her in all her walks and she calls him the "coughdrop",

chatters to him all the time and I'm bound to say excites him by giggling at him and makes him worse than ever. The day he . . . . .
PAGES MISSING

Feb 11th 1943, Alan, HQ 12 Corps, TW, to Sheila

Thursday

My Dear,

I'm looking forward to seeing my Dear Ones. I want my wee tribe about me and I miss Robert especially for you know he's a good wee boy and I like playing with him. But then David gets more interesting every time I come home and you are quite a nice wife too![1]

Oh Sheila you are the only sane and proper person I have ever met and I'm not quite normal without you. I'll probably phone you tomorrow night but in any case I shall be in with the four o'clock train from London arriving Wakefield at about 8.30 on Saturday. If Fishers can produce a taxi can you ask them to oblige.

I love you my dear I need you and want you badly. Alan

20th Feb 1943, Alan, 12 Corps, TW, to Sheila

Beloved,

I have neglected writing to you because I phoned and have been spending all my spare time getting the photos ready. You will be impressed I think and pleased with them.

I shall not be going away from here at all until 26th or so as there has been the inevitable shuffle of dates.

I've no particular news but I'm hoping to see Will Hay in "The Goose Steps Out" at the flicks tonight.

I'm so glad that the boys seem on the mend but am sorry to hear that Robert is as naughty as ever. Poor wee David. Salt is such a good emetic!

I am sending your photos already stuck in the albums and I'm sending one or two to your Mummy and Daddy. I managed to get a little paper yesterday which was a great help, especially as it's

---

[1] So Alan arrives Wakefield on leave Sat 13th Feb. David now 8 months.

rather nice paper.

I shall try to phone tomorrow night and see how the home front is bearing up.

Oh beloved I need you and especially at weekends I miss you. Alan

24th Feb 1943, **Sheila, Wakefield, to Alan**

Tuesday 8.30 pm

Dear One,

Hope your journey wasn't too awful and that you enjoyed yourself this morning! I'm getting near the end of my laborious little day and have just downed tools, I'm going to have something to eat, feed David early and go to bed to read. You know if it wasn't for David's feed I think I'd go to bed about 7. 30 when alone! I slept like a log last night, spread all over the bed so to speak! I expect you've had a dreadful night.

Robert is coughing a lot and I think he's in for a cold. Excuse short note but I was late in finishing up tonight and as I said also want to get supper and go up to read.

It was fine having you home but is almost too dreadful when you go away. I feel stupid with misery for hours before you go, but as soon as you do go, well I start looking forward to the next time.

Robert says he is happier when you are here! He has peered at me once or twice today and said "are you happy Mummy? Why are you all alone?" Sorry about the blots. Yours lovingly, Sheila

Feb 24th 1943, Alan, 12 Corps, TW, to Sheila

Wed 9.15 pm

Dear,

I have put through a call to you and hoping to get a quick line. I'm sending back some recent letters for you to keep for me. Beloved I like your letters.

I am much touched and amused by how much Robert enjoyed making pancakes.

I go out Friday - Saturday and then Monday until mid-March so I should probably phone on Saturday evening.

I'm very tired the last two days for I been terribly busy and I never get a moment to turn and think. I've been in the office until after midnight and look like being there again tonight at the same time. I'm getting a bit tired of sorting out other people's messes, or perhaps it is that I just can't work alongside people but must do it myself. However something always turns up whereby I get a baby to hold and clean him up and I get tired of that. So no doubt do you! Beloved you have a foolish old grouser for a husband. The only thing he is satisfied with in this life are his Dear one and his wee boys. Oh my dear I do need you when I'm busy; but then I need you when I'm idle too.

My one you and the boat and Achiltibuie are my post-war planning. A very selfish plan no doubt but a very harmless one, a very healing one for a battered old man and a very necessary one for his readjustment to sense and good things.

Oh Sheila think of me a lot and love me for I love you so much. I've never met anyone who was the same sort of person as you and I never shall. Kiss my boys beloved and tell them I'm due for leave on April 7th. I love you, I love you and I want to live my life with you Beloved. Alan

28th Feb 1943, Sheila, Wakefield, to Alan

4 o'clock

Dear One,

Thanks for phoning me, I was hoping you would. I don't think I can write much to you tonight it would be just all love letter. I'm sort of all wrapped round by your presence still and Oh! Beloved I think I shall die I love you so much. You know dear I always told you how terribly near I felt to you in the three months after Robert was born - well last weekend has made me feel like that again, it's a dreadful extra special feeling, for goodness knows I have loved you to distraction in between and in addition to all that I love you more than I've ever done and dear I am just going about in a sort of daze with it all.

To come back to earth our boys are very bouncing, David's three colossal teeth have already quite changed his smile and Robert has been very sweet to me today. I arrived home, as you know, unexpectedly last night and found Lannie in some of my clothes!

Dear, I hope you have a pleasant time on Saturday evening. I do so wish I could have been there. Beloved I must admit I'm terribly thankful you don't take people to dances no matter how correctly. I may be (I am) terribly jealous, but it's so much my privilege to go out with you that on top of all other things the war has brought us I find it hard to bear, but as all the other wives seem to survive it, there is perhaps something pretty odd about yours.

Robert is very keen to come to TW, and says will have to get a battery for his torch because of the tunnels. He is entranced with the new "wheels" and they simply saved my bacon in the middle of last night because he woke up and said "Oh! Have you have brought my toys to me from Tunbridge Wells." His lips started to tremble when I was making my excuses and the most awful look of desolation came over him. I made a frantic dive for my case and dug for the wheels and the situation was restored at once!

We are so hoping to see you next week. Yours ever, Sheila

P. S. You've no idea how you cheered me on the phone yesterday, when I told you I'd heard alarming rumours about our future. When Mrs. Sam told me at breakfast that Sam was quite convinced his next leave would be his last and that quite soon, you know I'm an everlasting fool but I'd had about two mouthfuls and not another crumb could I swallow.

As I said to you the other night it's plain madness. S.

1st March 1943, Sheila, Wakefield, to Alan

Monday

My Dear,

It seems a dreadfully long time since I've written to you but I've been up to the ears. I am really hoping devoutly that your mother doesn't take your hint and come to see me just now because when one has no, or very little, help one can just manage oneself but extra people, though delightful for company's sake, make a big difference to the day's work no matter how helpful they try to be.

Since coming Mother has been running round in short sharp circles all the time trying to help me and tonight looks positively exhausted.[1]

I was phoning Monica to ask for Anthony today - he whooped all night and she had violent toothache, it's a great life! Thank heaven our two are all right again. Doreen's friend came to tea yesterday afternoon. I was still feeling a bit seedy and could cheerfully have seen her in Jericho, but she insisted on coming!

The weather for the past fortnight has been like summer and it's been unfortunate that I and my family have never all been fit once all at the time. Today however I venture to consider myself cured and no further bulletins will be issued.

Robert is thrilled about you coming home for a whole week and is dreaming beautiful visions of Meccano on tap constantly for the whole week! David has lost his wheeze and is as fit as ever again.

I'm sorry you have been so fearfully and annoyingly busy, I always love you a little bit extra when things are slightly troublesome for you, because you need me more and Oh! Beloved I long for you to need me even twice as much as you do! It seems such a long time since we lived together even at Largs and my dear it's not good for me to live without you. I enjoyed the "South Sea Man" so much and am thoroughly enjoying "The China Clippers".

It was amazingly nice of you to get me a comb, you've no idea how much I am in need of one. Beloved you are good to me and I adore you. I'd positively still adore you if you blacked both my eyes! Love Sheila

P.S. Pen really driving me silly, excuse blots!

9th *Mar 1943*, Sheila, Wakefield, to Alan

Tuesday

My Dearest Man,

It's delightful to be on your mailing list again! I've had three letters in two days. I do hope your legs are better - bad legs are such

---

[1] So Mamie (Sheila's mother) is there in Wakefield on 1st March 43.

a nuisance! There's nothing new except that Robert and I are invited to tea at Betty Senior's on Thurs along with Monica and Anthony. Dr McD Smith says Anthony must be quite uninfectious now, so pray heaven he is right!

We had a long letter from Steven[1] yesterday saying thank you for the photo of David and enclosing some of Marion.

Only fourteen days now beloved. I stroke off one each night. I am asked to tell you that Robert can <u>almost</u> dress himself. He is looking forward greatly to the whole week. He spent a bloodthirsty time killing Germans this afternoon! I love you always. Sheila

10th March 1943, Sheila, Wakefield, to Alan

Wednesday

Dear One,

It's 4.45 PM and I'm sitting beside the fire and David is sitting on the floor playing delightfully with his toys and making violent attempts to crawl at intervals. Robert is sound asleep in bed having been very sick about an hour ago. I can't think why. He has been complaining of a sore tummy all day much as he did on that awful occasion at Farnborough. I suppose children have an odd upset now and then. When he wakes up later in the evening I'm going to take him up some very thin bread and butter on one of the best plates on the silver salver and some milk in a wine glass and I know he'll be as pleased as punch.

I have another woman coming is the day's news. Morris can't, but doubt if I shall keep her as she isn't too good. She is a pathetic little soul, a bundle of nerves, jumps a foot in the air whenever I speak to her and her old father beats her at the weekends!

Thanks for another letter written yesterday. I'm longing for news of your coming.

Must attend to large family now! All love, Sheila

---

[1] 'Steven' is Steven Faulds, Sheila's cousin. Marion Faulds is Steven's daughter.

13th *March 1943,* **Sheila, Wakefield, to Alan**

Dear One,

Thanks for letter and cheque. It does seem a long time since I last saw you. I wonder when you will be able to phone. Robert is all right again. David was most violently and pathetically sick yesterday and distinctly under the weather for a bit, then to *cap* everything I woke almost at midnight feeling awful and spent a most miserable night and got up wondering how I should ever get dressed, far less get through the day. However I am practically recovered and am now wondering if I dare eat anything! I'd like to know the reason of it all!

A lot of planes seem to go over these nights and we had sirens on Tuesday just as I was going to bed. Within a few minutes the phone rang - Miss Whittaker to see if I'd like her to come round! Such is the effect of the unusual, I declined as gracefully as I could think, but it was rather sweet of her. She also phoned this afternoon to see if she could take the children out, but this also I declined until some other day as truth to tell I didn't feel I had strength to spare getting the pram down and up the steps. My mind is pretty blank tonight and I've forgotten I know several things I intended saying to you. Mr Moulton brought us three eggs today (one for each of us) and made me promise faithfully to eat mine!

Mother had a visit from Bobby C. the other day. He was of course astounded that you weren't away with the other Largs people! All love, Sheila

P.S. Aunt Bet is dying at "Killin".

14th *Mar 1943,* **Sheila, Seamill, to Alan**

Monday

My Dear One,

It was nice of you to phone tonight "Knowing you to be wondering" - I was! I've lived the last two days in a little lurid hell of my own making, and sternly desisted from writing hoping it would pass.[1] I think I feel calmer now but I don't think I'll say anything about this week's issue. There is no use my crying over spilt milk and there's always the chance you may be right, although I can't see it.

I am so sorry I forgot to thank you for the cheque. I'm afraid I'm very remiss about such things, but I don't forget to ask for it if it doesn't turn up to time - do I! The weather is perfectly filthy.

I love the enlargement of "Robert at the gate" and thank you for the poem. It makes the photograph stand out somehow and I shall always connect it with what it suggested to you. It is rather adorable.

I'm so grateful for the poem "Camusglashlan" and was unfortunately immediately inspired to write one myself! However I have stuck in the middle and my muse has gone. Beloved even if the "babies"[2] are very deformed at first, send them up, I'll welcome them all. You made me think of Rieff or rather "Camusglashlan" so *invitingly*. It's strange how much we've bound up our dreams there. I like to think I took you there and conceived the idea of a house.[3]

I'm sorry I forgot to enclose Lannie's letter in my last but here it is. Yours ever, Sheila

27ᵗʰ Mar 1943, Alan, HQ 12 Corps, TW to Sheila

My Dear,

I hope your Anniversary Present arrived all right but I'm afraid you would not get it until the morning. I was away at Command all day yesterday and did not get back until 8 o'clock so my efforts to phone you were futile. I came in last night to find a note from James Peebles asking me to a party at his home last night. I was too tired to bother so phoned this morning and apologised.

Beloved I need very badly to live with you. It's only six years since we were married and of these 3 ½ have been war. Yet I can hardly remember a time when you were not my wife and I can't think how poor and thin life was without you. I am very much made

---

[1] Since her last letter Sheila has moved up to Wayside, the house at Seamill.
[2] The 'babies' are Alan's poems.
[3] Apparently the rebuilding of Camusglashlan was Sheila's idea.

to be married to you and I'm much in love with you and my boys. I'm so glad that May can help and Mrs Riggs very *humble*. Tuck into your tablets and drink milk.

Beloved I want to go off in the car with you. Alan

30th Mar 1943, Alan, HQ 12 Corps, TW, to Sheila
My Dear,

I'm going to phone you tonight and I had your letter this morning. I hope the wee woolly waistcoat was a pleasant surprise, fits reasonably well and allows for my wee girl's growth. I knew you liked that fine wool. It comes from mills in Hawick and cost 5 coupons. I sent you a padlock yesterday.

It's a most glorious morning and I'm feeling very fit although I've had a slight cold for the past few days. Last night we saw the "Defence of Moscow" and "Desert Victory" in a special show for the troops. They were very good indeed, especially Desert Victory. I was not at the opening of the club but Jim and I had a snack there on Sunday night. It's very clean and fresh and well lit and altogether I think a successful innovation.

Beloved I agree that the house[1] is the first consideration and I shall send you a list of the minimum work necessary to make it habitable in a day or two. I think it can be made habitable at comparatively small cost. Oh my beloved how lucky I am to have a dear woman who will always be young in the heart and who loves the things I love. My Dear I shall love you as long as I love life and thank my maker for you.

Kiss my boys and tell them I shall be home soon. Alan

5th Apr 1943, Sheila, Wakefield, to Alan
Dear One,

I intended this being posted tonight but just as I was starting supper Miss Perkins and Miss Burton arrived to visit me and by the time they departed the letter was of course still unwritten and the post had gone. I just didn't know what to decide about June, but

---

[1] The house referred to is Camusglashlan.

phoned tonight and said I'd go. I shall probably manage to arrange for Sister's help on the way up as she will be returning at the end of May.

About letting the house to the Hipsons,[1] I don't think it's necessary to call in the doubtful help of Savills and K. - do you? They seem pretty decent people and as it's for a short period it would pay us a lot better to do it ourselves and have the full amount of rent. I should tell them they would not have the use of either outhouse (washhouse full of coal) or garage, or cupboard next bathroom (can't face terrific clearing out of house) and we could lock up your wardrobe in spare room, if we can find the keys! And arranged like that it shouldn't be too much of an effort either to leave or come back to. All this of course before I've phoned them and they may have got a house by this time! However, if they haven't they'll be thankful to have this one.

The house at Seamill has a crib in it and I think the people are going to leave a pram all of which will be a great help.

Dear, it isn't long now till you come, don't love me less than the last time beloved. Sheila

P.S. If you can send cheque early in May I will be able to pay electricity account out of last month's housekeeping money. Robert has adopted a little boy about six called Robin Smallwood. He called him off the road one day to come in and play with him it seems! I don't know anything about him except that he lives somewhere in Castle Road and comes into play every morning and they get on very well together and Robert is in the seventh heaven!

10th Apr 1943, Alan, HQ 12 Corps, TW, to Sheila

My Dear,

I had this morning the greatest cash windfall which has ever fallen to my lot namely a cheque for £92-14-0 from Fountain Press for sale of 2,472 copies of "Build Your Own Enlarger" !!!!!!

You will admit it's a fantastic sum even after £47.7.0 is deducted

---

[1] So Sheila is back in Wakefield and seems to be planning the move to Wayside at Seamill near West Kilbride, in the meantime letting out 66 Manygates Lane.

for income tax. I have never had such a surprise in my life before as when I opened this letter. I sort of expected about £50 but it seemed too good to be true.

I think it's a very sound idea for you to go North for a month or two in the summer.[1] It would do you and the boys good and would be a great joy to your parents and mine.

Oh my Dear one it's so long and so indefinite before this war is over and I live with you again. I shall never grumble at my lot after the war as long as I can live with you and my boys.

My Dear I need you so much and want you so continually. It's just existing to be away like this. I'm looking forward to my leave more than I ever did before. I suppose it's being delayed makes each day more grudging.

My Dear kiss my big one and my wee one and tell them I'm coming home soon. I hope your tummy is keeping better and allowing you to take at least six tablets a day. Love Alan

P.S. Doreen had her tonsils out on Friday and I shall try to phone up tonight to find out how she is.

14th *Apr 1943*, **Sheila, Wakefield, to Alan**

Wednesday

Dear One,

I am so looking forward to seeing you on Friday. I never can't quite get rid of the feeling of guilt at abandoning my family, but it doesn't keep me back! Anyhow I can phone them and I'm not staying as long as you seem to think!

I intended leaving on Monday but may manage to wait until Tuesday. Thanks for a nice letter which came in today. I don't feel like writing much tonight beloved, I'm so full of the thought of the weekend.

Please don't try to meet me at the station. The Wakefield train will probably be as late in London as it was the last time and I will miss the obvious connections. Just get your work finished up as

---

[1] It sounds as if Sheila's last visit to Wayside was to arrange to "go north for a month or two" and escape Wakefield.

soon as possible and come and find me at the hotel.

I love you beloved. Sheila

P. S. Thanks for 'rail warrants'.

19ᵗʰ Apr 1943, Alan, HQ 12 Corps, TW, to Sheila

My Dear,

Just a note to say I arrived safely after a comfortable journey.

My Dear I've never loved you more than I do and I've never enjoyed your company more than this last week end. It's a wonderful thing to love someone so much and so anew - and to be loved.

I think a lot of my girl and my boys and I look forward with a dreadful longing to being with them for always.

Bless you my very dear Sheila and may the Gods that be kind to us. Alan

21ˢᵗ Apr 1943, Alan, HQ 12 Corps, TW, to Sheila

Wednesday

My Very Dear One,

I had a letter from Daddy this morning saying that Doreen was much better and is going up with Moira for a week to Glen Clova. Lucky people aren't they? You and I could do with a week there.

I enjoyed Random Harvest very much. It's a very sentimental story but Ronald Coleman was at his best. And he can be marvellous as you will remember when he played Sydney Carton in "A Tale of two Cities" and Greer Garson was very good too.

If you ever get a chance when it is in Wakefield, I strongly recommend you to see it.

Beloved do you remember how much we used to enjoy our trips to the flicks in Wakefield. Oh my Dear when you think of it how much we enjoyed so many things the condition always being that we did them together.

In fact there was nothing which we did together which does not stand out as good and desirable and happy. My Dear it just bears out what I feel so often that I'm only half complete when I'm not with you and that nothing tastes so good without you.

I am on duty tonight and am going early to bed to read Greek poetry. Doesn't it sound highbrow! I've taken a lot to Gilbert Murray since his description of the ideas of Greek beauty as being like to the lines of a yacht.

Some of his lines are marvellously compact and expressive - this couplet seems *markedly* to me.

> When Theseus, for the blood of human shed,
> Spoke doom of exile on himself and fled.[1]

Beloved I'd love to write poetry. I love you. Alan

22nd Apr 1943, Alan, HQ 12 Corps, TW, to Sheila

My Dear,

I hope the iron solution and *roof* arrived undamaged. Thank you for a letter this morning which warmed me up inside. Beloved we feel very much the same about each other and neither of us can imagine that the other can possibly love so much. Oh wee one I am queer in many ways but my constant anchor is my love for you. That is stable and more and real. Far more real than material things and premises which can be destroyed. Stable and more when with the passing years my outlook and opinions change and waver.

I hope my wee boy David is not going to start the restless evening racket again for it must be very wearing.

Kiss my Boy Robert and tell him I'll be home soon for a whole week and that I'm so glad he was kind to the horsey.

I love you. Alan

25th Apr 1943, Alan, HQ 12 Corps, TW, to Sheila

Tuesday

My Very Dear,

It's very nice to get a letter from the girl you adore telling you that she has fallen in love with you.

It tends to make me a bit cock-a-hoop and bumptious and aggressively cheerful and indeed why not? After all you are a very lovely person and all that man could desire and you love me. Oh

---

[1] Euripides, Hippolytus.

Beloved I must have written more love letters than any man alive. I've been longer in love too - no wonder I'm ageing under the strain.

I shall see what can be done locally to procure a tricycle or a wee car for the wob and I shall see if I can find a wee present for David [1] and I shall see if I can find a life of Byron for my one. I shall send on some of the Greek books to you. I have enjoyed them so much. It's good that we both enjoy reading for it will be such a pleasure when we are old. Every day brings leave closer and I'm going to enjoy myself. I must get out the wee tent and let Robert and David have a party in the garden.

It's funny to think of David upright. He will be delighted with himself. It's interesting that he should be able to do that before he could sit up by himself.

Well Sweetheart of mine I shall finish this and get it off by the midday mail. I love you very dearly, you only, always. Alan

30th Apr 1943, Alan, HQ 12 Corps, TW, to Sheila

My Beloved,

A week on Monday or Tuesday and I shall be with my Dear Ones. It seems a long time since the day when David was born[2] and I've been thinking of that day a lot. My dear you and I trust and have and understand each other. We have had worries and fear together as on that day and we have had joy on many other days. Now we have two sons; and they will have joys and sorrows, hopes and fears and the some of it all will be joy. It's a precious and wonderful thing to have had some hand in the fashioning of two people who will never cease to love living and we have done this and even if it never occurs to them to say to us thank you for having me we have the knowledge that we have made their joy possible.

To make them get the most from living we must try to let them be familiar with as many activities of men as possible for only by knowing and appreciating can you enjoy. So beloved they must swim and run and fish and read and feast their eyes on lovely things and they must hate to hurt or cause pain or destroy in thought or

---

[1] David now 1 year. First mention of the tricycle.
[2] David's birthday 30th April.

deed what is lovely and good. They are such fine wee fellows, so throbbing with interest that our task should not be difficult. Beloved, one of the reasons why we go on being more and more in love with each other is that we have these sons.

My beloved I've read all this over and it does not make sense; but I'm not going to tear it up because I feel strongly and you can read beyond the shape and content to understand that all I am trying to say is that I love you all, and loving I want to make happy.

I'm glad you have fixed to go up for June, July and August.[1] I shall sneak up for one 48 hours and as I said on the phone, I hope to get leave on May 10 or 11th and again about mid-July.

I'm going up to an inter-allied medical conference in London on Monday and I shall give your regards to Major Freiberg with whom I am having lunch.

I managed to get Wooley's 'Ur of the Chaldees'[2] for you and I'm trying to get Life of Byron but have not yet succeeded. I've also picked up some very amusing wee books, one called '*Zoson*'[3] is a little charmer in its way and is an account of travel in Middle East in last century. I shall dispatch it or bring it up with me.

It's raining and overcast today but the rain was badly needed. All the fruit blossom is out and the countryside is looking lovely.

My dear I think it must be the spring too that makes me want you so much. But the seasons don't really make any difference do they?
Alan

30th Apr 1943, Sheila, Wakefield to Alan

Friday

Dear One,

David has had a quiet very happy wee birthday, during which he has discovered how to sit up when rolling about on the floor! He has been so happy and good you'd almost have thought he knew it was his birthday!

---

[1] Seamill fixed for June, July and August.
[2] Sir Leonard Woolley. Alan's spelling is wrong. I remember Sheila enthusing about 'Ur of the Chaldees'.
[3] 'Zoson'. I cannot identify this. Could be Zoron.

The Hipsons have not got another house and seem eager for this one. I've so far only spoken to Mrs H. but they are coming to see me. I am hoping you will be able to phone at the weekend when I can discuss it with you.

We are going to Mac Vic's tomorrow afternoon. Robert is simply pathetic about that tricycle! Perhaps I shall manage to get a wee one up North.

I've had no word from Sister, she's a funny lady. Anyhow Biddy (Mary's sister) wants to come with me to Seamill and stay for a fortnight! She gets her holiday first half of June. This seems an excellent idea to me, particularly as the parents are going to Nethy Bridge from the 4th to 14th June.

Well Beloved it's getting very near leave time and I am aching to see you. Love Sheila

3rd May 1943, Sheila, Wakefield, to Alan

Monday

Beloved,

Next week gets nearer and nearer and I'm so longing for it. There never was a man so dreadfully needed. I got the books today thank you very much. I've just started on "Byron" which is the reason this letter will be brief!

The Hipsons are to let me know by Wednesday if they are taking the house. They have the offer of sharing a house with someone and though not keen I think the money question enters into things. Mrs H. came to see me yesterday.

The weather is beastly cold and unsettled and I'm just longing for some heat. My dear pray that nothing gets in the way of next week. Love Sheila

P.S. Ask Dawson to find (beg borrow or steal if necessary) some lime juice for the gin it's quite impossible here, even Jim can't get it from his wine man that he always goes to. S.

4th May 1943, Alan, HQ 12 Corps, TW, to Sheila

Dear,

I'm going to phone you in a short time but I thought I'd just write to make another break in the short time till I see you. Till today week, to be precise May 11th. And I'm scrounging 10 days on the grounds that due to my leave being overdue I will add on 48 hours as if I had not had a 48 hours since my last leave.

I had a grand day at the conference yesterday. I did not see Major Freiberg so no salt herrings for you. I went to the Royal Academy after the meeting and enjoyed it very much. I completely fell in love with a small bronze head of a boy. I coveted it very much indeed. It was of a child of about two - and the face was just changing from a baby face - but Oh I can't hope to describe it. I have written to the sculptor asking for a photograph because I do so want you to see it.

It's a lovely bright day again for a change but they wind is cold and it's freezing in the shade.

There are some lovely deep purple and white lilac banks in the garden and they are tossing around in the wind in and out of the sun so that I'm cheered merely by looking at them. I sent you some more books today and I have another very amusing one on Food which I shall bring up with me.

I had a rather indifferent dinner in Martinez[1] last night. I think it's gone off a good deal.

The two extra days stolen to be with you beloved are going to be very sweet. I rather think you are the most wonderful person I know. I rather think I love you and I'm certain I want to be with you every minute and it looks as if I'll spend my entire life a wee bit love-lorn. Kiss my boys and tell them I am coming home for a full 10 days. Alan

---

[1] Martinez was a Spanish Restaurant just off Regent Street in London, which Sheila loved and took us there at least once after the war. It steadily, and sadly, declined, becoming an old restaurant with ambience, but expensive and poor food. Closed years ago, about 1995 I suppose.

5th May 1943, Alan, HQ 12 Corps, TW, to Sheila

My Beloved,

Six days to go but time is really quite short now and I'm as excited as if I was going to be married. Oh Dear Sheila I love you such a lot.

I have no word of a tricycle yet but still have hopes. Dawson is trying to get lemon juice and I seem to remember you had difficulty in getting steel wool for pans so he is trying to get some of that too. Progress with Heinz Salad Cream is, as yet, nil.

Strange as it may seem I have not bought any books since I wrote last time.

I love you, Alan

23rd May 1943, Sheila, Wakefield, to Alan

Sunday

My Dear,

The address in West Kilbride is Wayside, Summerlea Rd, Seamill and the telephone no. W.K. 2312.

My battle with nature still goes on, I took a drawing pin out of David's mouth yesterday, just happened to notice him sitting chewing something!

The "Alexanders"[1] are driving me insane, there are hundreds of them. I sat in the sitting room only for a few minutes to listen to the news last night and was nearly ill when I found one trying to get up my sleeve.

It would do your heart good to see the joy "Robert's Hammer" has caused, not to mention the nails!

Tuesday 8.15 p.m.

Am now beginning to see daylight through the muddle of clearing out all drawers etc.[2] I got the tickets today and the luggage goes off tomorrow. I shall be very glad to be gone now things have got this length. One half protests bitterly at leaving. One thinks of so many happy associations, particularly not knowing how things

---

[1] What on earth are "Alexanders"? The word is clearly written out.

[2] It looks as if this was setting out to Seamills for a long stay.

will be when the time comes to return, and the other half as always feels that there is great relief in movement when extra worried about you. It's come at a fortunate time really this move for I don't know how I could have got through these weeks of wondering without some diversion.

Robert thinks I went to see the engine driver today to ask if he'd take him and is very thrilled. If he is naughty I just have to make for the phone to tell the engine driver and the situation is restored! He has finished all his nails and wants to know why you sent so few!

Biddy has let me down but Daisy is coming, had all plans made it seems and I think was praying Biddy wouldn't go. I'm hoping for a letter from you tomorrow and a little dreading it.

David has changed a bit ever since you left. He is much less grumpy and I breakfast in peace except that he is apt to stand upright in his chair at a moment's notice and sway about with a charming grin. He crawls all over the house and chases Robert with shouts of glee when Robert crawls with him. Also he won't sit still in his bath for a moment in spite of repeated submergings, trying to crawl with the water up to his chest and kneel with waves slopping around him. I've been forced to tie his blanket to each side of his crib at nights at about chest high so to speak and as a result he hasn't wakened until 9 the last two mornings.

Robert has returned to my room, he had a nightmare the other night and firmly refused to go back. He says it's fun sleeping in his own wee room when you are here but when you aren't he is going to sleep with me.

Poor boy I heard him rattling downstairs just as I was going to bed. He had no idea where he was and only knew he was dead scared and had dreamed something was wrong and badly wanted to spend the night not only in my room but in my bed. I seem to have a lot of boys who have nightmares and decide to finish the night in my bed! I love you.

Sheila

24th May 1943, Alan, HQ 12 Corps, TW, to Sheila

My Dear,

Please excuse the paper. Thank you very much for sending on the toilet goods which I foolishly left at home on Friday.

After two warm days it's coldish-ish today and raining furiously. I seem to have the beginnings of a cold but otherwise am very fit.

There is no special news about here - I developed the films last night and hope to print them tonight.

They look pretty good especially of Robert and David and Robert and Anthony on the swing.

I hope Robert's hammer arrived safely and that he has not murdered anyone yet.

I got two more Gilbert Murray's at a new bookshop. I found the Medea and Orpheus Tyrannus. I also got a first class life of Horace, a book on Celtic mythology, and a standard history of Rome.

The Ronald Storrs was a disappointment but you will find the bits about T.E.L.[1] very interesting - quite the best part of the book.

I am sending a little book by Rabindranath Tagore[2] - I shall be glad to hear if you consider it good or nonsense. I just can't make up my mind.

Oh wee One I wish I was back - it seems such a long time since I left Wakefield on Friday morning.

I'm sending Robert a P.C.[3]

I love you, Alan

25th May 1943, Alan, HQ 12 Corps, TW, to Sheila

Tuesday

My Dear,

Its 9.30 PM and I'm sitting up in bed suffering violently and full of whisky and Veganin[4]. I have great hopes however that the worst of my cold is over and that I shall be alright tomorrow.

---

[1] T.E.L. T E Lawrence (of Arabia)
[2] Rabindranath Tagore was a Bengali polymath who reshaped his region's literature and music.
[3] P.C. - Post Card
[4] Tablets with paracetamol, codeine & caffeine.

The photos are really quite good and I shall print the proper prints tomorrow or Thursday. I shall send samples to the McVicars.

I am wading through "Horace" with some difficulty and not finding it easy at all. The Medea, the other Euripides, is not so exciting as the others - it's clearly a less noted work than Iphigenia or Hippolyte but still exciting enough. The Chorus in Euripides is so superb. It seems to me to be the "incidental music" but so much less disturbing. How marvellous it is after a stormy inflamed theme for the slows to start quietly on a minor key and gradually change to a crescendo in a major key, preparing you for the next appearance of the players. Or alternatively to key down the tempo and sooth the listener for the next scene which may be a soliloquy requiring a *repose* of thought to properly accept it.

Beloved I do so hope you like these Euripides as I do. They have had an enormous effect on me. I found them strangely moving and disturbing. I'm no judge of poetry but I love Gilbert Murray's rhyming verse.

This quotation from "Horace" finds a very ready echo in me.

"English lyric verse without rhyme cannot ring".

How true it is and how futile the attempts to produce lyrics in the classic style from that clearly already did ring in blank verse.

Beloved your man is a bore but before he passes on he is going to write some poetry.

Wed 26th May

Dear, Last night's effervescence astonishes me. If you can read it will astonish you. I love you, Alan.

P.S. will you be able to send me address and telephone number.

27th May 1943, Alan, HQ 12 Corps, TW, to Sheila

My Very Dear,

I had such a charming long letter from you today and that together with speaking to you last night has cheered me up a lot. Ten hours sleep last night has made a new man of me and my cold today is definitely reaching its Cap Bon!

I'm so glad that Daisy is coming up with you. She is strong and sensible and should I think be very helpful.

The book accumulation continues. I have managed to get a complete Milton and a complete Byron in good condition, the ten volumes of William Morris (2/-) and a good 'Scott'.

I'm going off to a hospital today to see some interesting cases of Pneumonia and James Peebles is coming to consult me about his tummy and have tea with me this afternoon.

I'm now writing poetry and if my natural embarrassment at conception, confinement and delivery at my age can be overcome, you shall see the child.

Wee one I like you and I look at my new snaps of you and love you. Alan.

30th *May 1943*, **Sheila, Seamill, to Alan**

Saturday 11.30 pm

Dearest One,

It was so nice to speak to you tonight. Well the journey is safely and comfortably over. Robert is wonderfully happy, it's a nice house and if I could just stop expecting bad news from you I'd be rather pleased with myself. It's been a gloriously sunny day and we are all red and burnt.

Oh I wish you could see Robert on his tricycle. It's a particularly nice one and even has a wee bag of tools behind!

I'm very sleepy tonight for altho I tried last night I just couldn't sleep. I'll add to this in the morning.

I've got David for a room mate which cramps my style rather! Robert and Daisy are sharing another room (separate beds!) and Oh! Beloved there's a fine big double bed and large room we'll have when you come!

Sunday

It's pouring of rain today (is that Irish or Yorkshire or what) and very sad because it means Robert is *separated* from tricycle!

Sorry about last night's blots but this pen acts that way sometimes. I'm longing for a letter from you tomorrow.

I think Monica McV. has what N. *Gubbins* calls a "tender secret".

Mrs Cook's address is: 34 Beachway Avenue, Largs. On second thoughts I'll enclose the letter.

Dear One, the beginning of July seems a long way off, which means that I am a most unreasonable woman, but it's really your fault for being that kind of a man. I love you, Sheila[1]

31st May 1943, Sheila, Seamill, to Alan

Dear One,

The photos are rather lovely and it's grand to have them. The one of my husband hardly does him justice all the same! There are some rather sweet ones of Robert aren't there? Why, Oh! Why does my dear new fountain pen do this sort of thing![2]

Mother and Daddy returned to Glasgow early this morning and go off to Nethy Bridge on Friday.

I've been chasing food officers all day - pen started to throw blots all over the place which is worrying when in bed as I am.

The local food office only opens for an hour once a week, so as I can't see myself standing in the mob that makes a rush during that hour complete with family I decided to go to the Largs Food Office this afternoon. I only had to take Robert as Daisy is here until Wed and could be left the whole afternoon in charge of David. We had the usual trouble getting a bus but got there in the end and after visiting F.O. Robert wanted to see the house he used to live in so we walked along and gave "Barona" the once over. Walked slap into "Sibbald"[3] too but he didn't know us at all! It looks as if we've cured them of house letting for ever!

I think I'll try and get "Sister" for your July leave, what do you say?

---

[1] Sheila is about to set off for Wayside, Seamill, West Kilbride, Ayrshire.

[2] The letter is blotched with ink from her new pen.

[3] Sibbald is the owner of "Barona" where David was born. Sibbald pursued Sheila for money for various, disputed, damages after she had left. The letter changes from being written in ink to pencil after the blots bit. Sheila seems to have a lot of trouble with blots - no Biros in those days! Sounds as if the air was a lot cleaner than industrial Wakefield.

Beloved it's amazing how clean the children keep here, one can take them out anytime without all that awful cleaning up business and tide marks all over.

I'm in the middle of "Ur of the Chaldees" enjoying it very much. Tuesday

Nothing of interest to report. Had first lot of books from you today (Storrs etc.) and letter of the 27th sent on from Wakefield. I shall look forward to your "child" and no matter how astounding it may be it will be of deep interest to me. Oh! Dear one you'll never never quite know how dear you are.

I've been feeling desperately weary and sleepy since coming here, must be the "change of air" that people talk so much about!

Your family are flourishing. Yours ever. Sheila.

2nd Jun 1943 Alan, HQ 12 Corps, TW, to Sheila

Dearest One of Mine,

I was too tied up with people in the room to get through on the phone last night but I shall certainly get through tonight.

I had your letter yesterday and that cheered me up a good deal for I was for some reason or other depressed - probably a relic of the cold.

Do you wish me to send any Thermos flasks to you at Seamill? I'm sorry I have not yet been able to *refuel* my lighter, so I shall keep yours just now if I may.

I have purchased a most lovely Plato translation - I'll confess how much I paid for it when I see you! It's in same type of binding as the Lockhart[1] and in similar condition.

Do you remember how when we were talking about the books found in Lawrence's room at Clouds Hill[2] we remarked on the numbers by William Morris? Well I've just been reading a life of Wm Morris and it's most interesting to find that he was clearly the spiritual father of Lawrence's love for woodcuts, and fine paper and home printing and bookbinding. Most of Morris's work seems to

---

[1] John Gibson Lockhart, who wrote a much-admired biography of Walter Scott.
[2] Clouds Hill cottage belonged to T E Lawrence (of Arabia) and is open to the public today.

just miss the mark but some is very curious and stimulating. Do you wish me to send you any reading matter or can you not cope with it?

I've got an Everyman Macaulay's History in 3 vols which will be handy as a reference if anyone else like Gordon Daviot[1] or Lays of Scottish Cavaliers[2] should quote him.

I may still get off early in July as Sam hopes to get off before the evening. Poor Sam is back to Major and feeling rather aggrieved.

I'm longing to hear your comments on the photos for they seem to me to show two very nice boys and one dear Sheila. Alan

3rd Jun 1943, Sheila, Seamill, to Alan

Thursday 11 p.m.[3]

Dearest One,

A few more jokes like last nights on the telephone people's part and your wife will be a dead woman. I was awakened from very deep sleep by the tel bell and floundered downstairs in the dark not very sure if I was having a nightmare or it was the real thing. As I expected they said Tunbridge W wants you and I sat in a cold sweat and with such palpitations as I hadn't thought possible. Having spoken with you a few hours before I knew it must be something desperate to make you phone after midnight and I died many deaths before a voice at the other end regretted that Col Stevenson had left but offered to give him a message![4]

It's been a lovely day and I took the tribe to Ardneil Bay in the afternoon, Robert on his tricycle! We had a nice time there except that Robert wept because the sea water wasn't warm and David swallowed a lot of sand.

---

[1] Gordon Davoit was a pseudonym of Josephine Tey under which she wrote plays with historical themes. Josephine Tey was better known for her mystery novels.

[2] Lays of Scottish Cavaliers by was a collection of poems by William Aytoun. It included rousing titles such as 'Edinburg After Flodden' and 'The Burial March of Dundee'.

[3] I've dated this letter from Alan's letter of 2nd June and am confident the date is correct. Interesting that 1st class post arrived the day after posting.

[4] The opening paragraph of this letter illustrates Sheila's terror of learning that Alan might be part of the invasion force, what we now call D-Day.

Your mother is coming to see us tomorrow so I hope it's another good day.

The flag arrived this evening and is to be hoisted with due honours tomorrow.

My hands are indulging in their usual reaction to the sun only much worse. They really are terrible tonight.

Friday

Your mother has been with us all day but unfortunately it's been beastly wet and cold. I am at this moment (8 p.m.) sitting in front of a radiator wound up in a rug nearly chittering - what a climate!

I was so delighted to have your letter of the 2nd this afternoon I hadn't expected one today and your letters make such a difference and are a great help to me.

I think after what happened on a previous attempt, it would be a great mistake to trust the Thermos Fs to the ungentle hands of the post office and I have no real need of them for the moment.

Much as I long to be able to follow you in your reading it just isn't possible just now. I'm in the middle of Storrs. I wasted (?) last evening by reading a translation of a German novel. I have all Burton to digest and several other books I brought up including some of your Greek friends. In addition to which there are one or two books in the house I have visions of looking at. For example; "a Manual of Seamanship" ancient but full of "bends and hitches" etc.!

Gosh! Just remembered that a parcel from Wakefield came in this afternoon, when there was no time to open it - books! - No, eggs! A parcel from Lannie wrapped in paper that had at one time come from you to me and seeing your writing on it I had supposed it was books you'd sent on.

I'll enclose the letter. Kenny doesn't really seem to be cut out for the army does he? It's a mercy he is recovering.

I'll write to her when I finish this. You know I'm still shivering. I'm for whisky and bed tonight, a good excuse anyway!

Dear one it's only a fortnight and seems more like a year since you left me. Oh Beloved when shall we ever live together again. I get so dreadfully lonely for you and *dearest* the import of every day that dawns.

Yours ever, Sheila

4ᵗʰ Jun 1943, Alan, HQ 12 Corps, TW, to Sheila

9.15 pm

My Dear,

I'm sitting in the office waiting for a call to come through for its Robert's birthday and I just could not get an opportunity to phone you earlier. I hope you like the enlargement of Robert at the gate. At any rate it's better than the poem!

I enclose another wee poem with some hesitation but Oh it's good to have someone who won't laugh at my efforts. I'm going to practise and practise until I do produce some poetry.

It's very cold and wet tonight and only a handful dined in mess. I'm going up to dine at the something tomorrow night with Col Cohen (who is a very rich man and a race-horse owner). His wife is staying there over the week.

There is no further news about my going with Wiggy but he will be up in town at the beginning of the week and hopes to hear something.

I do hope I get through reasonably quickly on the phone and don't give you a fright by getting you out of bed. Talking of beds that double one you have sounds attractive.

There seems nothing now to prevent me going off right at the beginning of July. That will be six months from Jan 7ᵗʰ the date of my second last leave! And I shall get 10 days. Now I must try to write a story for Robert - I have not written him one for a very long time.

11 PM

Sorry beloved. I shall have to leave it tomorrow. I enclose "The Two Little Boys" for Roberts's competition . . . . PAGES MISSING

9ᵗʰ Jun 1943, Alan, HQ 12 Corps, TW, to Sheila

Dearest,

This will be a very short note for I want to catch the post and I've been pretty busy all day.

I had a long letter from Mummy today full of Robert and David and Sheila and how lucky a man I am to have you. Now I'm inclined to agree there.

I'm busy on a long poem on a most lovely fairy tale called - "A Coffee House in Surat". I think I shall be a poet or a shade by the time I'm finished. I adore you. Alan

P.S. This will shake you, it shook me! - I was phoned up today by an A.T.S. Officer aged I should think 20-22 to see if I'd go to a dance with her! Beloved what are girls coming to.

10ᵗʰ June 1943, Sheila, Wakefield, to Alan

Dear,

Perhaps it might be better if you were thoroughly nasty next time you are home and then I should not miss you so much! Our wee family is in excellent heart and David more bouncing every day.

I intended writing this letter to you last night but just as I'd finished my supper Miss Whitaker came to see if she could wait until Charlie came home as she had forgotten her key and was locked out. She stayed until after 10 and after I had tidied up and fed David I just couldn't keep my eyes open.

I hope the film was good on Tuesday evening. My days are so unvaried that is hard to think of anything to tell you about. Life has taken a hard twist in the last two days because David spits all his food at me and I don't know what to do! He starts rocking with laughter as soon as he sees me approaching with a cup and spoon and fires everything back at me amid yells of joy, until we are all covered with whatever it happens to be and I am almost in tears.

It rained last night and all morning but cleared in the afternoon and we had another long walk. For it's a very nice family I have got and I like them. If only you were with us I'd have my head and the clouds all the time.

I've written to Sister asking her to come for a few days of the week and I am hoping she'll know what to do with *solving* that spit![1] I love looking after David but I'll enjoy seeing someone else do it for a short time.

Well I'll stop, get cleaned up and to bed early, there's no limit almost to the amount I can sleep and it makes the time shorter. Yours ever, Sheila

11th Jun 1943, Alan, HQ 12 Corps, TW, to Sheila

My Dear, I'm going to phone you tonight and this will not reach you until Monday. By that time in fact on Sunday night, I hope to know definitely whether I go with Wiggy. I rather think I should have heard by now if I had been going.

I have your letter and poems and a lock of Wobitty hair this morning. I like your poem Beloved. Do you think we can eventually produce a joint one, or would that lead to divorce? Oh Dear One we are reactionaries - we want things as they were - our poetry hovers between that of the young who look forward and the old who look back.

I wonder whether we are going to be very scornful of changes after the war and become 'good old days' addicts. We must not let ourselves. I'm reading "Old Mortality"[2] at the moment. It's curious how Scott was torn between a respect for Claverhouse's character and a sympathy with the people together with the need for arousing the reader's pity in the book.

My poem, of epic length I fear - on the Coffee House in Surat, gets a few verses every day. It's very hard work and I'm exhausted after an hour of poetrification.

I had a T.A.B. inoculation last night which had surprisingly little effect on my health. I sweated a bit in bed but whether that was due to T.A.B or a hot sultry night I'm not sure.

My Beloved I'm constantly thinking of you worrying your head

---

[1] Alan notes in his diary 16th July "just administered corporal punishment for the first time to David (with good effect) for spitting food at me!". Times have changed!

[2] Old Mortality - Walter Scott book.

off in Seamill. Try not to sweetheart - July 2nd 3rd and 4th or 5th will see me with you for 9 days.

Will you find out when the morning trains leave St Enoch's for I shall travel overnight from London. Now I must go and have lunch. I love you. Alan

12th Jun 1943, Alan, HQ 12 Corps, TW, to Sheila

My Dear,

You are a dear person to have as a wife and it's ridiculous what a thrill it gives me to speak to you on the phone.

I always feel much more joyful and restful after I've spoken to you and last night was no exception.

I sat in the mess garden and chatted to Rutherford who is an academical, and Cohen until about 11 o'clock last night. Then I went to my billet and read Old Mortality until I finished it about midnight. I enjoyed it very much - especially the broad Scots dialogue and characterisation of lowland country types. Scot's analysis of Claverhouse, as I mentioned yesterday, is most interesting and the end of the book finds the hero who had fought with the Cameronians, and had at one time been condemned to be shot by Claverhouse, sympathising with him though not actually fighting with him. Romantics like Scot cannot *trust* a heroine. I think it needs a rather more cynical man to depict a woman!

I have the notes at the end of Scott's[1] novels. They are informative and chatty but even more interesting they show that Scott could, if he wished, deftly outline a character and stimulate the interest in him in a few words. That is surprising in light of the profligately of description in the body of the book.

I must get hold of his "Worthies" some time for Scott must have known and loved so many border folk. Perhaps his chief claim to the notice of posterity will be his records of these people.

Beloved this letter is positively a Desmond McCarthy-ish letter but I'm thinking and talking to you on paper and my pen is running away with me.

---

[1] Alan spells the writer as Scot or Scott with careless abandon. Properly, Sir Walter Scott.

The Coffee House in Surat moves ponderously on. Childbirth in Hell! I've changed the hero's name to Takid which tweaks a string in me.

It's so tempting to make word music with names like Tohid, Meugzin, Groflan, Caravanserai, Tokay (- Bass and Stout!) that I can hardly get on with the story!

Yes my Dear your man is *Skelly*! But not so *skelly[1]* that he does not love you very much.

I love my sons too. Alan

13th Jun 1943, Sheila, Seamill, to Alan

Dearly Beloved,

I don't know why but it seems as if this uncertainty as to your projected move had been with me for untold weeks instead just over one. I was sure I would hear tonight but nothing has happened. I would not think much of that in itself only I was awakened just after seven this morning with the phone and on answering it was confronted with only a barrage of crackling and collection of fearsome noises which I battled with until nearly deafened when I gave up and went thoughtfully upstairs. On my way up my eyes fell on the wee black box where the telephone wire enters the house and where dwell as you know a lot better than I all the terminals etc. and odds and ends to which the telephone is it seems ultra sensitive. Away at the back of my mind I seem to see Robert sitting beside the aforesaid W.B. box with a faraway look in his eyes and also at one side the Bakelite is broken halfway up. I unscrewed the top and found a drawing pin that had been pushed in, removed it and behold the phone was normal again!

You'd just phoned. When I stopped speaking to you I became aware that Robert had added his howls to David's. I'd left the pan of milk on the cooker and my head was splitting. Peace now restored and I'm going to get a nice hot water bottle and to bed. It's bitterly cold and wet as ever.

I just don't know what to think about your affairs and have

---

[1] Think he meant 'skellie' - old Scots word meaning 'squint-eyed' or having an odd way of looking at things.

decided it's better to refrain. I'm enjoying "Storrs" very much and my disappointment has worn off from the eighth chapter.

The phone was bad tonight but I gather you are having a hectic time. I'm glad your arm wasn't too bad. Yours ever, Sheila

15th Jun 1943, Sheila, Seamill, to Alan

My Dear,

Forgive me if I don't write much tonight. I still feel distinctly stunned and empty of feeling. It would be better not to write at all, but you are due a letter and will wonder if you don't get it.

Poor beloved, it will be hard for you to leave the boys just now. I hope you are not selling your camera, I think you should keep it.

No more just now dear. David is crying and I must go to him so will stop. Yours ever, Sheila

2nd Jul 1943, Alan, HQ 12 Corps, TW, to Sheila

My Dear,

I had a very good journey down. About 10 p.m. the Sleeping Car Attendant came in and said would anyone like a sleeper? I jumped at the chance and got the top berth in one of the new two berth 1st Class sleepers. I slept very well and it made a tremendous difference to be able to get some rest.

I'm going into a new billet which I have not seen yet.

There is not a single scrap of news about my future so I shall just wait and see.

I have written to Col *Ryles* asking him if he could meet me in London early next week.

Well my Dear another leave has come and gone. Each one seems to go more quickly than the last and just as I'm getting down to feel really at home with you all I have to come away.

I hope that you are having another good day. It's glorious here and very hot.

Broomhead has gone off for 48 hours and Sam is going up to London tonight.

I'm sending Robert a wee parcel to compensate for the sweets of his I ate.

Oh Sheila it seems so futile to try and write to tell you how much I love you when I cannot say it properly to you when I'm with you, but you do know Beloved how you are the breath and sorrow of existence for me. Alan

9th *Jul 1943*, **Sheila, Seamill, to Alan**

Thursday

Dear One,[1]

A week today since you left. You will think I have been very neglectful in writing I'm afraid, but I find it difficult to write just now somehow. Although I'm afraid in spite of my efforts I think of you as constantly as ever!

We did enjoy our two nights in Glasgow Robert and I, and much as we love David were glad of a short break!

I'm sorry I stood your hair on end last night. I didn't know it was a secretive affair. It's a pity the phone was so bad but fortunate at any rate that I could hear you all right. I've finished at last "Euripides and His Life" and could discuss it quite brightly with you but no doubt by the time I next see you it will for the most part have faded. I enjoyed it very much.

The Isabel Burton's look most fascinating and I'm going to read them next.

David has had his curls shorn off and looks greatly improved. Robert informed me late last night that "we just live for one another, don't we Mummy!"

I can find no trace of a Khaki Shirt and am wondering if you've found it. I had a letter from Ruth today. Bobby is in Tunisia.

I'll be thinking of you a lot this evening and wondering a lot. It's strange I was dreaming about Achiltibuie all last night and Daddy woke me by coming in this morning and putting the papers on my chest and so first thing I saw was enclosed.

I noticed in yesterday's paper that G. Gill had had a daughter (the second?). It was born in Kent so it looks as if he was down there. Your loving wife, Sheila

---

[1] Date calculated from Alan leaving Seamill. Alan had been on leave.

11th Jul 1943, Alan, HQ 12 Corps, TW, to Sheila

My Dear One,

At last the uncertainty has resolved. Broomhead is posted away and I stay here so that is that. I shall phone you tonight and let you know.

We go out in the field on Tuesday so I shall not be able to phone you but my address for letters (or wires if need be) will be as above.

So I shall come up for a 48 hours whenever I can and count the days until my next leave which will be due on Sept 20th.

Brigadier Lawson the new ADMS[1] arrived on Friday night and seems a grand type of chap.

Well my dear love the next thing for you to do is find a house for the winter. I hope you can find one.

It's a long dreary business this war and I don't see how it can be over under another 18 months but one never knows. I'm going to have a long holiday with you at Achiltibuie whenever it is over. It's very bad luck, that accident at Achiltibuie. They must have gone too close inshore near the tideways in the islands.

I have a most excellent find in a wee book which I shall read you in a day or two "A Summer in Skye" by Alec Smith written about 1850. It is beautifully written and most fascinating.

Oh my Dear - it's lonely for you and I am never quite right when we are apart and things are so little fun unless shared. It seems a very long time until leave is due but I shall get 48 hours and it's now 10 days since I came back[2] - it seems much longer than that.

I'm sending back one of your own letters and a letter from John Fergie, which please dispose of when you have read.

Well my Dear I'll write again tomorrow. I love you, Alan

12th Jul 1943, Sheila, Seamill, to Alan

Monday

My Dear One,

Had your letter of Saturday today and also the cherries. They are delicious but mortality fairly heavy about 50/50. You will be fed up

---

[1] ADMS – Assistant Director Medical Service.

[2] 10 days since Alan came back from Seamill so he came back 1st July.

at the continuation of your boredom at TW, but I feel a new woman in the temporary relief.

The weather is fearful hail and thunder and gale of wind today.

Robert has become very friendly and plays almost continually with a little boy of seven who lives two houses away - Peter McNab by name. He is an attractive child and they play well together. There is another infant of three, (only just I should say) a stoical wee being with red hair and plentiful freckles, who joins them as often as lies in his power, but is much imposed upon and usually departs howling!

Robert is hobbling about with a large bandage and wet dressing on his knee. Last Monday he was as usual out playing with Peter (both on their tricycles) when towards bedtime there were murderous yells which I confused as coming from *myself*! I found Peter with his arms round Roberts's middle trying to hoist him to his feet and Robert much too weak at the knees from seeing blood from his knee all over his sock and shoe, to do anything to help himself! It was quite a small graze really but the day he got the plaster off he fell on the same place again on the road and had a very nasty knee full of dirt and grit and of course "buckets of blood". Just a beginning of a series of such I suppose!

I take every second I can to read the life of "Burton" and I'm about halfway through the first volume, there is so much of his other writing in it and I find it most interesting.

Oh! Beloved why can't you be sitting reading with me tonight, what a tragic waste of time it all is at the least. I shall get on with the Burton's "Mecca Medina" after the life I think before starting on any of Euripides things. It's strange but I remember hearing the Alcestis done on the wireless years ago and being much impressed. I hadn't realised it was the Euripides until reading the E. and this times. You ask about the next winter and of course I don't know what on earth to do. If there is any chance of you still being where you are I certainly don't want to be in Glasgow, it's so much easier for you to get to Wakefield. Of course you will say there is no chance of your being there next winter but you have never been right in that respect yet, I don't think! It's all rather difficult and it would be so much easier to talk it over with you.

The house (66) being conveniently let,[1] if I had only Robert I'd have chanced it and tried to get a "But and Ben"[2] somewhere between London and Tunbridge for say September and October which would have enabled us to see you with luck once a week. Don't trouble to head me off from this idea. I can see every fault in it that you will and I haven't only got Robert! I shall write Hipson and tell him I cannot decide until the beginning of August and perhaps stall things long enough to see you again before deciding and if at that time it looks as though you were to stay put for a bit then I suppose the best thing for both of us is for me to return there.

I'm not worried about Hipson going in any case as there seems to be a shortage of furnished houses there, but he seems a good tenant and if I did not return it would be more convenient to let him continue over the period that I was digging myself in somewhere even if we wished our higher rent later on.

Anna is going to the letter box so I'll stop and give this to her as it's a beastly night. Yours ever. Sheila

16th Jul 1943, Alan, HQ 12 Corps, TW, to Sheila
Friday

My Dear, I'm sorry I did not write yesterday but I was nearly all day at a dentist in the town where we were billeted. I had the root x-rayed and then, it proving healthy, the nerve extracted! This was a trifle nasty but I'm so relieved to have it finished. I'm going up again on Tuesday to have the root prepared for the Crown.

It's wet this morning but we have had good weather and I'm feeling extremely well on it. The new Brig[3] is a cheerful robust sort

---

[1] So at this stage 66 Manygates Lane is let out to Hipson. This suggests they owned 66, but it was rented so must be a sub-let. We are obviously up at Wayside, Seamill, West Kilbride, for some time.

[2] But n Ben. The derivation is from the Scots language for a two-roomed cottage, The term has been used by archaeologists to describe a basic design of "outer room" conjoined with "inner room" as a residential building plan; the outer room, used as an antechamber or kitchen, is the **but**, while the inner room is the **ben**.

[3] Brigadier Lawson.

of man and very good to work with.

I had a very good long letter from you yesterday and it was a great joy to feel that you felt so happy about the news which I had phoned you. The war seems to be going tremendously well just now and it's the Russians who are to be thanked for most of it.

I'll enclose a note for Robert to commiserate with him on his knee.

If we ever have another boy (!!!) we should call him "Angus". Beloved we have done our share and I want my playmate too much to view with cheerfulness the prospect of more of a family.

I'm so glad you are enjoying 'Life of Burton' - it was a lucky find. I most heartily agree, why cannot I be sitting with you when you are reading.

Beloved I can be so relaxed and natural and happy at such times. Oh Dearest you are surely the nicest person in all the world to talk to.

It seems quite possible that "if you only had Robert" it would be feasible to try and get accommodation near me but I shall have to talk that over with you when I get up for I don't see how it can be done by letter.

I have been able to do quite a lot of reading since I came out and it's been most enjoyable. After all - when I'm not at home and can play about it's the most pleasant relaxation and requires the fewest tools and the scantest accommodation.

The Arabic is coming on slowly[1] and I sometimes get a glimmer of light!

I'm going to get down to authorship sooner or later.

Well Dearest I'll now pen a note for the Wob. Talk to him a lot about me for I love my family.

Love Alan

---

[1] I can't believe Alan is trying to learn Arabic, but that's what it says!

16th *Jul 1943*, **Sheila, Seamill to Alan**

Friday

My Dear,

How awful that the phone had to be like that tonight. I'd give so much to know what you were trying to tell me for of course I've never stopped wondering since. Sister departed tonight for a fortnight - whole week in England and the "fair week" when her husband is on holiday. I shall be thankful when it's over as it's a nightmare to me that you might want me to go down if anything happened and I tied hand and foot here, Oh! how I wish I could have heard you tonight.

The photos are a joy to have and you could do a lot more with a few of them. They are really dreadfully badly processed.

Well beloved I really can't write you a long letter these days I am afraid and you poor one must be really as much on edge as I am. Perhaps you will phone tomorrow night but I don't expect that will be possible. I love you. Sheila

17th *Jul 1943*, **Sheila, Seamill, to Alan**

Saturday

Dear One,

What a relief to speak to you tonight and at least not to hear any bad news. I am trying not to think of Col R but finding it impossible. It's been cold and dull today and I'm thinking longingly of our boiling afternoons on the shore.

David has been much more settled today but still very jumpy if anyone strange looks twice at him! I am so glad you had a comfortable journey. I forgot to ask for your eye tonight. I'm afraid I was so anxious for your news that I went almost dumb.

Unless my tooth forces me I won't go to Glasgow until the latter half of the week, as I don't feel like going off anywhere with your position so peculiar and you will most likely hear something in first half of week.

David woke at 6.45 this morning so yours truly is distinctly sleepy so will feed David early and get off.

It's as well you were not here this afternoon, the kitchen sink got blocked and Daddy spent about an hour floundering about under it and in the end it disgorged a teaspoon and a dreadful old dish cloth!

It's absurd to tell you that I miss you for I might as well tell you I'm alive.

Yours ever. Sheila

18th Jul 1943, Sheila, Seamill to Alan

Sunday

My Dear,

Thanks for another letter. I shall post your box of clothes back tomorrow. Poor beloved it must have been horrible to wake and find a tooth missing. I have nightmares to that effect occasionally and am always very relieved to wake and find them all there. I hope the ensuing visit to the Dentist wasn't too bad.

The weather has relented at last and the last three days have been beautiful tho not quite so hot as when you were here.

I'm writing this out in the garden just before dinner and Robert keeps walking over and talking at me.

"A Summer In Sky" arrived safely and will be read. I'm now about halfway through Vol 2. Isabel Burton and getting a trifle weary of same, although I' enjoyed it.

The family are here and will be for the week.

Aunt Bet died[1] this morning, she had been brought back to Bears Den as I think you knew.

I am especially longing for you today and would give a lot even for a few hours of your company. The boys are fine and enjoying the good weather. Yours ever, Sheila

P.S. I enclose electricity account. I arranged for the meter to be taken on the day I left but didn't hear if this had been done although I suppose it was. I can pay the account all right but you can straighten things out with the electricity people as I am lazy!

---

[1] Aunt Bet died, so this letter must be Sunday 18th July.

22nd *Jul 1943*, Sheila, Seamill to Alan

Thursday

My Dear,

I had a note from you today saying you might get up about August 8th. It's so lovely to have a date to look forward to and I hope it doesn't get put off too much.

I had the poem this morning and beloved I do so appreciate your sending it to me. I've only just had time to run through it and refuse comment until I have been over it carefully tonight. I like it. I can't tell how much but from my first glance over it I think there are parts you could improve on considerably. However more later. I feel very much that it's an impertinence on my part to suggest improvements on something I could not do myself, however you asked for it!

Daddy got his face rather badly cut and bruised in the foundry today, a bit of metal from a propeller hit him under and over his eye, cutting his cheek and giving him a dreadful black eye, It has given him a bit of a shake. Both the parents went up to Glasgow yesterday to attend Aunt Bet's funeral[1] and Daddy spent today at the works and is now here until Monday.

Robert and Peter were caught red-handed today by the people next door trying to get the goldfish out of the wee stone pond!

Beloved you will never know how I long for you. Sheila

23rd Jul 1943, Alan, HQ 12 Corps, TW, to Sheila

My Dear,

The weather is still foul and everything is damp and soggy but I'm feeling very fit and well.

You would not like camping here. I removed about twenty earwigs from my bed last night!

I had a tour of units with ADMS yesterday and managed to get a bath at field Ambulance.

I've no particular news but had a letter from Moira who is with the family in *Solen*. Moira is very well and had walked three miles! They are all enjoying themselves.

---

[1] Aunt Bet (Bethia) was Mamie's sister, Sheila's Aunt.

I'm going to the dentist again tonight and I shall indeed be glad to have the gap in my face filled in!

Oh my Beloved I have been thinking so much about Camusglashlan that I wake up in the morning surprised to find myself not at Rieff.

The after war holiday must be a long one and I must have you all to myself. I love you. Alan

25th *Jul 1943*, Sheila, Seamill, to Alan

Tuesday 8 p.m.

Dear One,

I've got the fidgets badly tonight. I'm longing to hear from you and yet dreading it a lot.

I'm making a third attempt to enclose Lannie's letter, I'd just finished writing to you last night when Nonie came in and I cleared my things up hurriedly and forgot. He paid his visit in his car if you please and had a great tale concocted for legitimate destination if he ran into trouble on the way - shades of the "Oxford Group"!

Today has at least been dry but not much else. There's a Corn Crake in the field making an awful noise.

Robert cut a lump off his hair this morning, some of which I enclose, said it was getting in his eyes!

You know the place we used to stay, near here - well it's just as packed with soldiers as in those days. I mention this because I seem to remember you thought otherwise.

Oh but this week is taking some getting through. I wish I had a placid disposition.

Why Oh why do I have to feel as I do about you. If I just first need you half as much I could still be a loving faithful wife and so much more comfortable. Yours ever. Sheila

P.S. don't worry about *it* - closed it's unfinished and there will be no more!

28th Jul 1943, Alan, 12 Corps, TW, to Sheila

My Dear,

I'm expecting the mail in at any moment and hoping for a letter. It's another glorious morning and I had breakfast in short sleeves under some trees.

I won the revolver competition last night so that I have scooped both rifle and revolver which is galling for "combatant" soldiers!

I'm going to be very glad to have that tooth out tomorrow and I hope it's not too obviously a crown. It could hardly be worse however than the one it replaced.

Just had a nice wee letter from you. I have not got Iphigenia. I think it is in Wakefield. It's so good when we both can enthuse over something together like "The Medea".

I hope you enjoy 'The *[Illegible]*'. I did and am at present reading Thierry's Norman Conquest. The foundation of this book to me is that he uses all the ancient non-Latinised names for historical figures thus Alaric the Goth becomes All-Rick (all strong or all-powerful).

I'm so glad you also are having good weather and delighted that you are able to record that David had a good day! He will be a good wee boy and he and Robert will have enormous fun together

I picked up Gilbert Murray's 'Five Stages of Greek Religion' a day or two ago. It's a bit heavy but stimulating. Do remember to ask if *Captain* Crawford got the books when you see him. Well my Dear I have only a couple of weeks now. I love you so much. Alan

30th Jul 1943, Cpl Hyslop 735533, W. R.A.M.C. 10th Field Hospital, Attached 102 General Hospital, Ormskirk, Lancs

Friday

Dear Mrs Stevenson,

I was with Colonel Stevenson at HQ 12 Corps until recently, when he mentioned that he was trying to get a book "Celtic Bards and Kings" by Borrow.

The enclosed would appear to be the book in question, except that it appears to be wholly concerned with Wales and the Welsh whereas Col Stevenson's interest is Scotland and the Scots.

A Liverpool bookseller put me in touch with an antiquarian bookseller in Caernarvon who, apparently, specialises in Celtic literature. The address of this bookseller is - J.R. Morris, 7, Y Bont Bridd, Caernarvon. He was able to supply the book quite quickly. Colonel Stevenson was about to move when I left 12 Corps. If he has done so, I trust he is comfortably settled down at his new location.

Please convey my regards to him when next you write. Cpls do not as a rule go around paying their regards to Lieut Colonels and the wives of Lieut Colonels: but then, so far as other ranks are concerned, your husband is an exceptional Lieut Colonel.

My very best wishes,

yours sincerely, W. *Hyslop*[1]

1st Aug 1943, **Alan, Cheltenham, to Sheila**

My Dear,

I'm sitting up in bed feeling very sleepy but I feel I must write to tell you of a most amusing day.

We left camp at 12, had lunch in TW, and set out here[2] arriving about 7 p.m. To our horror there was a slip up in our hotel bookings and there we were with no hotel in the place to take us in and Bank Holiday weekend.

Well it was a real heat wave and we were tired hungry and thirsty. We went to the police station and they tried everywhere and at last phoned a most important American General[3] to see if he had any room in a requisitioned hotel.

Then things happened. We were whisked up there, given two John Collins (gin, ginger beer ice and lemon) and shown to our rooms. Each is a marvel of luxury and has a private bath room which we made immediate use of.

Then down to a magnificent dinner beautifully served, then

---

[1] I must remark that Cpl Hyslop's writing is excellent and puts both Sheila and Alan to shame! How nice for Sheila to get a letter like this about her husband.

[2] 'here' being Cheltenham.

[3] This was General John Lee, USA Headquarters, Cheltenham. Alan is on his way to Tenby for a combined ops exercise.

played croquet, of all games, in the garden with the General and so to bed.

The change from our lot and hanging about the police station to this is astonishing. To complete it I found a wood bowl filled with bay leaves on my dressing table, three plums and a peach. Now are you jealous?

I must say these Yanks are hospitable. They just can't do enough to be kind.

I'm looking forward to the exercise and more to my previous 48 hours. Unfortunately we moved overnight last night and the mail had not arrived by the time we had to leave.

'We' by the way are Col Kennet, Col Ffoulkes and self. Kennet was a founder member of the desert patrol people mentioned in 'Lybian Sands'[1] and was captured at Tobruck but escaped. He is a grand chap.

Well my dear I'll try to get this posted in the morning. Oh my Love, only 8 days now till I hold you in my arms.

Alan

2nd Aug 1943, Alan, Esplanade Hotel, Tenby, South Wales, to Sheila

Dearest,

Just a note to tide you over until Sunday.[2] I'm sorry about Robert's cold.

I woke up this morning longing for you more than I've ever done in all my life. Oh my own dear and I need you badly. I'll wire when I'm arriving as soon as I know. I'm in bed and very sleepy.[3]

Your own loved one.

Alan

---

[1] Lybian is Alan's spelling. Book is 'Libyan Sands' by Ralph A Bagnold.

[2] On Sunday 6th August Sheila stayed with Alan at the Esplanade Hotel in Tenby, South Wales.

[3] Alan won both rifle and .38 revolver competitions at this camp.

5th Aug 1943, Sheila, Seamill, to Alan

Thursday

My Dear,

It was nice to hear you tonight. This was to be a longer letter than it's going to be because Miss Gott came in just as I was starting supper and has just departed so I'll make it a short note and get it posted tonight.

Had what seemed a brain wave after speaking to you tonight but I suppose it isn't or it would have occurred to you - why on earth if you succeeded in arriving tomorrow can't you go up and get your business in London done before leave starts? If you have the opening when talking with the General in London you might mention in passing that your whole soul is yearning for the medical side of things, altho I don't suppose he is the ideal person to make the approach to. "Postings" have been chopped and changed before.

I still feel if I had had the sense not to urge that course we might not be where we are now. It's annoying that I'm not free to come south and I feel it very much. However it's lucky that Sister is free at all.

Oh! Beloved I'm the most unbrave of wives and it almost reduces me to tears when I think of the terrific relief I would have known if your work could have been in a hospital. You know I'm almost dreading the joy of being with you again, this time - cowardly I know, but sometimes I feel my heart must crack.

Poor Beloved this after all (and to your misfortune) is becoming a long letter, I believe I shouldn't send it, but, so be it. David has now got support on either side for his two pathetically lonely lower teeth and the poor mite had to work quite hard to get them.

The weather looks settled fair for a bit, but of course in this part of the world one never can be sure. Yours ever, Sheila

13th Aug 1943, Sheila, Seamill, to Alan

Friday

Dear One,

Nice to speak to you tonight, but Oh! Dear, there was I all braced up to take your news and agree with you that all was for the best and I've had to deflate and it's got to be gone through again on Sunday. It's a good thing we aren't superstitious because it happens to be the 13th! It's lashing rain as usual tonight and so chilly and cheerless I've been driven into the kitchen where there is a nice fire and writing at the table. I fancy old Anna is rather pleased, she is very good to me and to the children.

I'm afraid I haven't written to you for a few days. I've been rather in a state of suspended animation waiting for your news. To answer your questions - no, the garage had done nothing up to my departure from Wakefield, and no I'm afraid I have not brought your bathing suit. It did cross my mind but I never got the length of the hunting for it, the improbability of hot enough weather coinciding with you leave and your inclination with either of them being too much for me.

I am just about to parcel up an outsize haggis and black pudding to send to Mrs Morris!

Fancy my husband being chased by the girls. I can see I'll have to have my face lifted one of these days. Gracious beloved. I'm sorry for them, for there's only one you in all the world and you for some odd reason belong to me. The trouble is my dear you don't look married. I shall be forced to get you to wear a ring in spite of your protests, after all I do! Well now for the haggis etc.

Your loving wife. Sheila

P.S. It's all very well to say you like the poem, but you needn't have cackled so dreadfully!

P.P.S. We are going to have tea with Miss Gott tomorrow. I shall be rather glad to see it over as David really isn't at the sociable age and very toothy - he got another lower one on Wednesday but is very secretive about it!

20th Aug 1943, Alan, HQ Corps, TW, to Sheila

My Very Dear,

Screwtape[1] and handkerchief arrived this morning - many thanks. It's still lovely weather here and I'm still exceptionally well. I did 7 miles across country yesterday and enjoyed my P.T. this morning.

Yesterday I purchased some amusing books - Quiller Couch's Art of Writing, a companion to Art of Reading which you have seen being exceptionally good. Then I got another volume of Fraser's Golden Bough - The Scapegoat, The Contemporaries of Marco Polo - being an account of some less ambitious travels, The Dialogues of Lucian with some dubious illustrating by *Blanch* and a curious old book of Ossianic Tales printed in Caxton type in 1789. I have been cutting out drink ever since I came back and bought the books with the proceeds.

I'm so glad you have found a home for September but you are not going to pay for it.

My interpretation of Ossian proceeds slowly but I am very determined about it.

I shall never rest until I can reach publication standard - then knowing my limitations I shall let it rest at one publication.

It's good to know that my boys are well; - it's good to know they are with you, for that is a privilege which carries with it so many happinesses. Oh my love they are lucky boys. Kiss them from me.

I love you. Alan

22nd Aug 1943, Alan, HQ 12 Corps, TW, to Sheila

My Dear,

I could not wait for my call to you to come through last night as I had to rush off for my party. The party was pretty terrible but really the Vicar and his wife are exceedingly nice people and tried very hard.

Sorry about my scruffy note last night.

---

[1] The Screwtape Letters by C.S. Lewis. Letters from a Senior Devil to a Junior Tempter.

I'm plugging away at Ossian[1] and hope to have a few samples for you to see soon. The difficulty is to transfer the flowery and profane Gaelic images into readable prose or verse.

I'm experimenting with treating the *apostrophes* and calls to arms of the heroes into separate metre almost like the Greek Choruses. This breaks the monotony and carries the interest over to the body of the tale.

I've been reading and re reading Euripides and I cannot help quoting this lovely chorus from Hippolytus to you.

> "Could I take me to some cavern for mine hiding,
> In the hill-tops where the Sun scarce hath trod;
> Or a cloud make the home of mine abiding,
> As a bird among the bird-droves of God!
> Could I wing me to my rest amid the roar
> Of the deep Adriatic on the shore,
> Where the waters of Eridanus are clear,
> And Phaëthon's sad sisters by his grave
> Weep into the river, and each tear
> Gleams, a drop of amber, in the wave.
>
> To the strand of the Daughters of the Sunset,
> The Apple-tree, the singing and the gold;
> Where the mariner must stay him from his onset,
> And the red wave is tranquil as of old;
> Yea, beyond that pillar of the End
> That Atlas guardeth, would I wend;
> Where a voice of living waters never ceaseth
> In God's quiet garden by the sea,
> And Earth, the ancient life-giver, increaseth
> Joy among the meadows, like a tree."[2]

---

[1] Ossian (Scottish Gaelic: Oisean) is the narrator and purported author of a cycle of epic poems published by the Scottish poet James Macpherson from 1760.
[2] "O for the wings of a Dove"

And this:-

"Then straight upon the team would terror fall
Howbeit the Prince, cool eyed and knowing well
Each changing mood a horse has gripped the reins
Hard in both hands; then as an oarsman strains
Up from the bench, so strained he on the thong,
Back in the chariot swinging."

Oh Beloved if I could write like that! It's better to hope and fail than never to hope at all!

Wee one of Mine your husband is a feckless fellow and never will be a success at anything but bear with him for he loves you and he is at least trying to do something. The trouble is that "something" changes so often.

Kiss my boys Beloved and tell them I love them so. Alan

24ᵗʰ Aug 1943, Alan, HQ 12 Corps, TW, to Sheila

My Dearest One,

It's another lovely morning and I'm very cheered by the wonderful news from Russia.[1] I can't see that Germany can last out another year at this rate.

I'm almost used now to getting up at 6:45 AM but I think I shall manage to get back to my old habits if I try hard enough!

The poetic impulse has left me and progress is nil!

Thank my boys for sending me their love. It's miserable to love a Daddy who just pops in and out and is much more interested in his wife than his sons.

Oh Beloved it's good to live with you and I need you badly. The evenings are so short now and last night it was cold and autumnish.

I love the Spring and I want to go to Camusglashlan with you in the spring when the nights are long gloamings and the sands hot in the daytime. My own Darling it won't be very long now. I love you. Alan

---

[1] The 'wonderful news from Russia' is their victory at the battle of Kursk. Although over 18 months of war lay ahead the Germans were now retreating.

28th Aug 1943, Alan, HQ 12 Corps, TW, to Sheila

Dear One,[1]

Thank you for this morning's letter. It's exciting to hear that David is trying to walk. How I wish I could pop up for the afternoon. I'm doing next best by making a bow and arrows for Robert!

It's very difficult speaking on the phone as you say; especially when it's impossible to say what you would like.

It looks as though I may get off on leave earlier, say about 27th but if you are going to Wakefield then I'll just wait and come down with you.

My telephone number by day. 3450 extension 161 and my billet for 45.

Well dearest it's getting closer and closer this leave in any event. I love you very much. Alan

30th Aug 1943, Alan, HQ 12 Corps, TW, to Sheila

My Dear,

I've had a quiet weekend and have been in bed both nights by 10 o'clock. I've been able to get in some solid reading and feel as if I had had a slight break from the boredom of ordinary work.

I hope to get a letter with your new address this morning for I cannot find the letter.

My first aid lectures daily at 7.15 A,M. continue. 6.30 A.M. is a barbarous hour to rise!

I have been writing to Grants the Booksellers in Edinburg and they are hoping to get W. J. Watson's "The Place names of Ross-shire" for me.

Dearest one I'm longing for my leave and the joy of being with my dear own ones. You are three very attractive people you know. Each of you is a joy in your own way and you all love me in your own way. So my happiness must always be entirely dependent on the happiness of you three.

---

[1] There is no year on the letter, only 28/8. However, if David is trying to walk he must be around 13 months at least so as he was born April 42 we can assume it is 1943.

Oh the joy of Camusglashlan when we all go beloved, can you imagine it without a gripping in the throat?

I enclose a couple of soap coupons. I have two new bars and one part worn so I'm very well off.

Will you please let me have the rent of the new house so that I can get that squared. I'll just wait now until I see what the post brings. It's now 9.30 A.M.

P.M.

Just spoke to you, will rush and try to get post. Love, Alan.

31st Aug 1943, Alan, HQ 12 Corps, TW, to Sheila

My Dear,

Two letters today and phoning you last night makes me feel right up to date with home affairs. I'm so sorry to hear about your sties and I trust they are improving.

It must have been grand to see "my second son" walking. He will be quite nimble by the time I get home.

I sent off 28 pounds of apples and 14 pounds of peaches to you today and I do hope they arrived safely.

The box will open easily if you just prise up the lid on the side away from the brass locks on the back of the lid.

The box - (made with a knife, a file, a hammer and a hacksaw blade, including the protected edges!) would be welcome sent back as soon as possible.

Well Dearest one, there is no news. I'll be out on exercise for a few days and will phone you the night before I go.

Give my love to our boys. How wealthy we are in our love and our boys.

Alan

9th Sep 1943, Alan, HQ 12 Corps, TW, to Sheila

My Dear,

I'm glad to hear that Robert is still progressing favourably and that the attack is mild. It's certainly would break up the winter for you to have the Lennon girl (I never can remember her name) and baby and it would be so helpful to be able to get out etc. without worry.

I've been pretty slack again but have busied myself with making boxes of all shapes and sizes out of odds and ends of wood which I have picked up lying about the building. It's so odd beloved and I picture them all going to Camusglashlan filled with our "toys". Then I have a splendid bow and arrow to bring back to Robert when I come on leave.

I may be up on an exercise in Lincolnshire about leave time. In which case I would come straight to Wakefield and perhaps manage to scrounge an extra half day or so. I shall send Robert a P.C.to cheer him up.

Oh Dearest Woman I love you and need you. You don't know at all how much. Alan

P.S. Sorry came without Cheque Book - will send later.

17ᵗʰ Sep 1943, Alan, HQ 12 Corps, TW, to Sheila

My Dear,

Another letter this morning - I'm doing well. I also had one from Mummy in which she tells me of seeing Robert and how fit and well he looks.

I'm pretty busy with the others away but it's good for makes the time pass more quickly. I was early in bed last night and read for a long time. Today I hope to get some of the Cox's Pippins which I got last year. They were very good and well packed.

Oh Dearest only about a fortnight now. Oh my Darling how I long to spend an evening in our own house with you.

Kiss my sons and tell them that they are fine fellows who have long future in front of them. I love you. Alan

15th Oct 1943, Sheila, 6 Crown Mans, to Alan

Friday

Dear One,[1]

I had a surprisingly comfortable journey up on Wednesday. An R.N.R. officer opposite dashed out and brought me tea and coffee at various stops. Had just left wife and child to go East. I got a taxi fairly easily and got in here just before 11 PM to find Lannie in bed with flu and Annabella tight! Yes my dear you may not believe it but she'd had her afternoon and evening off and got back thoroughly lit up and told them what she thought of them.

Before she reached the abusive stage she had been hugging Sister and telling her how she loved her. Just before I arrived she'd thrown herself into bed so I confine myself to administering bromide to Lannie and Luminal to Sister who was extremely shaken and retired myself about 1 AM.

Robert woke me at seven and chatted until in desperation I got up. David when he saw me made a wild dive and threw his arms round my neck and hugged me for ages. They are very comforting to a lonely woman these children of yours. Sister has gone and Lannie is up and about today. I have a streaming cold but it is just a head one and I'll be over the worst tomorrow.

I've ineffectually pursued several houses in the last two days and yesterday saw three unfurnished rooms for which they wanted 149 a month! Beloved I am trying very hard to be as good as you are about this separation and am determinedly looking forward with the firm motto of "no brooding". I am going to try to keep the brightness of the future constantly before me. There will be

---

[1] This Air Mail letter is addressed to "Lt Col A C Stevenson R.A.M.C. (38813) Draft Index letters R.C.Y.O.Y. A.P.O. no 4675". So Alan is 'in transit' to Africa and Sheila has no idea where he is at this stage. The address is some sort of army 'P.O. Box'. Sheila is in Glasgow in Mamie's (her mother's) flat. Alan had 24th to 29th 'Education Leave' with us in Seamill before sailing. Sheila left us in Glasgow and spent 3 days with Alan in Tunbridge Wells, then a night in the Lismoyne Hotel, Fleet, on 13th Oct before he caught the train to Southampton to join his ship.

moments when I shall fail and be as miserable and depressed as anyone can be I suppose, but that will not be usual. I have all the happiness in the world to look forward to and I'm not going to let myself be broken by a few months separation.

Saturday 16th

Cold almost gone and Lannie all right. Lannie's sister has been for tea. The children are in good form except that David is a bit toothy and hates his Paisley food! The parents aren't coming back for another week. The Army P.C. came in this a.m. Oh! Beloved I shall be so thankful when I hear you've arrived. I was speaking to Ruth tonight. Bobby is in Italy.

David now gets up on an armchair and Robert gives him a ticket and pushes him up and down the room pretending it's a bus, both enjoying themselves immensely!

Dear I got so many nice things to think of looking back over the last few weeks and I'm so looking forward to the arrival of the photographs and of course to a letter from you although that is bound to be a very distant thing as yet.

Robert talks so nicely and naturally of you it's a great joy. My love is all with you always. Keep yourself very safe for me beloved.

Sheila

17th Oct 1943, Alan, On Ship, to Sheila

My Dear,[1]

I'm writing this on the second day at sea and of course I cannot tell you anything about it nor will I be able to send you this letter by air mail as it's clearly going to be too bulky, for I intend to add to it as the days go by and post it, in addition to an air mail letter, after arrival. *make the letter worthwhile*

---

[1] Since there are no dates or clues I can only guess which of the 'On Ship' letters came first, so I have dated them between 16th and 30th October in what seems a logical sequence, but distinguished them with the 'On Ship' tag. I know from his diary that the ship moved out to anchor (in Spithead?) on 15th Oct. Alan last saw Sheila on 13th Oct and was in Accra 2nd Nov having flown 1,000 miles to get there after landing at Freetown, Liberia, on 1st November.

understands that no letters = anxiety + fear that partner might be dead

I do hope that I can get a letter or preferably a cable to you soon after arrival, as I know so well how you will worry until you hear from me.

Duff is here and Sparks and I am in a two berth cabin fitted with triple bunks to take six with a Col, a Lieut Col and two Majors. It's pretty hectic getting washed and dressed and due to the pressure of space on board it is very seldom that we can get a seat.

That's a bit of a curse because I have a cold in the head and it's bitterly cold on deck.

I have made no provision of warm clothes for the voyage and am longing for warmer latitudes.

At the moment my trunk and valise are lost which is rather distressing. I expect they will turn up for it would be a big blow. I have been told by someone that they arrived at the quayside but I doubt whether they did. They were parked in a luggage van at the station and I had no opportunity to check on them again.

I managed to get a salt water bath today but the lack of salt water soap made it a bit sticky.

What a long groan this is. To tell the truth my beloved I have been pretty much in the dumps since I left you. It's not possible to deceive oneself indefinitely. I need you too much and all that I'm interested in is bound up in you too completely for me ever to be quite happy while this separation lasts.

It gets more difficult as I get older and depend on you more. For the past year my Dear I've not been quite myself. I've been woolly headed and uncertain as to right and wrong. I've had no crusade to wage - a feeling that everything I did was merely a marking time for getting back to you; that as nothing I could do would alter that in any way, nothing was, as a result, much worth bothering about.

I must try to get out of that attitude of mind. I must keep myself clear headed and proper minded for your sake. For I want to come back to you fit for you. Oh my Dear I must.

Another Day

I could not write yesterday as I was completely hors de combat with one of my very fiercest colds. I'm gradually coming to the

Clare Markham

with what was said in Charles Pamell's what was said in Charles surface today but my voice is completely gone.

The weather has been very good and I'm longing to be able to go on deck again.

There seem to be hopes that this may be posted from an intermediate port. That would be fine for you would get it in a week or so.

One of my pieces of luggage, my valise has turned up so presumably the tin trunk is on board.

Cigarettes are ¾ for 100 and chocolate is not rationed on board. The most curious things turn out to be available for example sock suspenders. We hope to have oranges, apples and bananas after our first port of call.

I've enjoyed Laski's[1] "Reflections on the Revolution of our Time" immensely but the last few chapters were a bit confused due to my cold.

Oh my Beloved I hope you will manage to get a nice house. It has just struck me that, if you get an expensive one you will not be able to *cope* + Sister on your £40.

Please use Glyn Mills cheques to keep you square.

I must write a note to Robert to enclose in this. I feel that I rather deceived him and yet it would have meant nothing to him to try to explain why and how long I am going to be away.

It's terribly crowded here, the officer accommodation is really frightful. Junior officers are sleeping in hammocks with two blankets. They don't like it one little bit. Well my Dear I shall add more daily. Oh how I long for this war to be over.

9 PM

Just confirmed that there will be a post from the next port. This is great news and has cheered me up enormously for I do so want you to have news and not be worried. A couple of your Veganin have also cheered me up. I hope my photographs turned out reasonably well. Please try to get yours taken somehow and remember to send me on the snaps. I haven't anything except two

---

[1] Harold Laski (1893 - 1950), was a British political theorist & economist.

very bad snap prints which I found knocking about my writing case.

It's been much rougher today but warmer and I'm beginning to feel almost human again after my cold.

Oh Beloved it's far harder, this whole business for you, and I wish I could help. I feel so utterly helpless to do anything to make this separation easier for you.

I'm glad, terribly, terribly glad we have the boys. They are part of me left behind with you and they love you. I don't suppose it makes much difference that they are so young, for you never can confide fully in them no matter what age they are.

Oh my Sheila I'm going to be very selfish of your company after all this.

Another Day

I've just finished the letter for air mail and I'm going to finish this now. I've managed to get a seat in the crowed lounge. It's just a seething mass of people, playing bridge, talking, smoking and writing letters.

It's odd to be writing two letters to you, one of which you will receive probably a fortnight before the other.

My cold is passing off and I am a bit more clear headed.

Oh Beloved wish you were coming with me.

Bless you and my boys. Alan

18th Oct 1943, Alan, On Ship, to Sheila

My Dear,

There is very little that I can write about in this letter which will be censored.

I hope you had a good journey home and managed to get something to eat on the way and by no means least, obtained transport from the station.

Will you please tell Mummy that you have received this and that she may expect a card telling her of the address to which she should write.

I'm still very numbed my Dear and can't quite appreciate that I won't see you for so long. Let's hope for the unexpected and an earlier return than now seems possible. Cross your fingers and get Robert and David to cross theirs.

I came across this morning a very battered remnant of the white heather which you sent to me in France, firmly tied into my tin hat. I gave the cord an extra knot to keep it there.

Well Sheila you will know how difficult it is to write and how little there is to write at this stage. I could say so little to you for you know all I have to say. Oh Beloved I hope you are not sad and distressed. I shall add more to this later.

I think I shall just finish this off and post it for I'm getting no forwarder.

Dear I shall take the greatest care of myself. I'm a pretty canny person as you know and I won't do anything which would worry you if at all possible. Don't worry if you don't hear from me for six weeks or two months. I shall cable you if and when possible.

Tell Robert that I shall write to him as soon as I can and send him anything interesting I can find. Kiss David and tell him to be like his Mummy. I do so hope you get a nice home soon. Regards to Sister and Lannie. Oh my Dear you will always be in my thoughts.
Alan

20th Oct 1943, Sheila, 6 Crown Mans, to Alan

My Dear A week has gone and Oh! How I wish I knew where you were and if all is well with you. Still no word of a house and I'm beginning to feel it's pretty hopeless and considering a retreat to Wakefield.[1] The boys are very well and sweet. Yesterday I showed Robert a map of the world, where you've gone, where we live, America and Germany. Today he pointed them all out without the slightest hesitation, also various national flags which I'd shown him at the same time. He can remember anything at all if it interests him. I must get him a globe of the world although it's an impossible thing to take about. Kenny's wife is expecting a baby in April, I wonder where he'll be then. I got David a wee horse today and he is simply charmed, pushes it all over the place saying choo-choo and screams

---

[1] 'A week has gone' - confirms they parted 13th Oct.

and scratches if Robert tries to take it from him! You will be glad to hear I've recovered my health and no longer palpitate! I got myself some Minadex[1] and have finished one bottle and started on the second and am feeling heaps better.

Sunday 24th of October.   *Clare Mahepeace Article*

Several days nearer to seeing you again beloved, for that is the way we must think of it. The photos arrived on Thursday, but they are not very good, it's nice to have them all the same and I've got one looking at me now. Your letter arrived the same day and was a great surprise and treat.

Yesterday I had lunch at the auto club with the parents and met Mrs Robinson, Gordon R. (Who is going to Ceylon) Douglas Steven, Nonie and several others. I was most interested to hear some details of Wilfred. This afternoon Daddy and I took Robert down to the docks to see the cranes working etc. then onto the "works" where he (R) had an ecstatic time! David and he kiss each other good night through the bars of the crib now, it's rather sweet. The house hunting goes on unabated but there is no space for details. It's more workable here now as we've moved things out of the dining room and have it for our own. I have dreadfully little news this week. It's just drifted by somehow. Lannie walks the pram miles daily which is a joy. What a help it will be when we get a regular letter service established between us, or the other way round. I must never expect your letters to be very regular if you move about so much as you expected. I've not managed to read much since you left but am just finishing "Rhodes", quite good but somehow she doesn't seem to make him live. I've been once in Smith's but with Robert, so not for long. I'm hoping to get a few hours to myself tomorrow afternoon and will go in and have a look

embodied relatives + loved ones

---

[1] Minadex. A Glaxo drug providing a low dose of dexamethasone, a corticosteroid, used among many other things for treating shock. Sheila was clearly close to panic at the thought of Alan moving abroad, and was having palpitations. Alan had presumably recommended Minadex to take if he was moved. It seems to be no longer available - except in Brazil.

round. Jack Knox is trying to hunt up a book on West Africa[1] for me. As soon as I get your permanent address I'll send you some of the photos you took of us in the spring but they'll probably take a long time to get to you as they will have to go ordinary mail. After a few months we will get some poly photos done and you shall have the results however ghastly. Beloved, you are with me always and every day I think and plan for the time when you come back to stop. I think the last six months should go quickly, at any rate at this end.

I hope soon to be able to send you proper airmail letters, these are very cramping, but perhaps we can only send them. I don't know yet. Please let me know if my letters are censored although it doesn't make any difference really. There is to be a circus here at Xmas. Yours ever, Sheila

25th Oct 1943, Alan, On Ship, to Sheila

Dear,

We have just heard that we can send letters airmail from the first port so I shall send this by that method and another by ordinary mail. Thus you will get two letters. The other letter is a long one, too long for this. We are allowed three sheets. Well dear - all is well - a grimy overloaded boat - but that was to be expected. I'm longing to hear if you have a home and how you and my dear boys are keeping.

My Beloved I had a very depressed time after I left you. I cannot conceive that I shall ever be complete again away from you and I shall never leave you for one day or one night as long as I live unless it is absolutely necessary after the war.

I like living and only naturally I'm thrilled at the interesting times lying ahead of me. But if you were only with me beloved I should cast off years and be a child again in my joy. I shall miss you so much as my haven of rest and contentment. Mentally and physically I need you and there is an awful sense of tension and strain when I'm not with you which often returns again and again whenever I'm not heavily occupied on a particular job. I love you and respect and

---

[1] Alan is on ship now for Africa. Sheila apparently knows enough to be getting a book on West Africa, but perhaps not exactly where.

cherish you Sheila. You know how proud I am to be your husband. You have made one person in the world happier than he ever believed it would be possible to be. You have given the world two grand boys with an infinite capacity for being happy and spreading happiness. These two things alone Beloved are seemingly very common attributes of women. But in truth how few women succeed. I wonder how many are the mental friends of their husbands and their confidents and their hopes and fears as you are with me.

As far as I can see I'm not short of anything and the barbershop on the ship supplies such exciting things as chocolate, sock suspenders, brown boot polish, sweets, cigarettes at 3/- for 100 and so on.

The food is shocking - shades of our honeymoon. Oh my beloved did anyone ever have such a good one. If you can I'd be glad if you would send me on the book I was reading about the place I'm going near.

Tell Mummy you have received this and I have written to her by ordinary mail. I have only got enough stamps for this and there are no more to be purchased on the boat.

I'll add to this tomorrow Beloved. Oh my Dear I hope you are not worried about me and wondering all the time when you will hear from me. I'm so helpless to hurry things on. It's a glorious mild day. The sun is not out yet but it's warm enough for short sleeves on deck. Had a happy talk with civilian Pathologist from place I am going last night and heard an enormous amount from him. He and Political Officer, both very nice chaps, both invited me to come and see them whenever I felt inclined out there. It will be pleasant to do so and get out after an army mess for a bit.

It's a curse having such a susceptibility to fleas! I have picked up one each time I was in the hold looking for my luggage.

I wonder if you will get a house. An unfurnished house with bits and pieces would be fun but a dreadful amount of arranging and a nuisance when you wanted to move again.

Duff has been pretty groggy with Mal de Mer but is now up and about again.

I hope the palpitations have not been troublesome. Take Bromide and/or Luminal[1] if they are bad.

I wish we had settled the question of a good doctor before I left. I just cannot think of anyone. In three months' time David will require to be Schick tested[2] (pronounced sheek) after his three diphtheria injections.

If you can get any M.C.M. 100 or Johnson's Super fine grain developer will you please send me a tin or two. Also if and when you are at Wakefield the Leica manual would be a great joy. It is in the window bookcase.

My sinuses which were blocked and painful yesterday after a filthy cold are now much relieved after a couple of drops of Endrine in each nostril. Thank goodness the cold came early in the voyage. I should hate to arrive at my destination 'ah boonged up'.

My Dear, this will be the first of many letters which you get from me before I see you again. I do hope I can write reasonably freely and am not too tied up by censorship to make my letters interesting. I shall try to find out where Wilfred is and look him up and I shall give you every possible snitch of news. About my doings. Please tell me too all about you and the boys. Every little thing will interest me.

I love you and you know it my own one. I'm so glad you came down to Crookham with me for I enjoyed being with you.

Kiss my boys. Regards to Mamie and Jimmy.

Your loving husband. Alan

P.S. Will you get Rothman in Buchanan Street to send me 200 Paul Mall de Luxe each month. They will go at cheap rate. Use Glynn Mills cheque. Wait until you have proper address.

I adore you. Alan

---

[1] Luminal sounds alarming and is now used to prevent seizures. More references to 'palpitations' suggest Sheila was pretty frantic.

[2] Schick test - a test for susceptibility to Corynebacterium diphtheria toxin.

27th Oct 1943, Alan, On Ship, to Sheila

My Very Dear,[1]

It's infuriating not to be able to tell you of the places we visit. I can't even put a date on this and say anything except that we are "at sea".

It's a fine warm sunny day but we have not yet changed into tropical clothes. I do so hope the air-mail letters from the last port arrive soon. It's a fortnight since I left you behind me.[2] Oh My Dear I hope all is well with my dear ones.

I'm lying in my bunk for a change feeling pleasantly tired after tramping the decks since 7.30 this morning. My trunk has been found, covered over with the bags in the wrong hold.

Oh Beloved when I had my first banana I would have given such a lot to be able to send it to Robert. Bananas, limes, grapes, oranges, apples - we had them from the last port and they were a delight.

I've more or less recovered completely from my cold and now I'm in much better form. It's so miserable in an overcrowded cabin. I'll write more tomorrow.

"Tomorrow"

I've just come down from deck after dinner. It's almost too warm to stay on deck in spite of the ship's movement. Oh Beloved, will you ever forget the cool nights on which we walked around the cool deck on the Vanguard arm in arm. You in your flowered frock and as lovely as any flower that ever bloomed. I can't stay on deck without thinking of our honeymoon beloved.

The ship is now 'wet' and I had a large whisky before dinner tonight.

Next Day

I'm sitting sweating in every pore in the saloon. It's awfully hot

---

[1] The paper is 12.5 cm x 18.5 cm. It is thin and very poor quality and he only got three sheets so the ink soaks through the paper from each side and he is writing in tiny writing to make best use of space. A real challenge to read now!

[2] We know he 'left her' on 13th October 1943 so I can work out the date of the letter - a fortnight later is 27th October.

and even on the open deck it's close and muggy. "We" changed into tropical kit today but Sparks and I decided to leave it for one more day. Tomorrow however I shall have to change. We have several days to go and it gets hotter and hotter as we go "south and souther". I cannot conceive how it can be hotter but it seems it will. I'm beginning to be a faint yellow colour with Chloroquine[1] and it's the oddest thing to think that I should so remain until I see you again.

At the next port where we change for our final destination this letter will go off. I'm afraid however it won't go by air mail because I have no stamps and Heaven knows where I can get any.

I gave a lecture on Health in the Tropics this afternoon to about 300 officers and men. I nearly expired of Heat Stroke in the middle of it, which would have been a very bad example.

The days slip by and it's now 15 days since I saw you. I get up front and patrol the decks until breakfast at 8.45 AM. Then we have boat drill at 10.00 AM. I am in charge of a boat. Then we lunch at 12.45. Then a sleep till tea at 4. A walk until dinner at 7. A walk until tired then retire to saloon to sweat. I have played some bridge but get very tired of it.

Oh My darling how leisurely and without plan this life is. A very vegetable existence at last! Wee one I love you.

Next Day

We are still ploughing along and it's getting hotter and hotter! Even in shorts and shirt it's incredibly hot air in the middle of the day. I gave another lecture today and am due to give two more on Malaria.

We had quite a decent meal tonight for a change but oh was it hot in the blacked out saloon.

I expect to finish the first stage of my journey in a few days' time and post this letter. Oh I do hope I shall be able to cable you. All I care for just now is to get ashore and so start my 18 months[2] and to

---

[1] Chloroquine is an antimalarial. It is used both to prevent malaria and also as a treatment for acute malaria.

[2] So a tour is 18 months, but apparently the 18 months does not start until Alan actually gets there.

cable you to let you know I have arrived. This is such a messy letter! I hate writing on such miserable paper as this. I'll try also to get someone going ashore here to cable for me if at all possible. Oh Beloved I'm longing to hear from you.

I love you. Alan

29th Oct 1943, Sheila, 6 Crown Mans, to Alan

Saturday

My Dear Man,

Your family is all well and in good heart. Robert asks me to tell you that he is being a very good boy and eating all his crusts! David is coming on rapidly and runs about the house blowing a whistle and making a fearful noise. Lannie is still with me and will be for a week or so yet. Yesterday I went to see "Mission To Moscow" and enjoyed it thoroughly. We are having a spell of beautiful weather these days, but suppose will get a shock soon. I saw and had a long talk with Roy Young on Wed. He offered at once to see Daddy as he said it would make it easier for him (D) to see someone else having once broken the ice in a talk with him. He didn't however have very definite ideas on who would be the best person to see, but suggested a psychologist as being the most likely and named "Yellowlees"[1]. I agree with him but am rather terrified of the whole business and wish it were not my responsibility. I am however very thankful I've seen Roy and whatever the *aid* might be I couldn't but do otherwise but to take some step. Roy was not optimistic and I'm glad he had the wisdom to say so to me. I'll let you know how things develop. Daddy is a great deal the better of his holiday I think but is rather pathetic and depressed. Lannie has lovely story about the Boating tragedy last summer. The launch involved belonged to Willie McCleod of Tanera and he got it new some time since. Just after he got it however and before he ever had it out, they saw lights on it after dusk and nobody near it whatever. This happened on several nights and finished the boat as far as McCleod was concerned. He never set foot in it again and sold it to the professor

---

[1] Henry Yellowlees (1888 - 1971). Well-known psychologist and Glasgow graduate.

at the Hotel who was drowned the first time he took it out! I can't think of any suitable comment but couldn't resist telling you the story.

Have had letters from City Treasurer asking for your superannuation money. I am sending it on as I don't know how your balance stands.

31st Oct

I'm afraid I'm missing you dreadfully already and Oh how thankful I shall be when that cable arrives, I get odd moments of sheer panic. Beloved you are so utterly all important to me.

We had lunch at the club again yesterday (being Saturday) and went on to cinema afterwards, very poor show. Am re-reading "Behind God's Back" and am somewhat shaken by his opinion of the Gold Coast and if anyone else tells me it's the "White Man's Grave" I shall scream. When David's pram is left at the garage now, he walks home and up the stairs sometimes holding Robert's hand. They look so funny coming up the road together.

Beloved shall we try to go to Russia after the war? I do want to very badly but we've so much to do I don't know if we can fit everything in!

You can't imagine how many times I've read your last letter. Fortunately it's a good strong paper! I sent you some photos. Let me know if they turn up. All love, Sheila[1]

1st Nov 1943, Alan, [Freetown, Liberia] to Sheila

My Very Dear,

I have completed first part of my journey and continue tomorrow. I cannot say more. Today has been an amazing somersault from sweating in a blacked out ship to landing in this amazing place.

The colours, the amazingly cheerful Africans, the sweet smiles and the multitude of incongruous sights make me wonder whether this is part of the same world as I have just left. The trees, the fruit, the strange coloured birds all stand out like a living cross between

---

[1] Letter addressed to: Lt Col A.C. Stevenson RAMC (38813) A.D.H. G.HQ West African Forces A.P.O. 4657

a museum and a hothouse.

Oh my Darling One how you would love it all. I'm sitting at a table with a warm breeze flowing across the room. Cool black boys are chattering outside and my mosquito net is hung over my bed, the crickets are simply screaming outside.

The above is the full address for letters.[1] I am sending Mummy another letter like this so there is no need to let her know.

Well Beloved, no doubt I shall tire rapidly of all this but first impressions are certainly very exciting.

I hope you have some news of a house where you can live with my dear boys.

Tell Robert that Daddy saw a monkey today playing with a cat and eating a banana. I love you, O how I love you my Dear, Alan[2]

2nd Nov 1943, Alan, G.HQ.WAF, [Accra] to Sheila

My Very Own,

I have arrived safely and in very good health. I shall wire you in the morning. It's now 10.15 PM and I am in bed, having flown about 1,000 miles today. I'll just give you my day in full because it's an amusing one.

Got up and 4.00 AM in pitch black world and shaved and went to breakfast. Boy brought baggage and then led out into the total darkness to where the car was alleged to be. Got lost in lots of scrub then a sudden high wind and a cloud burst. Soaked to the skin, water pouring out of every pocket and into mosquito boots! Found a car and motored 20 miles or so to air-port.[3] Flew here in 7 hours with two stops, one at bush aerodrome and one a couple of hundred miles from here. Very pleasant and almost dry on arrival. Aerodrome baking but cool in plane. Met by car and so here. Changed clothes,

---

[1] This refers to the only postal address, not necessarily where he is. It is Lieut Col A.C. Stevenson, R.A.M.C. Medical Branch, G.HQ, West African Forces, Accra, Gold Coast.

[2] This must be the day before he flew 1000 miles to destination (Accra we now know) covered in letter dated 2nd Nov. Believe he disembarked in Freetown.

[3] The 'airport' was Robertsfield, a 'bush' aerodrome in Liberia built by the Americans. Alan flew to the RAF aerodrome at Tokoradi for Achimota.

boy ironed and produced as new - had bath. Went and had a drink with Wiggy in loggia of his mess.

Went to our own mess and had dinner with Downe. Sat on loggia of own mess after dinner and drank a mixture of orange and lemon squash off ice, which I prepared in the mess and is the local highball.

Now in my room - a guest room where I shall be until Thursday - in bed under a green mosquito net. A terrific party with drums and singing is going on outside - this just completes the African atmosphere. The work sounds just like what the doctor ordered and I'm thrilled. The crickets are singing away again as a backing to the pounding of the drums and yelling.

My boy tells me he won't be with me long for he only needs £2.10 to complete the purchase of his wife - price £20 - expensive as she can read! His name is Daniel.

I expect my heavy baggage to arrive by sea in a fortnight. Meanwhile I have my suitcase, my box and, of course, my gun. It's not nearly so warm as the ship and the spaciousness and privacy is a joy. It's just about right for sleeping with one blanket and my skin is quite dry tonight. My boy comes over and serves breakfast and I have cups of orange and tea at 7 AM tomorrow. Meanwhile my one I'm dreadfully sleepy and so goodnight.

3.11.43, 2.30 PM.

Well my dear one. One day of the tour is over[1] and another begins.

I'm sitting in my office and it's about the hottest time of the day. If it's never worse than this I won't complain. Had pau-pau (a sort of melon) followed by bacon and eggs for breakfast.

The work here[2] is obviously greater and more difficult than I have ever undertaken before and is going to take a lot of getting on top of, but it really is interesting.

---

[1] Day one of tour so his 18 months counts from 2nd Nov 1943.

[2] 'Here' is definitely Achimota, suburb of Accra, but Alan is not sure if he can say so. The address he gives is Lt Col AC Stevenson, Medical Branch, G.HQ West African Forces.

I do so hope that the cable which I sent you this morning arrives quickly and makes you get a surprise and relief at the quickness of my arrival.

Now my Beloved I won't wait any longer before posting this. I have not unravelled the postal arrangements yet but I shall tomorrow. I love you my Dear. Alan.

P.S. (1) will you show this to parents. (2) Sheets for bed cost 7/6 here!

2nd Nov 1943, Sheila, 6 Crown Mans, to Alan

My Dear.

Today I've done a spot of Christmas shopping for Robert! I've got a much desired "garage" with petrol pumps and cars. A decent size but awful rubbish of course, the mail van and letters and numbers in wood. He is getting very keen on knowing letters and recognises quite a few. Bill Stephens is going to Tunbridge Wells, pity he wasn't there when you were. I will only say of the house hunt that it continues and accounts for quite a bit of my time. Anyway it's been quite a benefit having no rent to pay after all my gaiety when you were here. I'm keeping my end up very well, but will I be thankful to get that cable.

I have been forced to get rid of Sister[1] under most unpleasant circumstances. When mother told Annabella to depart (on the excuse that Sister was coming back and we would need the extra room) she started a terrific tirade about the "two faced Judas" as she called her and said if I wouldn't believe her I should ask Miss McLennan. Of course I at once tackled Lannie who said she was thankful I'd spoken as she couldn't bring herself to tell me before and had been worried stiff about it. Evidently she hadn't been a day in the house before Sister started to tell her what dreadful people we all were and much of what she said was not only stupid gossip but pure and simple slander.

I can only give you a few of the highlights - you were the meanest

---

[1] The 'Sister' affair had a deep impact on Sheila, so much so that she was still writing about it in February 1945.

man in the world and I was the most greedy woman. During all the time she had been with us, all you had ever given her was a "box" of handkerchiefs from which I (in my greed) had removed two, making it two short of the doz you had intended for her. I had consistently underpaid her all the years she had been with us and starved her into the bargain, if there was anything particularly good to eat in the house I took it to my bedroom and consumed it there, so that she was forced to go to cafes to keep body and soul together. Upon both of them asking why on earth she stayed she replied that she had a sort of liking for you and that you had asked her to stay as she was so good to your children and you wanted to feel they were being properly brought up while you were away. She also said enough about Edna to Lannie to make me pretty sure she had something to do with that episode. That is not one quarter of the whole tale. Lannie's sister (Ina)[1] came in the day after Lannie arrived and went to lift David whereupon Sister said "Oh be careful you mustn't touch him, he has an appalling temper and will bite you". I have today seen Ina and verified this. As soon as we left here that Thursday she went to Annabella and said "you wouldn't have got that 10/- if Doctor hadn't made Mrs Stevenson give it to you, I was watching them and he gave it to her". It all sounds completely cracked to me. Annabella I would have doubted, but not Lannie and her sister and they all say they never thought such a wicked and dangerous woman could exist. I have written to her (she is due back in a week or two) telling her I cannot employ her again and threatening her with legal action if I have any reason to suppose she is continuing to slander myself and family. I will send you a copy of the letters. I'll have to start a new letter card.

5th Nov 1943, Sheila, 6 Crown Mans, to Alan
My Dear.

This is a continuation of the 2nd Nov card. I imagine the Sister affair will knock you back on your heels a bit, it has shaken me to

---

[1] I think this confirms that Lannie was Kenny McLennan's sister. I had not realised that Sheila's connections with the McLennans of Blairbuie were so strong. Lannie's sister is Ina.

the core! From all the details which Lannie has given me and a wealth of them from Annabella, it appears that the woman has been living with me in a state of (as you know) amiability and hating me all the time with a most evil hatred. It gives one a strange tingling shock to realise this. She also said it suited her to "stick in with me" because it was a job which left her free to visit her daughter whenever she wanted to! Well the poor silly woman, like her sister in the fairy tale, has killed the goose that laid the golden eggs. But Oh Beloved, to think I left the children with her.

5th Nov

Lannie departed today and I shall miss her badly but on the other hand am so fed up with people I think I shall enjoy being on my own for a while. Robert and David are fine and David tonight has another tooth.

Sunday

Beloved I was so surprised and relieved to get your cable yesterday. It was so unexpectedly soon and I wasn't anywhere near the state of worrying about it being overdue. I am pretty well up to my ears these days as so far we've no help at all, but it all makes the days go quickly and the children are a joy to work with. David has advanced so much even since you last saw him. I have had a cheque for a month and a half's rent from Hipson[1] which isn't too bad! I'll send it to G. Mills. I have advertised for mother's help or some reliable person to do a bit of pram pushing but the advert won't go in for three weeks! Don't, if it occurs, mention when writing to your people that drink was the cause of Anna's dismissal. I have simply told your mother what we told Annabella[2], namely that we needed the room. I have of course phoned your mother the good news of your cable. It will be such a thrill to have a letter from you beloved, and I won't have to wait such a long time as I thought. This is a dreadfully scrappy letter my dear, but it's been a queer week. I still shake all over when I think of Sister, but I'll soon be

---

[1] Hipson of course is renting the Wakefield house.
[2] Annabella's drinking is mentioned elsewhere. See 3rd Oct 1943.

able to put it to the back of my mind with the things that are past. The last two days have been frosty and the boys get all rosy and look extra bonny. Robert keeps telling me what a dreadful shame it is you have to be in Africa, but says you are going to stay with us for good when you come back and look after us! - here's hoping! I have difficulty in getting air mail weight envelopes so will just send off the two letter cards just now. I am wondering if you have got any of my letters yet. It's odd to think of you so far away. I love you beloved and need you very badly. Sheila.[1]

5th Nov 1943, Alan, WAF, [Accra] to Sheila

My Dear,

I'm hoping that the cable arrived safely and that all well. I wish I had asked you to cable me. I only really get one of these letters per week but until Christmas I get two per week. Also I believe that owing to some change in rate, these letters will now take about 14 - 21 days to reach you which is a pity. It's going to be difficult to decide what to put in these letters and what to send by ordinary mail for you will get this, for example, a month or so before a long letter which I sent yesterday. I'll just have to put the *big thoughts* in this and hope not to tantalise you by writing about something which I don't follow up in my ordinary letter.

Oh Dear I'm so longing for news from you and goodness knows when I shall get it for I have no idea when you will be able to write. I will possibly cable again soon and ask for you to reply.

The voyage in the ship was a bit of nightmare but after landing and one night at the port, Duffy and I flew down here in a day. It was an interesting flight in many ways for the drabness of the sand and bush seen from the air is unbelievable. This place is a paradise in comparison. I've completely fallen for the Picanins. The small boys and girls are really lovely and their carriage is so powerful. They carry nothing in their hands, but on their heads and I saw a small boy coming back from market yesterday solemnly walking along with a bottle of ink balanced neatly on his small round head.

---

[1] This letter was actually posted on 9th November.

My boy brings morning tea and orange at 7 AM - the tray on his head. At 4 o'clock in the afternoon he brings to my office a large tray with tea and banana and my S.D. Hat and takes away my sombrero.

The heat is not half as bad as below decks on the boat though we are starting the hot season now. Oh beloved I wish you were here to see and enjoy all this.

My Dear I hope you have a house and my sons are well. Do please remember the snaps and try to get your photograph taken.

You would not like the insects here though you would like the lizards, great green fellows with orange coloured body with orange coloured heads and orange tipped tails run about the walls all day.

Kiss my boys and love me. Alan

8ᵗʰ Nov 1943, Alan, WAF, [Accra] to Sheila

My Dear,

It's about 10 PM and I'm lying naked on the top of my bed inside the mosquito net and it's very hot. Each time I lift my hand the paper sticks to it. The nights here are much more amazing than the days. There is some breeze all day but none at night. Last night we had an open air cinema show "The Silver Fleet". It was weird to be sitting out in the blackness. Today I was in town and had my hair cut. I watched an entire village turn out to pull in the fishing net. The yells that greeted its arrival sounded like a try being scored at Murrayfield! Picanins were dancing in and out of the surf. They really are the most adorable young fellows you ever saw in your life. I sent you the second cable for I'm so anxious to hear you are all well and Duff, who travelled with me, has had two air letters. I shall send you a weekly E.F.M. telegram which is selected phrases just to let you know I'm well. I managed to scrounge this extra letter card. Dear I'll stop now because it's a bit tricky and the light is bad. I'm going to get that *finished*. No heavy luggage yet.

My Dear a week of my tour has gone.

9.11.43

I find it so hard not to say each morning "what a lovely morning".

My African boy just gapes, for of course every morning is the same. You would not like the beasties round here. Beatles, enormous earwigs, frogs, lizards, scorpions, are everywhere. My slippers are hung on hooks suspended from a string at night to avoid young things deciding to make a home there. There are a lot of snakes about but fortunately I have not seen any

Oh Beloved how I long to hear from you. It will be such a joy to get first word from you that you know I am here. Think of it, since October 13th I have absolutely no word at all.

I'm going down to try out my rifle on the range this evening and tomorrow evening I'm going to play tennis if I can borrow some balls. Could you keep your eyes open for the chance of any.

The surf is huge on the beach but I'm looking forward enormously to getting down and getting some bathing and sunbathing.

Tell Robert that whenever Daddy gets his trunk and camera things he will send him photographs of black boys. And monkeys and bananas!

My Dear 18 months is a terribly long time. Love me love me every month of it and know that I will come home very soon. Alan who loves you so much. Alan

11th Nov 1943, Alan, WAF, [Accra] to Sheila

My Very Dear,

It was a great joy to get your cable today and know that you are all well. I'm looking forward to your first letter. Ordinary letters take 10 weeks or so. Only letters like these come reasonably quickly - about 10 - 14 days.

Had three sets of tennis last night and feel much better for them. I was not playing well even by my standards. Today I have been having an afternoon off to buy bathing shorts, material for white shorts and hair cream. I'm longing for my heavy luggage but I'm afraid I will not see it for another 10 days or so. In the interval I'm going up country by train early next week.

I'm still thrilled and amazed by Africa and I'm feeling very fit as if on holiday. I've gone completely tee-total. It's funny I just can't face a drink out here although I drink two quarts of mixed lime and orange squash each day. I lost at least three quarts of sweat playing tennis yesterday. I'm rapidly getting very brown with the sun. It's so strong that you get sunburned through an airtex shirt.

As I came through town today we passed some Americans looking very untidy. My Ashanti driver muttered something and I asked him what he said. He replied "I see white wok-wok. Which being interpreted means white bushman. When a soldier is very untidy here the greatest insult you can hurl at him is wok-wok meaning you are a wild man from the bush.

The soldiers from Ashanti and Northern Territory are fine upstanding chaps, very proud of themselves and loving their soldiering. They are either Pagans or Mohammedens. The Pagan or M is apparently much more trustworthy than the mercenary fellow of the coast. He is a real Wiley Oriental Gentleman. They have a lovely pigeon expression for a thief. He is called "tieff boy". I saw convicts being marched back to barracks today in whitecaps and trousers. Their guards wore khaki fez, with maroon trousers and carried muskets dating back to the Ashanti wars. Must write small again. Work here is most interesting. It's so new and strange that I spend a lot of time concealing my ignorance. The areas are so enormous and the *decisions* so novel. There is so little shading here. A man is either well or pretty sick. Rich or poor, spotlessly clean or very dirty.

Well it's now 6 o'clock and bath time. I'll finish this tomorrow morning. I suppose it's the Wob's and David's bath time too for our time is one half hour later than yours.

12.11.43 10 PM

Today I'm beginning to feel a bit more comfortable in my room. I bought furniture from a man who was leaving and now have it well arranged in my room. I have also taken on his boy as the one I had while very good was always trying to do me over things he said he needed, washing soap, starch, fruit, tea etc. etc.

My new boy was with my predecessor for 18 months and is said to be very good. His name is Jeremiah, he is hideous to look at - coal black not just dark - with two curling tribal scars on each cheek. Perhaps he has a heart of gold. He is a pagan from Northwest Ashanti. Played tennis again today, three hard sets and sweated like bull. You learn to walk slowly here. If you run up a flight of stairs, you break out in a sweat. Tennis was a little better today but Oh my backhand.

Sorry this is such a scrawl but as I have said ordinary letters take such ages. I'm quite used to

The 'Boy' Jeremiah November 1943

black faces everywhere now. Even the little shrimps of tennis ball boys seem quite natural. They are lazy wee sods and today one of them was much hampered by flowing robes coming to I should think, 8 yards long. If you will send me patterns or prop cuttings of sizes I'll get shirts and pants made for Robert and David. We can only send home locally produced articles, so no silk stockings! Alan

13th Nov 1943, Sheila, 6 Crown Mans, to Alan
My Dear One,

Terrific surprise yesterday when I received the first of the letters you wrote at sea. Of course ordinary mail and the air mail one didn't come until today! You must have had a dreadfully miserable time with one of your star colds under these conditions and I'm glad to think it's now a thing of the past. I am longing to know if your tin trunk[1] turned up, its loss is too ghastly to contemplate. It certainly doesn't sound a pleasure cruise. I am told by the P.O. that there is no more air mail service to W. Africa apart from these letter cards and they seem so flimsy I can't imagine them ever arriving. I hope my cable found you and that by now you have had some letters. The boys are just splendid, you'd hardly know David he's come on so much and Robert is just the usual Robert and a little extra. Today he squared up to me with his fists up and said "I'll hit you on your bleeding nose". Probably school will have to come sooner than I intend! He knows all his letters now and when out walking stands at all the street name plates to spell out the letters. He is sporting a utility Harris Tweed coat and knee length turn down stockings, new bright Fair Isle gloves and looks quite the schoolboy. David is growing at a great rate and is almost up to Robert's shoulders, he is as beefy as ever. I have got a woman who is highly recommended coming next Thursday to take David out, she is going to come six afternoons a week and can stay the whole afternoon if and when I want. If she is any good this will be a great help and will let me get into town sometimes. I don't want anything more while I'm staying here and if and when I get a house I can look out for someone to stay in. I'm out for the maid type tho. I've finished with nannies! My domestic arrangements having been so suddenly and unexpectedly upset I have pretty well decided to stop here until after Christmas and see what things look like then. The departure of Annabella was a relief to me and altho the reason for her going upset mother considerably, she has as usual when things go wrong, risen to the occasion. We've shifted the furniture around a bit and really got on very well. I'd still like my own house but at this worst time of the year I am rather cowardly about launching out into a new abode with the children. They are a very great responsibility beloved, when you are so far away. I am reading "The Ivory Coast in the Earlies" by Aloysius Horn[2] but haven't got far enough yet to

---

[1] The tin trunk was at Camus full of army blankets. Maybe it still is.
[2] Alfred Aloysius Horn. Born Alfred Aloysius Smith. Also known as 'Trader Horn' and 'Zambesi Jack'. An ivory trader and adventurer.

say much about it. Beloved, I'm so glad you are going to be selfish of my company after the war, because there is nothing in the world I desire as much as yours.

14th Nov

Put Robert to bed at lunch time with a temp of 101. However tonight he is normal and as bright as a bee so we'll see what tomorrow brings forth. Aloysius Horn is proving most amusing. I'll send it to you when I've finished and when I am able to get into town will execute your commissions there! In case you are wondering about it I have no statement from G. Mills but my £40 came through all right. I just can't imagine how you can need me as I do you, but if only the war could be over when we meet again I will be content to wait. Beloved I'll add a line to this in the morning and give you news of Robert.

15th Nov

Robert's temp up again last night but that was I think to be expected. He is very cheery and if he runs anything of a temp today I'll get the doctor (I've heard of a good one) so don't worry. Your air mail card came in this am. Robert very thrilled about the monkey. I'll get some more letter cards today and send you an extra one. All Love, Sheila

14th Nov 1943, Alan, WAF, [Accra] to Sheila

Sunday

My Beloved,

It's hardly worth writing this because there will be so many intervening Air Mail Cards, but I just feel I want to write to you tonight and it will always be an unexpected letter popping in to cheer you up. I'm so longing for a letter from you.

I wonder if you have tried to send ordinary air mail letters - they just come by sea. Only air mail cards such as I send you go by air.

I'm busy and enjoying my work and as happy as I can be away from you. It's surprising how quickly I have become adjusted to this strange place and I'm glad I wrote down some impressions before the oddness wears off. Already I never notice an African and the surprising sight of a black finger on soup plate is now commonplace.

I can't quite get used to the absolute necessity of slowing down all my actions because of the heat. I never was a quick walker but here if you walk smartly you just break out in a sweat.

It's now about 11 P.M. and the rain is pouring down outside while flashes of blue sheet lightning dart through my open shutters. I'm stark naked inside my mosquito net but my skin is moist with sweat. I've been to an open air Cinema show in front of the mess. It was Herbert Marshall in 'The Young Idea' and was only second class.

Next week - Tuesday, I go inland on tour unless - the chance of a lifetime, I am allowed to go to an epidemic in a place some distance from here not under our control. There is great speculation as to whether a team of us will be sent. By the time you get this it will be stale news and won't worry you.

Oh my Darling how I long for you. Only just 14 days of my tour gone and such a long time to go.

18.11.43

My Dear I've not added to this for many days so I have in the interval sent two air mail cards. Oh how I long for that first letter from you.

I'm still extremely busy trying to understand all the ins and outs of the work here. It's so hard to visualize and yet I can't go on tour until I get things straight in my mind here.

I don't think I've got any other particular news so I'll post this and start another tonight.

Oh beloved it's a terrible terrible waste to be with you only at intervals from 1939 - 1945 from my age of 30 - 36.

I love you, Oh my Dear I love you. Alan

15th Nov 1943, Alan, WAF, [Accra] to Sheila

My Very Dear,

Still no letter from you. I wonder if by any chance you have sent ordinary Air Mail Letters. These go by ordinary Sea mail and take about two months. Only sheets like this obtainable in Post Office as shown on P.C. from Crookham come by air mail. I think it must be that for the others who came on the boat with me have had several letters.

I'm keeping very busy - so busy trying to get on top of things here that I cancelled my tour. I've a chance of going to see some yellow fever in a nearby place but we are waiting approval from our honeymoon friends.

I've been playing tennis most evenings and I'm slowly improving. We borrow some appalling balls with moth-eaten covers and so soft that you can almost make your fingers meet through them.

The mango season is arriving and they are delicious.

It's going to get steadily hotter apparently until February and it really is amazing in the middle of the day. I lie naked on my bed after lunch, and if I fall asleep, wake with little rivulets of sweat pouring down my face and arms. I don't seem to be going to get very yellow with Mepacrine, but I am getting very sunburned.

This place is simply hotching with insects and you would not like the earwigs, but you would love the birds, they are so gaily coloured.

The high whistle of crickets goes on all and every night. This is punctuated by bullfrog croaks and in the background usually the African drums - so much for the silence of the tropical night.

I expect to get my heavy luggage at the end of the week. Sparks may be coming here as P.A.D. M S. I've written to Wilfred Robinson telling him I shall look him up when I'm in Sierra Leone.

Oh beloved I'm so longing for a letter from you. I've got two pictures which won't ever go out of my brain. You walking away into the Lismoyne and two cheerful wee faces at the window in North Gardner Street,[1] you will send the snaps of them won't you, and please get photographed yourself. My Darling one I hope you

---

[1] Alan had stayed a day or so with Sheila in Farnborough and he finally parted from her on 13th Oct 43 at the Lismoyne Hotel in Crookham, Fleet, before leaving for Africa. David & I were in Glasgow at North Gardner Street, presumably with Mamie & Jimmy.

are not wearying too much and that you have a house.

Tell Robert I am very busy working as hard as I can to get home soon to you all.

Well Beloved I'll write again soon as I can get another of these blessed rationed cards. Tell the parents any news I sent.

Love me always. Alan

16th Nov 1943, Sheila, 6 Crown Mans, to Alan

My Dear.

Robert has been up today and is full of bounce, he now has a slight head cold. Today he tried very hard to write "Love Robert" on a Christmas Card to send to you, he tried so hard that he perspired and the card got more and more grubby. However we sent it on! He also licked the stamps, or rather spat on them, and I found them floating on the envelope. I wonder if you can know how I am envying you the heat and colour of Africa. It's been snowing here today and somehow there seems an awful lot of winter ahead. I'm afraid I haven't done anything about Christmas parcels for you beloved, there doesn't seem anything to send and just of late I haven't been able to get into town at all. Never mind we will soon be having our Christmas days together again and won't it be a novelty for you, for when I think of it you've never had a Christmas with two boys! Jim[1] has sent a card to Princess Terr from a camp in Germany, so he is safe at any rate. Give Col Duff my regards, I expect Sparks will have departed for his hinterland! I'm longing for a letter from your real destination, I expect the last one came from Freetown. It will also be nice to get one with a date on it. It's such a relief to me that Robert is better, I got quite a shock when his temp shot up for no apparent reason. I just daren't think how long it will be before I see you beloved. I keep telling myself, sometimes a bit wildly, how quickly time is passing and this is possibly the longest bit of all. You'll have a bit of strangeness and excitement to take you over the beginning anyhow so that the latter part will be the longest for you I expect. Never mind Dear One, we are well

---

[1] Jim was evidently a P O W in Germany. But I really don't know which Jim this was - I don't think it was McVicar.

launched now anyhow and after this is over I shall stick to you infinitely faster than a shadow. The parents and Robert send their love.

Yours ever, Sheila

20th Nov 1943, Sheila, 6 Crown Mans, to Alan

My Dear. I'm wondering if I dare look for a letter at the beginning of the week. It will then be a week since I heard from you. We are all well. Robert hasn't been out yet but is going tomorrow. I've had a heavy cold but am over the worst now. David is terribly fit and very sweet, much sweeter than he has ever been I think and it's dreadful that you should be missing him. If I ask him to dance he toddles over and puts the wireless on! He is at the stage of being very thrilled with puss cats, dogs and most of all barrage balloons[1] of which he never tires. I've had the woman I told you about pram pushing for the last four afternoons and that's been a great help particularly as I was able to stay in and nurse my cold. Robert asks me to tell you that he let David play with his train and tender for a while this afternoon! Sadie's baby arrived all right a few days ago - a boy. I am hoping to be able to get into town next week to see to your cigarettes etc. I'm afraid your wants aren't very promptly attended to. Isabel Burton leaves me standing! I've sent off the Nigeria book you asked for, also "The Ivory Coast in the Earlies" which I enjoyed very much.

I'm afraid I as usual have very little in the way of news, it's such a dead time of year and I am in a state of suspended animation when you are away. I take great longings for Wakefield (or rather our house) at times but am going to try to live them down until next autumn. I am awaiting news from Lannie about furnished houses Achiltibuie way. As soon as this Winter's over I'm going to sell the pram, also the large folding one in Wakefield and get a really tiny light thing that I can take about easily and then when you get home we'll be past that stage and be able to move about again without bother. Oh I do wonder if the war will be over when you come

---

[1] Clumsy big balloons tethered by a wire meant to snag German aircraft

home. I suppose it could be but it seems too good to be true. It's been milder today, a great relief to me. If you are feeling hot when you read this, think of me shivering here, I'm sure I'd rather be hot! I'm missing you dreadfully but the weeks are folding up and beloved the future is bright. I hope you are having a good time and I'm longing to hear something of it. I'll stop now and add a few lines if I hear from you on Monday.

Monday
No letter but one will turn up one of these days. Why do you and I have such rotten sinuses? I hope the boys don't have trouble that way, it does make a cold such a trouble. Robert and I are going into town this afternoon to try to get your developer. All love, Sheila

21ˢᵗ Nov 1943, Alan, WAF, [Accra] to Sheila
My Very Dear, it's a hot Sunday morning and I'm sitting in my office writing this in the interval of reams of paperwork. I expect to go off inland by road for five days tomorrow. I'm more or less acclimatised now, it's surprising how quickly one gets used to sleeping with, at most, a sheet, and to wake up in the morning and drink hot tea in brilliant sunshine.

I've been playing tennis every second night if I can manage to get the work done, and will go to the beach this afternoon. Jock Marshall, the Academical and friend of George Laird is coming to dinner and thence to see the Sunday evening film with me tonight. I have only spoken to him on the phone.

The work is tremendously interesting and makes me wish I had come out to the tropics as a young man. Robert and David must have the chance. Tommy Semple, one of a Pollokshields family (you may remember Margaret Semple at *Land* Bank) is in a hospital in these parts and I expect to see him soon. Duff and I are invited up tomorrow night for a drink with an amazing old girl who is a phonetics expert and is trying to produce a written version of a tone language. Many West African languages depends entirely on most subtle differences of tone for a meaning. This old soul, she looks about 65-70, we met at the Hospital (civil). Unfortunately I expect to be away.

I hope you got my 'all well' E.F.M. I've great hopes of my first letter from you this week.

My baggage has just arrived and Jeremiah has gone over to collect it. Then I'll be able to take photographs and to send them to you. Downe[1] has a Leica with a telescopic lens which he will lend me. Also a Leica Manual so don't bother to send.

Oh My Dear - three weeks have gone.[2] I love you. Alan

24th Nov 1943, Alan, WAF, [Kumasi] to Sheila

My Dear,

I'm writing this in a rest house well away in the real Africa. It's getting dark and I'm at a window where the sun is setting over hundreds of miles bush. We, Major *Collen* the D.A.D.H. and myself left on 22/11 and came one day by train, then yesterday by car, and today by car. Villages up here are the real African collections of mud huts and European clothing is hardly worn. We stopped on the way at one village and asked for bananas. A small girl clad only in two pieces of coloured cord, with a red tuft fore and aft, came darting out with a bunch of 19 bananas and shyly asked for "a penny". I gave her a thrupenny bit and she fairly jumped for joy. The main roads are fine - packed red ironstone, but the tracks would give Rieff a shake.

25/9

Beloved, just back at Lesley Sparks' unit on the way back and I find three letters waiting for me dated 1st, 18th, and 25th October, all airmail letter cards. What a great joy it is to hear all your news and that you love me and that my boys are well and that they love you and me and each other.

I had a pleasant evening last night, and this morning a marvellous day in Sleeping Sickness country with the World No 1 expert. I

---

[1] Col is the Viscount Downe. There are many further references to him. See Dramatis Personae

[2] Alan means three weeks of his tour have gone.

learned so much and I did enjoy myself. I took lots of photographs.

The Doctor has a black wife! and we had a drink with them before I left. On the road down we bought two bunches of bananas and six oranges for 2 pence. We came round a corner and saw about 30 Baboons rushing across the road. One had a wee baby monkey hanging round her neck. I was too late to get photographs as they rushed into the jungle. You never saw such stuff, great banana and coconut trees, wild cocoa bean trees and thorn and grass so thick that it's an impenetrable mass 8 feet high. Saw a snake this morning too. Don't you believe Beloved "Behind Gods Back". Negley Farson[1] never got beyond the port and had D.T.s[2] for a fortnight in European Hospital. I adore you. Alan

24th Nov 1943, Sheila, 6 Crown Mansions, to Alan
My Very Dear, Your letter of the 5th inst arrived today. We are all very fit and Robert is most amused about the black boy's way of carrying things and has transported several things today on his head! Today he all by himself made an aeroplane with his "meccano" it was an amazingly good effort and I think my most genuine admiration of it gave him great pleasure. We (R and I) went into town this afternoon and managed to get your m.c.m 100 so you at least know it's on the way. Somehow I'm simply aching for you tonight and the months ahead look pretty formidable. However once this winters over it will be easier I think and I shall be sending you winter woollies to come home in before we know where we are! David is colossal, I may be mistaken but he seems an outsize to me. He drinks milk like a calf, defends himself with primitive ferocity and is a very definite character. There is nothing solemn about him now however and he can see a joke with anyone! I'm writing this in bed while half asleep but I have a great urge to write to you. It's nice to think of a long letter coming from you by sea. I have so little news that these letter cards just about exhaust it.

---

[1] James Negley Farson, 1890-1960. Travel writer, journalist and alcoholic.
[2] D.T.s, for those unfamiliar with it, is Delirium Tremens, Latin for the "Shaking Frenzy". Delirium tremens can occur when you stop drinking alcohol after a period of heavy drinking, especially if you do not eat enough food.

Beloved I love you so completely but I've written of it so often I always fear getting tedious, altho I never tire of hearing that I am loved. We'll make up for all this lost time my dear and somehow or other we'll have a terrific time after the war. I'm relying on you to be honest in your letters and not let that exasperating "stiff upper lip" of yours run away with you. I want a true picture of how you are feeling about things and in yourself. At 7 am in the grim cold darkness this morning there was a wail from Robert "when is Daddy going to send me a banana"! I've had your statement from Glyn Mills which I've sent on. Your balance of Nov 6th was £140.12. That is after deduction of my £40 and not including cheque for £19 house rent which I have just sent them.

25th

Robert now insists on carrying things on his head outside and it's rather embarrassing! Beloved I'm deadly lonely for you and wish I could come to you, but even supposing I could I couldn't because of the children - life is complicated isn't it? It's light and frosty today it's 3.30 pm and I'm sitting at a table beside the fire and Robert is sitting beside me doing "transfers", David is out in his pram being pushed by Susan.

27th Nov

Your parents were here for tea this afternoon and the boys played up wonderfully! Robert read his a.b.c book to them and wrote his name (he can do it much better now) and everyone was very pleased including Robert! Then David came in and bounced around in a most winning way. He was wearing a new plain blue suit and did look rather adorable - but tough - oh dear me yes, your second son is tough alright! It was such a treat to wake up to your cable yesterday morning and made me feel very bright. Robert is very matter of fact about your being away and lays aside things for you to mend when you get back! He grows more and more loveable and persists in unshakeable devotion to David and I, even when we're nasty to him. David whacks him a lot and will hardly let him go near him, which is not surprising as up 'till now Robert has always pinched his toys. However that is coming to a stop for as I've said David is awful tough. Love Sheila

26th Nov 1943, Alan, WAF, [Accra] to Sheila

My Dear,

I'm writing this in the train, very rocky, and in continuation of the other letter you will receive by the same post. I want to try to answer some of the things in your letters. I'm so very sorry about the Sister business. There is just nothing to be said for it's completely disgusting. She has no justification at all and I'm afraid she is not completely sane. Thank God at least she never vented her spite on the children.

Tuck into the Minadex and look after yourself. It's such fun to read about Robert and the Atlas. No letters have been censored and that they very rarely are. Oh my Dear they are such brave letters of yours. We have a future always, a precious one, when we can look forward to being together. Can't make out whether my photo has arrived. I'm looking forward to the snaps you sent.

I'm looking forward to developing my photographs when I get back but I'll probably only be one day at HQ and then off on another short trip. Each station here is a medley of yells. Africans selling the most incredible varieties of food. Yam, pau-pau, coconut, *basheen*, bananas, plantains, oranges, tagine's, mango, bread, lumps of fish in cornflour, peppers, and so on. On the roofs of the small sheds which count as the station sit rows of vultures looking very depressed.

10 PM

Back home after a dirty and hot journey in the train. Constant temp 94° and humidity enormous. It was a joy to find Jeremiah waiting with clean clothes laid out, a cup of tea waiting and a bath newly filled. Wiggy is in hospital with a mild malaria but will be out in a couple of days. There were a couple of wild gold-miners on the train who arrived drunk after last night's party and consumed another bottle of whiskey each on the way down. Don't pay rent into my account but into yours. I'll settle up Wakefield arrears. This has been a relatively expensive month here with getting new kit, buying furniture and so on. But I'll be able to live on my local allowance all right. I'm glad you have the Roy Young business over but Oh my Dear it must have been rotten for you. I'm going to be really busy for a couple of days here writing my tour report and dealing with accumulated paperwork.

I'm hoping to develop one film at least tomorrow night. I'll need to get ice to cool the water to a reasonable temperature.

Oh My Dear One I love you and miss you so much to talk to. I'm terribly glad to have the boys. I get a great kick when any one says "have you a family?" and I say, in a sort of offhand way, yes two boys. It's pretty primitive this having boys. I saw a Hausa today walk along in stately fashion with a long stick and he had two sons in robes strung out behind him with calabashes on their heads and he was mighty proud.

Well my dear there is no more room to write but I love you and I buoy myself up with you and Reiff when I think how long a time is ahead.

Alan

28th Nov 1943, Alan, WAF, [Accra] to Sheila

My Very Dear,

I'm lying in bed after a long day of work and play and I'm very sleepy. I had three air mail cards tonight dated 2nd and 17th November. You have not at the time of your writing had any letters from here but as they were sent off on Nov 2nd and 4th you will have them by now. I worked all morning but after 3 o'clock it was so hot that I gave it up and had a Sunday afternoon off. I slept for a bit and then developed two films. One started at home and next finished last week in the north. While they dried I went out with my gun and shot some rats round a clearing where the natives have some pigs. Tonight we had our weekly film in the open.

Oh my Beloved I'm sorry you have not got a house but as you say, when you have no help it will be much nicer for you at North Gardner Street. It's a thrill to hear of Robert reading letters. I wish I could see his face when he sees the photographs.

Oh my Dear it's so good to get loving letters like those I received tonight. I love you so dearly that every word I get is liable to bring to my mind some dear memory and some hope and some fear.

Beloved my world and all I care for is with you.

29/4

Its 8.15 AM and a glorious morning. All the mornings are lovely from 7 o'clock or earlier until about 9.30 when it gets very hot. I have had breakfast and a stroll and now I'm getting down to work in the office.

I've a lot to do but I really feel as regards work that, except for the time I was with 1st Army when I did some useful stuff, I'm doing a better job here than I have ever done. It's so much more interesting that it doesn't feel like work at all. It's just fun for the most part.

Leslie Sparks is coming down to assist me and take the Medical Booking and routine statistical work off my hands.

I am going to try to print some photographs tonight if my bits for the enlarger arrive from the carpenter. I'm longing to send them to you. My Very own one I have read again and again your letters. It's so lovely to hear about the boys in your language - our language of love for them.

I'm glad Robert got over his cold and I hope the new woman proves a success.

Never mind about Christmas Parcels. I can get anything in the world here. I'll send you one when I have an opportunity of buying Kano cloth. Beloved I must not answer your letters in this as you won't get this for a couple of months. I'll reply in my air mail.

30/11

The first month gone Beloved and I hope quickly for you. It seems a terribly long time since I landed in Africa and I hope it will fly quicker than this in future.

I love you beloved. Alan

28th Nov 1943, Sheila, 6 Crown Mans, to Alan

My Dear, I expect this will reach you at the same time as the letter I finished last night. This has been a very cold day - the pram handle felt like a bar of ice! I've started house hunting again violently. I feel it's too much for mother us being here and anyway I'm not good at living anywhere except in my own domain. You have been (if possible) more than ever in my thoughts in the last few days beloved. Even knowing how completely I love you, I think you cannot know the way in which my whole existence is bent towards your return. You're almost constantly in my thoughts and my eyes are always on the future. One thought that I cannot bear is that we will be parted again. Pray very hard beloved that it will not happen. I do not feel the depression and bitterness of that Winter that you were in France. I do feel dreadfully alone, but having you to come to me at the end of these, already dwindling, months I have no business to feel depressed. It seems absurd to quote in this restricted space but I can't resist this bit of Wordsworth which you will remember I found in a magazine when we were travelling south together and which has remained in my mind ever since. It seems so apt - "There are in our existence spots of time, that with distinct pre-eminence retain a renovating virtue, whence .... Our minds are nourished and invisibly repaired."[1]

Thoughts and memories of you are a never failing source of nourishment and repair. I have had many "spots of time" with you, beloved. I don't usually stress the fact that I am proud of you, for my love, although it most certainly could be, is not based on pride. I am most naturally proud and glad of your attainments and of all that you are, but I also know that since ever I have known you, I have been most hopelessly in love, whatever you might have been. To begin with I cast my bread upon the water without thought except that I loved and never to anyone in this world was there such a wonderful return.

---

[1] Lovely bit of Wordsworth from The Prelude, Book 12th, Imagination and Taste, How Impaired and Restored.

Monday 29th

It's a wild bitterly cold day. You don't know how lucky you are! David is in particularly good form today and is really shouting us deaf. I found him trying to put coal on the fire, fortunately there was a fireguard! I am reading Esther I never got it started in the summer and then I put it away and forgot about it. I just asked Robert if there is anything he wants to say and he said "Please tell him I'm being a good boy and helping to wash the plates" Oh! How we wish he wouldn't!

Your loving wife. Sheila

3rd Dec 1943, Alan, WAF, [Accra] to Sheila

My Very Dear,

I've just received your cable sent on Nov 26th and it's fine to know all is well. It's odd how sensitive one is out here for I read "am fit and well" to include children. Will you use "all well here" or some such phrase please!!! Oh my Darling the whole day takes on a new complexion with a letter or a cable.

I sent to Kodak asking them to send me a lot of film and paper. My first enlargements are so good and there is so much of medical interest to photograph that I'm very excited. I have some marvellous photographs of yours already and I'm definitely going to write my M.D. thesis and illustrate it during the tour. I've told Kodak to send you the bill. Will you please pay with Glyn Mills cheque. By the way again I say be sure to pay Higgins' cheque to your account. You will have to pay rent and rates from them.

Will you get John Smith and Co to send me three Notebooks 10 inches x 8 inches with ruled right hand page and 1/10 inch graph paper on left.

I'm off tomorrow on a week trip and then I hope to get down again to do some work of my own. I'm just emerging from the slough of the routine work and getting the statistics run as I like them. Wiggy is very fit and energetic after his malaria bout.

Oh beloved it's so funny to have Roberts new photograph here. He is a handsome youth you know.

10 PM

Just been packing my bits and pieces (including camera) for my tour. My Darling, more people were having farewell parties in the mess tonight. It's a long long way until mine. Do you remember Cockburn, the queer fellow who succeeded me in Aldershot? He is out here and was down in these parts. He had chop (the name for all meals)[1] with me last night. He shot an elephant recently. I'll add a little in the morning before I leave. I love you beloved and I need you tonight and always.

Dec 5th

It's a strange morning for its dull! It's quite overcast though hot and sticky.

Oh my own Darling wouldn't it be wonderful if you could come with me today, it would be just the sort of thing you would enjoy.

Kiss my boys and tell them I think of them many times every day. Tell Robert that I'm going to send him the black boys photograph very soon now and that the men out here have bows and arrows.

Had letters from Mummy and Moira. Moira seems to have had a bad time again. Oh it's hard luck. I'm looking forward to the first sea-mail with home News.

As you say these flimsy cards are not very satisfactory. I love you Sheila and I don't need to be away from you to know it. Alan

4th Dec 1943, Sheila, 6 Crown Mansions, to Alan

My Dear One.

On Tuesday I received your letter of Nov 21st and today there arrived letters of the 11th and 15th of Nov which seems odd. I am very distressed over the non-arrival of my letters, it's most distressing and mysterious as I have of course always used the air letter cards. I treated myself to a cable today and feel a bit cheered. I hope you will cable when you do start hearing from me as it's a hopeless feeling writing letters that seemed to vanish. We should have arranged to number our letters and would always have known

---

[1] 'Chop' is a general word meaning money or food or sometimes 'ready' as in 'bath chop'.

if any went missing. We are very well. I think the junior members of the tribe grow every day. Apart from the children life is pretty uninteresting and of course it's such a deadly time of year - funny to talk about a "deadly time of year", when I'm with you no time in the year is that, they are all alive and happy in their own way. But just now when I'm only half alive and it's dark and gloomy outside, I would cheerfully contend with regiments of earwigs for a bit of excitement - I think! Your letters mean so much to me. I do hate to think of you going without, you must feel so very separated from us. My brain simply won't work tonight. Last night was full of foghorns and sirens on the river, dustbin men and Robert who had insomnia. I didn't sleep much! Oh! My dear I just can't imagine you in your new environment at all. Come back not very different and loving me a lot please, because I'm afraid I shall be appallingly unchanged. I think I'll sleep now and finish this tomorrow.

Sunday 5th Dec

Pretty foggy all day but it lifted for a little while in the afternoon and David got out. David has developed so much, you would love him. He is a stubborn as a mule but he has charm! I have today paid £13 to Glyn Mills, being another cheque from Hipson. If I ever want a cheque I shall let you know in these letters as goodness knows when the monthly statements will ever reach you. How I wish I could see Jeremiah! What fun we could have out of so many things, perhaps even the earwigs? if I could be there. However I'm doing a pretty good job of work here and I'll probably burst with pride when you come home and view your family. David is growing so rapidly that sometimes I think I'm seeing double when I see the two of them together. Just been speaking to your mother on the phone, she wants to take us to the circus which will be grand. Mother has booked for the pantomime for Jan, so I'll let you know the results! We've got a good woman in the mornings now so things are less hectic. Daisy has been out at 66 Manygates prospecting for moths and airing the room, she is still asking to come back to us, and I've had another letter from Mr Morris saying Mrs M is hoping to get back and they are getting a house over our way and he'll come and dig the garden for me and will never let me be short of coal. He says "you have been good to us and I want to do something in return". I am lucky to have people like these waiting for my return aren't I?

I love you terribly beloved, take care of yourself for us, Yours ever, Sheila

11th Dec 1943, Alan, WAF, [Accra] to Sheila

My Very Dear One,

I returned from tour yesterday to find a very welcome cable waiting. It should have crossed with one of mine for I sent one while staying with Col Bingham - (will you phone his wife - in telephone book in Athol Gardens and tell her I was with him and he was looking very well).

I had a good trip, had some dinghy sailing at two different places, surf bathing and was at the *General's* Mess in one area when he threw a party. I had two flights which I enjoyed and stayed with Tommy Semple. Had a cheery note from Wilfred and hope to go to see him about 27th of this month. I'm just dazzled by the terrific number of new sights and strange things I see. There is always something grotesque and odd.

I'm having the Attorney General here who travelled out on the boat with me and a Captain Dohan of American army to dinner with me tomorrow night. I have sent you by Sea mail a long letter and photographs.

We have had no air mail for a fortnight. I gather the service has been cut which is annoying. I hope you are getting mine. Your cable sent on 22nd of Nov arrived here on 7th Dec which is pretty shocking for H.L.T. Good to have anything though beloved though it doesn't make me think of you all any oftener.

I am feeling amazingly fit but touch wood. I'm brown to the waist and I'm putting on weight. The work is fine - an awful lot of it but really just what I had hoped. Tell Moira I stayed with Col Bingham and that he sends his regards and was extremely kind to me.

It's getting pretty hot, 90° in shade day and night, but here there is a breeze all day. At night it gets very sticky and I now sleep naked without a sheet. But the mornings are glorious and the heat really does not bother me except just before I go to bed. Whether due to (I think it is) getting so sunburnt or not, my skin is fine and I've not a trace of prickly heat which seems to bother many.

I walked 10 miles on Thursday, many in swamps bare to the waist. This afternoon I'm going surfing.

Beloved this is a letter of me enjoying myself and much on top of things. It's hard for you. I love you so much. Tell the boys I love you. Alan

12ᵗʰ Dec 1943, Sheila, 6 Crown Mansions, to Alan

Beloved, It's just on two months now since I left you. I can't say it's gone quickly, still it has gone and it's definitely two months less. I got your letter by ordinary mail last Tuesday (the 7th), it was quite a short one and you finished it on Nov 18th so you see they don't take as long as you thought, or perhaps this was just a lucky one. I was so glad to get your cable on Wednesday and to know that at least you are getting my letters. We are all well and the boys are just full of beans. David is quite a little boy now and has left his babyhood suddenly behind. It's such a lovable age and it's such a shame you are missing it. I'm very lonely for you beloved, but I'm so glad you are where you are. The other night I had a nightmare. I dreamed you were being sent back and woke shaking with fright and knew it would be infinitely worse for me if you were still "somewhere in England" and I in my usual waking nightmare of the spring.[1] I had a letter from Lannie the other day. They have had to destroy both the dogs for killing sheep and I regret to say "Brechin" started it! Also had letter from Monica, she is fairly well; the babe is expected about 7th Jan. Dr Thomas (Wakefield) is dead. He had retired and bought a house in *Sheverly* and only lived two months. I intended and forgot to fill-in the date of Robert's visit to the pantomime in my last letter, it's the 3rd Jan. So you can think of him then. Tennis balls are quite hopeless I'm afraid, there were

---

[1] This refers to Sheila's terror of Alan being "somewhere in England" training for the Second Front (what we now call the D-Day). Great secrecy surrounded the positions of the various British, American, Canadian and other units for invasion of France.

none made last year and are to be none this season either.

I asked Daddy to see if Nony (who still plays a lot) could do anything for me and his reply was to send me the Lawn Tennis Associations circular to clubs advising them where to send their old balls for reconditioning to keep the game alive. They won't take any more orders for the Weekly Herald or Bulletin so that's a flop too! The cigarettes however I attended to and they should arrive sometime and there after monthly - more or less! Kay and Nony came in yesterday afternoon. Kay had never seen the children. She has only had one letter from Bob (in Hong Kong) in two years. This ought to be a Christmassy one as it may arrive about that time. I don't feel at all Christmassy and I don't suppose you do either. The weather is very frosty now and somewhat foggy - I just had Muriel Moyes on phone offering to let me their flat! Mr M isn't making anything of it and they (Cindy and she) don't know when they will be able to leave Mrs Moyes and would like their flat occupied. It's a corner ground flat in Beaumont Gate, possibly you remember it. It was difficult to know what to say but I've to see it tomorrow. I don't like the idea of renting a house from friends but possibly that's foolish and she insists they don't worry a bit about the children, but wouldn't like to give it to someone they didn't know. I'll give you the results in my next letter.

Was speaking to Ruth sent last night (on phone) we are going to meet in the Malmaison some evening in Jan and give ourselves a night out. It's the only way we can think of seeing each other. She is so isolated on the other side of the town and we've both babies round our necks during the day! - I'm in bed now and thinking of getting down to "Latin American History" which is the latest "Historical" pamphlet to reach me, I must say it looks pretty tough! Murray Niven has got six months leave because of Mr Moyes'[1] illness as there was no one else to cope with the business. I'm rather hoping for a letter tomorrow morning, anyhow it's a nice idea to go to sleep with. Robert wants to know if you'll come home black and if not why! He met Santa Claus in a shop yesterday and was

---

[1] The Moyes' were some kind of cousins via Jimmy's sister.

astonished. I love you beloved always and you know it very well. Yours ever Sheila

17th Dec 1943, Alan, WAF, [Accra] to Sheila

My Own Dear One,

This week, the third without an airmail, I have had the photographs of the children and various magazines and letter you have re-directed. They had been a great joy - (photographs). They are the best snaps of you we have and I feel all warm and tender when I look at them.

I've been slugging like a black in the office this week but had a bathe last Sunday and tennis last night. The bathing and sunbathing does one a lot of good and the tennis I enjoy very much. I have been getting into the office each morning about 7.45 to get on with the work in cool and quiet.

Lesley Sparks is posted here as my assistant and should arrive early next week and he will take the routine work, which merely irritates me, off my hands.

Downe is in hospital with Malaria but not a severe attack. I have now stopped taking Chloroquine and am taking a new stuff, sulphur protein[1] which seems to be four times as effective as Chloroquine. Very few people get a severe attack if they take their Chloroquine regularly. The circulars from University and Academical Club are full of interesting news.

My Sgt Clerk here, Sgt Goodall, is a B.S.C. in Metallurgy of the University and was at Steven and Struthers several times under instruction.

Will you drop a note to Mrs Wigmore and tell her that Wiggy seems very fit to me and quite recovered from his mild malaria. He is a grand chap to work with and I find him especially helpful in backing up some bright ideas (if somewhat unorthodox!) which I get.

I'm reading very little just now I can't keep awake after 9 PM but I enjoy the "Place Names of Ross-shire" as a last morsel. Last

---

[1] This is Sulfapyridine, original UK spelling sulphapyridine; it is a sulfonamide antibacterial. At one time it was commonly referred to as M & B.

night I woke up and put on a blanket!!!

I had a fearful dream too - you and I were talking and you were leaving me and going to marry someone else and you were quite calm and collected about the whole thing - you simply said you liked him. I kept trying to persuade you to stay. The children did not seem to exist. Eventually I forcibly held you from going away and kissed you and then it was all right, but it gave me an awful fright.

Oh my Dear, I've become so dependent on you and part of me is with you so that without you I should have no feet on the ground, no affection, no belief that life can be lovely and good. Love me always and tell me you love me for I am hungry for it.

Tell my family I'm sorry that I have only this one letter card to send but that I've written by Sea Mail. Tell them I'm enjoying my work very much. Yes My Dear, with the exception of some of the work in 1st Army, I'm doing more useful work here than anywhere since the beginning of the war. Kiss my boys. Tell Robert and David that time is passing and I'll be back with you all.

I love you. Alan

19ᵗʰ Dec 1943, Alan, WAF, [Accra] to Sheila

My Dear,

There are terrific hopes that this will reach you for Christmas. A special mode of transit is available and we are each allowed one letter.

So a very Merry Christmas to you My Dear. May you have joy in our own loved boys and Merry Christmas to them too. Tell them an aeroplane came specially all the way with my love to you and them.

I been trying to adjust to Christmas here but it's impossible. The weather is the same every day. The sun rises and sets the same time. As I sit at my Christmas lunch, in bright sunshine, being careful not to move quickly and sweat, it will be cold with you. But believe me Sheila I'll be picturing you. Remember Robert with his train at Crookham? Oh Wee David you will have forgotten me already - except for what you tell him.

I have had a proper enlarger built by an African carpenter and I hope to use it soon. I've bought white enamel and am painting my bed and trunk as a preliminary.

I'll send you a photograph of my room when it is finished!

I've had an incredibly busy week and I'm tired tonight but tomorrow morning I'm going off in the car early for about 50 miles inland by a picturesque road and I've great hopes of getting some good photographs.

Well my beloved this is not a very connected letter. I'm in great hope of a mail tomorrow from you. There has been none for three weeks. Col Bingham is here and had chop with me tonight. Jeremiah can now darn socks - great triumph - no African can darn properly.

20/12/43

Beloved it's 6.45 and a glorious morning. There is calm and peace and the divine coolness every morning. After a long hot days and sticky nights, interrupted by fruit bats and queer unidentifiable yowls, it's marvellous to be awake now, shaved, clothed in clean shorts and shirt.

The birds now are just as at home and I wish you were here now. I'll get Downe to take a photograph of me when he comes out of Hospital.

Kiss Robert and David, and again a Merry Christmas and love, all my love, to you. Alan

19th Dec 1943, Sheila, 6 Crown Mansions, to Alan

Sunday

Dear One,[1]

Had your two letters written "up country" dated 24th and 26th Nov on Thursday last, fascinating letters and most welcome and am I envious! Robert has had another very heavy cold, started it last

---

[1] Sheila's letter is dated 19th Nov! Obviously Sheila cannot have received Alan's letters of 24th and 25th Nov if she is writing on 19th Nov. Also 19th Nov is a Friday. However, 19th Dec is a Sunday so I think that is actually the date and she just made an error.

Monday but is now almost wholly recovered altho he hasn't been out yet. Tomorrow he goes to the circus and I've been in terror in case he'd had to miss it. However, I've got a taxi to take us there and bring us back so all's well.

David has now got it (the cold) and is a little lump of choking streaming misery - or rather should be for he remains inexpressibly cheerful!

I've seen Muriel's house, and though too big in many ways it's very suitable. However, the family are very against my moving in the middle of winter with no help. Meanwhile I am looking for someone to stay in and they say (the McKies) I can have the flat any time, as if I don't take it they aren't going to bother letting it at all and will just leave it shut up. I think I'll try to get a wee house at W. Kilbride for April and May, but we'll see.

I want to get the children out of town as soon as the weather improves. I do wish you could see David, he is such a pickle, so loveable and learning new things every day. Each morning he goes into the bedroom and pulls down his waterproof and sou'wester, crams his sou'wester anyhow on his head and follows me about trailing his coat and bleating until I put it on. Then he makes for the front door and stands trying to open it and saying bye bye to anyone who passes and when none opens the door for him he trails about the house trying to enlist someone to help and refuses to take off his coat and hat for a good half hour. The other day I heard a silence, investigation discovered David sitting in a pool of water festooned with violets and with a vase in his lap grinning depreciatingly. When I scold him he never cries, or sticks out his lip as Robert used to do, but just glowers stolidly. Then when I stop he leans forward and very deliberately kisses me - the only time he ever does! But I could write you papers about David. Can't get Robert to take Cod Liver Oil but am getting him to take Crooks Halibut ditto.

Beloved I'm an escapist, I'm now pretending to myself that you'll be home a year in Jan which is when Wiggy will I suppose be due home, it's not a bad idea really to have a pretend game like that with oneself at this stage. Don't think you are becoming any less real to Robert as time goes on, he speaks of you as tho you were just round the corner!

Moira has been having a hard time but seems to be a bit better now. I'm sorry not to be able to get out to see her.

Dear One, I can't imagine really that we shall ever be allowed to live together without interruption, but I suppose we shall - then you will tell stories of W. Africa and say "these were the days" - or will you?

Monday

David much better and in great form. Robert and I are all set for the circus. Just two letters from you. One sea mail dated 2nd Nov and one air of 3rd Dec. It's a lovely surprise getting them so soon after the others. The reason I said "I am fit and well" on cable was because I couldn't find an "all well" in the selected phrases,[1] I thought you'd realise why it was so stilted and I'm so sorry to have worried you at all. I love you beloved and wish I could make my letters as interesting as yours. I'll reply to today's letter in my next. Robert sends his love. Sheila

21st Dec 1943, Alan, WAF, Achimota, to Sheila

My Own Beloved,

I've just had three love letters this week and I can't wait for the issue of Air Cards to answer them. You see my Dear it's good to be loved and as the only person whose love I care about is yours it's exciting to get letters like that from you.

Sheila do you realise what an influence you have had on me? I have known you for 13 years I have loved you for 11 years and have known that you love me for over 10 years. These 10 years my Dear have been a continual realisation of how splendid life can be. I'm pretty given to swaying from enthusiasm to depression, as you know, but you are something which is true and which never varies according to my mood.

---

[1] The reference to cable 'phrases'. Cables were charged by the word and expensive. However, to save money you could take standard phrases out of a book and use a reference code which was only one word - the code was changed back to the phrase at the other end.

My Dear, look at the joy Robert and David have in living. Look at the joy and happiness you have given me and pray that you may be long spared to live with me.

It's fine to feel that your letters are now in reply to those I sent from here. It's good to hear about a very tough David and Robert printing letters. One of the outstanding things I've learned from living in adult life continually with men is that I admire so few of them. The vast majority are dull and drab creatures with no real enthusiasms and with, to my mind, completely false ideas of what is worthwhile.

Naturally I immediately think when I meet a dullard how awful if Robert or David grew up like that after the love that cherished them. My Dear their lives are their own but they are never never going to be allowed to grow up with the idea that to write a clever business letter is an achievement, or that to sit in Glasgow coffee-room and talk Rugby and Cricket is a reasonable use of the time that is given to them on this earth.

My Dear you have had some terrible preachy letters since you met me.

I was an incredible bore when you met me on some topics and now I am on others. But I'm glad, I was so glad, oh so glad you tell me that you are never tired of being told that I adore you. For that means - that you love me.

Today I flew about 120 miles along the coast leaving at 7:45 AM and flew back in time for dinner.

What a joy it is and how peaceful and uneventful to fly in comparison with the hot dirty roads full of Africans, goats, fowls and 'Mammie Cars' (these are trucks packed to an overwhelming degree with African Women going to market. They are literally asleep on the floor with ragged layers going up to the roofs while arms and legs and cheery black faces[1] bulge out of the open sides. Their *orbital* speed is about 50 M P H.

I saw Tommy Semple this morning. I've been amazingly busy and I'm feeling pretty humble about my Medical Knowledge. There

---

[1] It is perhaps worth explaining to younger readers that Alan quite possibly had never seen a black man in his life before arriving in Africa.

is such an infinite number of new things to learn that I often wonder if it's not just hopeless. I've had to learn about so many new kinds food. Cassava, okra, mango, millet, yam, cocoyam, palm oil, plantain, groundnuts, cowpea, guava, and so on. People come into my office and say look for such and such troops we shall be short of millet and native rice may not give 21 units of polished rice.

Which means lots of calculations and eventually an answer about which I'm not sure. Then someone comes in and says can you tell me the number of officers invalided in West Africa in past three years due to malaria and how many of them were in each of 1st, 2nd or 3rd tours.

Well my predecessor was a whale for work and eventually departed with a nervous breakdown but he never had any information ready sorted out to meet such queries and I'm very gradually getting information together about a few of the common *queries*.

At the moment though the diet and rations are the most queer. Every tribe in W.A. has a different language. All have different food taboos. Some regard rice as a luxury, others will only eat millet.

The Mohammedens will not have pork, only sheep, goat or beef. While some regard rats as a great delicacy and in N.T., a little mild ritual cannibalism still goes on at an important man's funeral celebrations.

Last Sunday I went in with Findlay[1] to an African Doctor's house to see and photograph some cases of yaws and a suspected Yellow Fever. In his village there is a terrific scandal for the village God has departed (from his small mud shrine) and won't come back! The girls dance for him, cocks are slain by the dozen and goats are running out but still he remains obdurate. The best aspect of all is the terrific scandal which has arisen because a deputation was found praying for his return in the local Methodist Mission Church!

My Dear it's 9:30 PM and I'm in bed and trying to read about the vitamins in red palm oil before I go fast asleep. I'm tired, pleasantly and healthily tired, after a long day.

---

[1] Brigadier G.M. Findlay, C.B.E. Co-authored iInvestgations in the Chemotherapy of Malaria in West Africa'. December 1944.

Did I tell you the embarkation staff officer at the place I was at today was a Private in my Hygiene Section at the beginning of the war? Dear One, I think of you a lot and I'm glad of you.

22/12

Beloved there is a sudden change in weather today. It's terribly hot and dry and all book covers are curling back. The atmosphere is windy and dusty - in short the Harmattan[1] has arrived. At least it dries one's sweat for a change.

It's nearly Christmas and I can't send a cable for cables are stopped pro-tem.

Oh Beloved, I'm glad to have my tribal photographs. I love you. Alan

23rd Dec 1943, Sheila, 6 Crown Mansions, to Alan

Dear One,

It's between 10 and 11 PM. I'm sitting in my bedroom and for no particular reason I feel wide-awake, very full of life and very cheerful. My three boys all seem specially dear tonight. Robert is lying asleep and looking very beautiful. Now going to tell you a story which you'll think is a bit tall but it did happen - once or twice I've shown David your photos and said over and over again slowly, "that's Daddy Daddy but not for quite a fortnight. This morning however he came stotting out of my room holding your photo (which he'd taken from my dressing table) out in front of him and muttering all the time "Dad-I, Dad-I". He wandered right up the hall and out of my ken, without lifting his head, in complete absorption! Of course he could just as easily have said "bow wow" but the fact remains he didn't and it was rather sweet. Beloved I just have to think of our reunion and far off as it is, a wave of intense excitement sweeps over me. There's some strange alchemy at work between us beloved, when after all these years and life together I can feel faint even at the thought of one meeting

---

[1] Harmattan is a hot, dry wind from the North East.

Dec 25th

It's 8 PM the boys are asleep and another war Christmas is over for which I'm very thankful. For years now I have dreaded Christmas and New Year and this year the effort is greater than ever, the toys were so hopeless and one feels deadly un-festive and Oh! I'm just so glad it's over. David is endeavouring to cut his eye teeth and I didn't get any sleep until nearly 5 this morning. He seemed to have earache and I was worried stiff about him. Result I started the day in a daze and so did David. However, after breakfast he fell asleep on my knee and woke in about half an hour looking a bit better, after his lunchtime sleep he was full of beans and has gone off to bed tonight very happily. Robert had a nice day - a lot of turkey and toys - of a kind! This afternoon Nancy Fulton and Peter and her new little boy Ronald came for tea and Robert did enjoy their company. Robert's reactions to the circus are rather hard to put down because I am unsure of them. He was terribly thrilled at first but got rather bored towards the end and I fancy that only the fact that the Lions and Tigers came last stopped him from demanding to be taken home! We were a bit far away I think (seventh row upper circle) but don't tell your mother this! Just as the taxi drew up at the door when we got back he said "Mummy, I don't think I'll tell them anything about it until tomorrow, I'm too tired". Since then he has said little of it, although he insists if asked that "it was lovely". I paid Hipson's last two cheques into Glyn Mills as I was going to use their cheques to pay rent and rates, but if you prefer it I'll in future pay them into my own account and deal with them that way. It will be less confusing for you. I'm so glad your work is so interesting and the photographs promising well. I'll get the Smiths note books sent off. Had a very joyful letter from you today for Sunshine and Surf Riding and dinghy sailing. It arrived in the bleak coldness of a pitch dark morning when David and I were feeling distinctly subhuman and I got a comfortable feeling that I had evacuated you to a pleasant land! It's so nice to know you are well and happy beloved. If only it can stay like that for you all the time I shall be a very lucky woman. I wouldn't say I'm not envious - I am - Green! I'll phone Mrs *Topping* when I can trace her, she's not in the telephone book. I've had no time as things have been hectic. I hope you can read these letters of mine beloved. I get really cross eyed trying to get as much as possible into the space.

Dec 27th

David has been rather ill for the last two days beloved, but tonight he looks like his old self again. He was very feverish (102) all day yesterday and wheezy, I decided he had bronchitis and got the doctor, who said he had bronchitis with pneumonic tendencies and better have MandB[1] right away (this was in the evening). I managed to get a taxi and got into Boots to get him started on them right away, his temperature came right down with a bump in a few hours but I don't think he slept for 10 minutes of each the whole night, he didn't complain, but just flopped about in a dazed sort of way.........I am starting another card.

Continuation Air Mail Dec 27th

and insisted on sitting up most of the time staring into space - most weird, my hair was standing on end - however he was much brighter this morning altho the MandB was still very much on his mind. His temp has been normal all day so we stopped the MandB unless it rises again and his breathing is greatly improved. The Dr will be again tomorrow afternoon. He is Dr Burton recommended by Roy Young as the best practitioner in Glasgow and he is a youngish man and certainly has a charming way with children. I have not told your family where I heard of him because of course they don't know I've been in contact with Roy. I've just said I've heard him well spoken of. I'm feeling pretty limp and tired now that the worst seems to be over, but am hoping for a more peaceful night tonight. I certainly won't forget this Christmas in a hurry and Oh! how I've longed for the comfort of your presence in these last few days.

---

[1] MandB - This is Sulfapyridine, original UK spelling sulphapyridine, it is a sulfonamide antibacterial. At one time it was known as M&B.

I'll add the latest news to this after the doctor has been here tomorrow.

Tuesday this 28

Patient very much improved and his temp has stayed down. The doctor came at lunchtime and was very pleased with him, so much so that I'm beginning to wonder why I've been worrying so much! His ears are still a bit inflamed evidently and his eye teeth are dreadfully sore, but Dr says he can get out at end of week, however I'll certainly err on the safe side. Personally I think when he gets his teeth through he'll be quite different, remember how upset Robert was at Crookham with his?

I'm not going to try to fill up this letter beloved because I've got Susan here for two hours and she plays with David and as I had another very disturbed night last night I am going to take the chance of forty winks. I'm feeling very relieved and will enjoy a rest. Robert is fine and sends his love.

Beloved take care of yourself I am so lost without you. Sheila

25th Dec 1943, Alan, WAF, Achimota, to Sheila

My Dear One,

It's Christmas day and there will be great excitement with the boys. We had a very special extra airmail delivery and I had your letters of 6th and 14th of December. So with my pile last Sunday I'm really up-to-date and brimming with news. I also had letters from Mummy and Daddy and a Sea Mail of the letter from the Fountain Press.

It's good to feel really in letter communication and as soon as it's permitted I'll send you a cable.

I'll be thinking of you all today especially, and also on Jan 3rd for the circus. Yes it's grand to know that there is affection for you in Wakefield with *Davy* and Mrs Morris.

I wonder if Sister did have anything to do with Edna. I hear from Mummy that Dr Welsh has, miracle doctor, produced some tennis balls and they are on the way. I'll be so interested to hear if you get the Muriel Moyes flat.

Sheila, it's so fine to hear of my boy's doings and sayings and reactions but it's even better to hear them from you than from anyone else. I've been frantically busy but have had one game of tennis and won £2.10 in Sgts Mess sweep. I hope to manage the afternoon off to go swimming today. I have to go to a conference in another colony in the middle of this week but I should only be away a couple of days. I've sent you a couple of letters by surface mail. It's odd beloved but I never until now have had any doubt as to my ability to settle down as Dep M.O.H. Wakefield after the war until now. But this is so much more interesting, so stimulating mentally that I can hardly conceive of that now. The work here has started my wee brain box fair humming, and I never remember being so clear mentally, capable of such an output of decent work. No days ever long enough for me to finish the things I want to do. No new thing I see or hear fails to have a reaction in that I want to hear more, see more and try to find out the whys and wherefore.

I'm sorry to say that Wiggy has another attack of Malaria and is in hospital. It's not a bad one, but it's too soon after the last.

Sparks arrives tomorrow and Duff is well. I met *Alenter* Hopley (used to throw the javelin at University). He is A.P.M.

Had one trip last week, one day flew around 120 miles in the morning and flew back in the evening. Oh it's such a pleasant clean way of travel.

Beloved I had three love letters last week. I've replied to them in a long surface mail letter but Oh My Darling I've read them often and I'm so terribly glad that my wife can write me love letters after 10 and more years. I shall never, never believe that any marriage can be as wonderful as ours the parties happen to remain in love.

Oh my Dear don't you see that I'm perpetually loving you more. I've just never met another woman who came within measuring distance of you. You see, you are just Sheila - the girl I love the half of me without which the other half is useless. Alan

1944

Notes on 1944

1944 was the year we knew the Germans were beaten, but much bloody fighting lay ahead.

Of course, the great event was D-Day 6th June when the massive Allied armada landed on the beaches in Normandy. Sheila was thrilled though glad Alan was safely in Africa. Alan was nagged by the thought that he had a safe billet and should be in the fighting somewhere.

Sheila's great fear was that, when the Germans surrendered, Alan would be sent east to fight the Japanese. Indeed, a five-year spell in the east was very possible and we know from a separate diary that when asked if he would willingly accept such a posting he replied unhesitatingly that he would go whereever he was ordered. He did not tell Sheila this and I doubt if she ever saw his diary!

Alan in tropical uniform.
I still have the stick he holds.

Sheila again spends time at Wayside in Seamill, but in May 1944 moves to the rented farm in Nethybridge near Aviemore.

The address is:
Dell Farm, Nethybridge, Inverness-shire. She also rented 24 Queens Gate from the Moyes, a flat which was convenient.

Schofield, ACS (Alan,) Duff, Matron, Wigmore, Findlay, Archer.
Alan & colleagues in 1944 in Accra, Gold Coast (now Ghana).
All those sitting in the second row are mentioned in the Alan-Sheila letters.

Schofield: Major Schofield. Mentioned a number of times. He hadamoebic dysentery. When he came home he brought photos and scent for Sheila as he lived in Morfield near Wakefield. He came round and had tea. Alan warned that he was a confirmed pessimist.

Lt Col Alan Stevenson: ADH - Assistant Deputy Hygiene

Duff: Colonel Duff. He became a very good friend of Alan's and was "a good chap". Poor Duff was badly seasick on the awful voyage out to Africa, got prickly heat in the Gold Coast and became very depressed. He was then operated on for an internal obstruction, an old appendix operation gone wrong. He was invalided out in 1945 and came up to Wakefield to see Sheila, who took a liking to him.

Matron: Miss Stewart, Matron Local European Civil Hospital.

Wigmore: Brigadier James Buckley Aquilla Wigmore.

Findlay: Brigadier Findlay. A "laboratory man" in Alan's words. They wrote a medical article together.

Archer: Colonel Archer, the ADP

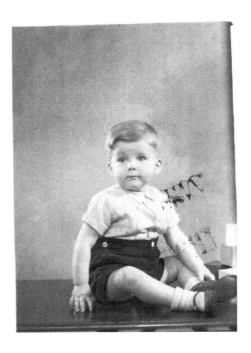

Love from David. you will be getting the other one later on, bigger than this. I hope you like me, it's a bit of a virgin not knowing ones Daddy very well it would be dreadful if you didn't know what I looked like.

FIGHTING MALARIA
IN WEST AFRICA

Daily Telegraph Reporter

DDT — dichlor-diphenyl-trichlore-thane, the powerful new "all purpose" insecticide—is being used with great success in the fight against malaria in West Africa.

Viscount Swinton, British Resident Minister there, described its new use when he addressed a Press conference in London yesterday.

"They have started experimenting with DDT against the malaria mosquito," he said. "I think it is going to be as damaging to them as it is to other things. It is a real killer. I wish we could use it against the Germans."

Lord Swinton told how two of the world's greatest anti-malaria experts were keeping R.A.F. airfields free from mosquitoes, and incidentally bringing new health to surrounding towns. **5 AUG 44**

1ˢᵗ Jan 1944, Alan, WAF, Achimota, to Sheila

My Beloved,

A happy New Year to you. We can now say "I'll see you next year". I've been longing for this card to write to you and now I seem to have nothing to say. I've had a Yachting World & Motor Boat & various letters readdressed from you but no surface mail from you. I have sent a watch by *Halpern*, our Polish M.O. here. It's one I bought for 15/- but I broke the hand trying to reset it & had not time to repair it before *Halpern* left. I should think you will easily get a new hand & it will please Robert. I've also sent you photographs by him & by ordinary mail. I also brought in the New Year asleep & have been down by plane again & spent a night with Col Bingham since I last wrote to you. I travelled in style with the minister for W.A. Lord Swinton in his private plane.

I was at the local races last Monday & got some good photographs & lost 10/- on fruitless "speculations". Oh my Dear I'm missing you & needing you & grudging you. I'll write more this evening.

2.1.44

It's 7.30 AM on a peaceful Sunday morning & I can close my eyes & imagine I'm at home. I shall be thinking of you all tomorrow at the Circus. Your wire arrived & I hope you got mine in time for New Year.

Leslie Sparks is here and full of cheer. Wiggie is out of Hospital again but I'm rather worried about him as he looks pretty tired. It's just the same as at home - he gets knocked up so easily. I've got a great ploy on here to buy some wood & let it season & then have it sent home after the war. It's dirt cheap - a beam of Mahogany which would cost about £7 at home is 5/- here, and it's very plentiful. Freight before the war was about £3 a ton & even if it was double that it would still be cheap at home. It would be grand for Camusglashlan & the boat. Beloved, I hope that the coming of New Year has cheered you. Here we are, married for nearly seven years, & we had 2½ years to live together. It's been many more kicks than halfpence for you <u>but</u> my Darling we <u>shall</u> live together again. I do hope that I can get a decent job after the war for I am getting too old to be bothered by money matters. The boys will have to be educated & so on but with a bit of luck I suppose I should be as well placed as anyone to get something good. It must allow us to live in the country.

My dear I shall never take to living in a city again. I have been wondering what to send you as a present. We are only allowed to send products of the country. There are only a limited number of good things. Kano cloth, smoked skin (Python), Leopard skins. Would you like smoked skin & could you get them made into shoes? If not if you send me an old shoe I shall have it copied.

Well my very own one I seem to have very little to say today. Wish a good new year to all the parents. I'll send a wee chit to Robert. I love you, Alan

Dear Robert,

I sent you photographs of a monkey; her name is Pepe & she climbs trees very quickly. She can eat a banana & throw nuts at me if she is annoyed.

I have been swimming in the sea. It's lovely & warm here. So warm that Daddy can stay in all afternoon & not feel cold. There are very big waves & you get a board of wood and float on them. The black boys have little boats hollowed out of the trunk of a tree & they are very clever at sailing in them.

Kiss Mummy & David for me. I love them & you very much. Daddy

1ˢᵗ Jan 1944, Sheila, 6 Crown Mansions, to Alan

My Dear,

I've had two letters from you since I last wrote, both arrived last Monday & one was your Christmas one so it was a very near miss. Yes I'll drop a note to Mrs. Wigmore when I have time and give her the good news of the Wig. I've had another hectic few days because David who on Tuesday had his first good night after being ill handed the ball over to Robert so to speak, who yelled with ear ache all Wednesday night and had a temp 100°. I phoned the doctor at 8

AM Thursday and he came right out, said inflammation of the middle ear, and gave him M & B & Sedonan ear drops & Aerfactone for his nose (which has never properly cleared). The poor old boy subsequently spent a very wretched day under the influence of M & B but in a very short time there was no more ear ache & at six the following morning after a wretched night his temp dropped & the slacking off of the M B gave him great relief. Today (Saturday) he has been up (simply insisted) in the one room and is very himself though not at all hungry. You would have laughed if you could have seen us last night, New Year's Eve or not. I went off to bed just after 10 & found Robert wide-awake & very Merry. He said Mummy, away & get some biscuits & milk and we will have a party. I got him some milk & I a whisky (in an effort to check a cold) & we had our party. I sat on the side of his bed & we toasted - first and foremost you, raising our glasses to your photographs and clinking them in the approved manner then the king & Mr Churchill & a host of others. When I'd come to the end of my wits for someone else, Robert said "what about God"? He was in one of his funniest moods and says "Oh! I do love you Sheila".

Sunday 2nd

I have a good report of your family today they seem fine both of them so I'm hoping my little run of bad luck is over.

I had your letter telling me of your daft dream that I was leaving you, I wonder if you realise just how daft it was! Oh! Beloved I do love you so. Funny to think of Sparks being with you, is he relieved!

Monday 3rd

The children are in bed & I'm sitting by the fire after a hectic day. Mother is in bed and I had to get the doctor today. He thinks she's just got flu but I'm sure I don't know, I don't think she's at all well, she's eating next to nothing and is losing weight rapidly. The Dr is coming again on Thursday and speaks of an x-ray to clear up the question of the discomfort in her middle, she however does not know of this. However we got to the pantomime this afternoon & Susan came in to take care of David & our morning woman came in the afternoon if you know what I mean so there were enough people in the house to let me out with an easy mind.

Did I tell you that Nancy and her two boys were coming with us! I asked that they go knowing what pleasure Robert would have at their company and he certainly did enjoy himself. I regret to say however that when the wolf (it was Red Riding Hood) approached Robert gave one wild yell & dived under his seat! How he got himself folded up into such a tiny ball I don't know but he refused to come to the surface until assured the wolf had departed for good! He was very good all the same.

My Dear I'm so tired of life without you, but every day is a day less and Oh! Beloved need me very badly because I'm just living for your return. I'll see about the boy's photos as soon as I can, I am free such a short time of the day & for the past few weeks there has always been someone ill & I have got nothing done. I have had a letter from Lannie saying no one in Achiltibuie will let their house because of income tax! I seem to be foiled everywhere I turn just now. I have hopes of a letter from you any day now even for tomorrow morning. David is more adorable than ever he dances with music now & is just as quick mentally as Robert, I mean of course in proportion to his age. They are both a great joy to me & could not possibly have more attractive children. I love you more than ever beloved. Sheila

P.S. I'm afraid this is a chef's breakfast I hope you can read it.

2nd Jan 1944, Alan, WAF, Achimota, to Sheila

My Dear,[1]

Two more letters from you yesterday. I'm glad that lots of people are coming to see you and hope the new help turns out well.

I shall try to look up Angus Taylor later this month. Hope you heard lots of things from Halpern which would let you know the kind of place this is. I'm glad he managed to get to see you.

---

[1] This letter is addressed to c/o Moyes, 24 Queens Gate, Glasgow. Sheila rented the Moyes Flat, from Muriel Moyes I think.

It's amazing to hear of you getting a surface mail so soon. It must have gone by air. I'm keeping very fit indeed these days, and it was very fortunate that the surface mail written in Hospital should reach you so soon. I hope you go to Achiltibuie Hotel. Love Alan

8th Jan 1944, Alan, WAF, Achimota, to Sheila

My Very Dear,

Your letter of *19th* Dec arrived yesterday. Isn't it a slow tedious process to get a reply on 8th Jan to letters I posted on 24th Nov. However it was grand to get it and your news. I've sent you several surface mails and three lots of photographs. Again I had a "Motor Boat" by the last surface mail. You said in the last letter, Jan 3rd, for the circus, but I gather you were going on the 20th.

It must be very difficult for you to decide about the flat of the McKies. It's grand to hear of David growing up & developing his own personality, it's so strange to hear of him wanting to go out & so on. I'm glad the colds were on the mend before you finished your letter. Oh Beloved how I enjoy them. None till now since December 23rd. Please write often, not only once a week. The Aerograph service is starting so although it would be no quicker, I should be able to write more often.

It's 9 o'clock & I'm in bed. I was at a farm a few miles away today watching my Trypanosome (Sleeping Sickness) team at work. I came back with the cart loaded with Pau Pau, tomatoes & pineapples. There is one on my table now which I have just started. It is a foot high & 9 inches across the base! Am playing a foursome tennis match tomorrow against the Engineers & am looking forward to it

Oh my Beloved the saving grace of all this is that the work is so interesting. I work very hard even by temperate climate standards but it's useful work & I like it. It is a great help having Sparks here to take the dull work away from me.

Have you had any word from Kodak about the film etc.? If not will you tell Wallace Eaton, 125 New Bond Street, to send me as much 35 mm Panchromatic film as they can spare. Also any more M.C.M. 100 or D.K. 20 will be welcome as I am doing a lot of useful photography in work & play. I got some grand photographs of insects but Oh bromide paper is expensive!

Sunday

Well my one it's 1:10 & I must dash off to lunch. It's very hot today T 104° after a cold night. Cold seems relative - room temp 70°!

I am going to have the afternoon off <u>not</u> because I should, the work is there, but because I'm stupid with work. I love you. Alan

(Enclosed) Dear Robert,

I hope you enjoyed the circus. You say a letter to Mummy & she will write it then you sign it. Love Daddy

9th Jan 1944, Sheila, 6 Crown Mansions, to Alan

My Very Dear,

It's a fortnight since I had a letter & I'm so looking forward to one. I've had a pretty hectic week but mother is now up 'tho looking dreadfully shaken. Her breaking down decided me definitely that I was going to move so I hope to get into Muriel's flat next week. Mrs Moyes died last Wednesday without ever knowing of Ian's death. Muriel however feels they can't go back to their flat just yet so I hope to be there until the end of March. I think it would be better to keep sending letters here dear but just do what you think best. I am now going to try for a house at W.K.[1] for April & May. Hazel Henderson[2] is coming to stay for 3 nights a week for a bit, she is doing massage at "The Anderson College" so it will save her the journey back to *Tarbert* every night & will be company for me. Susan can stay odd nights if I should want her.

I have at last sent off the note-books. I'm so sorry to take so long over them. But I couldn't get out, in fact I've only been out once in a fortnight! However that's all over now & Oh Beloved I'm so glad the children are well again. David has advanced today to size 6 in

---

[1] W.K. = West Kilbride.

[2] Hazel Henderson, (Elizabeth Hazel Henderson), Sheila's first cousin once removed. Hazel is 18 at this date. She married George Wilson in 1951.

shoes! & has been for his first outing without his pram. I had to run down to the shops yesterday afternoon & hadn't time to get the pram round (Susan's afternoon off) so I took David walking on his reins. He walked splendidly & was he pleased with himself. It was funny being out with two boys trotting alongside!

I had a letter from Miss Perkins this week, she says Dr Robinson has been home on leave. Steven has been very ill, evidently overdoing things badly. He has been in a nursing home for weeks & I've just had a very depressed letter from him saying he is to be taken to Peebles. Where by graded exercises he is to be allowed to walk again. Nancy knows less than I do as he won't write to her & May gives next to no information.

I've written to Mrs Wigmore, but can't trace Mrs Bingham at all. She is not in the phone book & Directory Inquiry know nothing of her. I'll try to find if Moira knows anything.

I've been reading a good book recently called "Brazilian Throne". I'll try to pick up a copy for our collection. I'm afraid I know nothing whatever about the Kings of Brazil.

Mother presented Robert with a little pearl grey flannel suit, blue & grey checked shirt & grey sleeveless pullover for Christmas. It will fit him in the summer & he looks adorable in it. David has cut one of his eye teeth today with none of the alarming symptoms Robert had at a like time & I am much relieved!

It's more & more of a heartbreak to me that you can't see David just now, he is the most joyous soul, gives kisses of a smacking heartiness & has just started to say "pease" when he wants anything. He is quite recovered & eating like a horse.

Oh! Beloved it's just on 3 months since I left you & it's a long long way to go yet. I've had a bad fit of missing you today. The last few weeks I've been so busy I haven't had much time to think about anything and you seemed so very far away, but today I feel you near again if you know what I mean in spite of all the miles between.

It's obvious I'll need another Letter Card, I'll just see if I've got one!

10th Jan 1944, Sheila, 6 Crown Mansions, to Alan

Yes Beloved,

I'm looking forward to my move at the end of the week, Friday or Saturday it will be. Robert is very thrilled at the thought of a move, he takes after his mother that way!

Steven & Struthers' horse & cart will come & move my things. I've mislaid my pen these days & write even worse with this one which I can't control at all. I've written Lannie telling her to send me name & address of the mysterious person who has a house to let only won't let it and in true Lannie style she persists in referring to him simply as "that man". I'll get in touch with him and see what can be done. I am paying Muriel £12 a month for her flat which is reasonable. I wonder if you managed to see Wilfred, his brother in law, the younger boy Davie, was killed last week, he was in the R.A.F.

You'd laugh if you could see Robert & his wee brother together! David is getting _fairly_ obedient and if told not to touch a particular thing the chances are he won't, except if Robert should be unwise enough to say "no" or "don't" to him, in that event the only way to stop David's immediate & fanatical determination to do the thing in question is to remove him bodily from the scene. His main rule in life is definitely to take no orders from Robert!

Beloved I'm sitting on my bed just thinking of turning in and I'm nearly asleep. I like writing to you when I'm alone & the house is quiet, but the drawback is by that time I usually am half asleep. It's turned very cold today after a mild spell, but so far we've really had a wonderfully mild winter.

Still no letter from you, I fear that there has been an air mail cut this end too, but here's hoping I'll get two or three at once.

11th Jan

Dreadfully cold morning very like snow. I'm going to the flat this afternoon to talk over a few things with Muriel & will take the chance of learning a few things. - Letter from you just come in. - Just read letter written on Christmas day. You still seem to be enjoying yourself more than ever, which is fine.

May I point out however for some considerable time you have been doubting your ability to settle down as Wakefield's Deputy M.O.H. It hasn't just struck you all of a sudden like & I fear if you think that you must have a touch of the sun!

Beloved I love you and well understand your feelings on the subject. So glad you are to get some tennis balls.

Dreadfully sorry about poor Wig, particularly as I was going to post today a nice bright little letter telling Mrs W how well he was. I shall not post it.

If you are thinking of staying out there we might as well come out right away don't you think! However the first 6 months, which is said to be always good, hasn't gone yet, perhaps I'd better wait a bit & see!

Oh my Dear it's so funny, I do love to think of you so happy & enjoying yourself, but I think a sort of primitive fear of the edge having been taken off your longing to come back to us. Dear me what crazy ideas one gets, just writing the foregoing has shown me how absurd it is. I'm so looking forward to the surface letters, but I suppose they will take weeks yet.

Yours ever, Sheila

11th Jan 1944, Alan, WAF, Cape St Mary, Gambia, to Sheila

My Beloved,

I'm writing this well over a thousand miles from where I wrote my last letter & yet I only left this morning. I'm up about a suspected case of Yellow Fever & as I flew up I was cursing & swearing that you were not there. For I sat in the Co-Pilot's seat all the way and I would have given lot to take over on my own set of controls for a bit. W Africa is pretty grim from the air. Miles of sand with a heavy surf then a lagoon & a village & a few dugout canoes then more sand. But always inland there is mangrove palm & then just bush.

Tonight my room looks onto a Veranda 50 feet above a strip of palms along the shore. The surf is booming in competition with the ever present cricket & in the morning I'm going to bathe before breakfast. I shall be away from HQ for a fortnight or so for I shall take the opportunity to do some touring up here so I'm hoping that there will be a collection on mail waiting for me. I bought a goatskin bag for, my suitcase being so heavy it takes too much of my 44 lbs which is the allowance. It's really very nice and will be useful at home. I have sent you some cloth & Robert some cufflinks, which I had promised him. My dear I love you & I'll write more tomorrow. Now I can hardly hold the pen for sleep.

12/1. 6:30 PM
Just about to have bath. Had a most interesting day. The weather here is wonderful. Just like Madeira - lovely and cool in the morning & evening & warm in the middle of the day. I've seen an extremely good selection of yaws, cerebral malaria, sleeping sickness, leprosy, yellow jack & so on. It really is a wonderful place for medicine.

Tonight I've been wandering along the beach and longing for you. Oh my Dear One you would love this life. The few women one sees out here are pretty miserable specimens. The trouble is that they are accustomed to do nothing all day & now they have to do some work to justify being here they seem more discontented than ever. Yet we could have a wonderful time beloved. But then we could anywhere my Dear.

Tell your Alan that I never go anywhere without the rotating plate gadget he made for me. I've had great pleasure from it. Graham Scott was in the hospital I'm staying at but he has just gone home. I shall be staying with Wilfred Robertson on my way home for a week or so & I'll let you know about him so that you can tell his wife.

It's strange I've just realised it but there is one coniferous tree outside the window. The first I've seen since I left home. The Africans here are completely abject from underfeeding & disease. How sad in such a lovely place. Kiss my dear Boys.

I love you. Alan

15th Jan 1944, Sheila, 24 Queens Gate, to Alan

My Dear One,

We moved in yesterday& after twenty-four hours of finding my way about & unpacking, tripping over David & Robert & being tripped over by them, surviving all the minor disasters of the first confused hours I am now feeling more at home and think my sanity is assured! If Sister, purged of her sins could have appeared she would have been most welcome, for whatever her faults, & they were hideous, she was a grand one to move with. It's so queer to have all this space at one's disposal, the hall itself is big enough to live in, & Robert & I have a huge bedroom with two Oriel windows. David sleeps in a large room next door with a door through from our room. Then there is a large spare bedroom, large dining room (which I shall not use), big kitchen, bathroom, cloakroom & cellar. It's pretty chilly of course but I think it's possibly better for the children - that way, at least I'm hoping so! Myself I don't like the cold at all so I am still most envious of you.

Robert likes his new home very much & makes the most incredible din rushing around all the wide open spaces of it.

David was frankly terrified of his change of home at first & if he lost sight of me nearly went out of his mind but he is settled down now.

Sunday 16th Jan

Feeling considerably more mistress of the situation today & I think I'm going to like it here very much. Hazel comes tomorrow evening & stays to Thursday, bed, breakfast & supper of course, of course she won't be in during the day. There is a bookcase full of good books here & at the moment I'm at Charles II by Arthur Bryant, also "And Quiet Flows the Don" by Solokhov. The Moyes had been wonderfully kind. The day I came into the house Mrs Moyes came with the most marvellous flowers for me & Muriel couldn't do enough to make me comfortable. With all their troubles thick upon them as it were I shall never forget how much thought they gave to make things as easy as possible for us.

This is a dreadfully scrappy letter, I'll try to write a better one during the week & tell you more the children's doings. It may be only baby fat but your younger son is getting enormous! He comes now when he bumps himself, running to get the sore bit kissed, just as Robert used to.

I wonder if you can picture at all where we are. It's a corner flat & although the door is in Queens Gate most of the windows are in Beaumont Gate (where I was born!) & looking onto Highborough Road. I can put David in his pram in the hall & walk straight out with him, there being only two or three low & widely spaced steps on the way. I think your parents are coming to tea on Saturday. So you will be getting a letter about the children I expect. They will see a difference in David for he alters every week just now. I can't think why my pen keeps blotting, please excuse it! Mother is looking a bit better and is out & about again. Myself beloved, I'm very fit, but aching very badly for you, still I'm not letting it get me down & am resolutely looking forward. Robert sends his love & wants me to tell you that he does the black out for me! All love, Sheila

18th Jan 1944, Alan, WAF, Freetown, Sierra Leone, to Sheila

My Beloved,

I'm staying at the Hospital with Wilfred Robinson having flown down here Sunday last. I'm just longing to get back to get my mail but I'll be here for another 4 or 5 days. I'm having a most interesting tour and learning more & more & more so that I feel ignorant & ignoranter & ignoranter for not having known it before. But it does pass the time seeing more places & stranger Africans & meeting new people all the time. It's now over 3 months since I left you my Dear & longer than I've ever been without seeing you (by the time you get this) even when I was in France. I look at the snaps a lot & I love you all.

Have you had my photograph from Farnborough? And when are you being taken? You can be taken to send to a husband overseas. Wilfred is very fit & sends his regards. Will you drop a note to his wife and tell her I saw him in excellent health. Tell me all about the boys when you write. Oh my Dear, I'm very proud of them. Conditions in the Africans in some of the places I have visited are really more terrible than one could ever have imagined. Riddled with disease, under nourished and as a result of the two, half-witted they live their short lives. It's the greatest piece of bunk ever suggested that we are good to our native peoples.

I saw 130 people in one village with such diseases as would fill a medical encyclopaedia & in that we graciously provide four underpaid doctors for ¼ million people. Do get hold of Richard Burton's wanderings in West Africa. See what he has to say about it - it's just getting worse ever since that was written in 1860.

There was a copy in John Smith's second hand section. Send it on when you have read it together with any other books of interest.

You might ask the photographic people for more MCM 100 from time to time & if Kodak have not written to you will you try to send me some film 35 mm for Leica.

Sorry to take up paper with that. O.C. Hospital here is Lt Col Gibbs whom I knew in Aldershot & I'm going to have dinner tomorrow with a chap called Ronald Hodge whom I have not seen since at school nearly 20 years ago! Heigh Ho Beloved, I'm nearly 35 - isn't it terrible. Still I am & feel ageless with you. Wouldn't it be terrible if you grew older & I did not?

I love you so my Dear, kiss the boys, love to parents. I hope to have a card to write them when I get back. Love Alan

20th Jan 1944, Sheila, 24 Queens Gate, to Alan

My Beloved,

I had your letter New Year's Day, today, & more than welcome it was. You mentioned you'd received no surface mail from me but you see I haven't sent any! There's no point in my doing so when it takes such ages & I can send as many Air Cards as I like. I haven't an awful lot of news beloved & I can't fill up paper with my longing for you which overshadows everything. I never seem to have a moment to call my own during the day & there is only the few hours of evening to read write letters, mend & all the odds and ends that one can't do with the children about. I'm awfully sorry all the same beloved if you been looking out for ordinary mail, but don't feel at all neglected, you are seldom out of my thoughts at all. The boys are fighting fit again, David has both his eye teeth through & eating like a horse. His dinner today consisted of - a rasher of bacon, a fried egg & a baked potato, then a good plate of pudding when he woke up an hour or so later! Robert has got the practical jokes craze, leaving things about where he knows I'll fall over them, then nearly splits his sides laughing. After I'd furiously attacked him tonight, having nearly fallen over a large bowl (David & all) which he'd left just outside the bathroom door, he said plaintively "well how do you be funny then", rather sweet!

The McVicar's daughter was born on January 2nd & is called Susan Carol. I had a letter today from Mrs MacDonald who says she knows Don would love to hear from you & his address is (Lt Col D C McDonald M.C., HQ Allied Military Government Region I. C.M.7.) He is in Sicily. My woman who was supposed to come in the mornings just hasn't turned up, however until I get someone, mother's one,[1] runs down and gives me a hand for a short time after that she's finished at number 6. It's such a huge flat & there is a great deal to be done, the floor space alone gives one plenty of exercise!

David is a funny wee soul, he is most savagely a "mother's boy" at the moment, but I expect he'll get over it soon now. Robert & he are able to play quite a bit together now & and Oh! Beloved - the noise! The other day I heard screams and & on investigation found Robert stumbling around the bedroom closely pursued by David who was hitting him remorselessly on the back of the head with the back of a hairbrush. Grinning from ear to ear!

Robert can rattle all through his alphabet now, you'd see a big difference in him in the few months you have been away. Oh! Beloved it's a dreadfully long time yet. Still as I said I'm glad you're away, the "second front" hangs like a cloud over everything these days & even with you away I feel the depression of it.

I'm going to start another card now & reply to some of the things

---

[1] This is exactly as written. Sheila means that Mamie's (Mother's) help would run down to give her a hand.

in your letter. I do hope the cable telling you of my move got to you quickly. I like to think you know where we are. S

22nd Jan 1944, Alan, WAF, Freetown, Sierra Leone, to Sheila

My Beloved,

I'm still with Wilfred Robinson but hope to go to G.H.Q in a few days. I have had a busy & Oh so interesting & (I really think) useful time here. So very many points of interest have arisen as a result of my tour. And so very many new things will begin as a result of it that I feel I'm being useful & that is the only way to have peace of mind.

I'm just longing to get back though for there should be a huge mail waiting for me. I've had a gay time here. On Thursday at a party for the departure home for one of my officers here, Wilfred & I took out four nurses from the hospital. I danced half a dance, I listened to the maudlin laments of a bearded Commander R.N. I had a grand talk with a Catholic White Father who has been here for 20 years. He was telling me about the Leopard Society & the Small Pox Society in which smallpox is worshipped as a god. I met a couple of chaps who had been on the boat with me & altogether had an amusing evening.

Last night I was dining with a Dr Turner, the guests were Commander Wilson, Dr & Mrs Hardy & a Miss Stewart, the Matron of the local European Civil Hospital. It was nice to dine in a house. They were all fond of music and were interested of all queer things in village life in Anglo Saxon England. I quoted a few quips from Thierry's Norman Conquest and Findlay's "Anglo or Saxon?" and was thereafter in the mob & found difficulty in persuading them that I knew nothing about it as I hadn't been there. Dr & Mrs Hardy are nice people. They have no children, live way up bush & she travels everywhere with him in the car on his district tours.

Oh my Dear, when I see anyone with his wife I at once think of you and get home rich. You must have your hands full with the boys & you must get very tired of it sometimes. But Beloved know that you are so good to them. I know that there is no one in all the world whom I'd rather have for my boys to know & love & learn from than you.

That is quite apart from your being my woman who are mine only & not the boys when I need you. It's going to be grand to be able to drop you a line often when I get back.

I'll be glad to be able to write to the parents oftener. Do let them know that I'm well and asking for them.

It's very moist & sticky here after my fresh air holiday last week but I had a glorious bathe in a surf free sandy bay yesterday. Oh how I love the warm water!

Well my dear tell the boys I'm very busy & that in the place I was last week I saw hundreds of monkeys & cranes & crocodiles & egrets and kyoto which is a little deer like Walt Disney's one.

Oh Sheila I love you and am always thinking of you. Alan[1]

23rd Jan 1944, Sheila, 24 Queens Gate, to Alan

My Dear One,[2]

Your parents were here yesterday & we had a pleasant afternoon. Robert was of course a host in himself and David, although horrified at first, became very convivial but wouldn't let them put a finger on him! Today I have been up to tea at Number 6 with the boys & they had a great time.

Monday

Another day gone & a very cold one too! Robert and I were in town this afternoon - the first time for weeks - we got David two new suits & a pretty woolly for Susan Carol. I'm sorry about "Wiggy". It doesn't seem as if he'd last the time - or does it? Seems a grand idea about the wood unless post-war freight is exceptionally heavy. I paid Kodak with a Glyn Mills cheque £6.13.6 for your things. Don't worry beloved about sending things home. The python skins are of course grand, but it would be quite impossible

---

[1] This letter is actually dated 22/1/43. However the postmark, though blurred, says '44' and it was with the 44 letters so I'm sure it is 44. Alan was in Tunbridge Wells in Jan 43.

[2] Card Address is 6 Crown Mansions, but Sheila is still at Queens Gate.

to get them made up these days, at any rate & I simply can't spare an old shoe to send out, one wears them until they fall to pieces just now & a python shoe would have to be a court one on much smarter lines than any I have now. The shoes now in the shops are appalling. I have arranged to have David's photo taken, but they are so short of film that it won't be done before March 1st. I'm going to have it tinted *they* 'Pettergrews' do it most beautifully. I shall take them in the suit he will wear & a piece of his hair the day after & I think it should be a success, so long as he doesn't scowl all the time!

I'm longing for a cable, I haven't had one for 26 days & so nice to feel one is up-to-date.

Wilfred's father-in-law (Mr Davie) dropped dead last Thursday just a fortnight after the boy was killed.

I've written to Mr McLeod (*Mason*) Polbain asking about his house, so will hope for the best. Kenny's wife wants to buy the pram which is difficult as I had hoped to get quite a lot for it! It would be funny to see our pram bumping young MacClennans about Blairbuie! I'm so glad I came to this house beloved & am really most comfortable & doing all of two persons work but with the children at any rate I am being well repaid by results, they are looking blooming.

I always forget to tell you how Daddy & Roy got on. Unfortunately Roy had to go to London just after I saw him & weeks went by before Daddy saw him, by which time I should think Roy was pretty vague about the whole thing. Anyhow he had him x-rayed most carefully again, & put him onto Dr Bennett he said was the G.P. he'd choose in all Glasgow & so far as I can gather there has been no repetition of the worst trouble since September but I am most unhappy about both parents, but I think there is nothing I can do at all, but stand by & look on, which is difficult to say the least of it.

I find having Hazel three nights a week a very mixed blessing & shall put an end to it as soon as I can. I'm afraid I am getting old & have little in common with sweet eighteen. Seems queer to think I decided on my life with you at that age. Oh! Beloved how I loved you & how much more I love you now.

Don't ever think Robert is in danger of forgetting you. You are very very real to him & he too is counting the months until you come back.

I just can't think how I shall spend the summer if I can't get the Polbain house, of course it would take a bit of getting to but once there I think it would be worth it.

Robert says to tell you he is a very good boy & a great help to me! Yours ever, Sheila

24th Jan 1944, Alan, WAF, Achimota, to Sheila

My Dear,

It was fine to come back here to your letter and the parcels of books (I cannot make out the names of the books, one parcel is developer)). It must have been a pretty hectic Christmas for you and I'm so glad that the boys are better. I can write as many of these things as I wish but they are not very "confidential". I've come back to a job of work which will keep me quiet for a bit!

I enjoyed seeing Wilfred. As you say he has improved a lot since his marriage. He took me to a party on Saturday night though I'm getting a bit old for such frivolity!

I cabled you today. It's nice to think of you on your own with the boys again and that you have a Doctor whom you like.

Had a note from John Fergie. Love Alan

25th Jan 1944, Alan, WAF, Achimota, to Sheila

Beloved,[1]

It's grand to be able to write to you so often. I had another two letters from you yesterday so I've really had a wonderful time since I got back.

My Own Sheila do you really for one minute consider because I like my work & play here that it could in 100 years take the keen edge of my appetite to get back to you! Beloved there is no answer

---

[1] Although this letter was started on 25/1/44, it was added to on 28/1/44 & with censorship unlikely to have been posted before 30/1/44. This just illustrates the difficulty in getting the letters sequential when the arrival dates can be so different.

except to say that I am never complete without you. You and Robert & David are my people, my very own and I love you all.

28.1.44

I've written you a long sea mail letter & sent some more photographs. It will be good to hear when you get my first sea mail letters. I'm rather overwhelmed with work since I came back. It has been an almighty rush to try to get up to date and unfortunately I may have to go off on Monday to be a member of the Court-Marshall of a Lt Col R.A.M.C.

It's pretty hot at nights just now and difficult to sleep as a result. I shot a snake with my rifle the other day. Great excitement but it turned out to be a harmless one!

Oh my Dear I'm looking forward to your next letters to me sure that you & the boys have taken no harm from your flu.

For Beloved that you & the boys are well means peace of mind for me. It's grand to think of you with a place of your own again & it will be fine to have the Henderson girls company at nights. She struck me as an exceptionally nice youngster. Glad to know that Doreen looks like getting into RNVR at last.[1]

Do you remember wee Staff Sgt *Gunderson* was my senior NCO at *Misterton*[2] in September 1939? Well he is out here as a *commercial* quartermaster & I'm looking forward to seeing him soon.

Well Beloved I'll get this off. I'm afraid it's not a very coherent newsy letter but I'll send you an Airgraph.

Yours always Alan

29th Jan 1944, Sheila, 24 Queens Gate, to Alan

Beloved,

Two letters from you on Thursday dated 8th & 11th Jan. Oh! To read of your wandering along the beach & longing for me drives

---

[1] R.N.V.R. is of course Royal Navy Volunteer Reserve.

[2] First mention of Misterton which I can't identify for certain. I'm pretty sure it is in north Lincolnshire, not far from Doncaster. But there are Mistertons in Nottinghamshire and Somerset. Mentioned again in Sheila's letter of 9th Feb.

me frantic! What fun we could have, & what a ghastly waste of precious & fleeting time this is. I wonder when the surface mail will put in an appearance, I do look forward to them. I'll try to write oftener, Oh! If only I were less busy & had a little more leisure, but I do get a lot more into these Air Cards than you do all the same! You get in about 55. I'll count at the end of this & see how many I get in! Moira & Doreen have been to tea this afternoon, the first time I'd seen them since you left & of course the first time they had seen the children. Moira said she couldn't get over how Robert had grown, of course David was quite new to them he'd developed so much. It's so funny David carries out simple commands now, will go and shut the door when asked, sit down, stand up etc. He's so good looking beloved I do wish you could see him. I'm going to get Robert a kilt (one of mine made down) & when it's ready, if David's coloured photo is a success, I'll have him done too. Meanwhile I'll have them Polyphotoed. I'm thrilled about the cloth & Robert asks daily when his "cuff links" are coming! Quaint to think of you with a goatskin bag. Glyn Mills statement from 21st Dec - 20th Jan came yesterday I'll send it to you surface mail with Roberts's letter. The balance is on 20th Jan. £212.

Sunday 30th

Another month nearly gone but what - of a time to go! Took boys up to No 6 for tea this afternoon. David now sits up at table and can drink unaided from a cup. Mother is going to take Robert for dinner tomorrow as I want to get into town before the bank closes & will have to do be ready to dash as soon as Susan comes to take David out. It's been a wonderful day, bright and mild as Spring & the crocus are coming out. No news of Achiltibuie house. If I don't get it I may return to Wakefield earlier than I intended. At the moment I mean to go back at the end August. I don't know when school starts, but I will want some time to get straightened out & get school things collected for Robert. I just don't imagine him in school cap and blazer! Muriel & Andy McKie are coming to spend an evening with me this week & probably Murray Niven. Inez Hay is coming back from London for good next week. She will be in Troon during the week & home at the weekends & I'm looking forward to seeing something of her. I'm expecting Ruth Tennant and her little boy to stay for a day or two soon. She is pretty down in the dumps & hasn't been too well, but we can have a good grouse together & it will be fun seeing the boys together.

I seem to have dreadfully little news this week dear, & I can't think of anything more at the moment. You have so many new things to write of but apart from the children things here are deadly monotonous. Oh! I ache for you all the time. Still on the whole time goes quickly & we are very comfortable.

I think I was at Tunbridge Wells with you this time last year beloved, it was a good time that & I am looking back on it tonight with greatest pleasure - Robert has just appeared (9.30 p.m.) nearly giving me a heart attack in the process! He is ultra bright & breezy and dreadfully chatty! He asks me if I think it would be "interesting" if I told you that he cut a bit out of the curtains! I put him back to bed & all is quiet again. There's a big bunch of snowdrops beside your photograph in my bedroom, a nice cool thing for you to think of out there! It's so nice to be in a furnished house where the furniture is really good & everything well chosen & tasteful, usually they are so awful. The annoying bit is that as Muriel says, we could have had this house in September if only they'd thought of it sooner. Did I tell you that Robert sings now? He starts whenever he wakes & goes on nearly all day except when he's asking questions, of which there are more than ever. His favourite at the moment is "This is the army Mr Jones" & as neither of us can get past it gets rather maddening! Most of his songs go on and on and are pure invention & give him great pleasure! Poor Robert he still talks about his *dog* waiting for him in Wakefield. Funny to think of the Mac Vic's with a new baby & a girl too - quite outside my ken that! O! Beloved I do hope I don't get so used to living alone that I'm difficult to live with after the war! That would be the last straw wouldn't it? No I don't think so, for I definitely wasn't made to live alone & I definitely was made to live with you so why worry? My dear I'm starting to blether, never mind I'm somewhere about my 92 line which shows you what can be done.

I'm glad to hear about the Airgraphs for I too am very starved for letters, many as I've had. To think we used to write daily! Surely after the war we won't have to write many more letters to each other. I've just realised with joy that Robert gets a tea ration when he is five! This is a most disjointed letter. Oh! Dear I wish I could just get on the boat & come & see you.

Love from the three of us, but especially me. Sheila

31st Jan 1944, Alan, WAF, Achimota, to Sheila
My Dear,[1]

I've no specific news but I'm hoping for another air mail letter soon. Do you think Crittal Windows[2] would be out of place at Camusglashlan? They should be readily obtainable after the war - also what about a balcony in front of the house? From which you will see I'm busy planning again for the croft. I've written to George Muir asking him to look out for a dinghy which can be used on Loch of Rieff.

Hope you like the new flat and are getting some help with the boys.

Have you had the photos from Farnborough yet?

Love to yourself & the boys. Alan

31st Jan 1944, Sheila, 24 Queens Gate, to Alan
Beloved,

I've been in town on my own this afternoon, David with Susan and Robert with mother. I visited the bank (balance very healthy). Took my kilt to Rowans who are going to remake it, then visited Smiths second-hand Department. I had a 21/- book token to dispose of & got - John Bunyan, "Maker of Myths", by Lindsay, "Goethe" H.W. Nevison. "The Far West Coast" Denton & "The Golden Thread" by P.M. Buck. The last calls itself a survey of the traditions of great literature & if it is well written & comes up to the

---

[1] On a tiny letter card. It was actually postmarked 2nd Feb 44 due to delay in getting Censor Stamp.
[2] Crittal Windows were 'off the shelf' metal window frames, inexpensive and easy to fit. They remain at Camusglashlan.

fascinating chapter headings should be good. "The Far West Coast" is the western coastline of America & deals with the discoveries of Captain Cook & Vancouver, Bering, *Meakes*, Quadra[1] & so on & looking good. All are like new but nothing much bindings except The Golden Thread which is flashy. When in Rowans I bought Robert a wee furry sporran, it's rather a nice one & he is terribly pleased with it. David keeps calling it a bow-wow & enrages Robert to the point of tears! Oh! How lovely if you were at the other side of the fire at night looking at my new books. Of course I haven't got your knack of picking up the right thing and haven't time to prowl much but I like to think of us with lots of books round us & always feel I'm buying them for the four of us. I must do something about the bookcase question before you get back.

Feb 2nd

Beautiful mild sunny day. Wasted afternoon interviewing women for morning work, some snag about all of them, the only two possible wanted to bring child along too! David trying to say "tram car" each time one passes, achieves something like "*dary c cra*".

Feb 3rd

Terrific day, three letters from you. I'll reply in detail in my weekend letter. Two were airmail & one surface with some photographs, they are I think very good & I love the one of Robert it's sweet.

I phoned Joan today & found she was just about to phone me having had a letter from Wilfred today, saying exactly the same things about you as you of him! Beloved at least one of my letters to you must have gone amissing for I wrote in November telling you of the arrival of your Farnborough photos. They are a joy to me but aren't really at all good. I've been so long away from you now that they seem all right, but when I got them a short time after seeing you I thought them very poor. I will start numbering my letters calling this number one & you will be able to tell if any go

---

[1] Quadra - Captain Juan Francisco Bodega y Quadra, Spanish Navy, circa 1785

astray. Muriel & Andy coming in tonight, the boys seem to be asleep, but I wouldn't put it past Robert to put in an appearance! Beloved I think I'm only now beginning to miss you properly, I thought it was bad enough before, this last week I've just ached & ached to be with you, it just isn't fair you should be out there without me. It seems Wilfred says it's usually at least 20 months before people get home & the thought of the few more months added on is awful. Sheila

3rd Feb 1944, Alan, WAF, Achimota, to Sheila

My Very Dear,

I've just come out of hospital today after being in for five days with flu. They thought I had malaria but it proved not. I felt an awful fraud for I was not really ill at all. However there it is. I wrote you two long surface mail letters while I was in Hospital & I hope they don't take too long to reach you. Sorry this letter is so messy but the African nursing orderly in Hospital managed to get some furniture wax on it.

Oh my beloved I'm longing for news again, the rotten air mail service which we have only seems to operate once a fortnight or so. I want to be sure that you did not go down badly with flu.

I expect that I shall go up country shortly but only for a couple of days to decide what to do about a place where there is much sleeping sickness.

When you get Airgraphs from me will you compare the times they take with the time taken by air-letters.

The bombing offensive seems terrific. I hope the Germans don't have a whack at Glasgow again.

Tell Robert Daddy is hoping to get him a model African canoe but that it will take a long time for big steamer boat to get it to him. I've sent you a small surprise via a friend. I love you very much Beloved. Alan

5th Feb 1944, Sheila, 6 Crown Mansions, to Alan

My Dear Beloved, another surprise letter from you today, posted on 3rd Jan. while yesterday's surface one left before Christmas!

Today's was full of stories in the questionable taste of which you apologise for! No need beloved I enjoyed them thoroughly and am pleased that you bothered to write them for me. Today I took David to the doctor for his long overdue immunisation. He let out one wild yell, but in the midst of it popped the toffee I offered him into his mouth & all was peace. I had a long talk with the doctor on what he was up against in dealing with the parents and now feel a great relief that I now have a confident in the matter for things are far from well and I am very worried. Muriel & Andy were here last night & we had a most pleasant evening. I do like them both. Andy asks me to tell you that the first colonial Sect. of Gambia, one George Churchill, is a great friend of his and he would like if you would look him up sometime if possible. I can't make out if you have read Burton's "Wanderings in W. Africa". I think not. I'll see if I can find a copy & will send it on when I've digested it. I don't think the copy you saw in Smith's is still there. Talking of books, some weeks ago I saw in Smith's a quaint old copy of Thierry's "Norman Conquest" in two Vols. calf with gold. I wondered when I got home why on earth I hadn't taken it for I seem to remember your copy is most ordinary. However weeks went by before I got back & it had gone only two days before!

I had the expected blow about the Achiltibuie houses, they just won't let & I simply don't know what to do with myself now. For two pins I'd go back to Wakefield at the end of March, but it does seem so silly to spend the summer there. There doesn't seem too much hope of a house at W.K. for April & May & it's very hard just to know what to do for the best. Oh! If only I could get myself & boys on a ship going your way - well we wouldn't take long to pack! Robert is growing and is very sweet. He took it into his head yesterday morning to leap from his bed across to mine before I was awake & landed right on top of me! I'm afraid I just hit out wildly in fright & he got a fair clout!

Nancy is going to cycle in soon & spend an evening with me. Hugh seems to write very little & never seems to have leave. All that very much between ourselves of course. I may be wrong & I hope I am.

There has been a burglary at the island (Loch Lomond) & all Bill's civilian clothes are gone!

So nice to know from your cable that you know we are here. I simply can't remember if I told you it had arrived two days after you sent it.

Sunday

David's arm is rather painful today & together with another tooth almost through, has made him rather unhappy.

We are all going up to have tea with Elspeth on Friday it will be amusing to see what David & Sheila say to each other. Just been phoning your people beloved. They are well. I'll write again tomorrow evening, it's bedtime now & I have to turn in early or I couldn't cope with the day! I love and appreciate my husband more & more as time goes by, there's just no one else to talk to in the real sense of the word, no one near me at all. Yours ever, Sheila

7th Feb 1944, Sheila, 6 Crown Mansions, to Alan

My Dear. I didn't get writing last night (Feb.) as I intended. I was late in getting the children to bed, having been in town in the afternoon. Then at 7.30 just after I'd finished tidying up a woman arrived to be interviewed. After that I'd just made & eaten my toasted cheese & cocoa when Nan Carrick phoned & talked for ¾ of an hour! When that was finished I'd still got my afternoon purchases of six books to open & examine. I went into Smiths for "Wanderings in W.A." which they are going to try to get for me & found they had a lot of new stuff in, so came home again weighed down! It's just after midday & I'm writing this on the mantelpiece to get out of the brats way! It's a very high mantelpiece & my arm's aching already. I've never time to write in the mornings & I don't know what's happened today. It's a glorious day & the children are, of a sudden, terribly good.

8.30 pm

Having read a life of Goethe I simply had to rush back to Smiths this afternoon & get a translation of "Faust". I must stop buying books. The half doz. I got yesterday are Howitt's "Literature & Romance of Northern Europe" which on glancing through seems to me to be quite a find, it was published in 1852 - "The Greek Tradition" by Thomson with an introduction by Gilbert Murray. - "Roman Days" by Viktor Rydberg (a Swede) & published in 1879. This last looks fascinating & is in an attractive old binding & two slim vols. of "Everyday Things in Archaic Greece" & ditto in Homeric Greece. These are by M & C Quenelle & are really advanced school books but I think will be most interesting to such as I, who am trying to educate myself & are profusely illustrated. I feel just about knee deep in books & when I'll get through them with so little time at my disposal I don't know. I think I'll send most of them out to you at once & you can send them back one by one as you finish them.

How you would have laughed if you could have seen Robert & I in town this afternoon. We were going into Lyons when unfortunately Robert spied a small boy coming from the toy dept. with a wooden tommy gun which made a glorious noise by means of a toothed wooden wheel which wound round against another piece of wood, if you know what I mean! Robert immediately lost all sense of decency & proportion & demanded to be taken to the toy dept. for a gun & got ready to scream if there were any signs of opposition. The place was crowded. I was in a hurry, the "tommy gun" was an ugly shapeless monstrosity but I gave in as gracefully as possible & we went to inspect guns! The price for this crude piece of wood was 15/-. Robert hugged it to himself his eyes full of tears & of course I bought it. It's nearly as big as himself & he's crazy about it! We proceeded along Sauchiehall St: Robert shooting people, including a considerable number of American Soldiers, en route. Everyone was very sweet about it, several ladies even announced themselves dead! Robert puffing along, the thing, tucked under his arm, gasped "Sheila, I'll very very soon be big enough to go & kill the Germans & he glowed at thought. I don't think he has been more than a few inches away from it ever since & has gone to sleep clutching it. I've never seen him display such enthusiasm over anything before!

Oh! Dear one I think of you so much, always you are with me, everything is for you & because of you. Your sons are very beautiful & very bright & I'm so glad I was able to give them to you. I'm getting Robert's Polyphoto done next week. Nan Carrick & Ann are coming to tea on Friday week. I wonder how Robert & Ann will get on! Nonie has asked if he can come & visit us some Saturday so I'm going to ask him on Saturday first, as there is nobody coming that day & I'm hoping to have Mrs Moyes & the McKies the following one. I'll write again at the weekend beloved. Your loving wife, Sheila

8th Feb 1944, Alan, WAF, Achimota, to Sheila

My Dear,

Have not had a letter for some time but have hopes in the next few days.

I am completely well again and much the better of my rest in hospital. I have just completed some amusing new photographs which I shall send you. Judging by your letters you have not yet received any surface mail sent from here. You may by now have heard from Captain *Holden* and you will hear from Major Morrison.

I have not had any word from parents for a long time. I shall be staying with Colonel Bingham again shortly and will get his wife's exact address. Love to your dear self and boys. Alan

9th Feb 1944, Alan, WAF, Achimota, to Sheila

My Very Dear,

We are having one of those bad periods when no mail is arriving and I hope that it is not the same your end.

I'm really busy with interesting work and the time creeps along insensibly. I shall never have finished the work I have to do in 18 months because it is never-ending but it does help to pass the time. I expect that Robert has advanced a lot in the four months since I saw him. I'm very fond of Robert my Dear. Of course I love David and will always love them both equally but I don't know him nearly so well. My Dear mixing with so many types of men in war time has not made me more tolerant but more critical. There are so few it seems to me, who manage to combine honesty with ability.

Oh my Dear it's four months since I reported at Aldershot. Much the longest time I've been away from you. I expect you are longing and aching for the winter to be over. It can't be any fun in Glasgow with fogs & blackout. I'm greatly hoping to get Doreen's tennis balls in the next few days. I have not played tennis since being in Hospital but I should start again soon. I hope that Robert's watch has arrived & that it is not too difficult to get it repaired. Had a note from Frankie in last post. "Overworked, everything very difficult" what a H of a life that man has.

Oh my Beloved kiss the boys for me & tell them there is someone in Africa whose heart is with you all. Alan

9th Feb 1944, Sheila, 6 Crown Mansions, to Alan

My Dear, I don't seem to be able to stop writing you this week! Andy McKie phoned me this morning to say he'd some good news for me. He said he'd just seen Mrs Taylor's sister You will remember Mrs S who came along to see us the day Sue left W.K. & Mrs Taylor was going back to Nigeria in April. By this time I was expecting to be offered a chance of a passage on the boat! However his idea was that I could get Mrs Taylor's house in W.K. I however refused as it's such a dreadfully steep garden and with David at his present stage would be hair raising. We had discovered in the course of conversation last week that the sister was a patient of his. I wonder what on earth Mrs T is doing about her children.

Yes beloved I should certainly be very disappointed if Robert or David ended up in a bank or something similar and I have a hunch they won't. Still if that were either ones idea & they wanted that kind of life badly (I can't imagine it!) I certainly wouldn't try to force them to something else. With brains and that subtle 'something else' one can get anywhere even through the medium of a bank. Can't remember Winston Churchill's friend's name who left him £20,000 recently, but he started as a bank clerk without a penny and must have had a pretty full and interesting life from all accounts. Still it's not my idea any more than yours.

Feb 12th

Col Holpen phoned me today, he was on his way to Forfar and is coming to see me on his way back about the 21st. I shall be most interested to see him. And he also said he'd been away <u>twenty</u> months. Beloved if you dare to be away more than eighteen I shall come & fetch you. Nonie was here this afternoon and Robert fairly put him through his paces, made him read to him and so on nearly all the time! David & Elspeth's wee girl were very funny yesterday. David who had never been in a room with another child of his own age was shocked to the core! Then they went to opposite sides of the room and started playing their own little games & took no notice of each other whatsoever! Elspeth & Sheila are coming here for tea on Tuesday. Graham Chee was killed in action a few days ago.

I've finished the first part of "Faust" and I'm afraid it just doesn't move me at all. It's spoken of as the masterwork of German literature so I presume I am missing something in it and I fancy it doesn't translate well. Also I have a feeling the one I picked up was a poor translation. However as it is I find it a great disappointment. I am now starting on "The Literature & Romance of Northern Europe". David now shakes his head when he's had enough of anything & says "no more". He got another tooth yesterday & has now just his four back ones to get.

I had visit from Lannie's sister last night. No district nurse has replaced Kenny's wife in Achiltibuie & the baby is expected beginning of April, I think their hair is near standing on end. As Ina said pathetically poor Lannie will have an awful time because it's just lambing time too! There's no one else left to see to the sheep so I have visions of Lannie in a glorious mix up between babies & sheep. I had a letter from you yesterday beloved, written on Jan 28th. Funny Sgt Gunner's son turning up there. What a lifetime it seems since Misterton. Col Holpen said on the phone "your husband he takes the most beautiful photographs of my snakes & things! You know he's getting quite bold with snakes." Dear man I love you & want you desperately to remember eighteen months & not a day more! Your eldest son has poked his Tommy Gun through the front door! Love Sheila

10th Feb 1944, Sheila, Wakefield, to Alan

[1] . . . . . going to school next winter and wouldn't it be fun ect. ect. He said "will my boyfriends look after me?" I said I suppose so but why? He said "well you know I wouldn't like to get lost!"

I was baking yesterday afternoon and Robert was driving me frantic, mixing up horrible little messes and insisting on putting them on to bake with my pancakes getting himself covered with flour from head to foot and making the devil's own mess. I got very cross I'm afraid and was perfectly poisonous to him. When I lifted him at 10 he rolled a sleepy head on my shoulder and murmured "Oh Mummy it was so lovely making pancakes with you." I could have wept!

Today I found him clipping Tilda's whiskers with the big scissors, she lying peacefully asleep the while.

Now for some supper, the next job is to clean up my bicycle, I've got it in the kitchen and it's really a disgrace.

I love you dear, Sheila

P. S. Do remember the clock!

P. P. S. If you can remember the name of the shop where you left the mirror I wish you'd drop them a note and tell them it will be collected some time. I'm terrified they sell it! S

11th Feb 1944, Alan, WAF, Achimota, to Sheila

My Very Dear,

I sent you an Airgraph when I received your last two air letters on 9.2.44. They were post marked 25/1/44.

Firstly Dear, I hope you did not think that I thought I was not getting enough letters. I merely wondered how long sea mail was taking. Every air mail that comes in has letters from you and Oh my Dear I'm a happy man to get them.

I'm glad David has now all his teeth. He must be a most adorable

---

[1] Arbitrarily dated as I started school in 1944. Could be any month. This is a single disconnected sheet from Sheila to Alan. I hope someday to pair it with missing 1st page.

age. It's amazing to hear of Robert playing practical jokes. I sent an Airgraph to Monica congratulating them on Susan Carol. I had an air letter from Mrs Thornhill at Tunbridge Wells. It was good of you to remember to send them a Christmas Card and they seem very bucked about it.

I shall write to McDonald. The boys made their usual good impression on the Parents. Dad's company seems to have gone down well. You will have had another cable in the interval of writing saying you had not had one recently & I shall send you one tomorrow. Had lunch yesterday with Dr Reid and his wife. Dr R came out on the boat with me. It was a great joy to be in a house for a change. I'm glad to hear Kodak are sending me stuff. I asked for 'the moon' from them and it looks as though I shall definitely have enough to last me throughout my tour. If it ever reaches me. It's a scandal how much is stolen and nothing is ever done about it. I hope you get good news from McLeod, Polbain.

I expect to go on tour again in about three weeks' time.

Oh my Dear it's good to think that Robert remembers me. Tell him I'm playing tennis tonight and that tomorrow I'm going surf-bathing. I have made a **magnificent** new enlarger out of duralumin junk from crashed aeroplanes. By the way was it your Dad who knew Major Mason, salvage officer here. If so who are the mutual friends?

I hope all the photographs have arrived safely giving you some idea of the scenes here.

I love you beloved and I know that you know that always. Alan

P.S. Have you had any sea mail or photos from me yet?

15th Feb 1944, Sheila, 6 Crown Mansions, to Alan

Dear Beloved. I had your cable of the 12th Inst. today & it's made me feel comfortable & up to date. Elspeth & Sheila were here this afternoon, also your mother who came in unexpectedly. She seems very fit and had been at the house making marmalade. Robert is perfectly sweet with Sheila, is so much more gentle with her than with David, takes an intense interest in her frocks & says she's his sweetheart & he does wish we could have a little girl. David was good with her today too, offering toys etc. Oh Beloved little girls do seem much easier than boys. Still I've got what I wanted although I must say at times I view boarding schools with great favour! Robert has his Polyphoto done on Thursday or Friday. Neil Carrick & Ann come on Sat. with Mrs Moyes & the McKies. Mrs Moyes has just phoned to say Murray Niven wants to come too. Robert will have a field day! Then round about Monday I expect Col Holpen & next Thurs Ruth Tenant & Donald are coming for a day. Wilfred's wife is coming over to see me soon & with all this entertaining I am kept extra busy, but I enjoy it and it's good for the children. If only it weren't such a job finding cake etc. I have engaged an ex housekeeper who is going to come daily starting on Monday (I hope) & who expresses her willingness to come away with me for the summer. She isn't old, has excellent references & I shall be most thankful to get someone to do the housework which becomes an increasing annoyance & burden to me.

I shall be having to leave here before I know where I am & I shall be sorry to go. It suits me admirably & I don't like to think of leaving except that it will mean the winter over & I considerably nearer to you. I am considerably enjoying Howitt's "Literature of Northern Europe". I wonder how you'll like it. Thank goodness they are going to clear the Germans out of the Casino Monastery now, it's infamous to sell flesh & blood for stone.

16th Feb

A very queer thing happened today. Your letter written mostly in Hospital & sent off surface mail on the 29th of Jan[1] arrived at lunch time. Now how on earth could an ordinary letter come so quickly? It's the most up to date one I've had. Oh Dear one I do hope you are alright now. Fortunately I had your cable yesterday so am not so worried as I should otherwise have been. It's just the old story of the willing horse getting the burden to bear you know & being you I suppose you'll go on and on doing it until you just can't any

---

[1] This letter is missing. It is possible Alan withdrew it.

longer. Why have you so much less help than your predecessor who, as you told me, left with a nervous breakdown? For God's sake don't go and ruin your health slogging like *two* blacks out there. I know you can probably do as much or as little as you like & I know how much you will want to do your best & probably re-arrange everything & I know it's all from the very best of motives, but take this as a warning, think for a moment that you are only passing by & leave something for the next man to sort out. Also it seems to me if you agitate enough you could get more help. You probably don't love me any more after all that! Oh! Beloved I so badly want to see you. I've so much to say tonight & I find I've run out of these cards. Roberts watch has arrived & he is delighted. Also very bucked with his letter. The photographs are lovely. Jeremiah is rather sweet. The Padre who did these cartoons must have been a genius. I think they're marvellous. I've sent cheque to R.G. Lewis for your things. Oh! I'm looking forward to seeing Capt. Holpen & hearing of you at first hand. More than that I'm longing for your next letter telling me how you are.

Your loving wife, Sheila

17th Feb 1944, Alan, WAF, Achimota, to Sheila

My Dear,

I have your letter of 2nd Feb, Kodak stuff and one lot of cigarettes has arrived. Funny you not receiving surface mail as I have already had replies to several letters.

Oh it's so fine to hear of the boys being so well. Good to hear that you will be seeing Ruth and Inez. Give them my regards. Stand rebuked about number of lines per letter!

I'm right back in ruddy good health again and look forward to using my new photographic stuff. I have made a new enlarger which is my best yet.

Had a terrific thunderstorm and rain the night before last. Lesley and Duff send regards.

I can't write sense in these Airgraphs. I'll try one to Robert. What about Achiltibuie Hotel? Love Alan

19ᵗʰ Feb 1944, Alan, WAF, Achimota, to Sheila

My Very Dear,

I've sent you a wee present for our Anniversary but I don't expect, in view of the great delay in my surface mail reaching you, that it will reach you in time. Even worse writing than usual but it's <u>very</u> sticky and my arm keeps lifting the paper between words. I've had a terrific mail in last few days. Kodak stuff arrived and tennis balls. I had a terrific singles last night with a good player and, as usual when playing with someone really good, I was on form. We had four sets and I won one 0-6 - 6-2 - 3-6 - 3-6. I'm not going on tour again for about a month & I'm taking it a bit more easy in the office. Tomorrow afternoon I hope to have my weekly swim and sun bathe.

20/2

I had your cable yesterday afternoon. It's a great joy to hear & I shall cable again to you in a week or so. Had a good tennis four last night but my swim today must give way to work. I have some new photographs to send you which will amuse you. Am having two people up from the local Hospital to dinner tonight. I was their guest on Friday night. I feel more & more beloved that you would appreciate being out here probably even more than I do. I would more & as much as you if you were here to share. It's extraordinary how used one becomes to black faces everywhere though they seem to annoy some people to the point of desperation! Jeremiah is a tower of strength and amused me very much when I had Dr & Mrs Reid to dine. He came to serve and I was getting worried when he was late & sent another boy for him. The boy came back & said "Jeremiah say he come soon he have bath". When he came he was polished, with Kiwi I think, in a snow white jacket and slacks immaculately ironed. I dashed him two shillings & a packet of cigarettes for the night's work & he was delighted.

Oh my Dear I wish, I wish you could be here. I love you & my boys very much.

Alan

My Dear,

Robert has had a letter from you today which is dated 28th Dec! These surface letters are very chancy affairs. So far the monkey photos have not arrived. We took the watch into the jewellers today and they are going to put a hand & strap on it. The more I look at your last lot of photos the more I realise how good they are. The Abouassi Coy Sgt Major & the old Hausa mohammedan are really extraordinarily fine, also The "Camusglashlan of the Tropics". Robert had his Polyphoto done last week, it will be four weeks before we get it. He was most eager to have it done for you, but was painfully self-conscious during the taking which only took a few minutes and was done by a girl who took no pains to put him at ease. They are simply snowed under with people and do the whole thing unbelievably mechanically & at top speed. I'll get mine done in the next week or so. Robert got measured for his kilt today and they are having more [*indelible*] dye tasters in the next day or two so we'll choose then. We had a nice afternoon on Saturday. Extraordinary to hear Robert talking to "Uncle Andrew" & "Uncle Murray"! Muriel has won Robert's heart & brought school things for him to cut out & they pasted chickens & flowers etc., which they cut out of coloured paper, onto other paper & made a big picture of which Robert is terribly proud & which has to hang on the wall! Murray is just the same, a little stouter & older looking, but the same amusing patter all the time. The more I see of Muriel & Andy the more I like them. Joan is going to try to come home this summer. Sadie is also thinking about coming home. Robert had a great afternoon with Nan Carrick's wee girl, they nearly brought the house down! They are exactly the same size. I'm looking forward to having Ruth & Donald on Thursday. My new daily came today & seems most pleasant, it's a great relief.

Now for today's Airgraph which left you on the 31St Jan. At first I thought Crittal windows for the croft sounded too awful, but having had the day to deliberate I think it's a sound idea. They would be easy to fit & I don't think they would be noticeably out of place. The veranda would need most careful consideration. It would <u>not</u> suit the house but would be most useful.

We are having a very cold spell of weather again, which doesn't suit me at all!

22nd

Robert has a very slight cold today & I've kept him in bed altho' he's not at all ill. David is getting so much easier & I feel much more free than I have done for a very long time. So far no sign of Capt. Holpen. I hope he manages to come. It's so nice to have an odd Airgraph coming in & breaks the time between letters.

Beloved we'll soon be in the sixth month of your absence & it's a long way yet. Still the war drags on so slowly & I don't want you back until things clear up a bit! All love, Sheila

22nd Feb 1944, Alan, WAF, Achimota, to Sheila

My Dear,

Just an extra note which will, I hope, reach you between our letters. I have quite a lot of new photographs including some of myself to send to you.

I do hope that the first of my surface mail letters have arrived.

I'm longing to know if you have got fixed up at Achiltibuie. I don't like to think of you having to go to Wakefield for the summer.

I'm trying to get a model African Canoe for Robert's birthday but I cannot think of anything for David.

I'm very fit my Dear & I hope so are all my Dear ones. Alan

25th Feb 1944, Sheila, 6 Crown Mansions, to Alan

Dear One. Your cable yesterday was a joy. It's sweet of you to suggest Achiltibuie Hotel but it doesn't appeal to me at all. The children would be much better in their own house & I'd never be able to get over to Reiff & Blairbuie at all. Ruth & Donald came yesterday & went off in the afternoon. Donald is simply <u>enormous</u>, a chip off the old block alright. He eats like a horse & makes our two look like little slim wisps, but I'm not at all envious, he's far too big. I enjoyed having them very much but am quite pleased to be alone again. It's dreadful but I am beginning to prefer being alone & I am quite resentful of anything that keeps me off my books! It's just as well of course but it seems funny to get that way. Perhaps all right for a short time but I most definitely no longer want anyone to live with me always excepting a maid of course.

Saturday

Two letters today beloved, one of the 9th & the other of the 11th inst. Grand to hear you are feeling fit again. I forgot to tell you Ruth went into town yesterday to get her hair cut & left Donald with us. She didn't tell him she was going but just slipped away which I object to on principle. When he discovered she was gone, which he very quickly did, he became simply frantic & sobbed for an hour & a half until she came back. He ranged through the house & at one point I missed him & discovered him clinging to the railings outside! I had to forcibly detach him & haul him screaming indoors. Robert had long since got fed up & it was obvious no help could be expected from him. David kept going up to him & pointing at him in amazement which enraged Donald still more. We were very thankful to welcome Ruth back! Today I have the chance of getting the house we were in last summer at Seamill (the first one) for six months or whatever part of that I desire. Mrs Kirkland phoned today to say she was going away from the middle of March & would it interest me. I may take it for April & May if she will take a reasonable rent. I didn't speak to her as of course she phoned 1915 but I've to phone her on Monday. I would be most relieved to have somewhere definite to remove myself to at the end of March when I think Muriel would like to get back here. My "daily" is just marvellous & I feel she is just too good to last. She is so sweet to the children & a splendid worker. Also refined & having spent 14 years in Canada has seen a little of the world & isn't so dead from the neck up as most. Beloved a dull red lino (30 Squares) if they aren't too expensive after the war would be nice for the croft wouldn't they? They're a good imitation of flags & would be nice with the white walls & a few rugs. Robert thinks purple curtains would be lovely! A cheque came from "The Fountain Press" yesterday for £37.2.6. I've sent it on to G. Mills. Your bank balance on the 16ᵗʰ inst. was £224.4.2. I've sent you the statement. They've had their windows blown out at Kensington Lodge. It's awfully cold now and has been snowing today. I'm just going to wallow in a <u>very</u> hot bath, & then to bed with "Northern Europe"! Nancy is coming in to spend Tuesday evening with me. You're more than loving wife. Sheila

27ᵗʰ Feb 1944, Alan, WAF, Achimota, to Sheila

My Dear One,

I wonder whether you will get this or the Airgraph first. I've read these three letters of last week many times and you cannot imagine what a joy it is to read about the boys. I only wish that they would write and tell me, with love and understanding, how my very Dear One is and what she does and says. My Dear I'm still thrilled at your buying books for four. It's fine to know that Joan phoned you and that you are starting to get my surface mail. I'm glad too that David has had his immunisation dose.

Tell Andy McKie I shall look up his friend Churchill in about two months' time.

Beloved don't send books until you have read them because I can't send them back! I'm only allowed one 5lb parcel every three months. I have been very busy making a single exposure Leica out

The Single Exposure Leica Camera

of the most lovely duralumin scrap. I've taken a great deal of care with it but I wish I was at home with the facilities of my workshop. Yesterday I was surfing, the waves were particularly large and strong so that standing up to my knees in water the waves broke a foot over my head. If you are knocked down, you just spin along helplessly like a piece of driftwood. Yet the Kroo fishermen launched an eight paddle canoe and coaxed it out through that surf. It was a superb bit of boat handling. They are very happy cheery folk the Kroos. They swim not like fish, but like birds! The polish on their skins when wet with water is quite astonishing and to see one surfing in on the top of a huge breaker without a board, arms going like flails and white teeth gleaming, is unforgettable.

Dear Sheila, I too am isolated and alone without you. I cannot speak to anyone but you about the things that really interest me and matter. We must fight to have a home in the country Beloved and when we close the doors and sit in the firelight all this will be forgotten.

Kiss my boys & know that I think of you and imagine you many many times a day.

28th Feb 1944, Sheila, 6 Crown Mansions, to Alan

My Dear One,

It's wonderful how time goes on, only one more day & then March, & if I go away at the end of March to W.K. I shall feel I am setting my face towards the summer & after that the last lap - next winter. Having lost a diamond from my engagement ring I have just been struggling with the insurance claim form! The weather is still dreadfully cold & all day I keep wanting to curl up & can't keep warm at night no matter how many blankets I pile on. Our children continue to flourish & are most attractive & David is at a most edible stage. He gets his photograph taken on Wednesday & I know it won't be a smiling one! David laughs a lot but never when he is not amused & I have a feeling that he will be anything but amused! I won't mind at all because his face is very perfect in repose. He has such a nice firm mouth. He still wrinkles up his nose in the same old way when he laughs. But Oh beloved, he is a headstrong wee blighter! He seems to understand nearly everything one says to him now & has a painfully good memory. Talking of memories, I said to Robert yesterday "shut your eyes & open your mouth & see what the queen will give you" a thing I never say & at once he said "Oh Sheila do you remember the last time you said that was last winter in Wakefield. Daddy was home on leave & I was sitting on his knee on the chair at the window in the sitting room, & you came into the room & said that & gave us raisins to eat". It was not the fact of

- 191 -

getting raisins that recalled it to him for we haven't had them for ages, I can just dimly remember the incident myself now. By the way are you getting the Rothmans cigarettes alright? Letter from Aunt Aggie[1] says they are pretty cold with bits of cardboard over their windows! Aileen & her wee boy have gone to live at Tunbridge Wells to be with Bill, now how on earth do they manage it? Ruth is getting very grey, I hope to goodness I don't before you come back.

1st March

Had very pleasant evening with Nancy last night. She can be very amusing about the boys. Tonight I am sitting awaiting the arrival of Muriel & Andy & one Donald Stewart whom I've never seen but is coming to advise them on some alterations they are going to make in the house. I've had a great day. In the morning I took David to have his photo done & we had a great time. It was the first time he'd been on a tramway car & he was petrified! We went into a shoe shop & went & got him a jersey & he suddenly expanded & became quite master of the situation & thoroughly enjoyed having his photo taken. We met your mother & Doreen by accident so they came to the photographing too! We nearly went to sleep in the car on the way home. In the afternoon I'd promised to take Robert into town to choose the tartan for his kilt & he kept me to my word so strictly that we went off in a blizzard of snow which started just after lunch & is now quite deep. We took ages getting in but it was good fun. We decided on the ancient Gordon tartan which is really attractive & quite different from the ordinary one. We also got a wee blue jacket & what with his wee Sporran, he's going to be an awful swell!

I had my kilt fitted today at the same time. It looks fine now after being remade. You'd be amazed beloved if you knew how much you were in my thoughts. Yours ever, Sheila

---

[1] Agnes Stephens née Steven. They are at Kensington Lodge, London, and suffering from the bombing.

3rd Mar 1944, Alan, WAF, Achimota, to Sheila

My Dear,[1]
This is just an extra note for I sent another yesterday and I've really nothing to say today. Last night there was a terrific thunderstorm with sheets of rain driving down. Wiggy was paddling around his room up to the ankles in water at 4 AM! (By the way he is much more fit again, you might like to tell his wife.) I had been playing bridge in the mess and arrived back in my room exactly as if I had dived into the sea fully clothed. It's beautifully fresh today. I'm plodding morosely through Grote's Greece. (remaining II volume). The chapters on society are extremely good.

Kiss my boys. Love Alan

3rd Mar 1944, Sheila, 24 Queens Gate, to Alan

My Dear One. I'm so hoping for a letter tomorrow. I haven't had one for a week now & I've been so lucky with them of late that I feel it's a very long time! No I'm wrong, on Wednesday the photos of Pepe etc. arrived & a note written on 27th Dec. so only now I know you didn't have any Christmas dinner! The photos are intensely interesting & I love the nice black boys. Robert announced tonight that he's seen God at the pantomime & refuses to change his mind! David is changing a lot these days & saying a lot of new words, such as - down, up, well, etc. & is terribly tickled about it. Robert is trying hard to make him talk. I had a message I had to go into town for this morning & took Robert leaving David with Mrs Burrows, when I got back wondering how on earth they'd got on I was met by two smiling faces & Mrs B announced with fervour "he's the best wee boy in the whole of Glasgow". She really is a nice person to have in the house & is still coming away with me! I had a nice evening with the McKie's & Donald Stewart on Wednesday. The latter thinks he remembers you at the "Academy". I am paying a professional visit to Andy on Monday as I've developed a large cavity at the back of one of my front teeth. I got Robert a wee waterproof wind breaker jacket today. He looks rather

---

[1] Date corrected to '44.

sweet in it & it will be fine for playing in the garden in when we leave here. It's still bitterly cold & a lot of snow still lying. Mrs Taylor phoned me last night on the eve of her departure & asked me to let you know she was on her way out & if you were ever in Lagos would you get in touch with them through the Education Dept. & she would write me a report on you! How I envy her going out, but it must be dreadfully hard to leave one's children. Having town to go shopping in with Robert of an afternoon, good book shops & hunting clothes for the children, has passed so many winter afternoons for me. All that was impossible at Wakefield. Also the friends, who have come to me here in the last few weeks, have helped greatly to make time go & I'm very glad I stayed in Glasgow this winter. The more I am with other people however the nearer I feel to you. The terrific contrast of my distance from everyone else in this world & my nearness to you is the more constantly underlined & it frightens me. Never forget beloved that you are everything to me & I look forward to your homecoming as to heaven on earth.

I do badly want a Golden Retriever puppy, but don't worry, I am determined to live dogless until the war ends. I have to wake Robert by force these mornings! Yesterday, after bellowing at him for a while, I threw a biscuit which hit him on the head & caused him to open one eye, he demanded (without result) breakfast in bed. He was very amused about his biscuit! Yours, Sheila.

6th Mar 1944, Sheila, 24 Queens Gate, to Alan

My Beloved,

I am very weary for the sound of your voice & the touch of your hand. It's so long since I felt the sense of divine security that your presence brings me & it must be so much longer before I can again know it. However I am still profoundly grateful that you are where you are & that makes this separation seem worthwhile & much easier for me. I got my tooth "mended" today & I think Robert is relieved - I know I am! I am going back to "Wayside" Summerlea Rd. W.K. for March & April & will go down on the 31st of this month. I'll send you a cable tomorrow to let you know well in advance. I have definitely refused it for the summer months as I will not pay the extortionate rent for theses months. I have told Daddy to write Mr Ross of Aviemore Hotel & some people he knows around Nethybridge & ask about possible cottages or farmhouses up there. Rents should be reasonable up that way just now with no cars on the road & it would be a nice change.

Yesterday & today have been milder which is a great relief as coal is very short at W.K. I trust it will be moderately warm by the time we get there.

March 8th

One Airgraph dated 2nd Feb & three today, two for me & one for Robert at which he was greatly delighted. The dates were Feb 8th & 17th. You & I don't seem to be able to accept the fact that Muriel is married - I made out a cheque to Muriel Moyes & you address all letters to c/o Moyes instead of McKie![1] G. Scott is home & is reputed to say he never wants to set eyes on W.A. again.

The boys are fine, Robert is very sweet & infinitely wicked. Sometimes I think I'm too hard on him, sometimes too soft. I shall be thankful when you are home & it's not all my responsibility. How much do leopard skins cost? So many people tell me I'm a fool not to have a coat when there is the chance of skins that I'm beginning to wonder if I am. My old fur coat is nearly in pieces. Mother collapsed again yesterday with temp, spinning head etc. doctor came today & said she was to stop in bed for four days. She is perfectly convinced she is not going to live long & it's pretty depressing. She certainly looks dreadfully ill, but it's the spirit more than the body I feel. Your father came & saw us for a short time on Saturday. He seems very fit & we enjoyed seeing him. Now that I have somewhere else to go I am looking forward to my next move. Of course having Mrs Burrows going with us makes all the difference & I can view the move calmly. Pray very hard for goodness sake that nothing happens to her! I am so looking forward to David having a garden to play in & Robert having the joy of his

---

[1] Muriel Moyes is married to Andy McKie the dentist. She seems to be keeping her maiden name.

tricycle again & the other boys to play with. I am weary tonight which is unusual nowadays & am going to bed early. Goodnight beloved. Perhaps I'll dream of you & be happy. I love you. Sheila

7ᵗʰ Mar 1944, Alan, WAF, Achimota, to Sheila

My Dear,

I'm still very much up to date with five letters received in the last fortnight and I hope to get some more shortly. I was bathing on Saturday and yesterday afternoon and now I'm pretty brown all over with an astonishingly white zone where my bathing pants protect. I have constructed for myself a single exposure Leica from scrap aluminium. It really is the most successful and well finished job I have ever done. I'm reading Grote's Greece & enjoying it and I've plenty of work to do in the office.

So you will see I have not time to weary. I have now quite a colony of white rats in an old shed about 40 yards from the office. I'm doing feeding experiments on them with various tribal diets. I have 50 more breeding cages and 20 cages of rats!

Oh Beloved you would laugh to see how orderly I am here & how I sit over my breakfast reading a book and how Jeremiah swoops on me with toast, marmalade or the coffee pot,

Jeremiah was off at a formal adoption of a daughter yesterday, the father acknowledging that it really was his. He turned up in immaculate white shorts and a pink silk shirt!

The surfing was magnificent yesterday. By going well out and getting onto the crest of the wave just as it broke we could get a run in of 150 yards. It is most exhilarating but I swallowed about half the Bight of Benin!

I'm longing to know whether you are going to the Achiltibuie Hotel. I'd like to think of you there for you would have company in the evenings and not have to think of domestic troubles for a bit.

A bit of me would be there with you! An extra bit I mean, over and above normally with you.

Oh my Dear I love you and longing for the day. Alan.

12th Mar 1944, Sheila, 24 Queens Gate, to Alan

Dear One,

I hope you get my cable telling you of our W.K. move quickly. Nan Carrick phoned me last night to say they'd got a house there for April & May. Now some more news - I've taken a farmhouse at Nethy Bridge for July & August. Robert is terribly thrilled at the prospect & says it will be fine if we want a drink of milk in the night we will just go to the back door & call the "cow man" to bring a cow along! I presume he means that we won't need to wait for bottles in the morning. Anyhow it should be ideal for the boys & the postmaster says the farm people are "the nicest people in Nethy Bridge" so it will probably be rather fun. I expect both lots of parents will come up to the hotel sometime when we are there. Robert has taken an acute desire to go fishing & is altogether set for a good summer. It's nice for you to think of that isn't it beloved? Think of both of them up to their necks in heather in Aug. David walks very well outside now, fairly strides along & is so pleased to be getting a big boy. I'm going to view a folding pram which is for sale on Tuesday & if I take it I'll sell the big one. You will see at once that you cannot have any more babies if we have no pram! Your parents had tea with us yesterday, we enjoyed seeing them & they seem very fit.

Monday 13th

Your air letter card of Feb 27th arrived today & was as joyfully welcomed as they always are. I forgot to tell you that on Sat Robert had a letter dated 12th Feb with photos of men climbing for coconuts & was most impressed. He knows when he takes in the letters if there is one addressed to him! I got his Polyphoto today & will send it on. I am going in to visit Andy tomorrow to have my teeth finished & am taking Robert too as he has developed a black bit on one of his back teeth which is distressing me considerably. Still it's nice to have someone as gentle as Andy to take him to. I'd hate to take him to someone I didn't know.

I'm getting a terrific kick out of our son David these days, he is developing so quickly now & saying new words every day. Oh! I wish they would get a move on with this never ending war & finish it off before you come back. I get very depressed over it sometimes for I'd made up my mind it would be over & soon you will only have a year to go!

Bill Buchanan is in Naples now.

I love you beloved & am in good heart, cheerful in the hope of a wonderful future in your company when all this will soon seem like a dream. Yours ever, Sheila.

13th Mar 1944, Alan, WAF, Achimota, to Sheila

My Dear,

I was delighted to have your cable saying that you were going to West Kilbride. It is a pleasant and convenient little house where there are some nice people who you know. Robert will be thrilled and it will do them both good to be at the sea.

Had letter today from Jim McVicar - a terrible time was had by all as might be expected when the new baby arrived. Also from Miss Burton with the usual. Still getting news about the personalities of Wakefield.

Still getting hotter and damper here but I'm very fit.

Love to Mamie & Jimmy and my own boys. Your husband, Alan

16th Mar 1944, Sheila, 24 Queens Gate, to Alan

Beloved,

Two Airgraphs this morning dated 22nd & 24th Feb. How nice it is to think we are going to get some photos of you. By the way if you can't send books back do you want me to send my small "finds" or keep them for our library & your homecoming? Nan & Hazel had lunch with me today & afterwards Robert & I went into town with them & did some shopping. It was a lovely spring day & I enjoyed seeing them.

I regret to say that Robert had his two back teeth filled on Tuesday. It has shaken me considerably as I was rather proud of his teeth, but Andy says they are soft. Robert I hasten to say thoroughly enjoyed the whole visit. Andy was wonderfully patient & good with him pretending the drill was an aeroplane, first a Spitfire, then a

Lancaster & so on & it was quite extraordinary to see Robert completely relaxed with his mouth very wide open & intensely interested in the whole proceedings. After it was over he worked the chair up & down many times, asked innumerable questions about instruments etc, examined the revolving basin with ecstatic interest & in the end I had to literally drag him away!

R & I are going to Troon tomorrow to get sketched on Airgraph forms to send you. The sketches only take three minutes but will amuse you. Mother had an Airgraph from you today. Nice of you. She is allowed up now but is to stay indoors for another week. Doctor says she has a very tired heart.

Well it's news time so I'll get on with David's sock while I listen. David can feed himself pretty well now but <u>will</u> do it with his left hand! He is <u>very</u> adorable. Beloved, won't he be amazed when he suddenly has a Daddy.

17th

Beloved I've had a grand day with letters. One air card Feb . . . & three surface letters 19th & 21st Feb, the necklace & a pile of photos & some of the dearest face in all the world too. I love the necklace, thank you beloved, I'll wear it & think of you extra times in the day whenever I see it. There is one of your self taken photos I like very much only it's not very clear - must have been a difficult operation. I'd like to have seen you garbed in two hankies, you must have looked fetching to say the least of it!

Oh beloved if you were only away for a year it wouldn't seem long now, but it's a grim thought another winter yet. You've no idea how I dread winters just now. David has studied your photos & seems quite satisfied! I love you, Sheila

18th Mar 1944, WAF, Achimota, to Sheila

My Dear,

I'm sending this to North Gardener Street as I don't know quite when it will reach you. I hope it gets to you before you go to W.K. Had two letters last week & have replied in a surface mail letter. I shall be interested to know how long these and the Airgraphs take to reach you. It's been extremely hot & sticky but the rains are not far off and we already had some showers.

I'm going away hunting for snails in a large river[1] starting at 7 AM tomorrow. Not so mad as it seems - trying to find which snails spread Bilharzia.

Bilhartzia Snail

I keep extremely well and the days pass quickly, it's now 4½ months since I arrived here and it does not seem anything like that. I'm going off on tour next week and when I get back it will be getting on for six months since I arrived. Always send your letters here for they will be kept for me or sent on to me.

My Dear the "Demobilisation" scheme is announced and here it is shortly to cheer you up.

1. Everyone gets so many marks.
2. Marks awarded for - in order of importance:
   1. Age
   2. Marriage
   3. No of children
   4. Service overseas
   5. Availability of job at base
3. Everyone then divided into classes according to number of marks.
4. After Germany finished start off by demobilising certain classes.
5. Men in these classes will be next home and demobbed if

---

[1] The 'large river' is the River Volta,

abroad no matter where they are serving.

6. Everyone going on Demob
7. 56 Days' pay & allowances
8. 1 Days' pay for each month of service overseas

My Dear I should stand pretty high in that classification.
I love you my Dear. Kiss the boys. Alan

20th Mar 1944, Alan, WAF, Achimota, to Sheila

My Very Dear,

This is an extra letter to tell you about a magnificent day I had yesterday. There is a disease here called Bilharzia which is common in patchy distribution. It causes nodules in the bladder and blood in urine. It is spread by organisms from infected urine getting into small fresh water snails. From these after an interval emerge another stage of the organism which swims about and burrows into the skin of another victim. The snails which transmit are not well known & I heard of a village where children passed blood in water & so we set off yesterday with Findlay, a lab man, & two Africans in a 3 ton lorry - sitting on basket chairs. Left at 7 AM & went 56 miles to a tiny village on a large river. Embarked on a launch & travelled 15 miles downstream, the river alive with life, crocodiles, lovely birds, & thousands of the riverside people fishing & bathing & playing in the water from tiny canoes. I was disappointed not to see Hippopotamus. We landed & walked six miles gathering bearers & small boys at each village where we stopped & paid duty calls on the chiefs. Eventually we got to our village & after being soaked with rain in a thunderstorm got down to it. We found plenty of snails and we found blood in the urine of the children. We came away loaded with specimens & reversed our steps to G.HQ I'm one shade more sunburnt & much richer in memory as a result of yesterday.

If I thought once I thought a thousand times of the wickedness of the waste that you were not there. You would have loved it my Beloved. The sandy islands in the river, the boiling sun and the children laughing & splashing & chasing each other in and out of the water. The glorious views round each bend of the river. The songs of the paddlers in the big passing canoes, the crazy sailing canoes. The bustards, the parrots, the cormorants & terns, the hornbills, the monkeys.

Oh my Beloved what a world. I'll send photographs. I love you. Alan

21st Mar 1944, Sheila, 24 Queens Gate, to Alan

Beloved,

Yesterday a surface mail of some grand photographs. I'm gloating over the ones of you standing outside a house & have spent quite a lot of time today dashing back & forward looking at them. They've made me long for you more than ever, which is rather dreadful as I was bad enough as it was!

I've sent off Roberts Polyphoto to you, I am having mine done on Friday. I've also sent you two tins of developer which will be a drop in the bucket!

I had a letter from Monica last week, they are all well. She has a maid of 14 who she says isn't much bigger than Anthony! Vera Hunter, or rather Calvert, had a daughter in Dublin last Jan. It seems she badly wanted a son. Andy & Muriel are coming in on Friday evening. They are fed to the teeth because after great difficulty they had managed to get into a hotel at Elie[1] for Easter only hearing last night the hotel could not take them. Then this morning we heard the shores of the Firth are banned indefinitely. I wonder what travel restrictions are coming & Robert is pathetically worried in case he does not get to Nethy Bridge. By the way, assuming we get there, one address from the beginning of June will be - c/o Kennedy, Dell Farm, Nethy Bridge, Inverness-shire. Oh & I almost forgot, Andy's friends name is not Churchill but Chamberlain, can't think why I confused them.

Robert had his kilt fitted yesterday& was very thrilled at the idea, then just before we were ready to start out, he suddenly developed a look of horror & said in an agonised voice "Mummy, will I have

---

[1] Elie and Earlsferry on the north coast of the Firth of Forth.

to take my trousers off" on being told that he definitely would he announced he wasn't going & got ready to bellow. In the end he agreed to proceed if the "lady" went out of the room while he removed his trousers. The lovely bit to me is that when he got there he was so entertained with his kilt that he completely forgot his modesty! In fact he stood in a trance while the "lady" de bagged him.

David is as adorable as ever & I'm sending on two photos as the tinted effort won't be ready for some time yet. It will soon be 25th beloved & if I love you more every year as I have done I'll be dotty when I'm 90. I'll write again at the weekend. Sheila.

23rd Mar 1944, Sheila, 24 Queens Gate, to Alan
Letter dictated by Robert as follows.
Dear Daddy.

The bananas will be bad by the time they get here so don't send them. I read "Rupert" every day in the "Daily Express" & I take the papers in every morning. We are going to do some packing today for West Kilbride. David & I were playing with the tea trolley today. I was giving David rides. Mummy was trying to cook our dinners & we were whizzing round the kitchen & getting in the way. We've got a pretty footstool here. I had my kilt tried on & I am to have a wee pair of tartan trews. I always light Sheila's cigarettes now. There are red & blue tram cars here and green ones. I think about you a lot & want you to come home in three more days. My David can build some castles with cardboard bricks. When Mummy takes me out & not David, David runs to where his coat hangs & says "me, me, me". We take him walking on the ground sometimes with reins.

Well there you are beloved, a few words from your first born. The other day he came rushing to me almost speechless with excitement to say he'd seen a "kilt with legs" - a man in trews! The letter you sent to me for the 25th arrived today you are just the only possible man in all the world & I did a wise thing seven years ago. Beloved, soon we'll have the first six months over & I always felt they would be the worst. As to the war. I don't know, but a queer

lot of things are bound to happen to it in a years' time. Yours always,
Sheila

25ᵗʰ Mar 1944, Alan, WAF, Achimota, to Sheila
My Very Dear,

This is our Wedding Anniversary and the end of seven years of
being married to you. It seems much shorter than that. I am leaving
here on tour in a couple of days but I've had a pleasant two days.
Today being Saturday I spent the afternoon bathing and sunbathing
on a beach without surf & therefore grand for swimming.

I bought for you last night a little carved ivory head which
pleased me very much. It's a curious head, half negroid & half
mongolised. Also I bought two pairs of sandals. They cost 3/- per
pair. I had three letters the night before I left. Unfortunately I did
not bring them with me and so cannot reply in detail.

I'm looking forward to the polyphotos. Grand to hear of Robert's
theological adventures (God at Pantomime). I shall try to look up
Angus Taylor.

My Dear sometimes I get worried about changing & not being
the same person who comes back to you. But I'm not worried any
more nor ever will be for I have suddenly realised that I have always
been two persons. Myself with you & a shop window dummy for
everyone else. I feel very much beloved as you do, so very far away
from anyone except you that it's frightening. I'm so happy that you
have an additional part of me with you in the shape of the boys.

Tell Robert that I hope to have my new photographs to send him
soon. It's amazing to know that he can read his own name. I'll write
him an Airgraph. Alan

P.S. Get Fraser Darling's Island Farm it's very good - send it to me.

25ᵗʰ Mar 1944, Alan, WAF, Achimota, to Robert
My Dear Robert,[1]

Hope you like being back at West Kilbride. You will be having

---

[1] They are again at Wayside.

fun on your tricycle & David will be getting big enough to play with you.

I'm glad to hear he can say a few words.

I shall tell Grandpa to show you how to fish. I was swimming in the sea today & the water was very warm. I saw cuttle fish & crabs, also some Terns or Sea Swallows which are birds which fly all the way here from Scotland.

Kiss Mummy & David for me please.

Love to you all. Daddy

26th Mar 1944, Alan, WAF, Ilaro, Nigeria, to Sheila

My Dear,

I was so sleepy when I wrote last night that, having another form, I am writing again today. I am sending you from here the small ivory head and slippers. I shall try to get you some Kano cloth. I am nearly through a copy of Fraser Darling's Island Farm and I advise you to get it.

I also have managed to get some old copies of a lovely magazine called "Nigeria". It is packed with interesting material and the photographs are superb.

I hope to send home shortly too a box with surplus kit which I do not require out here - overcoats etc. I shall get a good solid box to send the stuff in, for the box of lovely wood will always be useful.

Where do you suggest I send the box? To 6 North Gardener Street or to Wakefield? I'll slip a small present in for you! A Housa trader is coming to see me later this month with leopard skins. If I have any money left after my tour I shall get one.

Well my beloved I shall be longing more and more as the month goes on to get back for my mail. I have wired Mummy on her birthday (late I'm afraid) & will send her another small ivory head.

I shall soon be able to send David a P.C. wont I? Oh my Dear he sounds such a grand wee boy. It's fine to hear of he and Robert liking each other. I hope they will always like & admire each other. Do you think one will be best man at the other's wedding?

Beloved Camusglashlan calls me and I think a tremendous amount about what we shall do there. Fraser Darling's writings make me long all the more. I do so hope that Robert & David will like going there. They will. Love Alan

26th Mar 1944, Sheila, 24 Queens Gate, to Alan

Beloved,[1]

I wonder what you were doing yesterday, our anniversary. I had quite a pleasant day. I went out to lunch to the "club" with Daddy, then onto a film (George Formby) back to the club for tea & home at 5.30. Mother held the fort here. I gave David his dinner before & put him to bed, then Susan came at 2.30 to take him out till 4.30 so most of the time Mother had only Robert to contend with! I had the boys in their bath when Inez appeared & stayed most of the evening so I hadn't time to feel lonely anyhow. Had a nice evening with Muriel & Andy on Thursday & they pressed me so hard that I gave in & am going to the theatre with them next Wednesday. Mrs Burrows is coming to stop with the children & they are so good with her that I shall be quite happy. Muriel phoned today that if anything prevented Mrs B. Mrs Moyes said she would come down & Mother & Daddy have offered too. So everyone seems to have decided to see I get some entertainment! We are not going to W.K. until Monday April 3rd. Mrs Burrows can't get away until then, she has let her house & wants to see the people in. I am actually looking forward to the summer, particularly as shall have two changes of scene. I still have a mania for the nomadic life! I don't know how I should have survived your absence if it had entailed sitting in the one place all the time. I had my Polyphoto done on Friday so one of those days you'll be getting a shock. It will be a few weeks before it's ready, but next week I'll try to get into a place in town that does them while you wait. I'm just waiting to hear Churchill speak. I wonder what he'll have to say. Oh! I wish I could see the end of this weary war, the Italian business is so depressing. I've just realised I've hardly mentioned the boys - they & their mother are however fit & reasonably happy. But Robert & I often sigh for you to be with

---

[1] Sheila is back at Queens Gate.

us again. Whenever a letter (army letter) arrives David says "Daddy, Daddy" & gets so excited. Poor lamb he doesn't know what it's all about but he watches & tries to join in everything we do & a letter is our biggest event. Am getting mixed up with the P.M. Will finish later.

27th

Well the P.M. didn't cheer me any but I don't suppose he was trying! Your Airgraph of the 8th inst. arrived today also letter for Robert with photo of the African soldier & his family - it's just lovely.

So I'm to get a bald husband returned to me, how thankful you must be to have such a young wife! Beloved when you do come home I think I shall eat you. I long for you desperately & count the end of every day a step in the right direction. Yours always, Sheila

1st Apr 1944, Alan, WAF, Iboden, Nigeria, to Sheila

My Very Dear,

Five months of my tour gone today. It's still three weeks or so until I get back & receive any sort of letter from you & I'm longing for that though I'm enjoying my tour.

Oh my Beloved don't think me sort of romantically minded & so on, but I get a terrific kick out of seeing such a bewildering number of new places. I've motored some hundreds of miles in this country in the forest belt but today I set off for the fabled north. I think that you, like me, always wanted to hear the Muezzin calling the Faithful to prayer. Well now I've seen it and felt excluded from a huge world & civilization and conception of spiritual things.

I long so much that you could be here to see the strange sights & so make them twenty times as fascinating for me. This business of travel is wondrous in that I get a bigger & bigger appetite to see more. What a great privilege a man has who marches along with his cheerful mohammeden troops, they singing their marching songs. The music is half barbarous negroid & half eastern. One man chants in a loud high minor key & the rest say the chorus. But the chorus does not, like ours, come at regular intervals but irregularly.

Sometimes only one word is suddenly chanted, sometimes only a sudden cry "Ha" but the timing is perfect & the singing of the march is immense. They are great big children, bad children very often but likeable.

It's a joy to twit them & see a serious worried face suddenly split in half in an enormous smile.

Well my Dear this is an odd letter & I hope you know how much I wish you could share these things, Alan

3rd Apr 1944, Alan, WAF, Kaduna, Nigeria, to Sheila

My Very Dear,

I'm still on tour & enjoying myself very much. There are plenty of horses here and I was riding this afternoon. I watched a polo game and wished I was staying here to learn. It's a dry dry heat, so dry that my mouth, nose, & hair are dry & the paper is crumbling in protest. I walked fully eight miles on an inspection this morning & beyond a thirst like a camel after a Sahara trip would not have known I had walked at all for the dry heat is so invigorating.

Oh my Dear you would love it. This business of living abroad in peace time isn't all "beer & skittles" but shall I say it's beer!

The more I get around the more I marvel at the poor types which we as a nation produce. Miserable specimens who complain of the heat and curse the African who has much more guts & self-respect than he has. The number of people who manage to get themselves invalided home on grounds of psychoneurosis or some such phrase is preposterous.

It means they have no guts or self-respect. The more I think of it the more I am determined that Robert and David must have self-respect - the self-respect which says "I shall not, I could not possibly do that because I am myself the son of my parents and because it's wrong. There is too much philosophising about what is right & what is wrong & attempts to satisfy self-esteem in doing wrong by philosophic or sociological arguments and by confusing the clear cut difference between ill & well doing.

You know me too well beloved ever to worry about being a hard taskmaster to the boys. You know I may be bad tempered & unjust but not consistently harsh. <u>But</u> I shall try to make them that they are too proud to let the world know or see by any symptom when they are afraid of physical or mental hurt or in doubt about their own capacity to endure. The one boy must as a start be played off against the other - assisting one so that the other would not see his tears & so on.

Oh I love you & I've very little space to tell you but I love & cherish you more the more people I see. Alan

4th Apr 1944, Sheila, Seamill, to Alan

Well Beloved,

We arrived at Wayside yesterday & the boys are very thrilled & full of joy. I must say I feel rather uprooted! I had created quite a little life of my own in the big city & people were always dropping in & I had always plenty to amuse myself with, however it couldn't go on & I'll soon settle down. Your father came to see us on Saturday & Elspeth phoned to see if she could come & spend the evening & I enjoyed a full up last weekend. The heavy baggage doesn't arrive until tomorrow & it will be a great help when it does. David is sleeping strapped into a bed & being very good about it. We went down & looked at the sea this morning but, as was to be expected, I had to carry David most of the way back & he is no lightweight! We had a comfortable journey down & had the compartment to ourselves. David simply bounced about all the way & insisted on standing on his head, being caught in mid air several times as the train lurched along. There was a letter card waiting for me when I arrived & two more have come today. The dates are 20th, 23rd & 25th March. Last two very full of your "trip" & it's infuriating not to know where it's a trip too! Your first one all about your wonderful day hunting the snails. It sounds excellent to me & I agree about the "wicked waste", I expect I am becoming a bit unreal to you leading my quiet little day to day here in contrast to your goings on, but just imagine the queerness of in the middle of an ordinary busy day getting a letter telling of you voyaging along African Rivers, crocodiles & all - it's just fantastic.

Dear One, I expect we are bound to be both a little different when we meet again, I think one changes all the time, we probably wouldn't recognise ourselves of - well let's say seven years ago, but so long as you don't ever meet anyone you like more than me, I don't see it's going to make much difference. We will have all the joy of discovering each other again. If you are as sure of yourself as I am of myself you have nothing to worry about.

I am sending you a funny photograph. I just dashed into a funny wee shop in Renfield St one day & without being at all spruced up got taken in about 30 sec. I think it's a wee bit queer but that may be pure conceit. I wish so much I knew how long you were away for. I can't find a hint anywhere. Do you remember the queer girl next door? Well "Bill" is home from Tunis & they are married & he is at Troon & everything in the garden is lovely!

All the local children seem to have had a dreadful winter, scarlet fever, whooping cough, pneumonia & so on, so they don't seem any more healthy in the country after all! I'll try to get you the books at once. It's very cold here & it's a wild wet horrible night. I do wish summer would come. Oh, dear one I want you very badly, thank God I have the children. I love you, Sheila

5th Apr 1944, Alan, WAF, Kaduna, Nigeria, to Sheila
My Dear,

I am off today to stay with Ian McKenzie. It's still amazingly dry with a shade temperature of 108 F in the middle of the day but this dry heat is very bearable and indeed exhilarating. I'm enjoying my tour so much but Beloved I want to have 50 lives in order to be able to know more about so many things. I'm terribly interested in nutrition, in tribal markings & organisation, in the botany, in the geology, in malaria & so on but Oh my Dear my intellect is so limited and above all as you know my Dear I fritter away my energy on so many things rather than go bald headed for an important one. I'm afraid you will always have a busy but never a successful husband. However I've got down to one paper on Malaria prevention by drugs with Brigadier Findlay in which I have written entirely on my own the historical part. I dug that out in the local library. I rather think it will be a good paper & it is going to be submitted to The Lancet or Proceedings of Royal Society of Tropical Medicine.

I hope it's not too cold at Seamills & that you had a decent journey down. Tell Robert that there are plenty of donkeys here & some camels & that the men sit right on the back of the donkey so- The people are all Mohammedens and the men wear long white robes. Occasionally the odd pagan appears  wearing nothing at all or a few leaves! There are dates and coconuts at fantastically small prices. Oh Beloved I wish you were here. Alan

8ᵗʰ Apr 1944, Alan, WAF, Kano, Nigeria, to Sheila

Air Mail No 1

My Dear,

I had two good days with Ian McKenzie and am going back to him for one day on my way back. Now I am where the donkey is the chief mode of transport & where the camel is a common sight. The market is amazing. Turks & Northern men of West Africa rub shoulders with Southerners & men from Somaliland, from Congo & Gaboon, from Dakar & Khartoum. From Cairo & Algiers they stream in with people from Abyssinia and all have come with camels or donkeys all the way.

I have bought you: (1) Crocodile skin bag[1]. (2) Leather writing case or wallet. (3) A lovely saddle cloth from a Tuareg (yes a veiled one!). (4) Two large pieces of native cloth. (5) Two more cushion covers. (6) a weird Arabic charm which is said to have been "dug up" in a direction which embrace most of Egypt & the Sahara.

For the boys I have a couple of donkey bells and a serviette ring of local silver each.

You could change any money in Africa at the market but the favourite was the Maria Theresa Dollar.

---

[1] The picture is of the crocodile bag, now in the possession of Kim Shaddick.

Oh beloved this is a good country & you would love it. The people are horse lovers and a good pony complete with saddle etc. costs £6 to £10.

You pay 10/- a week, & for that the Arab boy keeps himself and the horse. Horses are not encouraged near European houses & he just brings the horse when you want it and in any case daily just for you to see it. As you may guess I have expended film at a phenomenal rate and am so hoping to have really good photographs - will start another sheet.

Air Mail No 2
Continuing from letter (1) of same date.

The Dye Pits. They are 20 feet deep & the dye is indigo & camel dung.
The cloth dye is locally woven coarse cotton

I got two photographs which I am desperately keen to see: 1. of an old Arab whom I mentioned, I think, in my last letter - sitting writing in his mud hut - writing verses of the Koran on wooden boards & 2. of a small girl of about 8 years with a tray of tapioca flour held on one hand. But oh I have dozens which promise well.

Oh Beloved by what cruel fate you are not here. How it would *joy* you to raise your hand and say "samu" to the passing Housaman[1] & be greeted with a smile and an upright hand & a "samu".

How you would love to come round the corner in the market where the saddle makers sit, suddenly to see the dye pits with blue cloth drying everywhere and each man sitting by the side of his pit shrouded from the sun by a small thatch of straw on the end of a pole. Then to see the stray sheep & donkeys & small boys and sober Mullahs, and wild looking Tuaregs in red robes and pagan bushmen in leather brown cloth - to see them all just before a caravan of camels.

My Dear it's completely & utterly wrong for while I love it so much you would appreciate it a thousand times more.

Oh Sheila, Sheila I miss you in midst of my pleasure. I suppose in that large walled in market today with 30,000 souls about me I wished every 100 yards that I could turn & see you & share it all.

Perhaps I'm sounding a bit mushy but I cannot understand who could see it and remain unmoved. Now to letter 3. Alan.

Air Mail Card No 3

My Dear,

The expenditure of letter cards is terrific but I want to get it down while it's fresh in my memory for I'm sleepy, having been travelling last night. I was at a leper colony yesterday and go to another on Monday. I have been & seen so much since I left G.HQ and have so much still to see. I'm going to see a Sleeping Sickness Settlement on 13th and I just wish I could tell you all the places I've been but censorship prevents me.

These Mohammeden places strike me chiefly in two ways. 1. They are so much as I had read about them - The prayer mats, the Muezzin & the dignity of the Arab type. 2. The likeness to the Bible atmosphere - the ass & the camel, the *skin* grain boy, the Mullah sitting expounding to a circle of boys.

My Dear it's missing you so much at times like this that make

---

[1] Housaman - this is the way Alan has written it but it should properly be Housa man. The Housa are mainly in North West Nigeria.

me know how much I need you as a friend as well as a loved one. Life can never be complete when we are separated like this.

Tell Robert all about the Camels & the Donkeys and how I have tasted dates below the clusters on the date palm. Tell him I have seen a hyena and the nest of a nightjar. Tell him that the little boys here never wear shoes and that the sun is so hot and the air so dry that the ground at midday nearly burns my foot unbearably through my shoes. Tell him that I think of him every day and never forget him or David and that I'm longing to be home and to sit him on my knee and tell him stories. Tell him that I love you all and tell him to kiss you from me. Alan

P.S. I'm as fit as a fiddle.[1]

8th Apr 1944, Sheila, Seamill, to Alan

What a lot of letters I've had since coming here beloved. Four letter cards, two surface mails (12th March & river photos) & today an Airgraph of March 16th. I'm looking forward <u>very</u> much to my sandals!

Oh I'm in such a ferment for them to get on with the war with Germany, the de-mob plans make one think a lot.

I've had a sore throat and slight temp for the last four days & was forced to get the doctor today as I didn't seem to get better altho I was able to carry on alright. He said I had to go to bed & I said it was just imposs. So he said he could quite see that, but to take things as easily as I could & on no account to go out for a few days. He gave me some sulphonamide to take every four hours & told me to tie a wet sock round my neck, to drink as much water as possible & I would feel much better by Monday. I think he's probably mad but I feel I've got my money's worth. I only hope the tablets aren't a near relation of M&B[2] & lay me out. Enough of my ailments but I've been feeling so depressed since coming here that I'm positively

---

[1] This is one long letter. It has taken 3 separate cards to get it all down. Alan's sprawling writing is part of the problem.

[2] M&B was a near relation to sulphonamide. Both were precursors of antibiotics such as penicillin.

relieved to find out I've been "proper poorly" to account for it.

The children are already looking so very much the better for the change, they were looking alright when they came but they are really blooming now. The only trial is there is Whooping Cough all around us. I made them pancakes the other night & David consumed five straight off! Mother is trying to get David a wee wooden tricycle thing as he is frantic to get on Roberts & it doesn't seem fair!

The only things I've got so far towards their birthdays are just a few wee cakes & candles, a thing I haven't seen for years.

Sunday 9th

I'm definitely recovering! I woke up extremely limp this morning & stayed in bed until 11 am to the profound astonishment of the boys, particularly David! At first he wouldn't come near me & it was fine, then he went off & fetched his bricks & got in beside me, covered himself up & started to build castles, then the acrobatics started & he fell out on his head & in the end it was sheer pleasure to get up! Mrs B took them out this afternoon & I had a sleep & I'm much better tonight.

I'll be glad to hear of your return from your "tour" but I expect you are having a fine time.

Your father was phoning last night, they all seem very well & I think they will try to get down to the Hydro for a weekend.

Oh! How I wish you could see the boys, they play so much together now & they are such a fine pair. I'm writing to enrol Robert for the Wakefield school for Sept. One has to make some sort of plans. I love you my dear one, more & more & more. Sheila

10th Apr 1944, Alan, On Train to Zarga, Nigeria, to Sheila
My Dear,

I have despatched two parcels to you today one with Kano cloth and leather to Steven & Struthers and one with horse cloth & sandals for you & Robert to 6 North Gardner Street. Oh beloved I hope you like the things. The Kano cloth is cheap and plentiful so if you like it I can send you more of that pattern or plain white or with blue stripes & patterns. It's rather fine for cushion covers, chair covers etc. or bedspreads and some it will look lovely at Achiltibuie. I have had the cloth washed so you need not fear smallpox! These slippers are slightly better than most but still crude. I have more to send the best being a really good cushion cover for a pouffe. It is square or rather rectangular in shape.

I came here yesterday after two days & nights in the train and was I glad to get out of it. We sat & sweated all the time while the red dust & wood smoke from the engine blew in & covered us with muck.

The only water on the train tasted of earth & the food was bad. However an old friend, a man called McKay who travelled out in the boat with me, came on half way & we formed a bridge four at which I lost 12/-! & that passed the time.

The scenery was very fine and at some stations the crowds were amazing. At one a crowd of pagan women were walking past with calabashes on their heads. They wore only a leaf in the front and an earthenware plate, about the size of a server, behind. The latter is in case while working in the fields a spirit should take advantage of them. If this happens they get twins which are most unlucky. Sweet int it? Love to Robert & David, Alan

13th Apr 1944, Alan, WAF, Zarga, Nigeria, to Sheila
My Beloved,

I'm writing this at about 3 P.M. sitting in a small & very hot Giddak (Housa for hut of mud) stripped to the waist with streams of sweat running down my face & chest. The temp is 106 F in shade. I left the place I wrote to you from last (rather reluctantly for it was a place to see more of). On 11/4 I went down to stay with Ian McKenzie again. Yesterday we got up early & went riding on Arab horses. We cantered out about four miles through bush & then had an all out gallop of a mile. Then we came back past some native villages.

At 10 A.M. we set off along a back track to see a man at a sleeping sickness dispensary 56 miles off. At mile 38 at 11.50 A.M. we stopped with petrol blockage. We wrestled with that until 3 P.M.

& eventually got a tow in to a tin miner's place. Then after wrestling further unsuccessfully we set off at 5.45 in a crazy old Chevrolet without lights for return to Ian's unit. We stopped another 15 miles or so on and changed to an old Ford with lights. We then paid a visit to an isolated agricultural office and finally got in at 10 P.M.

Today I am stiff!! I travelled down 50 miles here by road today and leave at midnight by train for the South, I hope to fly from there & then fly back to G.HQ You will see beloved that I am not to be pitied but much to be envied but Oh my Dear the waste of it all without you. I'm longing for my mail which will be waiting for me at G.HQ

I have not yet been able to send off your presents but I shall at the first opportunity. I love you. Alan

12th Apr 1944, Sheila, Seamill, to Alan

Beloved,

Its 6 months now since the day we parted, if it was only to be a year it would not seem so dreadfully long now & in any case six months is a good solid bit behind us. I'm nearly alright again, my throat doesn't hurt anymore, but is still inflamed & slow in clearing up.

The doctor has been here again today giving the boys their second dose of whooping cough vaccine, they are getting their final one on Monday. There are so very many "whoops" about that if seemed wise to me to take this precaution & the doctor is very keen about it. He says three doses are supposed to last a lifetime, the doctor in Glasgow who I spoke to about it, said it only lasted a few months! Have you any ideas on the subject - I'd be so pleased to know what you think. The doctor I have here, (a doctor White from Adrossan), is a short very stout man in spats & looks just like a "bookie". He has a great reputation, I'm not very sure what I think of him. He is very clever with his hands (which are fat & ugly) & brings pennies out of Roberts's mouth & from the back of his neck! Today he brought a large bandage out of the front of Robert's shirt, it amazes me almost as much as Robert! R. goes about shaking himself doubtfully for a while, not knowing what he may produce!

I have got "Island Farm" & have just finished it & will send it on. Smiths are trying to get "Mungo P's Travels". I wrote you a long letter about books the night before I left Glasgow & in the confusion of our departure it went missing. I am very vexed about it because I can't remember what I said (not that it would be such a great loss!) but it may have got posted in spite of me. Anyhow, Smiths so far haven't found Burtons Wanderings in W.A. I've got a copy of the Iliad in prose to stand by me at Nethy Bridge & several others which I'll talk about later. It's strange but my reading seems to be absolutely affected by the places or houses I am in. Queens Gate was to me an ideal place for reading & I could have tackled anything there, but here I simply can't settle down to anything serious at all. I'm enjoying "Island Farm" very much. I think F.D. is probably pretty fond of himself, but so are we all. Somehow or other it annoys me tonight to read how much nearer intellectually they are to the war than those who are in it physically.

April 13. (Continuation)

Also I can't help feeling he makes an awful song & dance about his broken leg. This is probably all wrong & tomorrow I may not see it that way, but to tell you the truth I don't think I've ever been so tired & heart weary of the war as I am today & my whole sympathy goes out to those who are in it physically & I can feel no admiration for a man who is so very near it <u>intellectually</u> & between you & me & the door post I don't see how he can bear to be there at all. You will laugh long & loud at this coming from me. The fact is I am glad you've been in the army, it would never have worked the other way. I've had this thought for a longer time than you'd suppose but it's taken me almost five years to say it. Even tonight when I have a black fit of depression about the length of the war & the long months of loneliness that lie ahead, when for some reason I feel so fed up that I'd like to kick the furniture, I still know that things are best as they are with us.

April 14th

Feeling a new woman today. Was in the village with the boys in the morning & David had his hair cut - he bellowed all the time. It's been a wet afternoon but Mrs B. has taken them out for a walk before supper as it's cleared a bit. This has enabled me to get the Ration Books filled up, a job which takes ages, & some letters attended to. I have a heap of mending waiting for me tonight. All the boys' buttons seem to have come off at once & all Roberts's socks are in holes - let's hope there's something good on the wireless!

I'm so thankful I'm moving up North for the summer, this place seems so positively urban & I ache for the "wide open spaces".

I think you should send your box to Wakefield as I intend going back there in Sept. Beloved you will remember that you'll need some heavy things for your journey home, won't you?

Robert sends an awful lot of love & is never done wishing you could come home. All Love, Sheila

16th Apr 1944, Sheila, Seamill, to Alan

Beloved,

I am so longing to hear that you are safely back from your tour. I do hope I don't have too long to wait. Mrs Burrows took the children out this afternoon & I decided it was time I had some slight exercise & cycled along & had tea with Aunt Daisy.[1] I'm quite stiff & tired tonight, either a bad throat takes all the stuffing out of one or I'm sadly out of condition! Actually I'm feeling all right again but must see that I get more exercise or I'll be hopeless when you get home!

Robert took a nasty toss off his tricycle today & is going to have a lovely black eye tomorrow I'm afraid. All one side of his face & forehead are grazed & his knee & wrist as well. I'm so sorry for him, but he is very good about it. Beloved I want you so badly tonight there's no use trying to finish this until tomorrow.

April 17th

A very dull day. Mrs B. in Glasgow until tomorrow so we've had

---

[1] At Crawford Lodge, Ardrossan. Daisy is a diminutive of Margaret.

the place to ourselves. Robert's face isn't too bad, it looks so much worse than it is. I do wish you could see the boys having dinner since coming here! It's amazing what they put away & they are both yelling for it about half an hour before it's ready. We are longing for a really fine day, it's remarkable how starved for sun I always feel in these parts.

I am deadly hard up for news for you down here, one day is almost exactly like another. I have had no word of the Blairbuie baby yet but should think it must have arrived by this time. I noticed the death of a Major Selkirk in the papers last week. I intended sending you the cutting but forgot until it was too late. You did know someone of that name I think.

The children are to have their final injection tomorrow & will they be glad! Oh! I forgot, Robert had an Airgraph today & was very bucked, it was the 25th of last month, so not startlingly up to date. Nice to think of you seeing the sea swallows, I wish I could be one for a bit!

Oh! Beloved do you think doctors will be at a disadvantage when demobilising starts, won't they hang on to them all to the bitter end?

Love me very much dear you don't know how much I need it. Yours ever, Sheila

18th Apr 1944, Alan, WAF, Enugu, Nigeria, to Sheila
My Very Dear,

I am missing you very badly tonight. I get times like this when it's more acute than usual and when I never for a moment stop thinking of you and the boys.

Oh Sheila I need you so much and I love you and want you badly. I enjoy so many things. I shall never have enough time in this life to read a thousandth of what I want to read nor to do thousandth of the things I would do but I am happy in doing many things and very content and grateful for the life that has been given to me; but beloved I cannot enjoy things properly without you.[1]

Oh my Dear you made a captive of me and kept a bit of me that

---

[1] Strange phrasing by Alan I know but it is as written.

is necessary for full enjoyment of all things. How I have loved for example, lying sweating on my bed this afternoon, reading Thackeray's "The Four Georges", but if I longed once to share it with you I longed a thousand times. I shall never get full savour of anything without you again. Oh Beloved love me always and love me terribly for I need you. You will never appreciate what you mean to me, you can never feel my inmost thoughts and know that tightness inside and that tightening of face which has been mine since I left you in Crookham. I can feel the tightness now and it will never leave me until I feel your cheek on mine again.

I have been visiting units today and hope to leave for the first part of my return journey on Thursday. It's very hot and sticky here after the North & tonight it's raining buckets.

I'm going out to dinner tonight and tomorrow night with units & to the local club on Wednesday.

You will know and remember this loving old poem my Dear:-

> LOVE not me for comely grace,[1]
> For my pleasing eye or face,
> Nor for any outward part,
> No, nor for my constant heart,
> For those may fail, or turn to ill,   . .
> So thou and I shall sever:
> Keep therefore a true woman's eye,
> And love me still, but know not why-
> So hast thou the same reason still
> To doat upon me ever!

More parcels went today, one via Daddy & one via Jimmy for I can't send more than one to one address nor more than *12* in volume in any one. I'm in love with you. Alan

18th Apr 1944, Sheila, Seamill, to Alan

My Dear,

Had an Airgraph today dated 26th March so I don't feel at all up-

---

[1] Poem by John Wilbye, 1574-1636.

to-date. I sent you a cable yesterday requesting one back. I've never felt worried about you until this tour. But this last week or two with no up-to-date news I've not been so happy, anyhow a cable will be nice and set me up for the next few weeks.

David grows every day & daily learns a few new words, he says "Mummy's Oh dear bébé" now just as Robert used to! His words include neck, wash, knee, toes, drink, toast, sun & (in a tone of horror and very high-pitched) mess. This applies when for instance he spills his milk. Anyhow yesterday I took him out just after a dreadfully heavy shower, the gutters were all running like rivers & the roads full of puddles, & David sat & yelled all the way up to the village "Oh mess, Oh mess, mess. He insists on calling Robert "Bobily" much to Robert's rage! Sometimes they are locked in each other's arms and kissing each other soulfully & the next moment may be spitting fury & squabbling over a trifle. But they are always together now & play really quite well. Roberts trews having arrived he is insisting on wearing his kilt tomorrow. I do so wish you could see him, he is really rather sweet & so proud of himself.

I have now got Mungo Park & will send him on, I'm reading West African Agent by S.R. Young. I don't think it's much good but I'll send it on.

The coal situation here is wretched, we & our neighbours have none at all at the moment & goodness knows when it will arrive.

My Polyphotos arrived yesterday so you will be getting a shock one of those days. In most of them I look like a sick calf & my hair is most peculiar, however brace yourself for a reminder of the girl you left behind you.

I was at the cinema on Wednesday & quite childishly enjoyed myself. I am looking forward to seeing The Life & Death of Col. Blimp which is coming next week. I am now going to concoct a nice thick sandwich & go into a huddle over a tiny radiator with "W. African Agent".

The weather is perfectly awful. Ian Jack (Aviemore) died of wounds in Italy the week before last.

Have you ever written to the Ross & Cromarty people again about the Croft? Beloved I love you dearly. Yours ever, Sheila

25th Apr 1944, Alan, WAF, Achimota, to Sheila

My Very Dear,

I'm writing back in my own room with two cables and no less than nine airmail letters from you. Firstly I'm so sorry you were worried & wanted a cable. I had sent one yesterday & sent another today including birthday greetings to David.

Now to complete my story and then answer your letters.

I had a stroke of luck getting a long drive back with Dr Harkness, the Director Medical Services (Civil), in his car; 500 miles in a day. I had two more days & got back here by air today.

I had a perfectly wonderful tour, very useful I hope, intensely interesting and I took over 200 photographs. I had tea with Mr & Mrs Angus Taylor yesterday & instructed her to write to you to tell you how well I was looking. Everyone remarks on it here.

I have received developer & cigarettes and the Fountain Press sent me a complimentary copy of my book as I had mentioned that I had not one here. They speak of a second edition and talk well of the sales.

Now to your letters:

14th March

I can send the books back as surplus kit. Sorry to hear of Robert's teeth but delighted to hear that he had a good introduction. Give him plenty of Cod Liver Oil or *odelin* but don't worry, the important thing is to keep the shape of his mouth by conserving his milk teeth. Tell him I'm so glad he has had his teeth attended to. I'm looking forward to the Airgraph sketch.

Glad to hear your mother is keeping better. Funny if David is left-handed. I'm so delighted that the necklace arrived. I was afraid it might get lost. I'm also glad about the photographs.

March 21st

Great news of Robert's Polyphotos being dispatched. Thanks for Nethy Bridge address. I'm greatly amused about Roberts's kilt. I love you too much my dear.

March 23rd (Robert's Letter)

I'll write to him but tell him I'm so glad he thinks of me because I think of him every day & often each day.

March 26

I'm so glad you managed to the theatre. Andy and Muriel are friends of mine for life from now on. They have been good to you.
Alan

25th Apr 1944, Alan, WAF, Achimota, to Sheila

Letter 2 Continues

Your Letter March 26th

Your own Polyphoto my beloved will be the most precious thing a boat has ever brought to West Africa.

4th April

My Dear I'm still your Alan and always will be - the one who is part of you and loves you more than anything else in the world. My Dear it was good of you to get your Polyphoto taken and I shall wait for it very impatiently.

8th April

Oh my Dear I wish I could have been there with you when you were ill with your throat. It must be awful with these boys booming around to feel as one feels with a sore throat - did you throw any books at them? It's grand to hear of the boys being better for the change & enjoying their food. I'm trying to arrange for you to get food sent from South Africa.

April 13th

I'm glad to hear that Robert & David are having vaccine. You might ask him to Schick Test David to see if diphtheria is OK.

I have not quite digested your feelings about why Fraser Darling should be in the Army & why you are glad I am. It's late my dearest beloved one & I'm tired and there are a few mosquitos cruising about so I'll digest it and write tomorrow. It's good you don't know how good to know that you are feeling better after your throat. I shall send the box to Wakefield. Poor old Robert falling off his tricycle. Oh I am glad, glad & happy to have you in charge of my own very dear boys. Only you can love them but not only that you are the one in all the world I'd choose for the specific purpose.

Neil Selkirk was one of the forwards in the University Team when I was Captain. I'm very very sorry to hear of his death.

Just to complete the letter - I've found three letters from Mummy & three from Daddy waiting for me.

I sent you a lot of parcels & I have great hopes you will like the things. Did you get the silk from Major Morrison?

The wet season has started & the insects are preposterous. Huge flies, ants, beetles & the weirdest *mongrels* of all sorts come flying round lights so that I cannot sit under the light for the blighters falling on my lap.

Oh I love you, Alan[1]

25th Apr 1944, Sheila, Seamill, to Alan

My Dearly Beloved,

I have two lovely mental pictures Robert today for you. He had his kilt on for the first time & although I say it myself he looked grand. The first flash is of he & Peter out playing, Robert with his kilt swirling, a buff coloured wind jacket, a tin hat on the back of his head, his fair hair sprouting out in front & a murderous looking toy rifle of Peter's, killing Germans wholesale.

The second episode is hard to explain but when in the village this morning I bought a small wedding present for Dorothy Anderson, & Robert took immediate possession of it & announced he was going to deliver it! It was a small antique silver ink stand with enamel lid & Robert, his hair newly brushed, his sporran straightened, the ink stand in a piece of tissue paper clutched in his hand, went hastily over his little speech of presentation & departed next door. The next thing I heard was a strangled whisper from Mrs Burrows (Robert simply calls her Burrows) who was cleaning the front windows & who was hissing; "Robert go on go on". The bearer of gifts had quite forgotten the dignity of his mission & was

---

[1] Strange grammar but as written.

playing with the goldfish in the Anderson's garden! In the end he rang the bell and vanished inside. Some time passed & I was just going round to collect him, dinner being ready, when the door opened & Robert emerged, a paper bag under his arm, his eyes fixed with fearful intensity on a plate with four pieces of chocolate cake held rigidly in front of him, & with never a backward glance or lifting of his head, made the journey back with the greatest of ease, & arrived the cake still on the plate & the bag (of nuts) intact. I have <u>never</u> seen him so pleased about anything. He was beside himself with joy. "They asked me into the house & Dorothy was delighted with the present & their carpets don't go right up to the wall like ours & Mrs Anderson said I wasn't to eat any nuts till I asked you, they haven't stair carpet clips on the carpet they've got rods. Look they gave us chocolate cake, the dirty dinner dishes were still on the table, I've got to take the plate back I'll just go now". Hours later I was horrified to hear Robert yelling at the top of his voice in the middle of the road "Oh Dorothy that was a lovely present I gave you, wasn't it?"

I took them to Ardneil Bay this afternoon. It was cold-ish but they had a fine time and came home with glowing cheeks to a big tea. Your family longs for you beloved,

Sheila

29th Apr 1944, Sheila, Seamill, to Alan

My Dear,

I was so happy to get your cable on Thursday & I've had three letters this week all full of your tour. I'm so glad it went so well.

Your father & mother & Moira were here this afternoon. So we had David's birthday today instead of tomorrow. We had lots for tea, but the nearest we got to a birthday cake was a jam roll with two candles stuck in it! Your family brought David various toys & he was delighted with everything. The boys are looking so fit it's a constant joy to me these days. It's such a dreadful responsibility for me, who never had anything to do with children, being left with them & you will never know how much I miss not having you to turn to. Mungo Pk's Travels has arrived but I know you won't grudge me the time I take to read it before it gets underway to you. I'm fully half way through & enjoying it so much. I went to see "The Life & Death of Col Blimp" this week & it's a splendid film. You will be getting a letter from your people reporting on the progress of the boys - I think they were suitably impressed. Moira was looking pretty frail, but I was so glad she managed to get down. I'll repeat my address from June onwards in case you should have lost it or in case it never got to you (which I suspect is the fate of some of my letters) it is - C/O Kennedy, Dell Farm, Nethy Bridge.

Oh beloved it's such a long time yet, how much easier a year would have been, still from the length of time I think this accursed war is going to take, the extra six months is, from my point of view, probably a blessing. I can't stop speculating on the meeting of David & his Daddy! Robert & I often dream of you, but Oh! dear me it's a crazy sort of life. I also often wonder if I shall meet you with or without the children, with, I should think for I can't imagine where I would leave them, but I think I'd rather be without, for I'm sure I'd be incapable of looking after them!

Robert has gained in weight since coming here & now weighs three st (with his clothes on). I must try to weigh David someday, but he won't stand still for a moment.

Your loving wife, Sheila

30th Apr 1944, Alan, WAF, Achimota, to Sheila

My Beloved,

Tomorrow I shall have completed nine months here. A long time and a long way to go but Oh my Darling I hope that you are less worried that you might have been.

I've had a very busy week after getting back from my tour. Parcels have come in and I have now enough film and developer to last me for my whole tour. I'm a bit worried about the expense but I'm hoping to recoup by sending some photographs to the "Times". I've now developed all my tour films and some are quite good.

I hope my cables arrived quickly and that my series of parcels start to trickle in in a month or so. Had a letter from Fountain Press talking about a new edition of the book and I have suggested to them that this is a good idea <u>and</u> that I write another one on "Home Made Fittings for Leica Cameras".

I'm finding it very hard to settle down to Office work after being away but I just have to do so there it is. I'm very much out of pocket after my tour but I hope to get back some in expenses. Incredibly I note that the cheques are always stamped on the back with the location of the bank. So much for security.

I do very badly want a couple of photograph albums and a negative storage booklet for six exposures of 35 mm film. Otherwise I shall never have a really good collection from here.

Could you oblige? Do it by post with Wallace Eaton. Any colour of album page in grey tones, not sepia.

Kiss the boys and tell them I love them & you, Alan

2nd May 1944, Alan, WAF, Achimota, to Sheila

My Beloved,

Six months and one day of my tour gone. The mail does not go until tomorrow this week & so I am able to reply to yours which came in last night. It was posted an April 22nd so the service is speeding up. Firstly I am so sorry that with a gap in letters and knowing I was on tour you were worried. I hope that the two cables reached you quickly. Oh my Dear! how I would love to see Robert in his kilt. I've now to look forward to photographs of you all. My Dearest Sheila I'm <u>much</u> more interested in yours than the boys though I love my boys as you well know. I have so many photographs to send you and it is infuriating that I cannot name the places.

After six months Dear I can honestly say that I have felt well out here and have enjoyed myself. Perhaps I'll change my tune. Nevertheless apart from periods of a day & night or two when I've felt tired and discouraged I've always been on top of my form, sometimes I feel inclined to sit on my bottom and answer old letters rather than fight & fight against people who prevaricate & are not really interested in doing things but only having on paper the insurance policy, "I recommended but no one carried out". It's dammed easy too to get a reputation on paper, but it's equally hard to force things through and get the work done. As I just put it in a report "It's the translation of a paper scheme to the actual anti-malarial drain, not the drawing up of the Malarial Scheme".

Well my Dear I love you and with you all things are possible. Kiss my proudest achievements (not paper schemes) for me, Alan

P.S. I have written to Cromarty Estates.[1]

4th May 1944, Alan, WAF, Achimota, to Sheila

Sea Mail

Woman who I like so much,

Here are advance guard of snaps from my tour. Will you show them to the small boys (whom I like so much) and tell them I'm pretty busy but time is passing.

I'm not proud of them as photographs. Talking of pride I'm very proud of being head of our "bush" tribe.

Oh My Dear it's 6.15 and I've just been told 'baf passed sa". Which means your bath is ready. So I shall "go for baf" then I shall "pass along for mess" & say "you bring one small ------ ----- ----- and one plenty big ginger savvy?" Then I shall "go for chop" and it's all very silly for what's the point in baths unless to feel nice for you? And what's the point of a nice drink on a warm balcony with the crickets chirruping without you?

Oh Sheila you are going to be spoiled for a very big change when I get back.

Alan

4th May 1944, Sheila, Seamill, to Alan

My Dear One,

Four letters from you last Monday all full of "the tour". Oh Beloved how I wish I could have been there, you just don't know how much I wish it. "Mungo Park is on its way to you now, I enjoyed it very much indeed and was sorry when it was done. It's infuriating that you can't mention any names of places, it would be

---

[1] Interesting reference to Cromarty Estates as it represents the opening of negotiations about Camusglashlan.

so interesting. The weather here is awful, gales & rain & more rain. I wonder we survive at all, it's turned very cold again as well. The Carricks have arrived for May & June. They have a nice little house at the Adrossan end of Seamill. They look like having an uneasy time as Nan says they are going home the moment the invasion starts! They are coming to tea tomorrow and Robert is looking forward to having Owen to play with.

Robert & I went to Crawford Lodge last Sunday & R enjoyed meeting Tilda's puppy[1], he just couldn't believe his eyes! Both boys are splendid, I weighed David the other day, he is 2 st. 4 lbs with a light coat on & he walked up the village & back without being in his pram once. I'll soon be able to do without the pram. I'm so looking forward to all the lovely things you have sent home & do hope they don't take too long. I am gasping for the sandals as footwear has become a distinct problem with me. I really haven't got very long here now, we go to Nethy B on the 31st & I shall probably go to Glasgow on the 28th or 29th as I have a few things to do in town before going north. I am deep in "The Far West Coast" & fascinated by the doings of Vitus Bering & Capt Cook. Mrs Bullersons can only go to Nethy B for June which is rather sad, but I shall probably find someone to do a spot of work up there. Oh I daren't think how much I'd like to be with you, how tired I am of Britain these days, with the war stretching back for years & nothing but the little daily round possible. Then I think of the children & how marvellous they are & I know how lucky I am, but so do get so ratty sometimes!

However time does go on and it's so good to feel that you are happy & interested and it's grand to know (roughly!) when we will see you again. By the way are the Rothmans cigarettes getting your length? Robert is getting positively monotonous the number of times he says plaintively "Oh! I do wish my Daddy would come home". It's so nice he really got to know you before you had to go. Poor old David just doesn't know what he's missing.

Love Sheila

---

[1] So Aunt Daisy was looking after Tilda at Crawford Lodge I wonder whose dog Tilda was.

8th May 1944, Sheila, Seamill, to Alan

My Dear One,

Your tribe is very well - all of it! I was delighted to receive another cable from you last Friday which means apart from anything else that even if I don't have another letter for a fortnight or three weeks I don't worry, nice things cables.

Mother & Daddy came down on Saturday & went back on Sunday, neither of them seem very fit, but it was nice to see them after five weeks & mother was so struck with David's likeness to you. She wasn't in the least trying to please me by saying the right thing, but I'm so very thrilled about it.

Murdo Malcolm Gillies MacLennan arrived at Blairbuie on April 20th.[1] His mother according to Lannie had a "very rough time" but all are very charmed with him although as Lannie naively remarks "the lambs are a full time job themselves". Kenny doesn't know when he will see him as of course all leave is stopped & he of course very fed up about it. Lannie is coming down to spend a fortnight with me at Dell Farm in July. Beloved there is so little to tell you of just now, these days are so very uneventful. Nan (Carrick) & her two children came to tea on Friday afternoon. Robert & Owen had a great time, but David was perfectly horrified at James (age 13 months) & nearly screamed the place down. James returned in kind & for a while things were chaotic. Even afterwards when David would come running into the room forgetting there was anything strange in it, he would shy like a horse when he saw James sitting on the rug. We are going to their home on Wed. Nan has just given up her ideas of nine children. & thinks (seriously) five would be enough. As they reckon with Nursing Home, specialists fees, special nurse & so on £140 as the cost simply of the arrival of a baby, the cut in the desired numbers isn't surprising! She is really worried about the curtailment of my family due to your absence! Oh Beloved I'm afraid I'm not that kind of woman at all. How I wish I could be getting the roof on the croft or doing something constructive this summer.

---

[1] The MacLennan family at Blairbuie keep cropping up in these letters. I have done a brief sketch of them in Appendix 7.

One doesn't seem to have done anything but existed for so long. It's such an odd period of tension & waiting in every way just now & no possible outlet but to break a few dishes! Surely this month can't pass without something sensational happening.

9th May

Another wet day, it's pathetic. Robert sends all his love & is glad you aren't forgetting him. Well I must steel myself & go out now! Yours always, Sheila

9th May 1944, Alan, WAF, Achimota, to Sheila

Letter Card 1 Tuesday

My Beloved,

I had your letter posted on 1st today so they are coming through well. I also had one from Mrs McKenzie dated 3rd. I'm so relieved to see that you've had my cable though you do not indicate that you have had both cables. By the way did you ever get the crepe de chine?[1]

I'm glad to hear that David had a good birthday even if the cake was a jam roll. Glad you are enjoying Mungo Park. There is no hurry in the world beloved about sending them. It's odd that we both should be thinking of how and where we shall meet. I too my dear want you all to myself for a little - the children can wait.

I've taken good note of the Nethybridge address. I was reading a good article by Seton Gordon[2] today on "The Old Caledonian Forest". He says the only remnants are to be found near Nethy Bridge.

I gave a talk to African Students last week on "A new Conception of Preventative Medicine" which seems to have gone down well as I have now been asked to repeat it at an African Club.

On Thursday I'm driving with Americans & on Friday Dr Bruce Wilson of Rockefeller is driving with me.

I'm simply bursting into authorship now. I have the following in

---

[1] Crêpe de Chine is a soft, fine, sometimes sheer fabric.
[2] Seton Gordon (1888-1927) was a well-known naturalist and photographer who published widely on the Highlands.

hand (if finished a different matter).

1. Chemosuppression of Malaria article with Brig Findlay.
2. A Model Malaria Oiling Scheme with a Czech called Chwatt.
3. A Dictionary of West African Foods.
4. Revision of Enlarger book.
5. New book on Leica Gadgets.
6. A series of essays developed for Penguin Series on Intellect & Character and the difficulty of choosing key men in a "service".

So my dear the wee brain's "fair buzzin" and no doubt you would say I was in a "difficult" stage if I was with you. I'm longing to hear of the parcels arriving & hear your comments on the articles. To above 6 you might add 7.

7. A series of photographs to sell to the Times and a reborn idea of local life in a photographic record of an Ashanti village for National Geographic Magazine - but Oh wee one, I'll have to start another card. . . . . .

Letter Card 2. 9th May 1944
To continue Beloved –
to continue a long recital of "me, me, me" I'm afraid.

Beloved you say pathetically in your letter "in case my letters never get to you - which I suspect is the fate of some of my letters". No, they all get to me I think & I hope I answer everything. As you will know by now I had great heaps of letters when I came back from tour.

David's proof photo arrived & I have it. I have it propped up in front of me now. Just killed a mosquito which I shall enclose (very squashed). It's a malaria carrier brand the first I have seen in my room since I came here although there are plenty of harmless ones. The D.D.M.S is pretty fit again but Major Grieg is in Hospital with a sharp attack of Malaria. Sparks is gone to another colony & Duff is covered all over with prickly heat and <u>very</u> depressed.

It has been powerful hot - uncontrolled sweats drip off your chin & runs down to form a dark patch in seat of pants!

Yes David is a dear, and <u>very</u> handsome beloved. It really is a most glorious age when their baby hands and faces contrast with coming boyishness. Hasn't he a firm little mouth?

My Dear I suppose today, as other days, I have thought of you twenty different times. Always wonder what you were doing or fancying I knew and day dreaming about it all.

David will get to know me & Robert will remember me but you are part of me always and beyond. Love me and love my boys beloved for we all feed on and are surrounded by your love.

Alan

10th May 1944, Sheila, Seamill, to Alan

My Beloved,

We had three letters from you on Tuesday. One for Robert & two for me. It's a terrific thrill to get a love letter from one's husband when one feels towards him as I do. I had a delightful surprise today - a letter from Mrs Taylor all full of you. It came quickly as it was only sent off on April 28th & is a great joy to me. Today I sent off the big pram to Achiltibuie. They had asked me to sell it to them (when finished with it) about six months ago so there was really no way out! I have however refused to take any payment for it as for one thing I don't believe in selling to friends & secondly they have done us a great many kindnesses & of a kind which as you know are difficult to repay. We went to tea with Nan yesterday & and afterwards to the shore where the children enjoyed themselves but personally I nearly froze. Nan's heart is still troubling her & she has to rest every afternoon for a while and gets very breathless.

May 14

Last two days we have seen some improvement in the weather & we have spent the afternoons on the shore. David had his first paddle today & loved it. I've only a fortnight here now as I intend going to Glasgow on Sunday the 28th & departing to Nethy Bridge on Wednesday the 31st. We all (Mrs B, the boys & I) went to Largs on Friday afternoon & had tea in Mackay's. I had to go to the Food Office & it was a chance to let David see a little of the world. It was the first time he had been in a restaurant - how different from Roberts early days! I am hoping to get to Largs on Tuesday afternoon to see "Tunisian Victory". Sitting on the shore that afternoon David insisted on wearing my sunglasses & had them on quite a while. I wonder if you can imagine how quaint he looked! We took a friend of Roberts with us. John is pretty dumb, bright red hair & covered with freckles & Roberts thinks he's just marvellous.

Beloved you been gone seven months now. It will be strange when we are together again & not counting the days any more. To me there is an extraordinary unreality in this life without you, there is such a large part of me not alive at all. I can't write any more just now beloved, I want you so much & it's so long yet.

Yours ever, Sheila

14th May 1944, Alan, WAF, Achimota, to Sheila

My Very Dear,

It's Sunday night & it's nearly 10 o'clock and I'm missing you. But for that matter it might be to 2 AM Thursday or 12 noon Friday. I'd still be missing you. I could not bear to go to the cinema tonight and I've been sitting drawing diagrams for the new book in my room. I've had a really busy week but today I sent off the Malaria suppression article to the Royal Society of Tropical Medicine (of which by the way I have just been elected Fellow) and the tropical development article to the Miniature Camera Magazine. Oh Beloveds my wee brain is buzzing at a terrific rate with ideas just now - they range from Sunday morning Bible readings with Robert to how I can possibly bathe with you in the cold water at Achiltibuie to how to produce Vitamin B from palm fruit kernels - to whether I shall try to sell photographs to the Times to the plan of an article for the National Geographic Magazine - to why I did not find West Africa sooner so as to share it with you - to the iniquity of a pimply faced youth plus wife whom I met yesterday. Seven months out in the Colonial Medical Services who is feathering his nest & ought to be in the Army.

Oh My Dear what awful letters I write to you. It will soon be Roberts's birthday & I have nothing to send him. Tell him the purse is for his birthday if it has arrived. My Beloveds it's such a long time until next spring. I wonder how you would like here. I suppose I like it most because of my work but My Dear I never see anything interesting without wanting to show it to you. I'll write again on Tuesday when I hope to have a letter. Kiss my sons. I love you, Alan

16th May 1944, Alan, WAF, Achimota, to Sheila

Letter Card

Dearest,

Here's another note begun two hours after my last. It's in anticipation of having another of yours to answer tonight & to tell you that I have today sent off to you 2 lbs tea, nine bars of milk chocolate, six handkerchiefs and two jelly powders. I would have sent more but I'm limited to 5 lbs gross weight. Say what you want when I get my next label. Any grocery - sugar, tea, tinned butter, cheese, chocolate etc. Is jelly powder any use to you? More later.

9.30 PM in bed

My Sheila - I have had your letter of 8th May posted on 10th May today, that's quick work isn't it. I've also had more developer, some cigarettes and above all Roberts Poly-photo. Oh my love what a funny wee boy he is! He really has an amazingly big mouth & sticking out ears - and his nose! But he is the nicest eldest son any man ever had & I love him so much. He is pleasantly firm looking for a boy of his age. Oh My Dear I want him to be a full-size person on his own.

I'm so tired of nonentities - Beloved I am terribly sleepy I just can't write more tonight except that I love you & wish you could see the thousands of glow-worms outside tonight.

17/5

Well My Dear another day nearer to you. It's going to be a hot one and damp after the rain. Glad to hear about MacLennans. I should write to them. Beloved I feel exactly like you about merely existing during this war & I want to get the roof on at Camusglashlan".

Great news from Italy. I hope that things will go well. I'll write to Robert. Love & more love, Alan

16th May 1944, Alan, WAF, Achimota, to Sheila

Letter Card

My Dear,

An extra mail came in yesterday with your air letter of the fourth (we still hope for more today or tomorrow). I'm so very glad you had four letters. I'm afraid you will be disappointed in the sandals - they are very crude but I shall see if I can do any better. I am amused to hear about the family - what a hell of a business life must be to Nan! David at 2 stone 4 pounds is now only 3 pounds lighter than Robert was when I left. I suppose this will be about the last letter to Seamill. It's pouring with rain and thundering like the crack of doom but it's cool, really cool & my skin's dry for the first time since coming out except when I was in the far dry north. Yes the cigarettes are reaching me & are very welcome.

I must write to Robert for it's a long time since I wrote to him. My dear last night I was lured off by the Science Master at a nearby college to listen to a gramophone recital of 36 records of a Bach Mass. I just lost interest completely & sat back with my eyes shut & thought of you and my sons for 2 ½ hours. My dear it did me so much good. I have to think of these lovely wee boys who love you and know that you love them.

Still I scrounged a good meal last night. All the college homes are really comfortable & the food is such a pleasant change.

It's really amazing how good the "boys" are at cooking and serving. They are infinitely better than maids - now that I'm used to the light-coloured insides of their hands!

Love Alan

16th May 1944, Sheila, Seamill to Alan

Dear One. Two cheery letters from you yesterday written on 25th of April. Robert has undertaken to double his usual daily dose of cod liver oil after hearing that you said it was good for him! Yes I'll get Dr White to Schick test David. By the way your doctor Harkness is a great friend of his - may I say it's a small world! I have not so far received any silk. I have had one parcel of white material but with nothing to connect it with Major Morrison. I thanked you for it weeks ago but it's possible the letter did not arrive. I'll send out the books now I know you can send them back - a regular Jew your wife is! It's been as cold as winter again today & it's very trying. I'm reading "The Roman Emperors In Marble" just now by Viktor Rydberg.[1] I don't suppose I remember one quarter of what I read but I'm always learning something & it's the most wonderful help in a lonely life. I have got to the stage when I simply cannot read a novel. I wouldn't tell anyone this it sounds so snobbish & I'm such a hopeless fool really but it is satisfying to be reading something worthwhile & a grand feeling to be learning things in a pleasant way. If only I could remember all the things that fascinate me when I read them for ever. Well I'm now going to concoct a nice fat sandwich. & get on with the "Emperors". I'll finish this later or tomorrow.

17th of May

I've been in town for a few hours today getting some shopping done as I think I'll have a bit of a rush getting everything done in the two days before we go to Nethy Bridge. I got back to two letters from you, 30th of April & 28th of May. I'll write Wallace Heaton about your albums etc.

I bought a good Atlas today, I've been missing one dreadfully when reading here & there won't be one at N.B. I wonder if your book man in T.Wells could get Burtons "Wanderings in W.Africa" I've given up hopes of Smith's. I'd write him but I can't think of his name - was it Law?

Well Beloveds I haven't been able to get any food worth mentioning all day, so I'm going to have a bacon and egg - yes two! I've got positively sore eyes through poring over my Atlas all the

---

[1] Swedish novelist and historian (1828-1895)

way down in the train.
I love you, Sheila

20ᵗʰ May 1944, Sheila, Seamill, to Alan

Beloved, I've ordered your albums & negative storage book from W.H. & hope they don't take too long to reach you. Today has been beautifully sunny though by no means a heatwave. Robert and I went to Largs this afternoon & went out in a wee boat! He has pleaded for ages to be taken out for our "row" & I just couldn't put off any longer. I wish you could have seen his face when he at last found himself bouncing about on the waves! To begin with he was somewhat anxious and belatedly asked "Mummy have you ever rowed a boat before & do you know how to turn?" He sat very stiffly all the time & I think was somewhat relieved to set foot safely on dry land, but is most anxious to go again. He was very friendly with a little boy called Ronnie last summer, but unfortunately Ronnie has moved to a house some distance away. Yesterday Ronnie and his mother, Mrs Meredith came to tea & the boys had a great time, it was a very wet day & the noise was deafening. Mrs M.is very Irish & quite amusing. She hasn't seen her husband who has been in India for years. They are cutting trains right & left just now. I shall heave a sigh of relief when we get to Nethy Bridge.

I phoned Dr W. yesterday to ask him to come & test David. He was very amazed & said it was most unusual & quite unnecessary but if it would set your mind at rest he would do it. Just another barmy G.P.! He said if you see "Joe" (Dr Harkness) again will you tell him he was asking for him.

My Beloved, I woke with such a dreadful longing for you this morning. Few men I think can ever have been so necessary to another human being as you are to me. Even though I may not stress it in every letter I never stop missing you, the ache is always there. How odd it will be to be happy again, but how wonderful that I know what real happiness is for I think many people never find it.
21st Sunday

Daddy & Mother arrived very unexpectedly this forenoon for the day. It's been a lovely day but still to me cold-ish. Daddy & Robert went to the shore for a while in the afternoon. It's just on 9 PM & David is still crying in his crib. I can't get him to sleep these bright nights.

Heard today that David Robinson & Robin Roxburgh are at the War Office now. I sent off a parcel of books to you a few days ago. Robert is longing for his canoe to arrive!

Yours ever, Sheila

22nd May 1944, Alan, WAF, Achimota, to Sheila

Letter Card

My Dear,

I am writing today because I'm off early tomorrow on tour for a couple of days and I will not get your next letter until I get back & this must catch the post.

I was away snail hunting all day yesterday. The same as the forest expedition only we were in a canoe with six paddles instead of a launch. It was a great day & I enjoyed myself thoroughly.

I have sent you a copy of the big paper on Malaria suppression. I can hardly keep awake today for I was out from 4.30 AM then yesterday until 10 P.M.

I'm playing tennis tonight, then having a drink with some American insect experts & I shall be off at 5.45 tomorrow. So Beloveds one of mine you will see that I don't have time to get into mischief! I've just read Andre Maurois' Disraeli & enjoyed it and am now hunting for "Ariel a Life of Shelley" by the same author. I am so pleased with our *tough* Robert's Poly-photo. And longing for yours. My Dear it's over seven months since I saw you and heard your voice. Oh my Dear it's too long. We must not lose each other's company for an instant after the war. Do you remember when you sent to say we ought to have our holidays apart?

Do you remember how I used to make you cross by insisting that we must have common hobbies & how I took up photography with that end in view - & then neglected you!

We have so many more links together now - Robert & David - Achiltibuie - the boat - our reading.

Did you know we were going to write a historical biography

together after the war. Whose shall it be, "Mary Queen of Scots" - "Cameron of Lochiel" - I'm immensely thrilled by a glimpse of Mrs Gladstone given in Maurois' Disraeli - in her diary she records engaging a servant & remarks "it took a very long time for William to decide & he did eventually on moral principles". It's fun to see someone as devoted as she can laugh at her idol. Oh I love you, Alan

28th May 1944, Alan, WAF, Achimota, to Sheila

Letter Card

My Very Dear,[1]

This week the sketches of you and Robert arrived and I loved them. They are not of course right but the artist has seen some of the charm of both of you. Your postcard photo also arrived and I did not like that at all. It is blurred and muddy and of course as you know I don't like your hair high up like that. The snaps I took at West Kilbride last year are my standby & I take them out and gaze at them very often. Oh my Dear how I long to see you.

I think you were wise about pram, it was much better to make it a gift.

I had a good short two-day tour and I set off on Tuesday again for another two days. I'm sending off a cable today for Roberts's birthday. When was our engagement, wasn't it July 6th. I've sent you three photographs today and I hope to have some more self-portraits to send in a week or so.

I'm really frantically busy just now trying to cope with work and books etc. I'm busy revising for a new addition of "Build Your Own Enlarger" and drafts for approval of a new book on "Leica Gadgets".

Oh Beloved if I could only make enough extra out of this writing to take a backwater job in the country how happy a life we could have. But Dear that's not what I really mean for we should always be happy together.

---

[1] We know from Alan's diary that he had just been notified he was being considered for Director of Medical Services of a division bound for Burma. Presumably he dared not mention this to Sheila.

I made a gesture in the last few days - not appearing too keen for a job - which troubles my conscience a bit but will ensure that I stay here & so let your mind be at ease.

Oh my beloved it's not easy having two loyalties. Kiss my boys, Alan

PS:
1. Sending to 6 North Gardener St but will send next one to catch you at Nethy Bridge.[1]
2. Am wearing my 1939 - 1943 Medal Ribbons.

28th May 1944, Sheila, Seamill, to Alan

Beloved,

I've been more days than usual without writing you. I hope it won't cause a gap at your end. It's been a full week packing and also I've been out quite a bit. Nan and Hazel came down on Monday I enjoyed seeing them and they are coming up to spend a week or so at Nethy Bridge. Mrs Meredith called on Tuesday evening and I went to the cinema with her on Thursday & to supper afterwards. Last night I went along to say goodbye to Aunt Daisy, didn't stay long & spent the rest of the evening with Nan (Carrick). Robert and I have been sharing a bed this week to avoid having too many dirty sheets to take away. He is really quite comfortable to sleep with now! I had two delightful letters from you the other day written on the 9th. The "Mosquito" arrived in as good order as could be expected & gave me a good laugh, in fact I sat and shook with laughter over that letter, the thought of Duff all over prickly heat somehow struck me as very funny at the time. I can see now it is anything but and please give him my sympathy. You must look quaint with a pool in the seat of your pants, even your youngest son would be horrified at that! I am so interested to hear of all you're doings & all your irons in the fire of authorship! I am hoping I won't object to your "difficult" stages (as you pathetically refer to them) any more. I have learned in a hard school to live alone & for one

---

[1] Actually it was not sent to 6 North Gardiner St but to Dell Farm, Nethybridge.

thing I should be more mentally self-supporting than I was & certainly when you aren't here I can lose myself in reading as I never could when first married. So will hope it will continue. Also it will be such a change to have a man to live with again that when you have a "cracked" spell I'll just remind myself what it was like without you & shut up!

I got an awful fright with David tonight. He slipped in the bath & hit his chin on the side. When I got him on his feet blood streaming down his chest & for a dreadful moment I thought his teeth must have gone through his tongue. Fortunately it was just a very gaping cut under his chin, where there is lots of baby fat, but did it bleed! A very little more in length & it would have had to be stitched. I sat holding cotton wool from a fresh packet I had on it, & as long as I left a little bit on it stopped bleeding, as soon as I took it away it opened up - result the wee soul is off to sleep with the wee white billy goat beard sticking on the foot of his chin & Robert is tickled to death! One of your parcels has arrived at Crown Mansions & I'm looking forward to seeing it tomorrow. Your tour photos arrived yesterday & are a great joy. Oh! Beloved I want to be there too. It's too late to start another card tonight. I'm off for a bath. We go with the afternoon train tomorrow. I love you. I love you, I love you, Sheila

1st Jun 1944, Sheila, Nethybridge, to Alan

Dear One,

Here we all are one more stage on the long journey back to you. It was nice to arrive yesterday & find a cable waiting for me. The journey up went off very well, much better than I expected! It's poured all day today which when one is settling in is rather trying. It's rather a gloomy house, but possibly when not surrounded by mist will be more attractive. Did I mention that Daddy & Mother were at the hotel for June? It's just over a mile away. David is thrilled with the hens, colours, fir cones etc. & Robert is glad we came. I'm going to get some vegetables into the garden (which is the usual highland apology) right away. Excuse pencil but I've no ink. The heavy luggage got stuck on the way & has just arrived so

I'll have to go & unpack. My sandals have arrived, thank you so much. I shall take them to the local cobbler & get him to trim an inch off the toe & they will be ideal. I love the little ivory head, it's clever isn't it? Oh Beloved I'm lonely tonight & fed up with myself & need you badly. Your parents & Moira came to 6 N Gardner St & had tea with us on Monday so you will be hearing another account of the boys! I'm enjoying the Nigeria magazine. A few days ago Smiths sent me Burton's "Wanderings in W. Africa" so I'll read it quickly & send it on. It's in very bad condition & they took 18/- for it! I've told Wallace Heaton to send you four photo albums & two negative storage ditto. I hope they arrive reasonably quickly, it's a long time since you had any kind of present from me!

June 2nd

I'm feeling much more settled today & think we will be very happy here. Last night my head ached & everything seemed awful, but today everything seems different. Daddy took us to Grantown in a taxi this afternoon (still raining!) & I got fish ordered to come by bus twice a week & generally got a lot of things straightened out.

Had letter from you today, telling of Tropical Medicine Fellowship & so on. All very interesting. Robert is going to have lunch at the Hotel on Sunday & Daddy has had a magnificent boat made for him at the works.[1] I've got him a little wooden tank which he badly wanted & mother has got him a sort of constructional toy that can be made into a boat or a train & also something else, I haven't seen it yet.

He's a strange wee chap Robert & he needs you even more than

---

[1] I well remember the 'boat'. I never realised it was made for me at Steven & Struthers. It was a model yacht with a thin metal keel. Every time I tried to sail it, it just capsized! Jimmy made two small lead weights for me, melting the lead on the fire in the kitchen, I think in a cooking pot but I image Sheila would have mentioned that if true. He made a sand mould and poured the liquid lead in outside the door. I know that cow's urine was the traditional binder for sand, I used it at Loughborough, and I wonder if Jimmy did. He drilled the keel and used wire to bind the weights to the bottom of the keel, one on each side. I was immensely impressed.

he knows which is saying a lot. I have great hopes of getting some riding & certainly it's grand cycling country. Love me terribly beloved, I just live to be with you again, Sheila

4 Jun 1944, Alan, WAF, Achimota, to Sheila

Letter Card

My Very Dear,

I'm afraid I have not been able to write very often recently for I've been away and have been wickedly busy. I returned last night to find your two letters of 16th & 20th May waiting for me. I have just had letter saying you had received the cloth. I'm afraid I thought it <u>was</u> silk. Oh my Dear I wish I could be back with you to read things with you. Mr Pratley of Halls Bookshop, Tunbridge Wells, has just sent me a Thierry's Norman Conquest and five of Gilbert Murray's Euripides. Thank you very much for arranging about albums & film storage book.

It must have been fun taking Robert in the rowing boat. I hope he will get plenty in the years to come. Dr White is batty! 20% of children are <u>not</u> fully protected by the usual course and if still Schick Test positive require an extra dose or two. I shall remember him to Dr Harkness when I'm next in these parts.

I've had a hectic week and am just beginning to recover from it this evening. I'm laying out large areas of swampy jungle for mosquito trials and I've had to travel by canoe & walk through the most appalling stuff with guides from village.

In places it is so dark under the foliage that you almost need a torch and at one stage I scrambled for five miles through swamp over tree trunks & wading up to my waist. It took me 4 ½ hours for that five miles! I've had three bush cutters with me to cut paths.

Some of the villages are very bad & the children having never seen a European fled yelling on my arrival. I hope my photos come out well. I was terrified at slipping in completely and ruining my camera.

I've got a very mild sort of dysentery & am very tired as I've had to make up arrears in the office all day but a good sleep will put me right. It's a funny life to be in the office one week and to be negotiating with an Omanhene (chief) for accommodating 25 labourers in his village the next!

I'm longing to hear of the first parcels of leather work arriving. If I can scrounge another letter card I'll write more later before the mail goes.

Oh Sheila I'm missing you & I need you tonight. Alan

4th Jun 1944, Alan, WAF, Achimota, to Sheila

Letter Card

My Beloved,

Just starting this second letter after dinner. It's 8.45 P.M. & I'm just off to bed. My indelicate complaint seems to be abating. Bless you my very Dear.

5/6/44 7.30 A.M.

I'm lying in bed clad only in a pair of pyjama trousers waiting for the news to come on army band speaker. I took a long time to get to sleep last night though I was very tired. So I read Thierry's Norman Conquest and am enjoying it just as much as when I first read it.

The complaint seems to have gone this morning.

The news of the capture of Rome is very welcome & I sincerely hope that it is succeeded by a quick jaunt North. It's awful this uncertainty about a second front & it's bad to be in this backwater when other men are proving themselves. I hope that it will soon all be over in Europe.

Well my Dear I seem to be depressing this morning. I'm not really, it's the effect of having a great deal to do & not seeing very well how I'm to do it. It's difficult to be away so much from the office and yet do a job properly and I do want to do a useful job here.

Oh my Beloved if I just could see you for half an hour, all my little troubles would vanish and all would be well. I love you so very much Sheila and these 4¼ years are a wicked waste of our short lives. I'm always so very glad we have the boys. Oh Beloved how good it is to have such children.

I found a passage in Gilbert Murray[1] which expresses very much one's tenderness for one's own wee ones.

"Thou little thing that curlest in my arms, what sweet scents cling about thy neck! Put up thy arms and climb about my neck, now kiss me lips to lips!"

I've had a windfall of three Airletter cards so I'll be able to write you more letters.

I must hurry up now & dress for I've dawdled over this until it is now 8.5.

Bless you my very dear own Dear, Alan

4th Jun 1944, Sheila, Nethybridge, to Alan

My Dear One your eldest son has passed his fifth birthday with a great deal of gusto & enjoyment. He was pleased about your cable & to know that you were thinking about him. He & I went to the Hotel for dinner & he had a huge meal & was thrilled with all his presents & is very proud to be five! David is very fit & sweet & today has the plaster off his chin. They would both feed the hens all day long. A great ploy of David's is getting in wood from the wood pile which is about fifty yds from the house. He trots back & forward with a bit under each arm blissfully enjoying himself. Yesterday he was pursued by a particularly cheeky hen expecting to be fed & had to be rescued in a high state of agitation! - It kept pecking at his knees. Still it rains, now 9 pm and the sun has come out & I too am tempted out but I love you very much & I'm writing instead.

The children since coming here simply won't go to sleep of nights & as David flops about until about 9 pm, gets his legs stuck through the bars of his cot & screams for assistance, it's a bit wearing & shortens my evenings which I look to as the peaceful spell of the day. Would you like me to try to get Burton's "A Mission to Gelele, King of Dahome" with notices of the so called 'Amazons', the Grand Customs, the yearly customs, the Human Sacrifices & The Negros Place in Nature? It's supposed to be his

---

[1] The Gilbert Murray quote, or rather translation, is from "The Trojan Women of Euripides".

most profound anthropological study, but may be as dry as dust for all I know.

I'm glad you are having it a bit cooler these days but according to Burton the worst times are after the rains!

Robert wore his new grey flannel suit & dark red tie which he is extremely proud of today & looked very sweet. Oh! Beloved what fun it will be when you come home & we can all go places together. I'm looking forward to Nan & Hazel coming up in July, Douglas & Nonie are coming to Boat of Garten for their holidays about the same time. Did I tell you that Uncle James & Violet are coming to the Hotel for July & Aug? I wish you could know how much I love & need you beloved - you never will & it seems a pity. Robert is very anxious about his canoe, which hasn't shown up yet. I do wish you could hear how well he pronounces it! Love from all your tribe, Sheila

Continuation of June 4th. NEW CARD

I was actually able to shed a few woollies & uncurl a bit. We have had venison broth for dinner. Robert thought it was very queer meat but David loved it. I had half an hour's heavenly peace afterwards with David asleep & Robert playing in the *well haven* about a hundred yds away audibly talking to himself but dulled by the distance to a gentle murmur. Then Robert & Daddy went to fish in the river & mother said she had to go to rescue them should they fall in & disentangle flies from the trees where they are half the time! David & I wandered down in the rear, made for the heavenly secluded sandy place & thoroughly enjoyed ourselves. We paddled & then I lay on the sand & David played around me with his pail (old can with handle) & spade (made Steven & Struthers). Then home over the fields carrying David from about half way, quite used to it now & somehow very pleased to be carrying him with his arms round my neck & his head on my shoulders, yawning occasionally & very contented. The farmer calling a greeting to us from the field where he was working, the deep blue & purple hills, the violets underfoot & the house (I note with relief that my kitchen fire still burns & hasn't died on me) in the distance with wood smoke rising lazily from the chimney are all the essence of peace & somehow I feel suddenly uncomfortable that I am enjoying this peace when they are coping with pilotless planes in the south. But unlike you I do not feel like going south! I get home & we get supper then Robert & the others return. Robert breathless & ecstatic with a minute salmon parr which he insists on my frying for his supper! Mother was much worried about his reactions to a fish being killed - she need not have been, he killed it himself with great gusto! Daddy on departing for the Hotel leaves instructions with Robert that the worms are to have a teaspoonful of cream tomorrow morning, which it seems will toughen them for Mondays fishing! I know it will be the first thing I will have to do in the morning. My gumboil has been very sore all week but is much better today - thank goodness. I am alone just now, but have maid coming at end of month. Now to sleep. I love you beloved & need you so much more than you can realise. Sheila

6th Jun 1944, Alan, WAF, Achimota, to Sheila

Letter Card

My Beloved,

Your letter posted 28th May arrived this morning & I'm answering it before I go tomorrow for ten days by road with Jeremiah, a tent, a 'chop' *bone* Primus Stoves, cookers, lamps & goodness know what not. I'm so glad to have your letter & be able to answer it before I leave. Oh my beloved it must be very hard to be living alone & the evenings must be the worst of it. I'm sorry to hear about poor old David's chin. Poor wee chap - I hope it heals quickly. I'm glad the tour photographs arrived. I knew you would at once long to be with me. Oh Sheila it's such an incredible opportunity for me to see so much at government expense but what a waste without you. I'm sure the reason for most women "withering" & wilting in the country is that they just don't go out enough. I'm as brown as a nut with being out so much & I feel so ridiculously healthy in comparison with the job office ghosts in the mess. I seldom wear a hat in the car & I often have an open car.

So the big-time, the Second Front, has come. It's odd to be here

& to listen to the wireless almost as if it was at times a huge exercise and at another time just H G Wells & at another History. You will be thankful that your interest is that of a Patriot only & not of a relative. It seems to have gone well so far and Oh Oh surely we deserve success and a merciful providence will stop all the suffering involved soon.

11 P.M.

My Dear I am just about to pop into bed. It's a sticky night but lovely out - a glorious full moon. The crickets are whistling away - it's extraordinary how one gets used to the continual high pitched shriek. Have had my tennis racquet repaired. The strings are the first repairs since 1934!

I have some snaps to send you including three of myself taken by my thread and matchstick method. I must write to Robert soon. Tell him I love him and kiss David's cut for me. I love you my own Dear Sheila, Alan

6th Jun 1944, Sheila, Nethybridge, to Alan

My Dear One,

I did enjoy the letters of the father of the "African Family"! They really are treasures. The latest photographs arrived this week, isn't the bush mother & baby splendid? Robert also had a letter & photos which pleased him very much. Then today arrived the parcel sent to Steven & Struthers. The bags are attractive & roomy. I haven't quite made up my mind about the bedspread. It's suffered a bit in the wash I think. I've looked at it a dozen times today & haven't decided yet what it is really intended for! It's too short for a bed but I'll think out a use for it yet. I feel it will be just right for something but what I don't yet know. Anyhow the parcel gave us a big thrill & thank you very much.

For once it's been fine today but is ending up with a wet evening. We went down to the river in the afternoon & the boys paddled happily for two hours. David is proceeding to cut his second back tooth having just produced all the bits of the other one. The top ones now then teething is at least over! I had a long letter from your mother today, but she sent it in a bag of tomatoes two of which burst, I can't tell you anything about it!

Robert & David had Airgraphs yesterday. David is terribly pleased at getting one handed to him & promptly put it in the coal scuttle & covered it up with wood! We had a great afternoon yesterday when we visited a Canadian Saw Mill nearby. The boys would have stopped for hours watching bull dozers (?) & all kinds of weird contraptions handling huge trees & making roads & so on. David chattering about "big lorries" a new one & numerous new words brought out in the excitement of the occasion. My Cockney maid is settling down well, she is a real Mrs Mop. Hopelessly harum-scarum, but means terribly well & has all the cheerfulness of her kind. The little girl has been taken over by Robert & they play houses & shops & houses endlessly!

Just heard Churchill on the Flying Bomb, sounds kind of grim & difficult to judge just what it's like. How I wish one could see the end of it all. Robert wants to know if you couldn't send a ship for us so that we could all go to Africa! He is getting quite annoyed at your staying away so long. I'm very short of news I'm afraid beloved. Love me a lot, Sheila

7th Jun 1944, Sheila, Nethybridge, to Alan

My Dear One,

So the 'second front' has at last got under way. It's hard to grasp the fact at all & my first reaction was to feel slightly sick. Oh! Beloved I do thank God you are far away & feel I have been dealt with kindly.

We are all much more settled here now & I've got used to cooking on an open fire & trotting about with a candle when David wakens in the night. It's really beautiful & we have the Abernathy Forest right at the backdoor & can take any of the innumerable paths through the pines & moor. Can you picture your small tribe ambling along a little white road through the heather with only the hills looking down, the wee one stopping every few yards to pick up "tones" & put them carefully in his trouser pockets - "tones in poc" he calls it - then hastening along after Robert with clucks of satisfaction over his latest find.

The hens are getting very bold due I suppose to the boys feeding them so much & they give David quite a lot of worry & he's had at least one good peck. He isn't what you could call frightened so much as indignant & at times overwhelmed - there are sixty of them!

I heard peculiar sounds from the kitchen this evening & could hear David running around. I found the hens overflowing in the back door & David retreating & advancing with the tide, making futile gestures & saying or rather whispering in a very small emotionally charged voice "shoo, shoo, Oh! de. Shoo, shoo". He just loves being here, they both do. Robert & I had lunch at the hotel today. He walked down with Daddy & I followed up later (it's a good mile & a bit) after giving David his dinner & putting him to bed, on my bicycle. By the time I arrived somewhat heated & blown about everyone was in the dining room. I proceeded to make an unobtrusive entrance, when, just as I slid in the door the silence was rent by a bellow from Robert seated in the middle of the room "Hurry up Mummy you're just in time".

The hills are a picture tonight & although 10 pm the sun is bright & I think I'll go for a short walk before turning in. I'm reading Fraser Darling's "Island Years" & it will keep me awake long after I go to bed.

Oh! Beloved may those coming battles in France go well & put an end to this insane existence. Think of us as happy here beloved & thinking of & loving you all the time.

Yours ever, Sheila

9th Jun 1944, Alan, WAF, Achimota, to Sheila

Letter Card 1

My Very Dear,

It would afford you a lot of amusement if you could see me now, for I am both togged up in mess kit with buttons polished and hair brushed. I'm sitting on the veranda of this school bungalow and there is one engineer about half a mile away, one district commissioner about ¾ a mile away, but no one else. From here, the evening being clear, I can see for miles over the jungly bush. The reason for the final touch, the jacket, is that last night I discovered that mosquitos could bite through shirts! However this reason being agreed the rest is just pure *thinking*. I have a bottle of VAT 69 Whisky & a bottle of soda water at my right hand. That the top button of my tunic is loosed we shall not put down to carelessness or casualness but merely to a studied negligence akin to the white tie just obviously not fastened with elastic behind!

I've been living out here on my own (+ Jeremiah) for two days now and I shall be here for another week. The only snag is that I cannot of course get any news of the war. I slept last night on the veranda and even though without sheets & clad only in pyjama trousers, I was too hot.

I shall be doing 10-15 miles each day in bush & it's great fun. I have one boy to cut, one to carry a haversack & map case & I often take pity on a small boy & let him carry the camera. At the end of the day I give the cutting boy & the guide-cum carrier a shilling each & the small boy gets twopence. It must be most mysterious to you why I have been doing all this on & off for a fortnight but Richardson has asked for some special mosquito destruction trials and I'm getting on with that. It's a great chance of seeing real bush. I have quite an army of African Soldiers with me and 50 bush cutters. The mosquitos are really appalling here.

I shall continue on another sheet I'm flush out of cards today. Love Alan

9th Jun 1944, Alan, WAF, Achimota, to Sheila

Letter Card 2

My Beloved,

The first half of this letter I drafted in such a form that you could, if you liked, send it to my people to read; for it would amuse them & I cannot spare another lettercard for them. Beloved if you could just suddenly embody on the wicker chair in front of me - Oh if you only could - Well for one thing I should probably "rape you"[1] for

---

[1] After careful consideration & input from David & Gill, studying the original handwritten text of Alan's letter (bad writing as usual) and Sheila's reply, I have

another I'd never let you disembody away from me again.

I'm working through Thierry's Norman Conquest again & liking it even more than last time. After dinner I hope to get down to writing out properly a lot of information on local news for West African Foods which I gathered today. I also have about 500 mosquitos to identify.

Oh Beloved a lowly thought has struck me - the united family face falling over the VAT 69 Whisky! Would they be worried. Reassure them somehow - I swear that in two nights I've had two "small" whiskys with "plenty long" sodas. I managed to borrow a Tilley Lamp so I have a very good light. I saw Tommy Single again just before I left G.HQ it's odd to have in front of me on the veranda the identical camp bed on which you slept at Rieff in 1938. Six years ago my love. I'll stop now for Jeremiah is hovering about trying to indicate that "chop" is passed. Also it's about to rain buckets as it has on & off all day.

10.6.44 7 P.M.

Scene exactly as yesterday - stage props identical.

Being tired of chop cooked in cocoa-nut oil I'm having corn on the cob & four boiled eggs for dinner and I <u>am</u> looking forward to them. The cook has just been in to say "What I pass master for breakfast chop". I have told him I want Paw-Paw & ginger and 3 "flied" egg.

I have only walked five miles today & I went down to the sea & bathed on the way back. I think I must start a surface mail letter as I have just one more card to last me a week.

I cannot find out anything about the invasion but I shall pay a call on the D.C. & see if he knows anything.

Kiss yourself from me, Alan

9th Jun 1944, Sheila, Nethybridge to Alan

Dear One,

It certainly knows how to rain here! By way of a change

---

settled to my satisfaction they actually were talking playfully about "rape". Not something one would do nowadays!

yesterday was fine & a glorious evening but today it's been at the old game again & the mist wrapped round us. It's been warm anyhow & this afternoon the parents who had come up & brought their lunch set out for the river (Nethy) with fishing rod & Robert & the yacht & David & I followed in our own way. The river is just under a mile from the house going across the fields & I've discovered a beautiful sandy place shallow on our side where the children can play in perfect safety & freedom. I have to manhandle David across the fields & am getting very used to carrying him long distances! He walks part of the way of course but it's heavy going for his short fat legs & he'll suddenly grasp me round the knees & insist on being carried. When he is walking it's slow progress for at least one field is carpeted with violets & buttercups & he pulls them & presents them to me all the way. When we do get to the river I can just sit back & let things go, he is so happy throwing stones in the water & sticks & it's a delight to watch him. Before I forget I must tell you he calls chickens "baba chooks" which I think rather perfect!

Daddy & Robert were playing in a wee burn near the house yesterday. Daddy was digging out a pool to make it deep enough for the boat. I was out in the fields with David & was surprised to find on returning that Robert was sporting a different set of clothes! He had been standing on the bank peering into the pool (very deep & muddy from the excavations previously mentioned) & had slipped & done a perfect nose dive in, only the Wellington boots left waving above the surface. He was very full of all "Jimmy" had done for him, how he'd hauled him out, taken him home, given him a bath & found clean clothes!

I must send you out Fraser D's Island Years, I've also got a newly published book by Cecil Beaton to send you. It's called British Photographers & is a history of photography which has had excellent reviews & might amuse you.

I've got wonderfully limbered up physically since coming up here & once again the miles mean nothing & I only get sleepy never tired. At times I feel absurdly young - as long as I don't pass a mirror - & want to run when going short distances outside, my legs just won't walk & it must look very silly!

Beloved I'll have definitely a few more lines & wrinkles & a few more white hairs when you return but I'm hopelessly young inside. There's no doubt this northland does buck one up. Robert is now very anxious about his canoe. I'm rather afraid it's got lost. Oh! My dear, I'm so in love with you & so lost without you. I hope you like me alright when you get back!

All love, Sheila

10th Jun 1944, Sheila, Nethybridge, to Alan

My Beloved,

I had two very nice letters from you on Saturday. Saturday was in fact a very nice day. David woke at 7 am. The sun was shining gloriously so I dressed myself & David & woke Robert with considerable difficulty. Then I sent Mrs Whitelands little girl down to the hotel on my bicycle with a note to Mamie to say I'd be at the 9.15 bus if she would like a jaunt to Aviemore (there is only one bus). We had some of our breakfast on the table & departed for the village eating the rest! Can you see us beloved, David sitting in his pram & Robert & I pushing & all eating rolls. A brilliant morning & not a soul about until we got to Nethy B. I arranged in the village for a car to meet us at bus when we got back at 12.30 so that we'd get back for lunch without too much effort. We had a nice bus ride, much enjoyed by two small boys. I did some shopping (no chemist for instance here) wandered around at the hotel grounds & came home laden with flowers & vegetables. The army are still in possession of the hotel altho' all gone from it & keep the vegetable garden going & get the proceeds. It sounds a queer story to me. The view from the hotel was perfect, the hills looking their best & I longed to shift my house there. We sat & ate chocolate & basked in the sun & generally enjoyed ourselves. It's fun to have two wee boys instead of one & a baby. The bus home was however too much for David who fell blissfully asleep! In the afternoon we had a picnic at the river - a fire & tea & all! - & the boys splashed in & out of the water all the time.

The parents left today but we are looking forward to your family arriving on Thursday.

I have not yet heard definitely that Miss Williams (Wakefield School) can take Robert as she is very full up & was waiting to see if the High School could relieve her of some of her pupils, but I expect definite word this week. If she is unable to take him before Christmas, I think I may try for a cottage either in the village or at Aviemore for Sept. & not return to Wakefield until mid Oct. I don't know how this strikes you but the boys do look so well on the life here. I shall possibly be alone in Sept. so want smaller house with electricity.

I manage very well thank you with the £40 & altho' when living in furnished houses I don't save a lot ends meet quite beautifully so don't worry about that. My bank balance has been healthier in these last nine months than for a year or so previously. Also in these parts there is nothing to spend money on in these parts except food which is very restful!

You'll never never know how much your wife loves you beloved, which I think is a pity, but you just couldn't possibly guess, Sheila

11th Jun 1944, Alan, WAF, Achimota, to Sheila

Letter Card

My Dear,

I'm continuing the two letter cards written from my bungalow. I must tell you some rather Rabelaisian stories which the District Commissioner told me about. An old Paramount Chief (Omanhene) in whose kingdom I am working has wife palaver. He has four wives and one was recently found enjoying herself with a boy of fifteen. The Omanhene came to the D.C. in great distress about it. The offence was committed just outside his boundaries so to get the boy convicted he would have to apply to a neighbouring Omanhene. He is most unwilling to tell the other chief about such a bad business so he would just have he thinks to let the boy off. But that's not all. His elders say he should put away his erring wife but the old man says she is quite the nicest wife he has ever had. So the poor chap is held in a cleft stick on both counts.

They have no idea of love and affection as we have. Wives are bought & when they leave their husbands their dowries go with them. The D.C. is also worried by a rich African who is a rubber buyer & is away for long periods. He has eight wives whom he hardly bothers to visit but keeps them in a walled in compound. When he goes off he employs a sort of private detective who tells him of goings on. His girls tend to climb out at night & go haywire & it's all noted down. Then the man comes back & sues all the correspondents for £15 each. At the last occasion the D.C. had to award him £45 & he doesn't know how to stop the palaver.

Their appetite in such matters is fantastic. Both Jeremiah and the cook have acquired temporary wives since we arrived - pair of dignified young women.

11.6.44 Sunday.

I hate to be so monotonous but it's 6.20 P.M. - I'm all dressed up again - jubla - jubla. and the VAT 69 are still with me.

Today I have acquired a "smallboy" who is appointed *really* for errands, fetching wood. The said smallboy is clearly terrified of me & hides when I approach.

Today I sent off the two airmail letters which should reach the port all right. One of my O.C's Hygiene Section came out to see me, brought me a case of beer and some army bread & the war news. It was decent of him to come out 55 miles.

The war news seems excellent and it looks as though we are quickly getting a good bridgehead built up. We shall undoubtedly get some tremendously ferocious assaults on it and I don't think the end in Europe is near yet. A lot depends on the success of the next Russian Offensive. I suppose in the end the Germans will rather hold them to the last & let us into Germany in hope of more lenient treatment. That would be a pity.

Today my labourers have not been working. I sat & worked at Ashanti names for foodstuffs with my African Survey Sgt Boating. He speaks Hausa and Ashanti and is a very clever chap. In the afternoon I showed Major Barber over some of "my back" and then went along to see the mouth of a big river to see whether a motor boat could get in to hurry up my work along it. I'm afraid I shall have to rely on canoes. It must have been an odd sight to see me, in a very small canoe with my camera clutched to my bosom, clad in white shorts and shirt and gum boots, pottering about the river mouth trying to make a crazy old African boatman, clad in a brown cloth plus a very natty soft hat, try to understand what I wanted.

I am enclosing some photographs which will interest you. Those of self are not too reassuring but in spite of being pop eyed I'm still sane. Oh Beloved you would so love all this. You above all women would enter into the fun of it & enjoy it I could take you to village after village where no white woman has been and show you places and ju-jus and scenes that you would love.

It's odd that I at 35 years of age should come out here and enjoy myself doing things which never seemed likely to be more than pleasant reading before. It's all so strangely "like a book".

I'm having chicken cooked in ground nut oil for dinner tonight. Having seen it I told Jeremiah to get the knives sharpened which was considered a very good joke.

Beloved you, as I, will be longing for me to be half way through my tour. I arrived here on Nov 1st so on August 1st I shall have reached the homeward run. What are you going to do after July when you leave Nethy Bridge?

My Dear I'm now going off to look at photographs of my Dear Ones.

9 P.M.

Just off to bed so I shall finish this in case I get an opportunity of sending it tomorrow.

Kiss Robert & David & tell them I love them. Oh my Beloved it's a long time, Alan

12th Jun 1944, Sheila, Nethybridge, to Alan

Dear One.

Your letter of May 16th came in today - not very good going! How lovely to think of that parcel of things on the way to us. Yes tea will be most helpful & the chocolate will be a luxury. I need the hankies too, I seem to lose an awful lot. About the next parcel, butter &

sugar would be a terrible joy. I don't suppose you remember much about rations but 2 ounces of butter a head doesn't go far - I'm not complaining but I can't get used to margarine & dislike it as much as ever. Then sugar is always a worry as the children need puddings every day, or at any rate expect them & I just can't stop liking it in my tea, the only thing I do like sweet. No doubt the jelly powder will go down very well with the children, anything different is so good. On the train coming up here a naval officer gave me a tin of pineapple juice for the boys, we took it on our milk pudding & it was the event for two days.

13th

Quite a fine day but very cold. Had a shower of hailstones in afternoon! Gave David his dinner then Robert & I hailed a passing truck from the lumber camp & went down to the hotel for overs by way of a change. Had lovely walk back on the other side of the river. Am very lazy tonight, it's fine & I intended going out on my bicycle but I've just been dozing in front of a wood fire. I've had quite a few aspirin in the last 24 hours in an effort to get peace from a sore swollen gum & I think they've made me a bit dopey but they are a lot of help. Your parents, Moira & Doreen are coming to the hotel on July 13th for two days. So here's hoping they get good weather. One can dare to hope that things are going reasonably well in France these days. I feel very far away from it here & you must feel in another world. The saving grace of my life since you left is that I'm so fully occupied. A day with the boys in close attendance leaves little time to ponder much of whether time is passing quickly

or slowly. Mother always says how she pities me in the evenings & cannot understand that I positively enjoy them! They are so short the evenings, the boys aren't in bed till 7 pm now & after I get things straightened out, make some supper & eat it there is very little time left for reading, writing & mending & I always seem to have several letters that must be written. I read a bit in bed of course but I can't keep awake very long & sleep really soundly. Excuse worse writing than usual, but you must be used to it! I love you & ache for you, Sheila

2th Jun 1944, Sheila, Nethybridge, to Alan

Beloved,

Roberts's purse, the charm, very welcome "fasteners" & the pouffé came yesterday morning. Robert was pleased but a little dumped because it wasn't his canoe! Oh! Please, please, please can I have a purse like Roberts? It is a perfect match for the crocodile bag (which I like more every time I look at it) & if you hadn't written Roberts name on it he would certainly have lost it to me!

The pouffé is very nice indeed & I like it. I sent you the cable today to say the leather had arrived. I have no news at all. Your sons are wonderfully fit & David develops every day & get easier all the time. He's just longing to be allowed to sleep with Robert & makes a dive into his bed when he gets his pyjamas on & has to be hauled out & taken to his own room. I tried them in the same room one night but was forced to separate them in the end. I think by next winter I shall manage to get them in together. I shall miss Robert in my room so will probably put it off until as far on in the winter as possible, when it won't be so long until I get my other room mate back! We are going to tea tomorrow with some English people & children who have taken a house not very far away to get away from flying bombs, there are quite a lot of people coming up now who have been bombed out. It's so very sad to have it starting all over again.

I expect your people will be pretty weary when they arrive (about 6 pm) tomorrow. I'll go down & see them in the evening. Glasgow fair is always such a hopeless time to travel. I've had no word from the school yet & just can't make up my mind about Sept. No use asking you what you think, it would be mid Aug before I heard. Had 19th June Airgraph this a.m. & look forward to letter at end of week. The Airgraphs take as long as surface mail! Robert's chief worry about going to school is that he can't tie his shoe laces so how will he get home at dinner time!

Your tribe all love you beloved, but one of them loves you beyond all reason.

Sheila

13th Jun 1944, Sheila, Nethybridge, to Alan

Beloved,

You've been gone 9 months today & I am regarding it as half way. Even if this isn't quite correct the extra fortnight won't make a lot of difference at the good end & I just can't wait any longer for half time! I've had such a wonderful day's mail. I've had two long sea letters & the tea, handkerchiefs etc. which are just grand. Thank you very very much for thinking of taking the trouble to send such a nice parcel. The letters were a joy. The photos - well all I can say is no wonder the small boy was afraid of you! Dear One, I'll live anywhere you want & where you are happy, I know I shall be also. I too love the country & when there get a great kick from a short visit to town. I think the only thing in the world I'd like to have been is an archaeologist, which is a bit irrelevant! But the places I most want to go to are Greece & Asia Minor & we must go there. Yes the idea of 60 days holiday are very attractive for although I go mostly in discomfort a lot on my two legs or better still bicycle & live mostly on bread there are places in the world I must and will see. Well beloved I'll add to this later. I must get the children ready to go out to tea with the Clarks.

Saturday 15th June

It's dreadfully cold & unsettled again. Your parents & Moira spent yesterday afternoon with us, & we are going to have lunch with them tomorrow. I see them often as I go along to the hotel any time I am down at the shops. It's such a shame they can't get about at all as there are such lovely spots all round but all have to be walked to, quite short distances really, but of course quite beyond your mother & Moira.

Poor Moira looks very frail indeed & I wish it would get a bit warmer while she is here. I had your cable of the 13th today & feel pleased with myself. Beloved in your long *sacrifice* letter you commented on your lack of close friends, but I am in the same position, for years you alone have filled my life & I am completely lost without you. I miss you even more than I fully realise & I think, for sometimes I get unbearably on edge & nearly bite even my very precious boy's heads off. It's such an awful age yet until you come but surely when it gets to the stage of just a . . . . . [1]

14ᵗʰ Jun 1944, Alan, WAF, Achimota, to Robert

My Dear Robert,

I'm afraid that it is a long time since I wrote to you but Sheila will have been telling you what I have been doing for I have written often to her. She will have said I was on a canoe on a river. The black boys cut down a large tree then they cut off the branches, take the bark off and hollow it out until it is the shape of the canoe you see in the photographs I send. I am outside my little home & Jeremiah is making my bed ready for the night. It's much nicer to sleep outside here for it is very hot at nights. Kiss David for me and tell him I hope he is learning to talk well.

Kiss Mummy too. Daddy

15ᵗʰ Jun 1944, Sheila, Nethybridge, to Alan

My Very Dear,

Yesterday I had your two interesting letters of 4th June. I do hope you don't get ill over your "mosquito trials" it all sounds bit grim & I hope your dysentery passed off as quickly as you hoped when you wrote. Last time you wrote of being very tired and wondering how you were going to get through everything you landed up in hospital & I await your next letter with some anxiety. I feel you can't be wholly well when you write of it being bad to be where you are when "other men are proving themselves". It's so absolutely lunatic for you of all people to be worrying about an extraordinary thing like that. If you were sitting here with me then I could understand, but as things are it's absurd & you know it. Then about the cryptic "gesture" about "a job" well I may as well be honest & say right away that I am glad in every bit of me that abstract loyalty did not win. I can't think it was your conscience that was worrying you so much as the idea that people would think you were funking it, which is of course inconceivable to anyone

---

[1] The Letter Card is full and stops abruptly. There must have been a 'follow up' but I don't have it.

knowing you even slightly. I understand that you are bound to have two loyalties, but it will help you to realise my attitude is not obscure if you ask yourself how you would react if I also developed another loyalty. Courage & bravery in men strike a response in me, the unstintingness & intensity of which has always been quite beyond my understanding & I am perfectly satisfied with my husband. I know him very well, he is the father of my sons & they too have every reason to be proud. I quite see & as a matter of fact wrote some time ago that you couldn't have remained at home during this affray, neither of us could have been happy, but don't for my sake beloved be miserable when there is no need.

Yesterday we went by bus to Aviemore with the parents as Daddy wanted to see Mr Ross (of the hotel) it was a nice change & we had an excellent tea in the little tea room. You never saw anything more desolate than the hotel, vacated but not given up by the military. The usual scene of broken windows & smashed woodwork & the grounds a wilderness. How on earth do they do it? Today we have felt it was almost summer! I was actually *[Illegible]* [1]

16th Jun 1944, Alan, WAF, Achimota, to Sheila

Sea Mail

My Very Dear,

It's 5 o'clock and I'm sitting stripped to the waist on the balcony of my bungalow after eight days out here. Tomorrow I go back to G.HQ. I shall be glad to get back to get your letters but I am well content to stay here and walk through the bush & go up and down in canoes & return for an early dinner here, some reading, some work and an early bed.

I've read through Island Farm which you sent me but oh beloved it is almost sore to read. I agree with you that it does not ring true in places. I for one could not write such a book for profit while my peers were in the services. I have no desire to meet Fraser Darling or even to see Tanera but reading it over again strengthens my determination, which has been growing ever since the war started,

---

[1] This letter just stops and there is another page somewhere, so let's hope it just turns up.

to live in the country after the war.

All my instincts shout out to me to grab you and get away from people. I will presently be getting pretty near forty when the war is over. My employment during the war had made it certain that my only line of advancement in medicine would be in Public Health. So employed I might, between 45 & 50, with a great deal of luck, get a post at £1,500 per annum. If the war had not come I might have gone a little further. Now that is not riches.

In the Highlands & Islands medical service I could earn between £900 & £1,200 according to the district. We would have a good life, a useful life and above all we could keep planning together the little things which make living so good.

The boys would have a healthy place to live. One can take holidays up to 60 days in the year in the Highlands & Islands service provided that a locum is found. In time if necessary we could get our own electric light plant going. Paraffin "fridges" are perfectly satisfactory. They are used in hundreds out here. We would have a telephone and a car. Think of the places where there are H&I Med Service doctors. Skye West, Torridon, Gairloch, Ullapool, Lochinver, Scourie, Tongue, Bettyhill & so on. Any one of them would be grand. Please tell me what you really think. Don't think I'm getting carried away and I'm certainly not suggesting that I feel that only in H&I would I be content. I have no ambition in my profession at all - none.

M.O.H of a Highland County would be next best. I wonder what unkind fate interfered so as not to let me even be considered for Ross-shire. That would have been a very pleasant job.

Well now to bath - it will be welcome for I have a devil of a lot of bites from various queer insects on me. I must say though that nothing out here compares with the midges of the Highlands.

Are my glasses rose tinted? No I know the answer now to killing & repelling midges.

I was reduced to stripping to the skin in bush today when a lot of red ants dropped off a tree. They are about 1/4 inch long and each has a red hot poker instead of a sting! The monkeys are very funny in the woods. You hear them often then you see them but they sometimes sit up a tree and simply foam at the mouth with rage at you.

7.15 P.M.

I've just written three Airgraphs, to Mummy, to Robert and to David. It's dark but my Tilley lamp gives a good light on the veranda. I wish the crickets did not make quite such a noise. The silent tropical night is all baloney. The frogs are croaking, the crickets are "clicking", whistling and screeching and there is a fruit bat in the distance making its unworldly yelling like a child being strangled ha, ha, ha, ha, ha, ha. HA!

I was presented with a basket full of oranges in a village today. The oranges were lying rotting all over the village & the headman said they seldom ate them. They are the most delicious sweet oranges I think I ever tasted. I also purchased sweet corns on the cob for twopence. This was gross profiteering.

I also got a dozen eggs here in the village. The eggs here are small. I'm having two corn cobs & six poached eggs for supper tonight. Inevitably the VAT 69 & soda bottle are at my right hand! It's very pleasant this drink of whisky soda as the sun goes down.

I'm looking forward to developing my seven films when I get back to G.HQ I hope to have enough shortly for a small article with photographs on the forest village folk.

Time is the great difficulty. It really is quite impossible to do all I want to do.

8.30 PM

Beloved the most amusing thing happened after dinner tonight. I had shown Jeremiah how to make coffee properly a couple of times - before that it was a question of whether I was getting coffee, stew or yellow water. Well my method was to heat a jug & put in the coffee, then pour boiling water on it & finally for want of anything better to filter it by means of an enamel funnel & a little cotton wool into my cup.

Tonight I said. "Now Jeremiah you pass coffee for me tonight". So after dinner a very nervous & important Jeremiah appeared &

the cook came to watch. He did it <u>exactly</u> as I had - perfectly only he put nothing in the funnel! When I asked him why he did not put in any cotton wool he replied. "no have de cotton wool master". It's so easy to forget how very ignorant the poor boys are and so easy to get angry with them. When they don't understand but rush off wildly & do something. Yet if one can have patience they are really most anxious to please. They are <u>very</u> lazy but there is something very likeable about them. They react very well to clownish jesting as when I sent Jeremiah to the cook the other day to enquire whether "his mammy ever go drop him on head when he was small picanini!" Old Jeremiah came back grinning from ear to ear & said "He say no sah".

As the mosquitos are very bad here I gave Jeremiah an old mosquito net for I did not want him down with an attack of malaria. He is very delighted with this.

They always take the hardest possible thing to sleep on. He sleeps on a concrete slab, the top of an old well under the bungalow (the bungalow is on stilts).

The net was suspended from above. They are very childish in the pleasure it gives them to imitate Europeans. A pair of boots which gives their feet hell will be worn on all possible occasions while some of the headdresses have to be seen to be believed. Gaudy diced red white and blue caps are very favoured while any kind of topee - some I think relics of last century - makes a man well dressed.

It's pitiful really. In one village I asked an English speaking boy to take me through bush to another village. He said "Massa wait small till I dress". Well he looked well with just a piece of calico print draped round him the corner thrown over his shoulder but he disappeared & emerging again wore an appalling pair of torn cheap khaki shorts & a cheap print shirt with its tail hanging down outside. Excuse the smears. They are drops of "flit"[1]. I was just clearing a path in the most incredible variety of insects which are attracted to the light.

---

[1] Flit was a popular liquid fly killer sprayed from a 'flit gun'.

You will remember that I'm keeping a diary I add to it from time to time. It is in the form of a letter to the boys but it has really developed into a letter to you.

Oh Sheila my Dear if you only knew how much you are in my mind. In the morning when I wake, dozens of times during the day & always I go to sleep thinking of you. I had a dreadful nightmare recently. We were not married & you were refusing to marry me. There was someone else who did not appear. The awfulness of it, the utter emptiness of everything, were terrible. Oh my Dear one I was stupid and absurdly possessive before we were married but I know now it was inevitable. You were so incredibly precious and valuable to me that I could not avoid being miserly in my outlook. It was in 1930 I suppose that I first met you and in 1932 (July) that I went to Dublin & I had asked you to marry me in late autumn 1932 12 years ago. How much we both must have changed in all things but in loving each other since then.[1]

I shall tell you something I've never told you before Beloved. When I left you the night I asked you to marry me, I for a few hours then and never since, felt sorry. I felt I had given up my freedom and tied myself up for I had great ambitions of doing things (even if I did pose as a lover of the vegetable existence). I did not sleep & really only the instant I saw you again did the feeling pass away never to return. When I saw you I accepted kismet[2]. I never liked to tell you for it always seemed wrong and disloyal but Oh my Dear precious Sheila it was just a very passing phase and I'm sure you felt the same.

I only knew you then as the loveliest person I'd ever seen, as a pleasant companion, as all I ever had imagined & wanted in the way of womanliness; yet it did not occur to me to want to kiss you. Oh

---

[1] So when they first met in 1930 Alan (born 27th Jan 1909) was 21 and Sheila (born 2nd August 1913) was 17. They got engaged when he was 23 & she 19. Alan at that stage had still about 5 years before he was fully qualified. I think this may have been at the root of Mamie's reservations about Alan being able to support her daughter when they got engaged.

[2] 'Kismet' of course means fate, destiny or fortune in a number of languages including Arabic and Turkish.

my Dear I'm glad you were my first woman. It made my standards so high that nothing else would do.

It will be at least 10 ½ months until I see you - less when this reaches you - but I know I have only to look into your eyes and hold you for a second in my arms for all the intervening period to be as naught and we to be to each other as before.

I shall be a very contented person after the war; and we beloved, as we grow older, will never I know have any troubles for there is and has been always too much frankness between us - too little restraint & artificiality to let the passing years change our affection. We have had very little restraint between us My Dear. No more than loving minds and opinions of our own and neither being submerged intellectually by the other.

Oh it's odd to be sitting out here and musing on the love I bear you and on the tenderness that comes over me whenever I think of you.

Never never doubt that I love you Sheila. Something nasty & bitter comes over me sometimes. Always when I have a guilty conscience about doing something not quite right. I have visited my spite at myself on you in the past but you have been patient & decent to me & I love you always. Oh Sheila I crave your respect first in all the world, then my own & then that of our children.

Yours will always be too easily come by while you love me. The children will be and rightly, critical of their father. You see out here I have no-one at all to whom I am myself for I'm only that to you.

As you know I have for some temperamental reason never had very close friends, never a friend any considerable degree closer to me than other people. You are all my friends and all my love and passion. I'm glad that Robert and David will have each other. It would have been so good for me to have a brother. Dear one I hope that when you get this letter it can convey to you however poorly how much I love and cherish you. My Dear I'm so much happier for writing it, it's good for me to melt from time to time into the atmosphere of goodness & peace and happiness which you have always, always conveyed to me.

Your loving husband, Alan

19ᵗʰ Jun 1944, Alan, WAF, Achimota, to Sheila

Letter Card

My Very Dear,

I returned here on 17ᵗʰ to find two letters awaiting me. I'm glad to hear you are settled at Dell Farm & hope the weather has improved & with it the apparent gloominess of the place. You will like the second pair of sandals better & I hope the leather work arrives safely. It's odd because the leather was sent before the others. I'm delighted to hear of you getting Burton's books & My Dear thank you very much for sending the albums. I'm looking forward immensely to getting my very large collection safely lodged. Oh it's odd, to think that if it is really so, that Robert misses me. I miss him you know. Had a long letter from Mummy. Robert & David mean so very much to Mummy & Daddy & her letter just reeks of the affection they have for you all. Your ears would tingle if you knew how she praises you and your boys. Oh Sweetheart of mine the Gods were very kind to me when I met you.

The rains continue & fungus grows in my shoes overnight! I had a wonderful time while I was away & hope to go back later this week for a few days. I'm enjoying Mungo Park. What an amazingly tough time he had and how he stuck at it! Oh Beloved I'd love to follow his route across the hinterland.

The "*Coasters Log*" is not very good. He had very little insight into the people & even I know much more now about their ways of living than he does.

It will be nice for you to have your parents & Aunt & Uncle near you.

I'll send another letter tomorrow when I hope to have another mail in. I'll also send photographs. I believe the ordinary mail letters are getting home nearly as quickly as the air mail cards.

Love Alan

19ᵗʰ Jun 1944, Sheila, Nethybridge, to Alan

Dear Beloved,

The last two days have been really summer & I am enjoying it! The only thing is that the flies have decided it's summer too, how wonderful to have hot weather & no flies in the house. The boys are having a great time, we spent this afternoon at the river & I am hoping to teach Robert to swim before the summer is out. I do so wish you could see them, Robert takes David away to gather fir cones for the fire or he will take him away up the wee burn (a very wee wee one!) near the house. I lost them for a short time this morning & in the end found them sitting side by side on a log near the hen house deep in what must have been a very peculiar conversation!

I'm sure you can't imagine that you have such a perfect second son as you have, it's such a joy to see him so big & beefy & full of fun after his poor start.

I am now in constant touch with Baylies about the car which they never looked near after last Oct until I gingered them up in the early spring, I won't let them rest again. They say it's alright but will deteriorate quickly unless the roof is put right. I've arranged for that to be done & altho' Sanderson says he won't pay believe me he will. He (Sanderson) says he wants to sell the house & would like me to buy it! [1] In any case he cannot in the terms of the agreement give us notice until Oct to become effective in April & even then couldn't put me out these days. I sent to Savill & K. sometime ago for a copy of the agreement & am well versed in everything particularly his responsibility for roofs!

I've just been cleaning three minute trout caught on the river this afternoon which I promised your eldest son for his breakfast & had quite forgotten about. Now I'm off to bed nicely weathered & glowing with the sun, I'd forgotten it felt so good. I lay on the sand for a long time with my eyes shut this afternoon trying to imagine I was at the croft. Beloved I wear the gold chain you sent me a great

---

[1] Alan's car was laid up in the garage at 66 Manygates Lane for the duration of the war, but the roof of the garage was leaking and Baylies (a local garage) had reported there was a danger this would damage the car, a convertible. On approaching the house's owner, Sanderson, he had refused to pay to repair the roof, so Sheila had sent to 'Savill & K' (lawyers or letting agency?) to check on the tenancy agreement. I had often wondered if the house was rented or if they owned it.

deal & it has been much admired.

Love Sheila

20th Jun 1944, Alan, WAF, Achimota, to Sheila

Letter Card

My Beloved,

Your letters dated June 7th & 9th have just arrived and only you could possibly realise how much pleasure they gave me. I'm so glad you are liking Nethy Bridge so much. Oh how I would love to join the tribe wandering through the paths in Abernethy Forest and picking up stones & violets. I'm glad you are happy there. I love the bits about David & the hens. Yes "Baba chooks" is just perfect.

It's grand to hear that you are feeling the tonic of Highland air again. I'm not worried about grey hairs & wrinkles: <u>firstly</u> ever since I have known you I have heard about them, <u>secondly</u> I've never seen them, <u>thirdly</u> something happens when I look at you that dissolves time & place & eternity & <u>fourthly</u> I don't care a dam about anything so long as you love me.

Poor old Robert falling into the burn - a very necessary part of his education! Yes Beloved two very nice letters for your good man to receive. I also had one from Bobby.

I'm afraid the leather bags, the leather cushions & the canoe must have been stolen. It's very annoying for they were the things I most wanted to get to you. I shall order another canoe but you will have to wait till I'm next in Malandain's country for the leather. I've enjoyed Mungo Park immensely. Much of his description is of ways of living totally unchanged today.

I've sent cheques to Wakefield Corporation for £80 for superannuation & to Income Tax Wakefield on Royalties for £39 so don't get a shock when the bank balance comes in. Are you managing it all on the £40? <u>Please </u>draw cheques for your extra needs.

I sent you & Robert photographs & I'm frantically trying to get time to sort out all I have. I love you very much, Alan

25th Jun 1944, Sheila, Nethybridge, to Alan

My Beloved,

It's over a week since I heard of you & I'm so spoilt with letters that I get quite fidgety when it gets over a week without one. I've got a miserable feeling you've been ill but I'm probably barmy. The Malaria Suppression paper has arrived & I enjoyed reading it although of course a good deal of it was above my head. Still as I say I did enjoy having the chance of reading it, thank you for sending it to me & I'll now dispatch it to Moira.

Beloved before I forget to tell you, the farmer's wife discovered Robert coming out of the hen house yesterday with a dripping can in his hand & found all her sitting hens soaking wet! On being collared he just said he didn't like eggs anyway.

We had a nice day on Saturday. We went down to the hotel about 11 am & found Daddy had ordered a car to take us to Grantown, I having casually remarked the day before that I'd have to go in some day. It was a lovely day & the children fortunately had their best bib & tuckers on although we had only intended calling at the hotel & coming straight home. The boys got their hair cut & I got a few things I needed & we got back to the hotel for lunch at 1.15. It was David's first effort at lunching out but he was very good & only howled once when he insisted on tasting my gin & lime! There are a lot of children at the hotel & they all played in the gardens afterwards for a while then the parents walked home with us & had tea here. David fell asleep very abruptly in his pram a thing he hasn't done since infancy & slept profoundly for about half an hour. I think he enjoyed his day more than anyone! He now says "Daddy in aff", "bread for chooks", "Oh! Look rain" - "Oh horse" or "man" Oh whatever it is & so on.

When peace comes I ask you solemnly not to let me flag from my fixed intention of either getting our cine camera repaired or as soon as possible getting a new one. It would be so dreadful when I got old to think I could see the children again as they were & the expressions on their faces & aliveness & had simply neglected the chance of preserving it.

Robert sends his love. Yours ever, Sheila

28th Jun 1944, Alan, WAF, Achimota, to Sheila

Letter Card

My Beloved,

I have delayed sending this hoping that the mail would be in from you in time to answer. It has not arrived & this must be posted today.

I was in High Society last night! I was invited to dine with Lord Swinton[1] the Resident Cabinet Minister & then to a concert. It was a very good dinner & the concert promised boldly "Songs by Major McLusky U.S. Army" - was superb. He is a professional opera singer and he sang Brahms songs and operatic Arias superbly. All society was there, the Governor and his wife, the senior service representatives. Some government officials. Prominent Africans & many half caste, quadroons & octoroons & some Syrians & Indians. The outstanding impression to me was the strangeness of seeing women of so many different colours!

But Beloved I wanted to have you there. There are too many "hard faced bitches" in this world & I love you.

I'm still here half time & bush cutting & swamp clearing the other half. I have been given a "jeep" to myself. That is a great convenience & makes me quite independent. I go back tomorrow for 10 days or so. I'm greatly hoping that your letters will come in today.

My Dear I don't think I've ever as long as I have lived been in such good form mentally. I find so much of engrossing interest everywhere. It's so odd to find that well over half of ones fellows are cursing & swearing at the climate & hoping for the day when they see Africa for the last time. I'm aching to get home but I should be sorry to think I'll never see W. A. again. Beloved in Celestial Spheres we shall join the Geographical Society. Oh I love you, Alan

1st Jul 1944, Sheila, Nethybridge to Alan

Letter Cards 1, 2 & 3

---

[1] Lord Swinton (Phillip Cunliffe-Lister) with the title of Minister Resident in West Africa was referred to by the African Press as Resident British Minister in West Africa.

My Beloved,[1]

I had your two lovely letters written from the shack bungalow on June 9th & they gave me great amusement! I should love to be "raped" in wicker chair in jungle setting, to add to my collection of odd places for such activities! I shall show the first letter to your family as requested but refuse to say anything about VAT 69 unless they show signs of obvious terror, or they will think surely that my unasked for reassurance probably covers some consternation of my own! In any case it's delicate ground for me to tread. But I feel they should have the pleasure of your letter. Beloved I love you just dreadfully & more & more & more. I shall be a complete clinging vine when you come home. The boys are very well. David has at last decided to get a move on with his last four teeth & has one through & the others showing signs of activity. He has however a very sore mouth & it's making him a bit pale & inclined to go about with his whole hand stuffed in his mouth! I had such a silly day yesterday. I rushed round & got things done here (maid arrived today thank goodness) then beat it down the mile & a bit to the shops with the children (Robert on tricycle) got my weekend ordering done then collected mother from the hotel & went along to see a most beautiful old house which she was keen for me to see as it's to let with attendance & they thought of going in the autumn & Daddy was trying to persuade me to go too & have a rest. However that's by the way, we saw the house & had an awful rush back to the hotel where we were having lunch. I got half way through mine including a gin & some foul fizzing lemon stuff & as suddenly as if I'd been poisoned I began to feel dreadful. My legs just got me the length of the parent's bed & there I remained for the next two hours prostrate with pain& nausea. Mother removed home two boys, a tricycle & a pram & at 4.30 Daddy removed me in a taxi, I convinced I was dying & was astonished at . . . . .

---

[1] This letter is actually three letter cards but written as a single letter.
Alan's letter, to which this replies, was sent on 9th June air letter card and arrived, or was replied to, 1st July. So it took around 20 days!

Continued on Letter card 2

managing to get the length of the taxi at all! Being shaken up in the car seemed to do me a power of good & after an hour or so in a chair I was ready for duty again! Today I'm a bit weak at the knees but otherwise fine. I think gin is a most virulent potion when mixed with certain things & remember your misery after taking it with orange juice at Britford. Anyway I blame the gin having felt very full of beans until half way through lunch.

It's a dreadful night raining in torrents, how wonderful it would be here with a half decent climate.

Perhaps by now the blow will have fallen & my Polyphotos will have arrived. I hope you aren't too nasty about it, because I've been very sweet about your photos & never ever said a word about the one with the hat turned up all round! I've sent off Wandering's in W.A. (Burton). I shall be very interested to hear what you think of it for I must confess I found it distinctly tedious. Probably having seen the places will carry you through it with more gusto. Of course there are interesting bits but the style is very poor. I've just finished rather a dull book on "Sheridan". I'll send it on too. I've written to Smith's asking them to send you Darling's "Island Years". I know you'll enjoy it.

You'll soon have been away for 9 months beloved & I'll feel a corner turned, but it does seem a long time only to be half way. The maid I spoke of as having arrived is Mrs Whitelaw, a cockney, who worked for mother in the mornings last winter & for a short time came to me at Queens Gate. She liked being with us so volunteered to come up here for two months on hearing of Mrs Burrows defection. She has had to bring her twelve year old daughter with her but it's a big house & she seems a nice child & plays beautifully with Robert. Also they will be company for each other, any normal maid would never stand the isolation here. Mrs B. nearly swooned when she discovered she'd have to use her legs to cover the mile to the twice a week picture house & decided after a fortnight instead of the month, that she was going home.

I told her she could pay her own way back in that case & then she contrived to lose her wages . . . . .

Continued on Letter card 3

on her way to the station & after sending a small boy up with a note to that effect & nothing forthcoming from me, a policeman arrived to ask me about her as she had reported the loss & he seemed to think there was something fishy about the story. I asked if she was stuck at the station but he said no she had plenty of money to get home & when I told him why she was getting left to find her own way he said "Oh! She's one of those is she" then asked where her husband was, which seemed beside the point, but as I only knew he was somewhere in Canada wasn't much help. So that was the end of Burrows. She had lost interest in the children & everything else latterly altho' she was very good with them at first. I think she had a secret sorrow. Happy indeed are those who employ no one. Anyhow there's nothing dour about Mrs Whitelaw & I hope she lasts the two months! I don't know why I'm so appallingly gossipy tonight beloved, I expect you quite limp by this time.

Gracious I nearly forgot to thank you for your cable. Strange it was sent off the day I sent you asking for one. I'd been some time without a letter & I was longing for up to date news that all was well with you. Bill Stephens is still in this country. The K.L.[1] people are all sleeping in the kitchen in an effort to keep out of the way of flying bombs. It's hard to know how bad things are but one has the feeling they are quite trying.

Sunday 2nd

It's been a lovely day for a change & we've had two fine walks. I'm just back from the hotel having cycled down for dinner. It's the first time I've been down in the evening & I've enjoyed the change. Mrs Kennedy is going to send us a turkey & a tree next Christmas - nothing like preparing in advance!

Well Dear I'm very very sleepy now & I'm just going to drop into bed read "*N. Gubliners*"[2] & then to sleep. I wish I could dream of you more, when I do they are always such impossible dreams & situations. I love you, Sheila

---

[1] Kensington Lodge, Oaklands Park - Surrey, I think.
[2] I have no idea what she was reading. Just can't make it out. Dubliners?

5th Jul 1944, Alan, WAF, Achimota, to Sheila

Letter Card

My Very Dear,

I had to leave G.HQ before the last mail, which was delayed, had arrived & so I'm not able to answer any letters. I have been sweating on the top line on this anti-malarial experiment which is extremely important & seems to be giving Richardson a nervous breakdown. The rain has been terrific about 2- 3 <u>inches</u> a day & I have been completely soaked every day since Friday. Even the Jeep cannot tackle the flooding & I just have to flounder along on Shank's mare. The innumerable small troubles of getting people paid, especially my labourers, & keeping the lorries & motor bikes on the road would be a sick headache alone. But the two sergeant entomologists I have with me are both *nice* BScs & <u>highly</u> educated, nevertheless they have as much push & guts as lice. They moan like sick children when anything goes wrong & wait with great patience for me to come & <u>do</u> something about it. However the work slowly progresses & my only outstanding troubles are two complaints that my labourers stole. A. Sugar Cane & B. Corn cobs from fields & a police charge of attempted rape by one of my African Soldiers! Well boys will be boys & no doubt it will all come right.

Oh Beloved I'm longing for news of you. What are you going to do after the end of this month? Could you stay on at Nethybridge?

Four days ago I completed eight months & I'm romping along toward the halfway mark. I'm wondering if the latest parcels have arrived. I have some South African jam & marmalade parcelled up ready to send to you.

Tell Robert I'm very busy but will write soon & tell him all about the black men with whom I'm working here.

Kiss them both, I love you, Alan

7th Jul 1944, Sheila, Nethybridge, to Alan

Letter Card

My Dear,

I have had a letter from Steven[1] asking if you would like a job in Carlisle. I shall give you word for word the part of the letter dealing with the subject as follows -

"I don't know Alan's position in regard to Wakefield but the M.O.H. for the city of Carlisle is very ill & will never be back at work. I wondered if you would be interested in me keeping you alive to the possibilities. I know of one case when someone in the forces applied for and has been appointed to a job which he will take up after the war. It is likely that the appointment will be deferred till after the war, but if it were advertised just now what is Alan's position? I should be thrilled with the prospect of your coming here - of course Alan maybe does not want to leave Wakefield or may feel bound to go back. I don't know but there is no harm in letting you know of the prospect. Actually the M.O.H. may die so don't say anything to outsiders yet. It feels too like waiting for dead men's shoes but I should hate to think we had missed an opportunity. The salary is I believe about £1,200."

Well beloved there it is, you may look at it & say simply "no good", on the other hand you may feel you want to say to me "what do you think". If you know at once it's no good you need take no notice of the following for you know that I shall be in complete agreement with you. What I think, is this - If it is possible to live outside the city boundaries I think it's a pretty sound idea, because 1. You do not wish to put the clock back & work in Wakefield. 2. While not our ideal geographically, we would have a much better chance of stepping off from there in time to something nearer it, than you would after the war with the civilian appointment as assistant of Wakefield. 3. The salary is almost double is it not to what you would return to? I am presuming that the alternative is to start off again at Wakefield & try for a change from there which

---

[1] This is Steven Faulds, grandson of John Steven & Agnes Henderson, brother of Nancy (Agnes) Faulds, thus Steven & Nancy were Sheila's cousins. Nancy was a great childhood friend of Sheila's.

might well take many months.

I may be quite wrong & you need have no hesitation in correcting me. I know how you want to live in the country, so do I, but there are nice places a few miles out of Carlisle & it is in the centre of good country. Anyhow I shall hear what you think. Meanwhile I shall write Steven & tell him you are in no way tied to Wakefield but that we wish to live in the country & what are the chances of that. If you wish to write to him his address is "Eden Chester" Warwick Bridge, Cumberland.

If you come to an immediate decision in the matter it might be as well to cable me. Say "Eden Chester yes" or "Eden Chester no" & I could tell Steven at once. All Love, Sheila

8th Jul 1944, Alan, WAF, Achimota, to Sheila

Letter Card 1

My Very Dear Sheila,

I returned by air today after another week in bush. I went straight to the office for your letters and oh the joy to find no less than seven from you. Five air cards, the photos and the Wakefield Corporation one.

I am only here for a few days & then off again & I'm going to have a hectic time here. Firstly Beloved I'm <u>very</u> fit, never fitter. Everyone says "by Jove Steve you <u>do</u> look well" when I come back.

I'm so brown with being out while everyone else is so pale, especially in this wet season, that I feel like a lion amongst lambs when people grumble about prickly heat & such bothers. So you need not worry that I am about to go into hospital! My cable would have crossed with yours so you would not be worried for long.

I'll answer your letters tomorrow for tonight I'm just rocking with sleep. I spent all morning in a mangrove swamp and then flew back. But Oh my precious one I'm taking your photographs to bed with me. I am <u>so</u> glad to have them at last.

Sunday 9/7

Now, well slept and having broken the back of the accumulated work I can begin answering your letters. The first is that of June 4th.

It's so lovely to read about David & Robert playing in wee burns. I can still feel the joy & peace of such plays thirty years ago (Beloved I'm definitely an old man) and oh why did I miss the excitement at the wee salmon parr.

Yours of June 12th. I'll send more sugar & try butter. I have jam & marmalade and I shall send it off. I hope your swollen gum did not cause any more trouble. Beloved you need me to look after you.

15th June.

All I can say is "love me still & know not why" for beloved your man falls so very much below your opinion of him. Aviemore Hotel now sounds in a terrible state. I adore you, Alan

9th Jul 1944, Alan, WAF, Achimota, to Sheila
Letter Card - Continuing No 1 of 8th & 9th

My Dear,

Your next letter is dated 19th June. Oh I hope Robert does learn to swim for then David will follow suit. Tell him I hope he can learn soon for when I come back we will all be going in wee boats and then if he is to go out in a boat by himself he must be able to swim.

It's good to hear how well David is growing up. Beloved remember when you said "But there will never be another Robert". How true - there never will be but in another sense how wrong - they are both loved for themselves.

Thank you very much for seeing about the car. I don't like Sanderson's talk of a sale. I'd hate to be homeless! If in doubt ask Baylies to take the car away and store it in their own garage. Why not ask Sanderson what he wants for the house. It would be a reasonable investment - through a Building Society - if not too expensive.

I'm glad you wear my chain - it's pure gold as you are but not fine enough for so dear a neck as yours.

25th June (Your letter)

I'm so sorry that you were worried about the delayed mail & I hope my cable & letters arrived soon to put your mind at rest. I liked the story of Robert & the wet hens!

Beloved my first present to you after the war is a 16mm cine camera - it's a promise. The anthropology of the "tribe" must I agree be recorded.

Now I must get on with some more work. The files have piled up while I have been writing. I've had a terrific amount of real bush work in the last month but it's been fun & an experience I'd hate to have missed. I'll tell you all about it in a surface mail letter which I shall write tonight. Kiss my boys, Alan

9th Jul 1944, Alan, WAF, Achimota, to Sheila

Sea Mail

My Very Own Dear,

As I promised in the second of my air letters today I am writing a longer letter to tell you of my doings. But firstly more about your photographs. I like them Beloved. They are like you & therefore attractive & bright & nice. It's a pity the numbers are not on them for I'd so love an enlargement. True to your instincts you have cut out all which you do not think flattering. I must just make an enlargement from the prints.

Its 8.30 PM & the cinema is on but I'm back to write to you & then read the grand books you sent to me. I'm reading the Golden Thread & then I'm going to tackle "Northern Antiquities". Oh Sheila how many men have wives who would send so many books which cry out to be read.

I've just been flooded out in my experimental area. Fifteen inches of rain in five days changed the landscape a bit.

Then one of the bridges in the small road leading to the villages was broken down by one of my lorries and simply floated away on the flood! Just to cap that I had a sergeant marooned in a village surrounded by water without a mosquito net and without food. It teemed & poured until everything was either soaking or covered with mould. The most weird insects appeared & birds & small animals driven out by the floods were buzzing about in the open. It washed away nearly all of my carefully marked mosquito breeding places and so spoiled a large slice of work.

I expect to be able to stay only for a few days out this time. I want to get back here for a spell for there are so many things to do.

My Dear sleep is overwhelming me & I'm going to bed. I can't keep my eyes open.

10.7.44 8.20 AM

Sorry my Dear about last night - I read in bed for about one minute then turned over & did not wake until 6.45 AM.

Have had breakfast and am about to start the day's work. Beloved you would so love the mornings here. The air is so soft and warm. I get up & wander about my room drinking tea and shaving slowly. Then I go up to breakfast & dawdle over that. Dear I want desperately to take you overseas after the war to see things with me. I'm sending you a booklet "Introducing West Africa" which will interest you.

Just discovered a number on the back of the Polyphoto "50550". Well now to work. Kiss my boys, Alan

12ᵗʰ Jul 1944, Alan, WAF, Achimota, to Sheila

Air Mail

My Beloved,

I had three letters last night and I'm particularly glad to have them firstly because I could answer them & get today's mail & secondly because I hope to be back here for the next batch next Tuesday.

The film albums have arrived and are exactly what I wanted but did not even hope for in war time. Thank you very much.

I'm so sorry to hear of your bad time at the hotel. Oh my dear you need me to look after you. I hope there have been no returns. I hope David's mouth is better too.

You are very good sending books to me and I really enjoy them so much. It's bad luck about your servant difficulties. I hope the new one is a success.

Have you any plans for August onwards? Try to keep in the country if you can.

I've been trying frantically to get my book amendments and additions finished. I have not managed but will take the stuff out to bush with me. There I'm always so wrapped in the blessed tiredness that follows exercise in the open air that in the evenings I'm only just able to stagger to bed at 9 o'clock. Professor *Burton* my constant companion now is a grand old boy. He is so knowledgeable about all nature and is so very well read. He is fortunately (or says he is) pleased with my preliminary work and Wiggy who was very worried over the importance of it all is delighted. I have the four new appendices for the book and one new chapter. As all first edition is now sold there will probably be quite a decent cheque coming to you for the six months ending June.

Well sweetheart mine. Remember I love living, I enjoy myself, I am interested in many things but I have one passion. My own, dear, you. Alan

15th & 16th Jul 1944, Sheila, Nethybridge, to Alan

Air Mails 1, 2 & 3

[The first of the two Lettercards, Saturday 15th July, is missing]
Continuation - Air Mail 2
. . . . . few months it will suddenly fly. I do wish I could count on the war being over but I'm not very optimistic. Beloved I'm sure you'll find something good in the job line after the war & I don't mean good only money sense. I must say the prospect of life as the wife of a G.P. in Scourie appals me! The country definitely yes, I agree fully but there is a happy medium. I don't think your growing sons would be very impressed with a home in just such a hinterland as that and what about schooling before you could pack them off to boarding school. I've seen enough highland school bumpkins going red in the face & tying themselves into knots since coming here to make me quite strong on the subject. We would thoroughly enjoy (at least I should) a year or so on a Fraser Darlingish island all the same but where is the excuse? A highland county would be excellent but I should think extremely difficult to land. This sounds odd after my meek announcement in the earlier part of my letter that I'll live anywhere you want but I still mean it & you know I

would. Only after spending night after night wrapped in mist & coldness here & thinking what a godforsaken spot it will be in the winter, Scourie & Bettyhill shook me considerably! The trouble is I simply can't imagine us settled anywhere for keeps, can you? I have very pleasant memories of the south which may, I admit may be a little enchanted by distance, but I did like it. The obvious glaring drawback to it is its distance from the north, which is I think quite a tragedy.

Oh! Beloved I love you. Do you remember how I loathed Wakefield at first & how unhappy I made you? I can't really feel I'm the same person as that shadowy foolish girl. I've learnt a lot the hard way since then. I do really think I'll be easier to live with now. Of course we've lived entirely different existences in the past few years, whether you desired it or no you've been places & seen things. I altho' profoundly grateful for the privilege of bringing up our children have been leading a necessarily monastic existence & sometimes do feel like seeing a little life before I'm quite grey & bespectacled. By "life" I don't mean anything very vivid but after five years of worry depression & fear I feel it would be distinctly beneficial to be within a few hours distance anyway of some of the simple diversions of life. Anyway it's very difficult to know what one does feel or want these days, when everything's upside down. All I am sure I do want is you home & then I'll be so new-fangled with having a husband I'll probably agree with . . . . .

Continuation - Lettercard 3
. . . . . everything you say! Oh I'd like to talk to you tonight. Beloved I really am quite amiable & I'll make our home any old where you like after all that's my job. I'm not a good woman but I do know some of my shortcomings & I do know that I am not cut out for membership of that band of women, which as you know I admire very much, wives of General Practitioners. I always felt that in Public Health I had a very lucky escape from a life which, as I loved you, it was very much on the cards would have come my way. On the other hand I would feel dammed to eternity if I thought I had dictated your life to you. Oh! Beloved I'm in such a muddle! Just

come home & everything will straighten out.

Your father & I had a mouse hunt in the sitting room yesterday. It was an outsize mouse. Your mother & Moira stationed themselves at the windows & we got down to it. I made a flying grab at it & fell full length, skinning my knee like a small girl & it got mixed up with your father's feet & with his feet about the poor mouse hadn't much chance & I was downright sorry for it. Well I'm almost asleep & it's really dark so I'm going upstairs to my candles. It's grand now that David can join us at table & what a difference at supper when two small boys sit & eat their eggs & bread & I sit & knit or just sit, very pleased that I'm not stuffing porridge into an unwilling baby. Sunday 16th

It's been a fine day & we've enjoyed some slight heat. We went down for lunch to the hotel & it all went off extra well. David behaved wonderfully well & was no trouble at all at lunch & astonished your people at the amount he put away! We sat in the gardens until tea time & the children played about beautifully & I was very bucked that they were so good for I know they can be otherwise! I didn't get back here until about 6 pm & was just putting two weary boys to bed, when Nonie arrived. He had cycled over from B. of Garten[1] where he arrived yesterday with a friend of Douglas Steven's. Douglas is due in a day or two. He (Nonie) had half an hour here then off again to be back to the hotel in time for dinner. I am going over to have tea with them on Wednesday. Your family are coming up for tea tomorrow. Beloved, know that I love you completely & always & for ever. Sheila[2]

16th Jul 1944, Alan, WAF, Achimota, to Sheila

Sea Mail

My Very Dear,

I've been back here from G. HQ since last Wednesday (12th) and oh such a lot has happened since then. I'll just tell you all about it

---

[1] B of G is Boat of Garten on River Spey.
[2] Much of this letter was distinctly emotional. The original, unlike Sheila's other letters with blots and a number of crossings out, is plainly written with some exasperation.

so you will have an idea of how I spend my time these days.

Well I arrived by air with Prof Burton about 2 o'clock. At 3 o'clock I started out to some of my administrative areas with a young engineer officer who was with me to see a broken bridge. I returned to the Hospital where I am staying about 7.30.

Alan. Bridge repair work at Winneba.

On Thursday I went out to the areas and got labourers on to strengthen and repair small bridges which had been damaged by floods. This was so that the heavy lorries could get down the track to repair the big bridge. On Friday ditto, found my soldiers (Europeans & Africans) and labourers. Had a lot of trouble with some of the bridges & ditched the Jeep twice.

Saturday

This was a very heavy long day in bush spotting mosquito breeding places and later seeing a new bridge placed in position by the engineers.

Today

I have been out mosquito breeding spotting again with the professor & took him to his vast delight on a river in a canoe.

Beloved when I had had a shower tonight & changed & was standing feeling all clean & cool in my shirt & shorts. I began to brush my hair & I hardly recognised myself in the mirror. Somehow I suppose I must have brushed my hair but I cannot remember seeing myself in a mirror for a very long time. I am a deep mahogany colour with the sun. My hair is getting fair again & I'm getting fat! I knew that I weighed 11 st 10 in a thin shirt & shorts but I must be more than that now. It's quite monotonous how when I get back to G.HQ people remark on how well I am. I suppose I've never felt fitter. I'm sure you would say I was looking better than I've ever looked except after five weeks in Achiltibuie.

This climate invigorates me, not as with so many people - the reverse. I <u>think</u> better & I really have worked physically hard in the past two months.

Oh Beloved if you could see me getting out of my Jeep in shorts & gum boots & hatless - I never take a driver - in one of these villages where I am well known. The folk come trooping out of their huts & two or three always bring me a present. A pineapple, some eggs, a few oranges or limes & so on are brought up & handed to me with great big smiles & greetings, which in the Nzema a speaking villages is "ya"-oh.

The women give an odd sort of curtsey when they give me anything & the men have much natural grace & dignity. Then the children will say 'ride motor'? And I take them on for a mile or so - as many as a dozen in & on the Jeep to the next village or a mile or so on the track. Then I drop them & they troop off happily back.

Paying out my labourers is really amazing - they are of a dozen different tribes & many have unpronounceable names. My efforts at calling out "Hassan Sarachanchi" or "K'tinga Fra-Fra" cause peals of laughter and then after a bit much of this I come on a pay roll name like "Brandy" just Brandy or Small Boy Koko (the classical funny names both seen by me in print are Lance Corporal Small Glass Ball and Private Bloody Fool).

Perhaps I enjoy all this so much because of the pure novelty & because it's so incredibly like what one read about West Africa - I don't know. What I do know is that I like the Africans. They are such cheerful happy go lucky toughs. Can you imagine a soldiers payout at home when a soldier advances to the table & salutes smartly & is given his pay & then asks (as he is entitled) for a further advance of pay - on being asked why he says he is in great debt due to the high cost of living (meaning women) in the village. On my refusing he salutes smartly & about turns. As he marches away I am horror stricken to see that he has no trousers on! I roar "Yao, come back here". He about turns smartly showing unmentionable parts protruding from a pair of minute bathing drawers under his hanging shirt. "Yao, where are your trousers?" "Master I no have chop one day two day - marrying take shorts for chop". Well even if it's all a lie he deserved his advance & got it.

Monday Jul 17th

I'm longing to get back to G.HQ for the air mail which will be in tomorrow, but I won't manage until Friday or Saturday.

The rains have abated meanwhile and the weather is delightful. Not too hot but with brilliant sun shine all day.

Oh My Dear I'm longing to hear what you are going to do after the end of this month. I suppose I had better send this letter to 6 North Gardner Street. I visited Ashly *Govan* who is Chief of Police here. Mummy met his mother in Bridge of Allan. You will be able to do some detective work[1] as to where I am.

I have two coconuts to send to the boys and I have sent you more tea & sugar & some marmalade. I'm trying very hard to get hold of some South African butter so as to be able to send it to you.

Now I must get down to breakfast.

Sheila I've had to write too many letters to you - surely we shall be able to live together in peace after the war instead of this

---

[1] The comment about the 'detective work' reminds us that Alan was never able to say where he actually was! The address Sheila writes to names no country or town, only W.A.F (West African Forces). Only on 31st July, see later letter, is it revealed that the G.H.Q is in Accra, Gold Coast (now Ghana).

miserable business of being separated.

I love you always & always, Alan

18th Jul 1944, Alan, WAF, Achimota, to Sheila

Air Mail

My Very Dear,

I expect that the ordinary letter I sent you yesterday will reach you as soon as this. I'm longing to get back to G.HQ to get your letters which will have arrived today.

I have told you all of my doings in the ordinary letter but today I was flying in a small plane seeing my work from the air. It was grand to see it all in the sun, the thick forest & the tiny paths after sweating there for so long. I'm extremely fit these days. This open air life makes twice the man of me as regards feeling fit.

I'm so wondering beloved what you are going to do after the end of this month. I'm longing to hear more about my boys. You know beloved I think they are "good uns" & I hope they grow up to continue to be as much of a joy to us as they promise. Oh the wicked waste of being away now!

I'm enjoying Antiquities of Northern Europe & will be glad to get back to G.H.Q to get on with the others you sent. The cigarettes are arriving regularly. This is a very disconnected sort of letter. I'm sorry beloved - I'll finish it later, somehow I seem to have nothing to say tonight.

8.40 P.M.

Well Beloved, I've had a good dinner and am getting that overwhelming sleepiness which always comes over me these nights after a day in the open. I shall be up and out at 6 A.M. tomorrow.

I'm terribly fond of my jeep.[1] What a joy it would be at Rieff. I think it could be taken all the way to Camusglashlan - but who wants cars at Camusglashlan? That's our place, not a cars place.

---

[1] Random capital letters, for example Jeep & jeep? I reproduce them as written.

Oh Beloved I would that B.F. at Strathpeffer[1] would hurry up and answer my letter. I love you, Alan[2]

20th Jul 1944, Sheila, Nethybridge, to Alan

20th Jul 1944, Sheila, Nethybridge, to Alan

3 Air Mails

My Very Dear,

Your people left today & on the whole they had wonderful weather for their six days, the last four being perfect. We all went into Grantown by car on Tuesday afternoon, had tea, got the boys hair cut etc. You will be having letters I expect telling you their impressions of the boys! Yesterday was really a most wonderful day for which I was duly thankful as I'd *arranged* to cycle over to Boat of G. & have tea with the boys at the hotel. I made up orange juice, a parcel of cakes & sent Mrs W, Irene & the children off to the sands on the Nethy & departed with an easy mind. I had a lovely run over & thoroughly enjoyed the exercise. They are coming over to collect me tomorrow morning & climb the "Cairngorm".[3] We can cycle from here six or seven miles over the most lovely tracks until we are nearly at Loch Morlich & then strike the hill track.

I'll delay sending this until tomorrow night & be able to tell you what kind of a day we had.

Uncle James & Violet are at the hotel now & I am going to dine with them on Saturday evening. All of which will show you that I'm having quite a gay week & it all helps to make the time pass more quickly which of course is very much my chief aim these days.

Beloved the saddle cloth & sandals have arrived. The cloth is beautiful, but there is no help for it now. You'll have to get me a

---

[1] Strathpeffer is in Ross & Cromarty not far from Inverness. The 'BF' at Strathpeffer is Lord Tarbert, son of the Earl of Cromartie who Alan had written to about the Camusglashlan lease.

[2] I do wonder sometimes how on earth the censor passed Alan's letters. He can't possibly have been able to read them! Were I a censor I should have refused them.

[3] Cairngorm. It was then a long walk up from Coylumbridge to Loch Morlich and on to Glenmore Lodge up an unpaved track. Now it is a busy tarred road and the whole area is disfigured by ski lifts.

horse to put under it! I've worn the sandals constantly ever since they arrived a few days ago & they are a godsend for which I return a very genuine vote of thanks.

Robert's are sweet but a trifle on the big size.

You remember the charms you sent me? I don't know if you ever thought of them being worn, but the greenish blue glass one makes a very lovely ornament. Nonie is going to try to take some photographs for you of the children & I. I hope they come out but he doesn't seem too sure of his film, which is pretty old.

I am being hailed by David who has just awakened from his afternoon nap. More tomorrow.

Saturday (22nd)

Had terrific day yesterday, cycled close on 25 miles & got almost to the top of Cairngorm as well, will start another letter -
Continuation – Letter Card 2

It was a hopeless day for climbing really, mist well down on the hills when we started but bits of blue kept appearing & we thought it would clear. We cycled the first 8 miles round the back of beyond over tracks which were so bad that at times they were like the bed of a stream & delivered a great deal of amusements at each other's acrobatics. The only casualty was Douglas's friend Jimmy Stuart who got a nasty smash on his knee. He, incidentally was a bit of a moan the whole way, first his brakes were on the point of giving out, he was always sure we were on the wrong track (in spite of maps & compass), when climbing he maintained nearly the whole way we were on the wrong hill & when coming down announced that his knees usually gave out! Then to crown all he was in a great state in case he'd be late for his dinner.

The state of the tracks being so bad it took us two hours to cover the first nine miles, which brought us almost to Glenmore Lodge at the far end of Loch Morlich. We managed to cycle another mile into the hills, then had lunch & started to climb. About half way up we were repaid by lovely views of the lochs & Rothiemurchus then entered the mists & saw nothing else at all. I was very fed up for the view from the top is supposed to be pretty fine & one looks down into the famous Loch Avon on the other side. Within about strolling distance of the top the mist was so dense & there seemed so little possibility of it lifting we decided to call it a day, although we'd have gone on for the satisfaction of doing what we'd set out to if I hadn't been voting on the call it a day side, as I was beginning to worry about not getting back for the children's bed time. We came down arguing animatedly all the way as to direction & I must say altho' J.Stuart worried unceasingly & vocally about it's getting lost I never knew a compass which helped people less! That is with the possible exception of J.S. who was still agitated about his dinner. Then the difficulty arose about getting home as of course we weren't making for the same places & the time factor was becoming acute & the thought of the roads we'd already come over was not tempting at the end of a day & they insisted if I went back that way they would too.

Continuation – Letter Card 3

This was trying as I'd nothing to feed them on when we arrived here! Anyhow I decided it would pay me for the sake of better roads to go round by B. of Garten although it involved a good few more miles. We took the Slugan Pass over from Loch Morlich which was a lovely run & came out a few miles Aviemore side of B. of G. where I shed my escort with the exception of Nonie who came on another three miles leaving me with only another three to go. The last mile here just about finished me being uphill all the way!

I found David washed & in his dressing gown & full of beans but Robert had sternly resisted all efforts to wash him & said he was having nothing done till I came in. I got them into bed & got down to my supper enveloped with an aching weariness & a most wonderful sense of wellbeing. Then after a short interval a hot bath & bed & the end of a good day. Yes, I'm stiff alright today! It's strange beloved but since you went away I've never felt you so near to me as yesterday. It was as if you walked at my shoulder all the time & gave me a sense of detached happiness. I had leisure to think of so many things we have done together & memories came thick & fast. Do you remember the funny bath we had in the river at Loch

Morlich before we were married? I nearly brought home a Gordon Setter puppy but was restrained! I hope you aren't very bored by this silly account of my doings, but Oh! beloved I'm so very much in love with you & I need you to talk to.

I hope by now you will realise I am here until the end of Aug. I can't think how the mistake arose.

Sunday

The boys are very fit & we are just going out for a walk. I had dinner with Uncle J. & Violet last night, they send their regards. I am less stiff today but there are still traces! David is making great strides with his talking & is now putting small sentences of three or four words together. Excuse messy letters, no excuse that I can think of! Love me beloved because I need you more than life. Sheila

23rd Jul 1944, Alan, WAF, Achimota, to Sheila

Air Mail

My Very Dear,

I came back here last night to find three letters from you of 6th, 10th & 19th <u>Jun.</u> presumably you mean July. Unfortunately you gave no indication of your whereabouts at the end of the month so I shall have to send this to North Gardener Street. The cable about the leather was also here. I'm glad it arrived safely & that you like it. I liked your wee card about the bedspread! Just you wait until you see the one on my bed at present, its colours clash with my deep pink pyjamas which I'm trying to wear out and the design is <u>horrible</u>.

Oh Beloved I do so enjoy reading about Robert & David & oh I nearly forgot Robert's photograph in the kilt arrived. He really is adorable with that tough wee face & the kilt. How typical of Mummy - the letter with the tomatoes.

I'll write and explain to Robert about my being delayed. I'll get you a purse like the crocodile bag. It's a pity that the sewing is rough but it's a nice skin and a snip fastener of some kind will make it much more carryable.

Oh it's fun to hear of Robert & David trying to sleep together. What beautiful things they are our Dear Sons.

My show is going well and Duff tells me that <u>Wiggy</u> expects to get a C.B.E. out of it! I'm <u>very</u> much held up in my books. It's my being so busy. I'm too tired after a long day to force myself to concentrate.

But Oh Beloved I'm so fit and full of beans this morning. It's now 12 noon & I've been pouring out letters & drafts since 8 A.M. without hesitation. My mind is so clear due to my physical well being. Beloved as regards where you stay. Don't go back to Wakefield in a hurry. Make the most of the Scotland & Country air for you & the boys. Robert will pick up schooling soon enough. Or send him to the local school to get used to it.

Another letter following. I adore you, Alan

26th Jul 1944, Alan, WAF, Achimota, to Sheila

3 Air Mails

Beloved,[1]

It's grand to have three whole letters from you today for I go off for a few days in the morning. Your letters are all dated June 13th but must be July 13th. Now I'll go quickly through the various points in your letters and then get more discursive. Firstly I love you. That My Very Dear is <u>most</u> important.

I'm so glad the tea arrived safely - it bodes well for the other two similar parcels en route and one packed ready to send. I'm so glad that the family managed up - I have a letter from Mummy just brimming over with delight at seeing you all and Oh Beloved so pathetically saying several times how pleased they all are that the boys seem to like them.

My Dear can you imagine how exciting it is to think of two dear boys sitting down to tea. I'm sitting in my room with my tea beside me but outside the window is a pomegranate bush & at the door are paw-paws and scarlet begonias.

<u>NOW</u> for the big what should we do discussion. You know my

---

[1] This is one letter sent as three separate Air Mails.

dear it's really funny but we are going through the same stage as before we were married. Few go through that twice! Supposing we were arguing about the subject it would be easier to approach for then I could formulate minimum requirements as the diplomatists say. My lists of such needs could be put alongside yours & by crossing out common desires we could bargain away our <u>peculiar</u> demands against each other. But we are not having an argument - so what?

I'll try to put down honestly what I long for more than anything in the future as I muse out here and as I dream myself to sleep at nights.

Firstly (you will be surprised to read) <u>you</u> are always in the plan. No you - no plan - no compromise on that point. Secondly the plan must be capable of improvement & alteration as time goes by - with the exception of <u>you</u> (wouldn't it save space moving from now on to be algebraical & equate you to X. So hereinafter you equals X).

Air Letter Card 2

To Continue. The plan must be capable of alteration with possible increase in income, with the boys growing up & away from us, with our future infirmity in that we shall not be able to climb trees indefinitely. Our plan must not be so rigid that with decrease or increase in income etc. etc. it does not work. I require as income the equivalent of £1500 per annum at pre-war values. I want leisure to read & go in the car & walk & talk & love all with X. I want leisure undisturbed for five weeks each year. Some years for Rieff, some for Asia Minor.

I want a self contained house with a big garage, a big workshop, not overlooked in the country within 25 miles of a (small) town. The garden must have grass for tea, a heated green house (for my post-war interest in Botany). The house must have a living room - where we sit in the evening - surrounded by bookshelves - there must be a good radiogram with good records & two of the easiest chairs in the world. In the garage ready for use will be all the kit we need to rush off to Camusglashlan at any time.

As to the boys Beloved I'm more and more convinced of the

importance of their education. I mean that in the most general way. They must be equipped to find interest in their surroundings everywhere. They must taste of every fun & joy from that of doing nothing to that of doing something for the very reason that it's hard and tiring and repugnant. They must be incalculated with the faith in an ultimate truth, in a future good and beautiful which however absurd or defamed glitters through the mist of sordidness. Let them be cynics to the world at large, let them falter and try to deceive themselves, if they have the faith they always have a future.

My Dear I'll never be too dogmatic if I can with them, but they <u>must</u> believe in the good and the bad. Their formal education will have to be arranged when the time comes and according to where -

Air Mail Letter Card 3

- we may be but given reasonable intelligence, which I think they have, what is important is to round their characters and prevent them from slipping to the extremes (which are either the result of lack of intelligence or of training) of dogmatism or of mental inertia or through lack of decisiveness.

Well My Beloved - we are no forwarder. I agree so entirely with you. Where we are together there is a home I'll take you to Asia Minor my Beloved. Don't think I'm coming home under the impression I'm getting old and want to "settle down". If it was not for the boys I'd have asked you to come out here long ago. For I like West Africa & I like the Africans. Perhaps I'd not like to stay in one place, I want to wander deep in the hinterland along the country Mungo Park travelled. I'm greatly hoping for local leave soon & a grand American, a Major Farrell (who is an entomologist) & I have planned to go way up country & then spend 14 days coming down the Volta in a canoe.

I agree with you about Archaeology Dear but I tend to the Anthropological side. That why I have such a yearning to publish the few bits & pieces I picked up among the Nzema people.

I've finished the additions to the book and it is being typed. Mr Farr of the Fountain Press is sending on to you some photographs I sent to him. I have made a start with the Leica Gadgets book. Well beloved three promises to you.

1. Present of *[Illegible]*
2. No G.P.
3. Asia Minor

I'll add a fourth - I'll always love you & cherish you above all persons & all things & all desires in the world.

Tell the boys I love them both & I love you & kiss them from me. Tell them I'm half way now and that I think of getting home to them many times every day. I'm glad I came here. Nowhere else <u>at</u> <u>all</u> is there a definite tour. I love you Sheila, Alan[1]

26th Jul 1944, Sheila, Nethybridge, to Alan

My Very Dear,

Your tribe is very well & the younger section of it growing at a great rate. The weather for the past week has been very poor. I have had no letter from you for over a week now so I have nothing to reply to. We are going to tea with Uncle James & Violet on Friday which I am rather dreading as the children are by no means used to them yet & find Violet rather alarming!

Uncle Wilson died very suddenly yesterday.[2] He hadn't been feeling very well lately & had a heart attack in the afternoon. Did I tell you that Uncle David[3] (Daddy's youngest brother) died about four weeks ago? He also had heart attack & neither Daddy or any of the others knew anything until they saw his death in the papers several days after the funeral. In its way in spite of the odd

---

[1] This letter was addressed to 6 North Gardener Street but re-directed to Dell Farm, Nethybridge.

[2] Uncle Wilson was John Wilson Steven, Jimmy's brother. He also was a Brassfounder. Married to Jean Allan Mollison.

[3] Uncle David Marshall Steven died 16th June 1944 in Skelmorlie near Largs, Ayr. His death was registered by his 2nd wife, Jessie Steven nee Donnachie. She married him in 1939 when she was 38 & he 63. She worked as a typist in a Bronzefoundry and was a spinster. The Bronzefoundry was surely Steven & Struthers. So we have the picture of the scandal & he & she were estranged from the family ever after. His 1st wife was Isabella May McCulloch who he married in 1915 but was divorced in August 1938. Isabella McCulloch remained close to the family and Sheila remembered her as Aunt Isa, so family were on her side.

circumstances & estrangement it was a great shock to him as in the old days he & Uncle D. had been great friends. The death of Uncle Wilson however will, I imagine, have shaken him badly. [1]

I do wish you could hear your youngest son talking. He is becoming a complete chatterbox. He has however great difficulty with his own name & calls himself "Daybilay". It's so odd to hear him saying "shut door, coldy wind" exactly as Robert used to do! He is what is known in our home town as being "wick"! Robert is looking just splendid, but is unfortunately dreading going to school, he has an appalling amount of worries about it, such as the impossibility of his ever getting home to dinner because he can't tie his shoe laces! I think the first day will cure everything but my heart bleeds terribly for him & I do ache for you to be with us when he goes. Perhaps you could write him an ultra-cheery letter on the subject. Anyhow he is having a lovely summer & most children seem to love it when they do go.

I am so hoping for a letter from you tomorrow. I sent you a cable yesterday. Altho' I'm dreading another war winter I find myself looking almost eagerly for signs of Autumn, so that I can think, now only the winter to face & then he comes.

I love you beloved, I am a different being when living with you & look forward to your return every hour of the day. Sheila

30th Jul 1944, Sheila, Nethybridge, to Alan

Beloved,

Fate was kind yesterday & sent me three letters from you of 8th, 9th & 12th inst. Also the W.A. Booklet which is most interesting. It's good, very good, to hear of you feeling so fit, may it continue so beloved.

We are also all very fit. David has turned pale again & his top gums are inflamed (last two teeth) but he is full of beans. The village is full of measles but I see no reason why it should visit us. We got a windfall of rasps & strawberries on Friday. I made as

---

[1] Both uncles who died were Jimmy's brothers. There were four brothers of whom Jimmy was the 3rd. I think this meant that Jimmy was the only surviving brother but I can't trace the death of his eldest brother William Steven born 1863.

much jam as I could & longed for the sugar from W.A! I was convinced the children would be ill as fresh fruit is such a rarity, but no, they came through smiling. I have simply no news at all for this letter, one day is almost exactly like another. I go down about twice a week & have dinner with Uncle James. The parents are coming to the hotel in the middle of Aug until the end of the month. I'm glad the albums arrived safely. I don't seem to be able to concentrate on reading these days. I take spells like that. Food is very easy up here. I get fish sent by bus from Grantown twice a week & the butcher is almost embarrassingly good to me. Also of course as many eggs as I can use.

David is beginning to enjoy looking at picture books. Thank goodness you will be home to help with story time! Robert asked me casually the other night if, when we all got old & died, another world started! They were both paddling at the river this afternoon, it was sunless but sultry & we might have been alone in the world.

Any word about the croft yet? Lannie says she thinks she will be able to come back to Wakefield with me when I go for a few weeks. It would be a great help.

Love always, Sheila

31st Jul 1944, Alan, WAF, Accra, to Sheila
Air Letter Card

My Very Dear,

Please note new official address.[1] The "West African Forces" comes last. I came back from my jungle on Saturday (29th) and go off again the day after tomorrow. From now on, there are two air mail deliveries a week here and two collections so you should get letters from me at shorter intervals. When I came back there was some sea mail waiting including the enlargements of David's photograph. It's not very flattering to a very handsome chap is it? My Article on Tropical Development etc. has been accepted by the Miniature Camera Magazine and the malaria *[Illegible]* one by the

---

[1] New Official Address is: Lieut Col A.C. Stevenson RAMC, G.H.Q, West African Forces, Accra, Gold Coast. At last Sheila officially knew where he was.

Journal Royal Soc. Trop Med & Hygiene.[1] I'm especially pleased about the acceptance of the former because it was dashed off in <u>one</u> evening. I brought back with me Col Jameson-Carr[2] who is an amazing man of 62. He was on reserve of R.M.U.R. Medical Service[3] Pre-War. Was too old to be called up, so joined as a private in Chasseurs Alpine of French Army.[4] Eventually he escaped from France & is employed at War Office as a Meteorologist. He has been everywhere, fought in South American Revolutions, knew [*Illegible*] & so on.

I'm sending back one small box of books to 66 Manygates Lane & will warn Hipson of its arrival. When you come to open next boxes you will find nuts & bolts & small wheels & 'junk' which I have accumulated here. I can't bear to part with it & it will be <u>very</u> useful after the war.

I have nominated you as my by proxy voter for any general election. I have no hesitation in saying vote for me as you vote for yourself. I was delighted to get your cable telling me you were staying on at Nethybridge.

The boys are having a lovely summer and beloved you are sowing the seeds of love of the country in them. I'm sending off a

---

[1] David has a copy of G.M. Findlay & A.C. Stevenson's 'Investigations in the Chemotherapy of Malaria in West Africa. II Malaria Suppression - Quinine and Mepracrine, 'Annals of Tropical Medicine & Parasitology, Vol 38. Nos. 3 & 4, 168-87. Dec. 30 1944.
Received for publication 9th June 1844. Acknowledgements to Brig J.B.A. Wigmore. In the collection Alan gave to David this is numbered as '1' - his first 'academic' article. See letter 30th March 1945 where Alan promises to send a copy to Sheila.
[2] Dr George Jameson-Carr, born 1885; Living in Hampshire in 1911. In 1918 a Surgeon Lieutenant in the Royal Navy. In 1931 making a living as a doctor on passenger liners criss crossing the Atlantic. He was briefly notorious in 1931 as he had treated & befriended a young 'socialite' who was murdered & thrown overboard from a liner. When questioned he said there was no romantic attachment between them - he never felt romantic attachment towards girls he had first met while pumping out their stomachs. In 1940-41 Lieutenant RAMC.
[3] R.M.U.R. Medical Service - unidentified.
[4] Chasseurs Alpin of French Army. The elite mountain infantry of the French Army.

coconut to them & I've sent you some more jam & marmalade.

Will you please, please love me, Alan

1st Aug 1944, Alan, WAF, Accra, to Sheila

Air Mail

My Beloved,

I'm in the Home Straight - I pass the half way mark today. I have your three letters of July 20th and one from Daddy of 26th which is very quick work.

Oh my dear how glad I was to hear of you having a little time from the boys and climbing the Cairngorm. It sounds lovely and oh my Beloved I <u>was</u> at your shoulder, I'm never far from there you know. Do I remember our little bothy at Morlich? Could I ever forget it. Do you remember how we started undressing on opposite sides of a bush? It's a lovely countryside and I'm very happy to know of my dear ones being there.

I'm delighted to hear that the last of the Nigeria packages have arrived. I just could not resist the horse cloth no matter how useless it was. I'm glad you are using the charm as an ornament. It certainly is unusual.

If I can get more I'll try to have them mounted by local goldsmiths. It's good to hear of Robert waiting for his Dear One to come in to put him to bed. He goes up in my estimation.

I was very sorry indeed to hear from Daddy about your Uncle Wilson's death. Your father will feel it very much. I'll not write for by the time my letter could arrive they will be over the trying time of dealing with correspondence.

Beloved your letters are most merry - when I see your dear writing on my desk I just can't wait but tear them open and go through them. Later I read them carefully & always have a last read in bed before I go to sleep.

I'm still enjoying Jamieson Carr's company. He tells me Col *Ryles* is back in London. I've dropped him a note. I am bidden to dinner on Friday but shall be "in bush" by then.

Kiss my boys. I love you, Alan

4Th Aug 1944, Sheila, Nethybridge, to Alan

My Dear,

It's afternoon. I'm sitting on the sand beside the river & two naked little boys are playing round me & its baking hot. The last 6 days have been wonderful but I suppose it can't last much longer. Even David is deep shades of brown & pink now & looking so bonny. I wish you could see the two of them today, they both have print suits on, blue trousers with striped tops & blue collars & cuffs. Robert has worn his for (David has just put his finger in the blot above!) two summers already & David's is a hand down from Roberts extreme youth but they are both very nice yet & look sweet dressed alike.

Their hair is exactly the same colour & if this weather continues will soon be white! We had strawberries & cream for dinner and are getting them quite often. Excuse this awful letter but so many things are happening around & David empties odd cans of water over my feet, which makes me jump in spite of the heat! I've been very remiss in writing this week & missed your usual mid-week letter, the fine weather seems to be bad for letter writing. I brought this one to the river as I am going to have dinner with Uncle James tonight & I'll be too sleepy when I get in.

Robert was out hay making until 9 pm last night. It was such a perfect evening & he was so happy I just couldn't bring him in. I expect memories of his stay here will stay with him.[1]

Measles I regret to say creeps nearer & nearer & one of the Kennedy (farm) boys is just starting it, Robert has been playing with him but never at very close quarters so I'm just hoping for the best. David is wallowing about in the shallows, he refuses to wet his bathing suit & will only sit in the water in nothing at all. If water gets on his bathing suit he rushes up to me in great distress & says "oh! Look look, bay suit wet - oh! Shame".

Today arrived the red leather oblong pouffé with decoration of python skin & I really terribly do like it beloved, I haven't seen one

---

[1] The memories have indeed stayed with me all my life & I remember the hay making and riding on top of the hay on the cart, which had metal rimmed wheels, with the farmhands as the old horse pulled it along. It was bliss.

that shape before. Time is getting on beloved & the news is good. All my love, Sheila.

5th Aug 1944, Alan, WAF, Accra, to Sheila

Air Mail, Saturday

My Very Dear,

I'm lying in bed under my net listening to the news on the wireless and wondering how long Germany can last. I think that for once my prophecy of autumn 1944 may not be far out.

I was late in getting back here tonight & the plane took off & landed in the dark. It was most enjoyable to have the experience. I only went away by air yesterday morning, so as you will see I can get about a bit. It was grand to have your letter of Jul 26th waiting on my table. The first benefit this was of the new bi-weekly airmail.

My Dear I shall never quite be able to accept that you can love me so much as you seem to - badly put but you know what I mean. It's good also good to have a letter from the woman I respect and love so dearly telling me that she loves me. I love to hear about my boys & I love news from you and from Mummy.

Don't worry about Robert. I won't say how I want Robert to be temperamentally for I just want him to be Robert & I shall write to him. He would not be of the temper I hope he is if he was not apprehensive of novelty so early in his experience. He is not a stolid chap. David sounds such a funny fussy wee fellow - he's about the age Robert was at the Malt House. How adorable he was fussing about with his pail and spade. More tomorrow Beloved but I had to write tonight, now I'm tired. I was away at 6 AM today, motored 40 miles, paddled through Mangrove Swamp & came out on a heavenly beach with my two African Soldiers. I just threw off my clothes and rushed into the water - you would have loved that[1]

6th Aug 1944, Sheila, Nethybridge, to Alan

My Beloved, this is the seventh final day of a most glorious week. Before I forget I must tell you that I have worn the last pair of

---

[1] Entirely run out of writing space so no salutation.

sandals you sent a great deal & during the last week constantly. I don't know what I would have done without them. The news also is extraordinarily good these days & even I, a confirmed pessimist as to the length of the war, feel a great hope that I cannot keep down.

William Kennedy has definitely got measles, the doctor was here yesterday, so I fear the worst as Robert was playing with him up to the day he took ill. I am feeling rather fed up for the boys are both so fit & it would come just at the end of the holiday & David is too young for these things. Still they may miss it, one never knows. Roberts's school starts on Sept 13th I have given notice to Hicksons. I shall spend a week or so in Glasgow after leaving here and intend going south about Sept 10th. They will probably take measles about the end of this month & we will be detained here, so be prepared!

I could tear my hair with vexation that you can't even get a glimpse of David these days, I am afraid I'm rather crazy about him but there is no doubt he is at an adorable age. Can you see him ambling through the hot fields these sunny days, very brief bright green bathing suit revealing all of a pair of very fat brown legs. A spade in one hand and a pail in the other. He is surrounded by bright yellow "Burdock" pink "clover" & "Blue Bonnets" & thousands of bees are droning like organ music. He stops every few yards to fill his can with clover heads or examine a bee and he can walk all the way to the river and back now with no effort at all. Strange how imperceptibly they grow, I had almost forgotten how much of the way I had to carry him when first we came.

Uncle John sent me a terrific box of vegetables and tomatoes & a large bunch of lovely black grapes for my birthday this week. I nearly dropped with surprise, it must be nearly 20 years since he has given me a present or exchanged a letter with me! We see Uncle James every other day & I dined with them again on Friday evening. Your sea mail letter 18th July telling me what you are doing in the bush came within a day of the air mail one!

I just had a cheque from Fountain Press for £33-9/- which I shall send to G.Mills. It's nice to have a successful author in the tribe! Beloved, I love you dearly, Sheila

7th Aug 1944, Alan, WAF, Accra to Sheila

Air Letter

My Very Dear,

I am wondering if I shall get the letter tomorrow for you will not know of the bi-weekly service yet and I had one on Friday. I've had a busy week in the office but have cleared most of it and will now take it easy until I get off on Wednesday. I'm sending home various boxes of surplus kit. Please open them all - they will go to 66 - in when you arrive. There are books, my bedsheets & towels and so on. You will find plenty of interest.

Burtons wandering in West Africa arrived yesterday together with the British Photographers. I've enjoyed the latter enormously and the former I have just started. His remarks on Madeira are priceless. Another consignment of cigarettes also arrived. I'm working very hard on the new book on Leica Gadgets and have great hopes of its being accepted.

I'm longing to hear whether the Times accepts my Nigerian efforts. Beloved I am beginning to wonder whether by any chance the war will be over when I come back to you.

The G.O.C. in C[1]. ordered Wiggy to appoint me O.C.[2] of a big General Hospital (rank full Colonel) but I have asked to be excused. I don't know whether I, in doing so, have cooked my goose, but the idea of sticking for the rest of my tour in one place acting as schoolmaster to Doctors & Nurses was too terrible. I have an interesting job now & I'd give a lot for promotion but not to that kind of job.

It's an old man's job & a dull old man at that. Wiggy has however sent to War Office an official recommendation for promotion to D.D.H.[3]

Oh Beloved do you laugh when you get these egotistical letters from me.

---

[1] General Officer Commanding in Chief
[2] Officer Commanding
[3] I think D.D.H. is Deputy Director of Health.

Beloved whereas yours is the respect I covet, paradoxically I don't mind your laughing at me, Alan

8th Aug 1944, Alan, WAF, Accra, to Sheila

Air Mail

My Beloved,

Your letter of July 30 came in tonight and a letter from Doreen dated August 3rd. My letters of 8th, 9th & 12th only reaching you on 29th is slow work. We are told the delay is due to censor office in the U.K. Sorry to hear of David's teething.

My letter from Doreen and another from Moira tell me that Moira is to have a course of penicillin. I don't think we can have too much hope in such a chronic condition but I never wished and prayed for anything more than that Moira should regain her health.

I'm glad that the food situation is not too bad. I feel so glad that you are staying where you are just now. Now Beloved a big apology. I forgot your birthday. I am so sorry but many happy returns and may we not spend any more of your birthdays apart. Oh Beloved what a waste this all is. I am in one of my down moods tonight. I'm missing you, I'm missing the children and nine months seems such a long time. I would not mind if it was certain to be the finish when I get back.

Funnily enough like you I'm off reading and after office today I was strengthening my big wooden trunk with metal band for sending it home. The African carpenters just ruin the most lovely wood by slovenly work. They drive wire nails in askew through lovely mahogany.

I'm enjoying Burton but I think it's pretty much of a pot boiler. As I know so many of the places he mentions it's fun. For example I have tramped the mangrove swamp of the "fetid *Balkan* shore in Freetown. I have been in Cape Coast, *Koomerada*, Dixcove, Butte & so on that it's fascinating to see how little they have changed. Old Burton had no great respect for the African! Well my darling I'm in bed and its 9 PM. I am going to read more Burton and get off to sleep. I wrote an opening letter to Robert on the school theme today. Oh my darling I love you, Alan

9th Aug 1944, Sheila, Nethybridge, to Alan

Beloved,

Yesterday I had three letter cards and one sea letter from you dated respectively 23rd, 25th, & 16th July. One letter card of the series 1,2,3 is missing but I expect it will catch up today & will reply to them when it does. Anyhow they are all delightful letters & a joy. I like the sound of your dealings with a trouserless soldier. Your leave ploy of canoeing down the Volta sounds just fine & although I should like to be there I shall heave a sigh of unutterable relief when it's all over!

I am getting as much fruit locally as I can use. Yesterday I picked as many & more wild raspberries as we could use for dinner, they are amazingly plentiful and of a good size, while their flavour is superior to the cultivated ones.

I departed in torrents of rain yesterday to cycle into Grantown to get orange juice for the children, but found to my horror that it was only issued between 9 and 3 & I didn't get there until 3.30. It's only given out one day a week so that means no more until next Tuesday. Anyhow I got plenty of chocolate and we haven't been able to get any here for weeks. It cleared just as I got there & I had a good run home arriving just ahead of a thunderstorm. I am cycling over to Aviemore tomorrow afternoon to call on Mr & Mrs *Vernon* (he christened Robert) who are on holiday there just now.

One of our amusements these days is watching tree felling in the nearby forest. They are now working quite close to the house & it's fascinating to watch, altho it hurts me terribly to see fine trees which one has got to know & have associations with being destroyed. The work is all done by Newfoundlanders & Canadians. Italian prisoners work in the fields not far off & when the sun shines they sing most beautifully.

The doctor came in two days ago after visiting William Kennedy to look at the boys mouths, he says you can see spots on their gums a full week before any other symptoms, but so far there is nothing. He is a queer bird, I had heard his praises sung all over the place but hadn't met him until last week. He is reputed to have a wonderful gift of diagnosis & obviously thinks so himself. He has studied in America, France & Germany & lord knows where & quite frankly tells one he is much better than anyone else because he was fortunately placed & had no need of money & was able to study & work for £1 a week for years. One runs into queer people, but he is <u>very</u> nice with the children & I feel a certain confidence in him rather in spite of himself. Sheila

10th Aug 1944, Sheila, Nethybridge, to Alan

Dear One, the missing letter of the post-war planning group arrived today. Beloved these last few letters have made my longing for you even more acute than usual & I've fallen in love with you yet again. All last night I tried to find you in my dreams, often in different & strange places I could see & was near to you sometime in the same room but there was always some reason why I shouldn't have been there & you looked coldly at me & showed no sign of recognition. I had the most terrible longing to touch you but never could. I'm hoping for better luck tonight!

Yes we must have a house & garden which is not overlooked. I cannot imagine us in a semi-detached villa at all although I suppose at one time the idea was not odd to us, but now definitely we must live somewhere quite apart.

I have a lovely idea for our more elderly lives - when you have retired & are giving your time to writing etc. we will go for two or three months, one year to Spain, one to Italy, one to Greece & so on & take a cottage in the country, rents I imagine will be very small & we will live quite alone with perhaps a female to come & scrub now and again. The boys will come out to us when they can & if they wish to & will have an ideal base for discovering & learning to know the different countries from. Housekeeping under the varying conditions will keep me from getting dull & should be highly amusing & your writing will benefit extraordinarily from the complete change.

We can have all kinds of expeditions from our cottage, for of course we shall be tough old folks & able to enjoy plenty of exercise. The worst of it is we shall probably fall in love with, say, a cottage in Spain & not want to go any farther & then there is always the Croft to attend to between. Oh! My dear, our lives aren't going to be nearly long enough & on top of that there is this dreadful waste of time.

I am very tickled over your liking my Polyphoto. I didn't cut out the missing ones from conceit but because everyone had said the whole thing was so awful I didn't dare risk your comments on the worst ones. If you care to send me the one you like I'll get you an enlargement, but as I think it would probably be a bit of a nuisance to you.

Will you keep letters which refer to the doings of the boys?

I love you, Sheila

12th Aug 1944, Alan, WAF, Accra, to Sheila

Air Mail

Dear One,

Back again here by air tonight to find your letter of Aug 4th. Now in bed & blessing the wife who writes to me so much & such good letters. What a fine time the boys are having, how lucky they are to have a mother whose great interest they are. Oh Beloved reared by those who love them and love each other they are fortunate. The idea of them both dressed alike & the shade of hair the same is delicious. I'm glad the pouffé arrived and met with approval. Slow but sure seems to be the Army P.O. motto. That parcel has taken four and a half months. More tomorrow my dear. Sleep is overwhelming me.

14/8

By the way have you had the books from the Reprint Society. I have the receipt for my cheque & instructions to send you certain books and a monthly selection for a year. You can regard that as your birthday present! I have some new quite good photographs which I shall send you. I expect you have by now had those sent on by Mr Farr of the Fountain Press. Oh Sheila words are such helpless things to express how I feel about you and the boys.

I know how I feel & I think about you so much, but when I dash to try & get it down I just then realise I cannot ever let you know.

Beloved all my experience in living & talking & meeting other people; in searching their recorded thoughts in books and in maturing in my own judgement & opinions - all make me understand more how fortunate I am to have met you, to have known you and to have two sons with you. I'll often disappoint you & hurt you but Oh my Dear the devil is in all of us and I love you always & always.

Two fair little heads come into my mind fifty times a day and elusive glimpses of your eyes torment me. Beloveds I shall always be your very own man - I can't think of anything I shall want when I'm back with you. Alan

14th Aug 1944, Sheila, Nethybridge, to Alan

My Dear. My news is extra sparse this week but we are all very well and in good heart. The weather is definitely broken & after one week of summer the need for fires is with us again. How I loved and revelled in that one hot week. I should have been born in some sunny lazy southern clime for I never get enough of it & always feel want.

David's right hand top molar is now showing four points through the gum. So won't take long now, he is very sweet about it all.

He came rushing through the house this morning, grabbed my hand & towed me towards the back door, saying "wee fright, come see wee fright". Aunt Violet was standing in the garden trying to tempt the boys with chocolate. David always refers to her as "wee fright" & runs for his life, little does she know! Robert had accepted the chocolate but apart from that things were at a standstill. It's strange how stand offish the children are to them & they try so hard!

I had a letter from Mrs Hipson the other day, saying Sandal[1] was full of evacuees & she must warn me they were expecting a mother & baby any day. It looks as if I were going back to deal with the new situation!

Your photos have arrived from the Fountain Press - they are just splendid, what did they say to you about them?

---

[1] Sandal being the district of Wakefield 66 Manygates Lane was in.

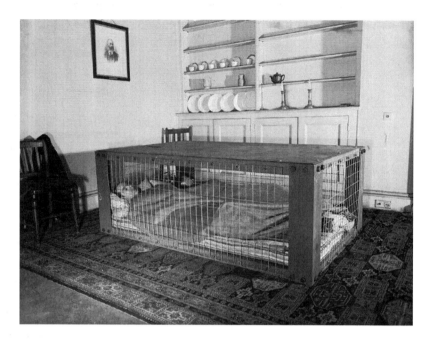

A Morrison Shelter

I have written to Nancy[1] to ask if she & Susan would like to stay with me for a bit this winter. She and Bunty & the babies are sleeping under a Morrison Shelter[2] in the dining room & Aunt A & Uncle W in the kitchen & having quite a hectic time.

The wireless here has given out & I feel dreadfully lost without the 9 PM News. I almost eat the paper when it arrives.

You have been gone 10 months now Beloved & soon life will take on a new tempo for me as your homecoming gets within a reasonable distance. Robert asks so often "how long now" & it's so

---

[1] Nancy Stephens, cousin.

[2] A Morrison Shelter was a sort of metal cage you could assemble yourself in a room. It had a little side door and when being bombed you crawled into it. If the bomb brought the house down you could, in theory, sit in there until the Air Raid Wardens removed the rubble & got you out. Not so good if the building caught fire though. And no good against a direct hit. The sleeping man looks quite relaxed.

impossible for him even yet to grasp the idea of months.

Love me very much when you do come beloved, I'm kind of built up on that.

Yours ever, Sheila

16th Aug 1944, Alan, WAF, Accra, to Sheila

Air Mail

My Very Dear,

Two exciting letters from you today. Do you know I have never had a mail without a letter from you and there now being two deliveries a week I felt sure that, you not knowing, could not possibly have a letter in this post.

The suggestion about Carlisle is very exciting and I would certainly like it. It's a reasonable place and the surrounding country is fine and it's handy for Scotland. It's also near several good schools. The Solway too is good and being a County Borough it's a good jumping off ground for better.

I gather that you too would like the idea and Oh Beloved I do appreciate how decent you are in suggesting that I go ahead & consult you afterwards. It's fun to have a wife who continually brings waves of fondness over me. As to your points 1,2,3 etc. I agree.

As you know I worry rather at going back to live on £700 per annum & if it had not been for the war I should with luck have had £1,000 by now. There is no chance of Frankie going and in any case I have no wish to stay in Wakefield, happy as we were there. I shall write to Steven and cable you tomorrow.

One great advantage would be that I'm almost certain that release of an M.O.H[1] would be more rapid from the Army than of a deputy M.O.H. It does strike one as just too reasonable though that they would keep a job open. I shall tell Steven that subject to the live outside proviso I will apply for the job if advertised & I'll give him an outline of my experience.

---

[1] MOH - Medical Officer of Health in Local Government

I am delighted about the £33-9-0 in royalties. I've now had £202.16.0 from that silly wee book. It's odd to think it all started in Crookham when I rather diffidently sent the article to "The Amateur Photographer" each six months. I think - well that's the end but I get 15% not 10% on the second edition and that may well go with a bang immediately post war. If the other book is accepted and goes well & I can keep producing this sort of stuff it may mean quite a lot in the future.

I do hope that the boys don't get measles but it is probable that they will it's very infectious. My only advice is to keep them in bed (if you can!) for four days after the temperature settles and if they get ear trouble to get a specialist.

I love to hear your raving about David. It really is a lovely age. It won't be so long now until I can purr with you over the tribe. I'll risk sending this to Dell Farm although the letters are taking a long time to get home just now. I'm here until Friday when I'm "going for bush" again. I like the bush people. The bush African is a good chap and very much the gentleman.

I killed a sheep in the jeep last week. I stopped at the next village and finding it was the head man's I went to see him & asked him how much it was worth. His reply was - through an interpreter, that he would not accept any money - it was very good of me to tell him - *the vast majority never looked near the village [Illegible].* I left with a present of a pineapple.

Kiss the boys & tell them I love them nearly as much as you. Alan

P.S. In case you wonder - Measles. Isolation period 10-14 days. Rash appears on 4th day. Starts like heavy cold.

17th Aug 1944, Sheila, Nethybridge, to Alan

My Very Dear,

Your letters of 31st July & 1st August arrived yesterday, also the glorious poem "West African Nightmare"! What nice letters you write your wife beloved & how near I feel to you.

The parents arrived at the hotel yesterday, Daddy looking very white & tired, but looks better already today. He is feeling Uncle

Wilson's death a lot. David simply takes possession of Daddy & takes him all over the place by the hand & in comparison almost ignores mother.

Nethy Bridge had some sad excitement this week. On Monday evening about 10.30 a Wellington with full bombload crashed on the ridge between here and the Cairngorm. The explosion naturally was terrific. The R.A.F. arrived in force the next day & although the place was full of people only too full of morbid details, Robert fortunately didn't realise anything unusual was going on and never asked one question about it.

I am reading in bed these nights "The Poets of The Greek Anthology", a collection of essays & translations by F.A.Wright. I couldn't for the life of me read it during the day, but find it an excellent bedtime book & have enjoyed it very much.

It's excellent news that the M.C. Magazine has accepted your article although it seems the wrong place for an article with such a title. Go on & prosper beloved. I am delighted that that side of your activities is also meeting with success.

In the last fine weather I have gained 4 pounds, at this rate I shall be 8 stone before I leave here, being only 2 lbs off it, & I've never in my life been 8 St! I must warn you however that I don't think I carry weight well & I'm getting a double chin!

The boys are in terrific form. I was just about to heave a sigh of relief at the end of this week when the measles fortnight would have been up, but today the other Kennedy boy has started it & I wouldn't swear Robert hasn't been near him in the last two weeks! It's an awful job keeping children away from each other when they live so close at hand. Ian (the one who has it now) takes Robert rides in the cart & in spite of measles or anything else Robert would risk anything for a cart ride!

I reprimanded Robert for something today & he turned round stuck out his tongue & said "says you"!

I love you dearly, Sheila

18th Aug 1944, Alan, WAF, Accra, to Sheila

Air Mail

My Very Dear,

Just an extra note to let you know I'm fit. I hope the cable went through quickly to you. I'm away from G.H.Q just now & came along here by plane today.

I have a new idea for articles for journals. Photographic article series on making of different types of native boats. I saw surf boats being made today.

Oh Beloved for your peace of mind I hope the boys won't get the measles.

I'm still very thrilled at the job in Carlisle. The more I think of it the better it sounds. Strangely enough you know I've often thought of Carlisle as a reasonable sort of place. I wonder - has it any second-hand bookshops?

It's 10:55 PM - isn't the news wonderful, the Americans reaching Paris - and I'm very sleepy after a longish day out in the open air. Dear one tell Robert I love him & keep reminding him of me for I miss him a lot. Love and more love. Alan

Dear Robert,

Just a small letter inside Sheila's letter. I know you are having a fine time still and I expect that you will be back in Glasgow by the time you get this. Time is passing and quite soon I shall be finished with the black boys & ready to come back to you.

Kiss Sheila & David for me and tell them both how much I love them. Daddy

22nd Aug 1944, Alan, WAF, Accra, to Sheila

Air Mail

My Very Dear,[1]

I do not go back to G H Q until tomorrow so Friday's and today's mail will be waiting for me. I have an extremely heavy head cold

---

[1] Redirected from c/o Steven, North Gardner St to Nethybridge.

at the moment. It seems so odd out here but it's the real thing alright. You will be glad you are not here to have books thrown at you!

I've been out all day - a very strong hot sun today and now bathed and waiting for chop. I'm writing to catch tomorrow's mail. I hope you got the cable all right & I'm still very bucked by the news from Steven. I wonder if by any chance I would be released when I get back. That just seems too wonderful to contemplate. Oh I am so tired of being half the time here & half at G.HQ It makes planning ahead of my work quite impossible. However I suppose I must do what I can - I can see an O.B.E. away in the distance!

By the way I have not had any bank statements for a bit. It may just be the delay in sea mail but I'd like to have them.

I am so hoping you have escaped measles. It would be dreadful if you all went down together.

I suppose I'd better address this to North Gardner Street. I am sorry for I hoped you would stay at Nethybridge until October or so. Oh Beloved think of six weeks leave in about 9 months' time. 9 long months though.

I am sorry that this is such a jumbly letter but I'm all stuffed up & cannot think.

Kiss the boys & know I love you always. Alan

25th Aug 1944, Alan, WAF, Accra, to Sheila

Air Mail

My Very Dear,

Back last night to two posts & three letters from my Beloved. Oh my Dear it's grand to hear of you all well but what a fantastic waste it is me being everywhere but with you. I am very tired of buzzing to & from my experiment but my cold seems to be on the high road to recovery - I'm playing tennis tonight so I have little excuse for complaint.

26 Aug

In bed 1.15 a.m. isn't the news wonderful. Another Russian encirclement on the Danube Delta. I think that the European war really may be over this year.

I played very bad tennis last night. I was tired & flat footed but it cheered me up for I needed it. When I get back here my table is packed high with files & I have a devil of a slog but for most of them that is that.

I always have someone or other staying with me to look after. Nowadays after being with someone for around 48 hours I can bear it no longer. It seems to me that so many people with pretentions to eminence spend all their time trying to impress on you the facets of their character. This playing a role gets very annoying. Each one is shooting a line so that they may be known and not forgotten when honours & promotions arrive.

Beloved you have a sorry old husband but one who loves you very much. I'm having Dr & Mrs Reid and Mr & Mrs Louis to dinner tomorrow night. I owe them hospitality and it's a good chance being here this weekend.

Will you tell my dear Robert that I'm terribly sorry about canoe and being away so long. I hope he is not forgetting his Daddy for I love him very much. Beloved I'm the luckiest man on earth to have you and Robert & David & prospects of earning a reasonable living & I know it very well. Perhaps perhaps perhaps I won't need to go away again when I get home.

Beloved I'm a bit of a loose thread when I'm not with you & I never needed you more than now. Alan

29th Aug 1944, Alan, WAF, Accra, to Sheila

Air Mail

My Very Dear,[1]

Just a hasty note. I am away again at the moment and I'm just off to bed. I've had a couple of Americans to dine tonight, one Major Farrell whom I have mentioned before. I'm going to be stiff tomorrow because I played hockey this afternoon. I'm longing to get back to Accra as usual for my mail but I shall not be back until Saturday. Oh my dear I'm tired of travelling so much. My cold has

---

[1] Sent c/o Steven, 6 North Gardner St, Glasgow. Forwarded to 66 Manygates Lane, Sandal, Wakefield, 15th Sept 44.

gone though I'm still a bit sniffily. I wrote to Robert before I left Accra the second edition of the letter on going to school. Oh Beloved I'm so glad that you have been with my boys so much. I like them to love you and I like you to love them. I feel that all I want of my boys is for them to be as like you as possible. What more could I ever ask them that they in nature would be like the sweetest dearest person in the world. Will you always remember that Beloved. I shall never never be able to repay you for how good you have been to me and them during this war.

I had a very successful dinner party on Sunday night before I left. Dr & Mrs Reid and Mr & Mrs Louis (Louis is the attorney general). They are all nice people and I was glad to be able to pay off my hospitality in one swoop but Oh Beloved I missed you terribly when I saw other men with their wives.

I am distressed to hear about the evacuees in Wakefield but perhaps they will be gone by the time you get back. I'm sorry you are not staying longer at the Nethybridge & Oh I wish I was with you wherever you are to relax and to help you.

David will be wanting to go to school with Robert. He must be very sweet if he is anything like as sweet as Robert was at his age - at the Malt House.

Do you remember how he played with his spade & pail? I love you, Alan.

P.S. Just thought 5 years ago tonight I was with you.

31st Aug 1944, Sheila, Nethybridge, to Alan
My Very Dear,

This will only be a few lines I'm afraid as I've still quite a bit to do tonight before the big exodus tomorrow. Children & I lunched with the parents at the hotel today. David is thoroughly adapted to hotel meals now & enters into the festive spirit with a bang so to speak!

I have put on weight steadily since coming here & have attained the previously unattainable peak of 8 stone!

I had a letter from you yesterday which came in eight days! I do hope your cold clears up quickly.

The Carlisle man is dead, so we await news of either the advertisement or the elevation of the deputy (whom Steven says is a futile person) until the end of the war.

I'm off to make sandwiches for tomorrow so excuse more beloved. I love you dearly, Sheila

3rd Sep 1944, Alan, WAF, Accra, to Sheila

Air Mail

My Very Dear

Five years, but not much longer I hope, I've been in the Army. Oh what useful years gone phut. I have your letter of Aug 17th - but the one before that is possibly lost. Your letter was waiting when I returned here last night. I'm so glad to hear you are putting on weight. I hope you reach your eight stones. I was getting quite worried about you. These two boys were very hard work on you my own Beloved.

Sorry to hear about the crash. There is a terrific wastage of good lives in this war but Oh isn't the news perfectly wonderful.

Bad luck about more risk of measles. Any news about Sanderson & the house? It's good to hear of Robert enjoying rides in the farm cart but distressing to hear of "says you"! I've had an interesting time the last few days with Professor Hiebron the Scientific Adviser to Ministry of Supply. Col Ryles sends his very kindest regards to Mrs Stevenson and the children. Lesley Sparks writing from Nigeria sends regards to "your very charming & soigné[1] lady". This is a scrappy letter.

Heard a good joke. The common saying about African women here is that "they get whiter & whiter every day you are in W.A. Two old planters were talking over a drink. One had been out 20 years & the other 30. The first said to the older man "do you notice these black women getting whiter & whiter every day?" The man who had been out 30 years replied "what black women?"

---

[1] soigné, means dressed very elegantly; well groomed.

I've been lazy about sending you photographs recently but I shall send some today. Well my very dear One; ten months completed - soon it will be a year & possibly the war will be over when I get back. It only remains to get M.O.H. Carlisle for the picture to be perfect. I am just aching to see the boys and to hear them talk

My longing for you is just not able to be expressed in any possible way. Oh Dearest Sheila how terribly happy you have made one man. I love you, Alan

3ʳᵈ Sep 1944, Alan, WAF, Accra, to Sheila

9.15 pm, Sea Mail

My Very Dear,

I'm in bed - could not be bothered to go to the weekly cinema tonight. I like going out with you, but I get so bored without you unless an exceptionally good flick. I was playing tennis this afternoon & was playing well for me. The ball seemed always to be in the right place when I hit at it and that made the difference. I played four sets and lost about 7 lbs of fluid. It is hotting up again after the relatively cool weather & I shall be very glad to savour the thrill of sleeping outside a net & with blankets again.

It is so queer to hear the old names in the news bulletins. Le Mans, Evreux, Lisieux, Amiens, Arras, Douai, Tournai. I wonder if my microscope is safe in the cellar at Seclin. I wonder if M. Renelle who owns the shop is a prisoner in Germany. I wonder if Madam & her small boys are still at Seclin. The last time I saw the place was on "the way back".[1] The little town was half ruined. There was a notice in the Renelle stationary shop window, "Madame has gone to her sister at Hellemmes". A pathetic notice for her husband who was in the French army and stationed in Lille. We have been lucky My Dear and no sum can ever add together the suffering caused by Germany within even our own memory.

I am reading slowly through the Koran. It's very lengthy & difficult to understand but it's very beautiful too. It's a fine faith in that it is alive and vital in the lives of its adherents. Out here I've

---

[1] "on the way back" obviously refers to the retreat to Dunkirk.

so often come across a Muhammadan at prayer on his little mat. Not "in the market place" but at noon beside a little bush path or on the sea shore. I've also been reading Mary Kingsley's "Travels in West Africa" & "West African Studies". She had a pretty vivid imagination. Her life is full of snakes, leopards & elephants. I've seen plenty of snakes but not the others so far but she hardly took a step without trampling on a snake & meeting a leopard. She was a great girl though. Travelled in complete Edwardian costume with bonnets & umbrella. She must have been pretty sweaty & smelt something awful.

I'm sending off a box of books, clothing, towels, sheets etc. tomorrow to Wakefield. It is padlocked. Key herewith and screwed down. Mr Whitelaw will remove the screws for you. The sheets & towels I do not need and will be useful. Don't buy any until I get back because I have "plenty, plenty".

Major Schofield from our office goes home shortly & I may persuade him to take some scent for me which I have purchased from French territory via a gentleman known as the Omanhene of Nzema.

Oh Sheila mine I wonder how long the Germans and Japs will last. I do not want to go away again but don't build up your hopes too much. I gather from Col Ryles that he did not enjoy himself in August. I'm busy with my wee tools just now making boxes for screws and I'm ordering the wood tomorrow to make a folding table for the boat or/and Camusglashlan. I've still had no reply from Strathpeffer. Perhaps that's good news for he has always previously refused at once & said nothing.

Well my very dear it's 10 PM & I think I shall go off to sleep. I'm pleasantly tired after my tennis and the old eyes are watering with yawning. What an infernal number of letters I've written to you Beloved. Oh I shall be glad to hold you in my arms & kiss you & tell you more than any letter.

7:30 AM 4th Sept

Still in bed. I heard the news of Finland's capitulation at 6.30 and have been lying reading with the sun streaming in through the open shutters. I get a pot of tea at 6.45 and I lie & drink cup after cup being thoroughly lazy.

You will find a terribly lazy man comes back to you, but you won't find him discontented. I have great hopes of a really good bag for you today. There is a Czech refugee in Accra who has an African half caste wife. He makes some very fine bags etc. and he promised me to have some crocodile in for inspection this week. Mummy wants some bags like the ones I sent you from Kano & Zaria. Oh Beloved I wish I could send you all the things in such profusion here, clothes, scent, shoes, food etc, etc. etc. I shall try to pack the scent bottle with some underwear if I can get courage to buy the stuff. I never see in shops anything that you wear. Are you Victorian in such matters?

Beloved I wish I could see your face when you get to this! Well it's time to get up. I am all smiley writing to you and very much in love. Alan

3rd Sep 1944, Sheila, 6 Crown Mansions, to Alan

My Dear,[1]

Five years ago today![2] Isn't the news splendid & exciting & Oh! Beloved it does almost look as 'tho' it might be all tidied up before you come home.

We had a very funny journey up here Friday. The taxi forgot to call for us & in the end we all frantically piled into a passing timber lorry (empty but very high!) whose driver & I were nodding acquaintances of three months standing. He very decently said he would go right out of his way and take us all the way to the station. However before we got to the crossroads we met the belated taxi & the whole circus transferred. I informed the taxi driver I would take great pleasure in wringing his neck & we tumbled onto the train with about half a minute to spare & found the parents with one foot on & one off so to speak & Mother maintaining that nothing would have induced her to move if we hadn't turned up. We spent the entire journey in the corridor & it wasn't nearly as bad as it sounds

---

[1] Addressed c/o Steven
[2] Five years ago - that Britain had gone to war with Germany.

as the boys had room to trot up & down & counting Mrs Whitelaw & Irene there were five of us for them to play with & I thank my stars we weren't cooped up in a crowded stuffy compartment.

The children were very good & David thoroughly enjoyed himself & had a long sleep on Mrs W's knee, both perched on top of somebody's kitbag. On arriving at Buchanan Street I found to my horror that my expanding suitcase was not on the van, but the porter soothed me by pointing to several others who had lost luggage & said it would come in on the next train in 20 minutes. It did but I haven't the least idea why and after spending an hour at the station between waiting for the luggage & taxi we did in the end all arrive here! I plan to travel to Wakefield next Sunday (the 10th) & Nan Henderson is coming with me which is fine. Your family are coming to visit us on Wednesday.

Thank you very much indeed for my birthday gift! When the Churchill book arrived I thought there must have been some mistake & was very puzzled. Your letter telling me about it must have gone missing. David is growing up fast, he can converse in a limited way now & is very chatty & bubbling over with new words and phrases every day.

My blessings on you beloveds for wanting to live in the country. It feels dreadful being back in town.

All love Sheila

6th Sep 1944, Alan, WAF, Accra, to Sheila

Sea Mail

My Very Dear,

There was not a letter in the post from you today but one from Mummy written on 27th August. She is in very good form though very worried about Moira & Doreen. She is hoping to see you on your way through.

I shall write to 6 N. Gardner Street because I just don't know where you are at the moment. Had a very pleasant dinner at Louis's last night. Probably only overseas will the full old fashioned dinner survive for there is no servant problem and the civilians seem to be able to make their cooks really function. It was a delicious meal beautifully served on a polished mahogany table at least 2 inches thick of solid wood.

Tonight I'm playing tennis and then Major McDonald the microbiologist & Farrell my American opposite number are coming to have dinner with me. Such a world of gaiety!

Well my dear as you know when I've bits and pieces to play about with, or books, time never hangs on my hands but dining with people makes another evening whisk by, another of the 240 or so until I have you to sit with and then I think I shall be so relaxed and be so happy that I shall go unconscious (That is "swoon"!). So you must lay on smelling salts against my return.

Talking of smelling salts please tell me in your letters following so that I can get some:

1. Shade of powder you use
2. Type of face cream you want
3. Colour of silk stockings
4. Size of your feet
5. Colour of underwear & type required
6. Any other relevant information on "luxury goods" required by you.

It's not important Beloved for I believe there is a shade of powder out here known as "African Pearl" which is the colour of chicory.

Oh Beloved everything I see I want to buy & send to you. I want to have a letter from me every day arriving at you so that you are constantly being subject to the propaganda of how much I love you.

I've just got some five boat fittings from the salvage dump and I carefully hoard them away. How I'm ever going to get them home I just don't know!

What is Kenny McLennan doing these days? Is he still at Huddersfield? Tell him to buy a dinghy for me. We must have a dinghy for Loch Rieff and heaven alone knows how we shall be able to get one after the war. I don't think we shall be able to get one under about £35 now but you never know. It's a pity I did not buy that one before the war with sails complete for £19. Do you remember I had just sold my camera to buy it?

Well my Dear I'm afraid eight months is a long time but at least 10 months was longer. I love you, Alan

7th Sep 1944, Alan, WAF, Accra, to Sheila

Air Mail

My Very Dear,[1]

Letters are expected today & this is begun, just so that you will get a quick answer! I'm off tomorrow in a new Jeep to my experiments and I'll get this off before I go.

10:20 PM

Had your last minute letter from Nethybridge. Oh Beloved I wish I could be there to help you when the family required to be moved. I'm glad you had a letter in eight days from me. I hope this gets to you as fast. I shall try to get someone from some people going home by air at the weekend to write to you and tell you they saw me fit and well.

I took a Branch Photograph[2] the other day & I shall send you a copy. Oh Beloved I wonder what will happen about Carlisle, it seems very unlikely to me that they would hold the position for a man they have never seen.

I'm off at 5:30 AM tomorrow so I'm going off to sleep very soon. As usual at this time I am terribly sleepy but I've had lots of exercise today for I have been very busy walking over the local malaria scheme and buzzing about in the office trying to get things through for my departure tomorrow.

Jock Marshall is back at Achintu from leave. I think he wrote to you or Mummy when he was in U.K.

Well Beloved I shall be beginning to think about demanding a relief soon. We demand five months ahead. I feel though that I want some local leave first to help to pass the time but it's very difficult to fit in. I'm needing you very badly beloved and Oh how I long for the months to pass. Tell Robert & David I love them & kiss them both. I love you, Alan

---

[1] Forwarded from 6 North Gardner St to 66 Manygates Lane.
[2] I think this is the photograph I have in the 1944 introduction.

8th Sep 1944, Sheila, 6 Crown Mansions, to Alan

My Dear,

I'm afraid I missed your mid-week letter this week, but it's been an impossible sort of week & I know you'll forgive me. Robert started a heavy cold on Sunday which I of course decided was measles & got the Doctor. However it remained only a cold. David took it on Monday & Daddy & I on Tuesday & now Mother has it. It was a most violent infection but has now almost gone, but it's been quite a hectic week. Your family came to tea on Wednesday. I spent the morning in bed weeping buckets & with a terrific sty in my eye to help me look really smart. I got myself up and received my in-laws with a vacant eye I'm afraid. I only felt half there if you know what I mean. However the boys weren't too sniffy by that time & were very sweet. David wasn't at all shy & they were very pleased. Yesterday morning my head was clear but I felt so limp I just lay and looked at the roof all morning. In the afternoon I put my clothes on with a terrible effort & went and had a tooth filled. Mother being the last to take it got left with the boys to contend with the two mornings I didn't get up! Anyhow we are all right now & ready for the next stage of our journey on Sunday which I will be very glad to have behind me! Mother has got Robert a wee school bag & it won't be long now before he starts. He refuses to be at all interested or thrilled at the idea! I got David a sweet winter coat today soft green.

I'm so glad Nan is coming to Wakefield with me. She is such cheerful company & will be such a standby the first day or two.

Nethybridge seems already very far away. In spite of my loneliness for you I shall always have very happy memories of the place, it is so closely connected with the amazing development of my dearly beloved David in these three months.

Robert too had lovely time there & always something to interest him. Excuse this disjointed letter my brain isn't very bright yet although the rest of me is all better!

I love you – Sheila

12th Sep 1944, Alan, WAF, Accra, to Sheila

Air Mail

My Dear,[1]

I've no letters to reply to as being in Takoradi[2] my mail will have gone to Accra and there was no letter in Friday's post. I'm anxious to know when you are going to Wakefield & how you find the evacuee problem there. A Major James a Rhodesian who will be in U.K. shortly by air will send a letter to you letting you know I'm really fit and he is bringing you some Kirby grips, fasteners, hooks & eyes etc. I don't know if they are still in short supply.

I shall be going back to Accra about Friday or Saturday and I'm then going to have one more visit here before Oct 1st & then for Sierra Leone leave & Gambia.[3] I am if anything fitter than usual just now and at the moment I am just cooling and drying off after a shower preparatory to changing. Major O'Toole & I are going to dine at RAF with Group Capt Hill and Major James who are due here shortly.

I am also dining at our RAF mess tomorrow with Wing Commander Black. On return to Accra I have to dine with Jock Marshall, back from UK & Mr & Mrs Cansdale. Cansdale is deputy in forestry department and is an authority on Gold Coast animals.

I hope you are getting letters oftener with the bi-weekly air service. Nearly half of the 11th month is gone beloved & it won't be very long until a year has passed. it's 11 months since I said goodbye to you outside the Malthouse at Crookham.

Oh my very own Dear this is a waste and I hope that the war in Europe is soon over for I'm very desirous of being a civilian again and being one of the small tribe or gang, family or party or whatever you like to call it of the dearest people in all the world.

Dear don't get too fat - moderation in all things!

Love Alan

---

[1] Forwarded from 6 North Gardner St to 66 Manygates Lane
[2] Takoradi is half of Secondi-Takoradi in Western Region, Ghana (Gold Coast).
[3] Censorship seems to have eased up a lot. Alan is chatting openly about his travels. U-Boats defeated and no Germans at all in Africa, I suppose.

13th Sep 1944, Sheila, Wakefield, to Alan

Well Beloved, we're home! I just can't tell you how pleased I am to lie back in our own place. Yes I'm dog tired, but so peaceful somehow to have the struggle & worry of getting back & Robert to school over. Nan went back to Glasgow yesterday. Our eldest son has put in his first day at school. If the McVicars hadn't phoned me at 8 AM he would never have got there as we were all dead to the world! Jim & Anthony called for us at 5 to 9 & we all set off. Of course I had to take David along as there was no one to leave him with. All went well until we got to the school gate and Robert put his feet together & would go no farther. He then threw his arms round me and howled. As Jim pointed out & I well knew if we didn't get him in today all would be lost, so we simply hoisted him over the door step & I just don't know when Jim went away! I had a dreadful few minutes & in the end left with the school ma'am assuring me she was quite used to such moments & all would be well. The door slammed and we were out on the road with Robert's yells ringing all along the way.

David at this point suddenly began to howl for Robert, having been an astonished silent spectator of the unusual scene. To make a long story short I was so busy the rest of the morning I had little time to brood over Robert except to be thankful they hadn't phoned for me to take him home. When David and I went for him at midday he was happily seated at a little green table on a little green chair (with eleven other little ones) happily & proudly ready to show the motor car he had drawn & informed me that I needn't bring him tomorrow he could easily come himself! I really think he is lucky, the two teachers are young & bright & kindly there are lots of toys & pictures, a rocking horse & a nice bright fire. Anthony has been promoted upstairs with the older children. They have half a pint of milk & take something to eat with them for their break at 10 PM.

I have a new woman (Mrs Goose!) coming tomorrow morning. I'll give you all the other news late later, I'm sleeping on my feet & just off a hot bath.

Oh Dear one I love you, Sheila

15th Sep 1944, Alan, WAF, Accra, to Sheila

Air Mail

My Very Dear,

There were two letters waiting for me on my return today from Tokorodi. I'm terribly sorry to hear that you all had colds in Glasgow. Oh my Beloved it really was a shame after your holiday. Oh My Dear you will never know what it means to me to hear you indulge in your joy in "my dearly loved David". How lucky we have been my Dear to have our love for each other and our two very dear boys.

I had a road trip for a change today in my jeep and I have a sore rear tonight!

I saw a new canoe for Robert almost completed yesterday & it should be ready for my return to Tokorodi on Tuesday. I hope it arrives safely. I expect you will be seeing a shoal of parcels from now on, and my two boxes in about six weeks time.

I love sending you things my Dear & hope the silk stockings arrive. I have some scent going off to you tomorrow. Do tell me if the stockings are any good.

Beloved this was to have been a long letter but I'm just blind with sleep & I'll find it in the morning when I'm more serviceable.

16.9.44

Woke at 6.30 this morning and was sorry to hear in the news about flying bombs. I expect it's the last fling & this German senseless hatred will not do them any good afterwards.

Your cousins will be getting very excited about Jim now. Poor chap he must have had a bad time.

I'm sending you separately an amusing letter from one of my labourers and "puff for Stevenson" from the War Office Experiment Committee.

Today I have a heap of work to do and I'm starting now 8 o'clock to try to get a good start.

Oh Beloved, I'm continually lazy & have many things to do which should have been done before. Kiss my Dear Boys.

Love Alan

16th Sep 1944, Sheila, Wakefield, to Alan

My Very Dear. A letter from you today the first for almost a fortnight - so I feel at ease again. I am gradually getting straightened out again here & enjoying the process. It will take a long time to get everything right & will keep me going for months I think, but it's such a wonderful feeling to think that I'm getting ready for you coming home & not, as the last time I was here, living in dread every day of your going away. I'm having the sweep Friday afternoon & Robert is thrilled at the prospect - I'm not! Robert is fed up because it's Saturday & he can't go to school! Oh! Beloveds I am so thankful to have got that hurdle over, you can't imagine how it worried me. He won't hear of me fetching him home now so I just watch at the crossroads & he comes trotting along with his wee bag on his back & his wee scarlet cap at a rakish angle on his head, very full of importance & ready for a big dinner. We are going to tea at McVicar's tomorrow, Monica came to see me for a while last night & she & Anthony & Susan came for tea on Tuesday. Susan is very sweet & good, but at the moment I'm not envious at all, as I'm revelling in having no pram etc. to contend with & freedom of movement in that I can just walk straight out to the shops with the boys & Oh! Everything is so much easier. Funny to think when Robert was David's age David was on his way. I have met one of Fishers drivers, a man the name of "Ayre", who was here before the war & has just been discharged from the Air Force after an accident. He is back with Fishers & is coming up next week to go over the car with another man from Fishers (Bailey's are hopeless) & I think I'll get them to take it to the garage as I feel another winter here will finish it. The man who was to repair the roof has been electrocuted & it's almost collapsing.

Steven is coming to Manchester on the 25th & wants to come over here for the night & have a chat with me. The Deputy has been appointed until the end of the war. Steven says the city boundary extends for 3 miles & they are only four miles out & and quite in the country, but I'll get a lot of information if he comes on the 25th.

I'm reading Aristophanes "Frogs" & enjoying it immensely. I hope you enjoy Poets of the G. anthology as much as I did. I don't understand half of this Greek stuff & the other half I expect goes in one ear out the other but I find it a most wonderful relaxation & enjoyment to read, & can get beautifully lost in it.

Love from all the tribe but most of all from me. Sheila

20th Sep 1944, Sheila, Wakefield, to Alan

My Very Dear. I've just been talking on the phone to Group Capt. Hill. How very stimulating to hear such first-hand news of you like that, thank you for thinking of it. The drive to get the house in order & get myself out of the muddle I got myself into. I have opened scores of parcels mostly my own. I think we need a mansion for all our stuff. Most of your books parcels I shall leave tied up as there is simply nowhere for them to go & they will keep better that way. As it is I filled the wardrobe in the maids room with books & tonight when I opened the door to get one out they all fell out on my toes, however I am long past the swearing stage. The curb in the sitting room is still in excellent condition which says a lot for you.

I had a visit from "Frankie" on Sunday morning. I had to phone him on Saturday evening about a letter which had come for you from a surgical officer in Leeds Infirmary about a patient you were supposed to have recently sent in! It was all Greek to Frankie but he said he'd just call and see us and collect the letter. He is the same as ever, sweet with the children but oh! So gloomy.

The boys are terrific & Oh! The noise! David is a real tough nut & I found him chasing Robert with a hatpin yesterday, Robert yelling blue murder! He fairly pushes and hits out for himself & has only to walk up to Robert with his mouth slightly open & Robert flees screaming David is going to bite him. They really are terribly fond of each other all the same & one would be so lost without the other.

Robert has a very small idea of self-defence which I am endeavouring to cure! Anthony, for instance (who really is rather a poisonous youth) simply cannot keep his hands to himself & thumps & wallops Robert continually. I've told Robert that unless he gives him a good clout in return I won't take him to see Anthony again. The poor child is horrified at the idea of such violence, but

I've explained that Anthony will stop doing it just as soon as he meets with resistance & I think R. sorrowfully admits to the need. I will just report what happens. Robert is a rare & adorable child with no temper whatever.

Your letter of the 7th came in this A.M. Don't be late in "demanding your relief". I have been rather dampened by so many stories of people who only got home from W.A. months overdue.

Had sweep today and painters coming to distemper our bedroom (which is filthy) on Monday. Yours ever, Sheila

22nd Sep 1944, Alan, WAF, Accra to Sheila

Air Mail

Beloved,

I returned home by jeep last night with a very sore seat. The letter about Robert's first day at school was waiting for me and Oh my Dear I was glad to have it. It seems to have gone well & I fancy he is very fellow to enjoy these early years at school because he likes doing things and will very quickly learn enjoy what he is learning.

It's fine to know of your journeys being over though I am sorry to think of you in the city. I have sent you all my best prints via Schofield who lives at Morley & will I hope come & see you. The prints were fading out here. My surplus prints are half spoilt etc. etc.

I presented to the mess for sale & they raised £3.15 for the Red Cross! It's very difficult when everyone keeps asking you for prints of photographs. Beloved I hope that a constant stream of parcels will be arriving telling you that I'm always thinking of you. I have sent a good many of one sort or another & I'm hoping that the jam etc. has arrived.

Oh my very own dear will you know ever how much I love you. I'm very thrilled by the wireless this morning. It looks as though I might be released when I get back & increases in pay will be very welcome though I don't know what they will amount to. However beloved you will get back a man who loves you and adores you more than ever and will always love you more & more as the years go by, Alan

Air Mail 1

My Dear,

I have written to General Finney and Col Blake asking them for testimonials for it seems to me that I never know when I may require them in applying for a job and it might take a little time when I require them urgently.

I have enclosed to each a stamped addressed envelope to send them to you. Perhaps you would be good enough to copy them onto an air letter at leisure and preserve the originals. Also some time when you are in Wakefield you might get six copies of each made in the typewriting shop in Wood Street (between Crockett's the Dyers and the ironmongers shop).

Also will you ask the wireless shop (in Kirkgate opposite or nearly opposite the old cinema) whether they now have our Decca wireless set.

I'm sending another trunk back by M.F.O. I made a strong crate and it opens at one end allowing the trunk to be slid out. The end that opens looks like this and I have put a dab of white paint over the only screws necessary to open the end.

The box will always be useful and the crate is of hardwood designed later to form part of a trailer for the car!

The tin without a label contains beef steak pie! All odd pieces of junk - very precious - will you please shoot into the tool shed or another convenient out of the way corner.

I can just see you your face when you open these boxes. I've included everything that might be useful. One pair of drill trousers & old underwear which will make dusters.

Oh it's such fun to be sending stuff home & for you to be there to receive it. Sorry about so many boxes but they will be reusable for our removal from Wakefield.

I'm sorry to write such an ordinary letter! By the way as you are enjoying the Greek stuff just now, get hold of Arnold Campbell's Horace which is among the books I sent from Tunbridge Wells. The introduction is first-class and there is a good general dissertation on poetry. Oh I love you, Alan

23rd Sep 1944, Alan, WAF, Accra to Sheila

Air Mail 2

My Very Own Sweetheart,

I had another letter yesterday written on Sept 16th which is quick work. I'm so sorry that you had a fortnight without a letter. You will I hope have had some since, as well as my cable. The mental picture of Robert in a wee red cap at a rake-ish angle trotting home from school keeps returning to me. Yes it must be a relief to have Robert at school & David able to go to Wakefield when necessary. I'm glad of the news about Fishers men & the car. By all means get it into a garage.

I get 300 miles leave petrol when I come back and I think it's worth getting the car going because it would do it good and would just take us for example to Carlisle (and some extra) so that from there we could get a decent connection to Achiltibuie.

If by any chance they can cope tell them to remove the front axle and reline the brakes. The track rod is not Alvis pattern but one is probably available from Alvis.

I'm so glad you are enjoying "The Frogs". I was as astounded & delighted when I first read it in Tunbridge Wells and I feel exactly as you do about this Greek literature browsing. I've no previous knowledge and get very lost but in all ways it's a great relaxation to browse about these old pages. It's easy to understand how Classical Scholars become soaked in the controversies about texts and translations & so on. Try dipping into the Jowett's Plato in tiny doses. It is so thought provoking as it has had so much influence on Ancient & Modern thought.

I'm sure we are going to end up with a most lovely library of books Beloved and oh the joy of sharing the pleasure in books & thoughts with you. I love you, I love you always, Alan

24th Sep 1944, Alan, WAF, Accra to Sheila

Air Mail

Beloved,

I forgot two things in my letter "telling you to do things" which I sent yesterday. The first is enclosed which is a missive handed to me by my Jeep mechanic who had asked me to get his shirt changed. I told him I would speak to the quartermaster about it & then forgot. You will admit it's a gem and should be preserved.

The second is that in a trunk I'm sending off today is an ebony walking stick. It's a present for Mummy so will you send it on sometime.

I'm particularly fit this morning and well it's another day started - another day nearer to you. Alan

P.S. Second thoughts Beloved I've sent letter to Daddy & asked him to have typewritten copies & then sent on.

25th Sep 1944, Alan, WAF, Accra, to Sheila

Air Mail

Dearest One,

Herewith some snaps, the key of a box coming home & another "order". The last is that in addition to the stick for Mummy there is a palm stick for Daddy in that box. Don't expect it for a couple of months.

Beloveds such great things are happening in Holland and I'm out here. Thank God for it for your peace of mind but you know how I must feel about it. But all I really care about in all the world is your love and your good opinion and perhaps to have been in early is earnest of willingness. For even if I had not had to go as you know I would have been compelled to go so that Robert when he grows up would not have wondered.

I had a letter from Steven and have replied to him. I'll now write a note for Robert. I adore you, Alan

27th Sep 1944, Sheila, Wakefield, to Alan

My very Dear Man. You have been sadly neglected recently as far as letters go but always beloveds you are in my thoughts. I've been pretty well up to the ears for the last week, the boys have both had colds again & I've had a spate of visitors, Monica one evening, Miss Whitaker the next & Steven last night, this with the sweep &

the painters & having to attend Coker with the tooth Andy[1] filled too hurriedly before I left Glasgow & which has been annoying me, on top of the daily round has I'm afraid made me miss my weekend letter to you. I've had so much to catch up with in the evenings. I enjoyed having Steven last night. We spent this morning with Dr Sutherland at County Hall & came back here for lunch. He has just left for the London train, & is coming back again in January when he has a meeting in Leeds. He is most terribly keen for you getting to Carlisle. Oh! Beloved, I just don't mind as long as I'm with you. You can't have any idea of the intensity of my longing for your presence. I just won't think of you're going away again, so you may as well make up your mind about that. I'm not strong enough to go on & on without you. Don't you imagine it's the boys that have been the strain on me, it's the lack of you & the worry about you for over five years now that tells. The boys, with you to advise & love me, would be no strain at all, so don't put it on to them. I'm looking forward with gusto to the parcels arriving. I had the latest batch of photos from you yesterday. I like the Medical Branch! Is that Duff next to you?

I wrote to Steven some time ago telling him I had had to discharge Sister B. under very unfortunate circumstances & would be interested in any information about her past he might happen to find out. He was all agog to hear what had happened & wanted to know what we had missed out of the house! She is evidently of most evil reputation in C. & the famous Nursing Home which she lost all her savings in was a brothel in which she & daughter played a most active role & which was the subject of a big police raid! - To be continued.

Continued Sept 27th on second Air Mail

I think this information should not be passed on to our families, if it makes you feel as hot & bothered as it does me you will understand why! The daughter is illegitimate & Steven says as a child was kept in a filthy condition. It is only on recent enquiry he

---

[1] Andy McKee, dentist in Glasgow. Not a relative as far as I know.

has discovered the truth of the "Nursing Home" but he says it's worried him for years to know why we employed her & he & May have often discussed whether they should warn us about her or no! She was sacked from C. Infirmary & so on. Incidentally I wonder where Edna comes in in all this because Sister arranged for her to go & see the daughter!

Robert is at school again after his second cold & David is just in the middle of his. I just don't know what to do about it all, but have doubled their Cod Oil doses.

The news is depressing these days it's somehow unbelievable that at this airborne landing in Holland should flop. Oh! My Dear if you could know how I hang on the news & oh! If you could know how I need you.

Beloved don't worry about my getting too fat, I should think I've lost most of my summer gain already. Certainly when life does not suit me physically, if I put on any weight at all, it's when I'm getting exercise as at Nethybridge. What about yourself you look pretty comfortable!

Oh! I wonder will this winter ever pass, it seems such a long way to go. Beloved, I shall be quite helpless with joy and relief when I see you. Wilfred R. should be coming home quite soon now. How I envy the three months start he has on you.

Must wake David from his afternoon nap now. Dear One I've never longed for you more than just now.

Yours ever, Sheila

28th Sep 1944, Alan, WAF, Accra, to Sheila

2 Air Mails

My Very Own Beloved,

I left Accra two days ago & so missed my mail. I hope to go back in a couple of days' time & then I'm off to Wilfred's part of the world for ten days or so. Then I'm going to settle at Accra for a month or so & try to get local leave about Christmas. I have a photograph to send you of Roberts's canoe which will give you an idea how the masts go up. I do hope it arrives for Christmas. I'm so longing for my mail for further news of Robert at school. I can't remember whereabouts the school is but I love to think of you all at 66.

I'm wondering whether you have heard from Group Capt. Hill and Major Talbot yet. Oh Most Dear of Women I like to think of you hearing of or from me very very often.

The weather is hotting up again but I spent an hour on the beach. Surf, sun & ordinary bathing. You would have loved it. Native places are dirty & dusty but the sea was sparkling green and white and altogether lovely. It's at such times when there is loveliness about that I ache for you to be here to share it all.

Oh wee woman it's dreadful to love someone so much.

Will you come with me on bush tours after the war? You know by car to Tiflis or to Keira, Nerve, Bokhara, Tashkent, Kokand and Kakarla? Love Alan

30th Sep 1944, Alan, WAF, Accra, to Sheila
2 Letter Cards

My Beloved, Eleven months on the coast completed tonight. I am back in Accra having come along in my jeep tonight. It's a166 miles in the jeep and I'm getting tired of that road, lovely though it is in places. A letter from you was waiting for me - written on September 20th and posted on 23rd. It must have reached here yesterday so Saturday seems to be one day for posting and the other is Wednesday.

I'm glad you are settling in but sorry you have so much palaver with sweeps, painters etc.

I'm glad Group Captain Hill phoned & you should have your wee present which was brought in the same plane by now. By the way have you received any jam or anything yet. I have sent you seven or eight parcels. You don't say if you had a letter in my cable. Mummy says in her letter that a letter for you from me was re-addressed by your mother on 18th so it would reach you.

I must believe you beloved when you say the boys are terribly fond of each other but their behaviour with hat pins etc. rather belies that! It sounds too as if Robert will have to have boxing lessons at an early stage. It's odd but when I think of it he does not fly into rages. I'm so longing to see David, he seems to be developing equally along his own way into a grand chap.

So sorry, I see you do mention my letter of 7th. Don't you pay any attention to stories of long tours. 99% are regular to a day & Duff who was along for a drink tonight was just talking of that & we are going to try & wangle our way into the April home trip.

Sorry we have so much stuff especially books and so little room. Oh I wonder what job I'll get after the war and much more difficult - what house! My trip to Wilfred's part of the . . . . .

Air Mail Card 2

. . . . . world is off. I've too much to do here and I must postpone it for another month. I'm going to settle down here until 14th so perhaps I'll be able to send you decent letters, for my recent ones have been very scrappy. I find it almost impossible to settle to a letter in Takoradi. Well now to bed to read "small small" and then to go to sleep thinking of you as I always do.

1/10/44

Well my beloved I slept like a log last night and feel better for it today. It is very tiring driving a Jeep with the temperature at 98° and a strong sun. It's extraordinary though how one gets used to heat & of course it's fine to be only in shorts & open necked shirt for one can sweat like a pig & it doesn't matter.

I'm going to play tennis at 4.30 and then to have an evening writing, or rather typing, photographic articles. I wish I had my typewriter here but I can usually get an office one in the evenings.

11 Months, what a long time my Dear. Oh I hope this is the end but I'm not very high in the release categories after all. I think that there is a good deal of International back-biting about the release of British Soldiers. I wish the Americans & Russians would remember that we have been in 26 months & 20 months respectively longer than they have. Well my dear we shall see but unless the European war finishes this year there is I should imagine no hope at all of getting out when I come back.

Tell me all or anything Robert says about school & tell him I too said he was to give Anthony a good bang on the nose followed by a clip on the left ear.

Give David a big hug & tell him about that mysterious man called his Daddy.

I love you, Alan

1ˢᵗ Oct 1944, Sheila, Wakefield, to Alan

My Dear. So many things to thank you for! Firstly the jam, six tins of it! Do you realise that for months I won't have to buy any jam & will be able to get sugar instead. The ration is 2 lbs of jam per head & one can have ½ lb sugar for each pound of jam which just makes all the difference in the world. Now the stockings, Kirby grips, fasteners and hooks! The last three are unobtainable & a godsend, but the stockings are a joy & I positively stroked them. The colour on the first sight looked dark, but they are so fine that when on they are quite light. I shall be terrified to wear them! Just imagine getting so excited over one pair of stockings - what a war! Also I have *Sala missed* Lagos letter which I shall preserve as appreciation of your "arduous & excellent work". I can well imagine the thoroughness of its execution. The boys have taken to wakening earlier in the morning these days. I think it must be with the alarm clock going off just after 7 AM week they have already got into the habit of wakening at that time. It extremely trying on a Sunday & I ache for one of the long lies we had on Sunday morning before the war! The McVicar's have been here to tea & as I've no help on Sundays & started the day at the crack of dawn I am now (8 PM) so sleepy I can hardly keep my eyes open & it must be much after before I'm in bed! I slept yesterday afternoon battling with the jungle outside. The amount of times I've tried to get this garden into order is amazing, but never before have I been assisted by two boys!

David chatters away all day and has started asking questions! "How do that? what this for?" & so on.

The war picture isn't looking nearly so bright these days, I mean for a speedy finish. I sat alone and wept when the news of Arnhem[1]

---

[1] Battle of Arnhem 1944. Operation Market Garden. A British-inspired attempt to capture bridges at Arnhem in Holland spearheaded by British and Polish

came through on Wednesday night. It had seemed for so many months we had passed the stage of our men being overpowered & annihilated, and it all started so wonderfully & we'd watched the great glittering air fleets go over & prayed for their success, which seemed certain.

Robert brings home windmills & spinning tops made with cardboard & glue. He is happy at school, but longing for holidays! All my love beloved, Sheila

3rd Oct 1944, Alan, WAF, Accra, to Sheila

Air Mail

My Dear,

Can you feel what it means when I write that? For I have written so many letters to you and I always wonder if I can tell you in any way how much I love & need you. I had an afternoon off today. First I set off with Archer (the A.D.P.) to try to find that crocodile purse which you wanted to go with your bag. This was not a successful search as I could not get another purse like Roberts. I however managed to get a couple of small note cases made out of whole baby crocodile skins. They are rather nice & I'll send you both. If you don't want both give one to Moira for Christmas. Then we had a bathe. The surf was grand and gave a run of 100 yards or so. Then we went to the club, had a game of snooker & a drink and then back to find two letters from you posted on sept 27th.

Your revelations about Sister Brown are almost unbelievable. I don't suppose Steven would have mentioned such a dreadful business unless he was absolutely sure of his facts. There was an occasion at Largs when you were spending a night in Glasgow when I was annoyed with Sister but I just thought she was a silly old woman and never mentioned it to you, but I am loath to believe that there was any question of an organised business. She probably was quite amoral but - well. I don't know but it all sounds too fantastic.

Isn't it rotten luck about the boy's colds. You are wise to double

---

parachute and glider troops. German resistance was grossly underestimated and the operation was a disaster.

the Cod Oil dose. Sorry to hear about your tooth. What help have you in the house?

I'm so glad you had the break of seeing Steven & it's good to know he will be back in January.

Yes that's Duff next to me. He is a good chap & he and I have been very best of friends out here.

You sound a wee bit under the weather My Beloved. I hope it's only "sound". Oh Sheila how silly it is to write of loving you and longing for you when I'm just filled with a feeling of wanting to see you and put my head on your lap and kiss you.

I'm getting a bit in need of leave and I'm saying that because I'm incredibly lazy & idle these days. I day dream too much of you & the rest of the "tribe".

I love you, Alan

4th Oct 1944, Sheila, Wakefield, to Alan

Beloved,

Soon, very soon, a year will have passed since I set eyes on you. How terrible this seemed, yet somehow it has gone by & soon we shall be on the last lap.

The clearing up process here continues. The car departs on Friday for repairs as you indicated & a dry home for the winter. The upholstery is pretty mouldy & fusty but thank the lord the engine turns over sweetly. Thus one job which brought me back here is underway. Another thing which was worrying me was moths. It was not an unnecessary worry & if I hadn't come you would have to have remained in the Army for lack of civilian clothes! The clearing of your clothes, hanging them out etc. has taken quite a time. Your black coat had a hole on the shoulder. I've sent it to be invisibly mended, they were just making a start on all your clothes, none are damaged, with the exception of your evening suit (tails) which is quite beyond hope! A skirt I left had the front completely eaten away & on taking the dining room curtains down they were discovered full of eggs!

I have your lovely photographs & letter of the 25th Sept. also letter to Robert. Robert is getting excited at the prospect of your return & I hear him telling David of it when I'm not in the room. This afternoon he had his arm round David's shoulders explaining at length how the car was going away to be made ready for your homecoming & how we were all going away in it soon. David was looking very profound & impressed.

Yesterday I discovered David lying on his tummy on the floor turning over the pages of the Atlas (which he quite unaccountably loves) & muttering "Daddy in the pink bit".

Robert seems to have settled down at school very happily now. We had one or two storms in the first fortnight, but I was dreadfully firm & he has accepted the inevitable for which I am thankful, for it takes it out of one! Oh! Beloveds, how I long for your company with no shadow of separation, it's been such a long time & I wasn't made tough. I love you. Sheila

5th Oct 1944, Alan, WAF, Accra, to Sheila

Sea Mail

My Beloved,

Enclosed cutting will be of interest. I'm looking forward to the next mail to be sure you all have not caught colds again. I'm enjoying the restfulness of staying here for a bit instead of gadding about and I'm busy making myself a new and bigger camera to take ¼ plate negatives.

The war seems to be going a little better in Europe & so my hopes rise of getting out the sooner. I'm in class 16 as regards release & so I should think it will be touch and go whether I get out after the European war if it applies to Doctors, for I would not be surprised if there was a snag there, although there are plenty of Doctors at home who could now be called up.

I think that at the psychological moment it would be wise to ask Frankie to apply for me and I shall write to him telling him so. He is a funny bird though & I don't know how it would strike him.

Well Beloveds this is just an extra note & I hope it will come in at and on time when you will not have had another for a few days.

I love you always & always. Alan

5th Oct 1944, Sheila, Wakefield, to Alan

My Dear,

I wrote you last night but there were several things I forgot to say, one will be a surprise for you - Robert is starting to lose his front teeth! He came running to me on Monday morning to show his right lower front tooth loose. I was panic stricken! I packed him off to school & thought it out. There he was just over five & his front tooth waggling all over the place. I phoned Cocker, he said oh! It's all right, I've known them lose them as young as four & as late as ten. Further examination when he came home from school discovered the other new tooth poking up behind. He will look funny for a bit!

Our old friend Mr Morton is dead & we miss seeing him going about very much. I had a visit from Miss Burton the other day. She is very funny, says she isn't working hard at all, the Department is in such a complete muddle it just isn't worth it!

Cocker the dentist asked to be remembered to you. I have been to him twice since coming here having had the trouble with the tooth Andy filled very hurriedly just before I came down. Cocker & I can't see eye to eye about it. I said the filling was loose & he said it must be the tooth I felt loose & probably I was getting an abscess, rushed me off & X-Rayed me. I knew there was no abscess & the filling is loose say what he likes. However it's stopped hurting so I'll keep it for Andy!

Miss Burton tells me Mrs *Hershing* is having another baby! Have your letter of 23rd Sept. & will send copies of testimonials as requested & will also have copies made. I got Hipson to collect the Decca wireless & have just managed to get a battery so am well off in the radio line.

I make no promises to open out any more parcels to find Horace, there is no room anywhere for an extra collar stud!

Monica is coming up this evening & I'm in the middle of painting the dining room mantelpiece, so must not start another letter. I love you beloveds & time flies. Sheila

8th Oct 1944, Sheila, Wakefield, to Alan

Beloved,

A year ago almost to the day we were in Wakefield on our way to Crookham. I really think it doesn't seem like a year but the next six months seem a long long time. Still I'm glad you're not due home yet,[1] and Beloved if you say anything else about how awful it is being out there when things are doing elsewhere I shall start getting very tiresome about being tied here to the children when I also could just as easily be doing very different things elsewhere.

There is a rumour that Frankie is about to become engaged, but I haven't been told definitely to whom!

Can you by any chance get curtain runners out your way? You know the wee wheel things that slip on to the curtain rail.

The County M.O's job here is about to be advertised. Jim is very concerned that you aren't here to get it! We were down at the McVicar's for tea today. Robert hasn't come to the scratch about hitting Anthony yet I'm sorry to say, but David makes up for him & has had a few heroic cracks at Anthony already, he simply bristles with self-defence if Anthony gets rough with him.

It's a blessed relief having the "dim out"[2] instead of the "black out". I've got the old black out frames out in the shed & am afraid to part with them just in case! However they take up so much room I know I shall lose patience one day & throw them at the salvage man.

I told you didn't I that I had a nice letter from Major Talbot in Sept. & a few days ago I had one from an S.H.Thayer from Salisbury. Thus I feel very well informed about you & they all send good reports!

A book I would like sent back particularly is "Poets of the Greek Anthology" but I expect you'll manage to send them all back.

Well dear one I must go & find some supper. Oh! It will be wonderful to have you about the place again beloved, you will

---

[1] Sheila feared that if Alan got home too soon he might be assigned to the European campaign with its fierce fighting, or to the Far East.

[2] Presumably as the only risk now was from V1 and V2 rockets which couldn't see lights anyway!

never believe how much you are missed - I love you too much.
Sheila

10th Oct 1944, Alan, WAF, Accra, to Sheila

2 Air Mails

My Very Own Sheila,

Two letters (1st & 4th Oct) came in this afternoon. I am terribly cheered up by them because - well I don't know quite why but you are talking of the jam and the stockings and David & his Daddy coming home - but I'll go through each letter now & comment.

I'll send more jam forthwith and I shall try to find someone else to take more stockings. I'm afraid it's the only colour they have. When I come home we shall have a long lie in on Sunday if it means sending the boys to a kennel for the weekend!

Yes Arnhem was a sad disappointment. So many good chaps - the best of them all go in wars. The filthy Hun goes on and on building up hatred and I shall never be able to feel anything but hatred for him. The desecration of his impact on so many lovely things material and spiritual has lasted too long. How many homes are shells of homes, how many people will go down to their graves aching and drawn by the loss of all that they lived for.

Just noticed your second letter caught the post at 11 AM on Thursday 5th October and I received it at 3.30 p.m. on Tuesday 10th October. Great work.

I can't tell you how delighted I am about the car. It's a very good engine in that car and ever since the brave days at The Sound when I fitted new piston rings & carburettor it has done 24-25 M P G in the long run which is really good. The only snag was the stiff steering and that will be cured by the axle being straightened. It's good of you Dearest to go to the trouble.

We must keep that car for a long time and not waste money on inflated priced cars after the war.

The moths sound dreadful. My poor tail coat! Well my Dear I can get another but it must be nice to take you out with. Oh to hold you in my arms & dance beloved. Oh my Dear I can feel you now. Another letter follows. Alan

My Dear,

Oh how very precious it is to hear of Robert telling David about me coming home and the car. And David's prattle too. Surely there never was a luckier man.

I'm not going to finish this now but leave it until I'm in bed at night.

I wish you could see my room tonight. It's terribly untidy for there is a chaotic mixture of workshop & photographs going on. I'm busy making a table lighter to send to you and the *news* is wonderful!

Kiss Robert & David & tell them their Daddy thinks their Mummy the most loved and kind and dear person in all the world.

10.30 p.m.

I'm late abed tonight but I've been enlarging. For your information the atmosphere in the room is awful - terrible! I'm trying to get a series of the Gold Coast Castles. You will get more details about them in the little yellow book I sent you soon after I arrived here. They are all in lovely situations. Scenery is not West Africa's strong point. It's the coast only where natural scenery is really at its best. The castles have all been built on natural mounds at the sea and either overlook African towns or most lovely palm fringed beaches where the large surf breaks. Beloved many of them have rent houses in them and nothing else. How wonderful it would be to be going spending weekends there with you. I can't imagine anyone who would appreciate the grandeur of them in the starlight or in the glorious tropical mornings, more than you. Oh I want 20 lives so long as they are all with you or do you think you could stand that! How many babies per life? Oh Sheila I wish you could feel me longing for you tonight. Alan

10th Oct 1944, Sheila, Wakefield, to Alan

Dear One,

Today your letters of the 30th Sept. & 3rd inst. Also the coconuts & Miniature Camera Magazine with your most interesting article.

I've had a tremendous kick out of it beloved & I'm so thrilled about having a husband who can write. Remember me to Duff, I took a liking to him during the brief time he was with us.

Robert is now minus tooth & it alters him amazingly. However the other one is through & will push up fast. He'll probably have the two upper front ones missing when you come home & David will steal all the limelight for manly beauty! David flies into to terrific almost *clear* eyed rages - or rather they look as if they were going to be terrific, but in almost 30 seconds he rushes to me saying "Mummy kiss Dayblay", on being kissed he fetches a dreadful sigh, says "all better now" & wanders away as happy as a lark!

Robert doesn't say an awful lot about what he does at school, but he is very impressed by a John Nicholls who is the smallest boy in the school & by far the naughtiest!

He (Robert) is in heaven the day they make things (cardboard, glue & so on) & comes home radiant complete with the article made. There is a concert in December & they all have to do something, sing or recite or take part in a play. I know I shall go through agonies before we get it over! Robert is horrified at the idea.

I have by no means finished with the history of Sister Brown & have yet to hear Mr Dunlop's version - the ear, nose & throat specialist she was so keen on. You would be surprised I think if you knew the extreme bitterness of my feeling on the subject. I have no idea what happened at Largs when I was away, but she told people that whenever she saw you "something came over her" & you were the reason she stayed with me. Also that you begged her to stand by the children when you were away as it would be such a relief to you to know there was a responsible person in charge. This was told me independently by three different people.

Excuse this very messy letter beloved, Robert has been oiling his tricycle with the sweetest wee oil can I couldn't resist buying him & I think he got some on this letter.

I can't think why you don't come high on the release categories, if you can add a year of age to every two months service you will be well over 60 & automatically first-out. There must be more to it than meets the eye I suppose.

I am not & have not been under the weather & I love you very dearly. Sheila

13th Oct 1944, Alan, WAF, Accra, to Sheila

Air Mail

My Very Dear,

Having the Office Typewriter in my room tonight for writing an article I thought I would give you the treat of a letter which you could read! As I'm going off for a few days tomorrow I was 'specially glad to have your 'extra' letter tonight. It is the one written on 5th Oct. poor old Robert and his teeth. It is earlier than usual but it does not matter when it occurs so long as he gets a good set of second ones. I'm terribly sorry to hear about Mr Moulton. He was a quite exceptional man and anyone who was as good to you as he was has an especial place in my affection. I'm glad that Miss Burton came to see you. She is a decent soul and has always written to me ever since I went away and kept me in touch with the local scandal. I hope that your tooth is now settled and is not giving you any more trouble. Cocker is a funny bird but, I think a good dentist.

Oh I am so glad you have the Decca for it will let you have it in your room if you wanted and you will not have to lug it out. Sorry about the crowded condition of the house. I'll not bring home any collar studs in case there is no room for them! What you will say when my various trunks and boxes arrive I hate to think, and when you open them and find them full of 'Valuables' consisting of more 'Junk' for my workshop your language will be rich.

Heavens I've been typing hard for ages and the space is not filling up. Curse it too I've just wasted the letter G which would have filled its own wee bit.

I had some fun on the wireless tonight with the man in the next room Col Gilbert. When I heard he was going to broadcast on teaching of English to Africans I suggested he should start with "can you hear me mother"? I must stop now for it's too late to type.

In the middle of his talk he said now suppose I said "can you hear me Steve" that would be five words.

Beloved I can't really type a letter to you, I have become so used to writing to you dreamily while thinking of you and wondering what you are doing. It's a sort of communication with you which does not go with type writing.

Oh Beloved I hope you will save up just enough coal for us to sit before the fire in the sitting room and bring down our things and undress in front of the blazing fire. Oh Sheila I can think of so many lovely nights when we had coffee and talked and got out Atlases for the route to Greece and so on. Remember always I'm the very same man unchanged in any important way from the man who first (over the course of an hour's monologue) told you he loved you.

I must now pack my bag & get to bed for my plane leaves early. I'm coming back by road at the end of next week.

I hope Robert got the photograph of the canoe (and more important the canoe).

Bless you Beloved and Bless all my tribe. Alan

14th Oct 1944, Sheila, Wakefield, to Alan

A year yesterday beloved & oh! How I long for the next six months to go by. I had your letter (sea?) Of the 5th inst. today with cutting about D.D.T. I had realised that that was probably what you were playing with. Good idea to write to Frankie, for heaven's sake do. How you arrive in Cat. 16 I just don't know, it certainly doesn't work out that way when an averagely intelligent person (me!) reads the papers. Frankie is nearly scatty which of course is usual. They have & can get no Deputy & the old assistant seems pretty hopeless. They seem to have had a drug addict as Deputy for a short time (I had this very hush hush from Miss Burton!) Which seems to have shaken Frankie to the core. I think he could be relied upon to send quite an agonising appeal for you. Let me know when you write because I promised to have him to tea & will put off until I know your letter must have reached him & have the pleasure of hearing what he says!

I am thoroughly depressed about the war at the moment & can see it going on & on & on. I've also completely got the pip over the demobilisation business which I had thought was going to turn out so well for you & dammit on paper it did. People who were in at the beginning could surely be replaced at the end of five & a half or six years. If men don't take everything lying down the Government will take more care of them. It will end with the censor opening this & your dear one being charged with sedition! All the same if there's any question of them taking you away again I think I'll kill someone.

Apart from all this I'm very well thank you. The boys are fine but Robert says he is not going back to school because they are starting to teach him sums & he doesn't like them at all!

The car has been removed (did I tell you?) It's gone to a mechanic off Kirkgate who works for Fishers & he seems a real nice man. The engine is perfectly all right, but leather naturally very mouldy.

I've made a lovely cake today with your coconuts & iced it too! You who have been away from it cannot imagine how marvellous it is to get a new & almost forgotten flavour again. McVickers coming tomorrow. I love you always, Sheila

15ᵗʰ Oct 1944, Sheila, Wakefield, to Alan

My Dear, I can't resist writing an extra letter tonight. It's been a busy day, I've no help on Sundays & the McVicar's have been to tea. However everything, the baking included, went well and we had a very merry tea party. The boys nearly deafened us, David is quite as tough as the older ones & at one point Jim had to detach him from Antony's nose, to which he was clinging with the determination of a bulldog! Oh! Beloved if only I could keep David at the age he is until you get back, he is so perfect just now & nothing will ever make up for what you've missed of him these last six months. He is so full of fun & so gloriously unaffected yet. I heard him telling his teddy bear (which he takes to bed and calls his darling) tonight "Daddy coming home darling. Daddy coming home". He is partial to men always & asks to sit next to Jim at table. I really am grateful for the McVicar's, we know them pretty well now & they are such a help in making the weekends pass. Also Monica comes up one evening each week & when one is busy it's too much of an effort to cultivate new people.

I am so relieved that Greece is to escape more damage & Athens will still be there for us to enjoy. We will get there beloved.

I can't settle to read these days and have been falling back on the wireless. Funny how I get these spells. I think it's when I'm happiest & least worried I read best. I'm so frantic about the fast dwindling chances of the war finishing this year & your position in getting out, but I can't concentrate these evenings & have to keep myself occupied. Oh! Dearest on earth I do wish I didn't need you so badly, but I can't remember any time now when I didn't.

I have a daily woman about my age & enormously fat & lazy. She wanders in at 9.30 & departs immediately after lunch & often before it if she feels inclined! However I haven't the energy to change & am going to try to keep my tongue in my cheek until after Christmas anyhow. All the same, time is going very quickly & Oh! Beloved, life will be such fun again when you are home.

You'll find Robert a chip off the old block, happy as a lark if he has a hammer & nails & the wee saw I got him. He sounds just like you outside! Oh the news is on & it sounds good. You've a crazy wife beloved but oh! How she loves you. Sheila

17ᵗʰ Oct 1944, Alan, WAF, Accra, to Sheila

Air Mail

My Very Dear,

Being away I have no letter to reply to but I have an account of an interesting day to give you, so here is an extra letter. On Monday, having to be at a place called Princes[1] I did what I have wanted to do for a long time, walked the 7 miles to a place called Akwidaa & back. In late 17th century the Prussians thought they would break

---

[1] 'Princes' refers to Princes Town, Gold Coast. On 1st January 1681, a Brandenburger expedition of two ships commanded by Otto Friedrich von der Groeben, arrived in the Gold Coast, and began to build a strong fort between Axim and the Cape of Three Points. The fort was completed in 1683 and was renamed Fort Gross-Friedrichsburg in honour of Prince Frederick William I, Elector of Brandenburg. Because the Fort Groß Friedrichsburg was named after a Prince, it has been referred to as: Ft. Friedrichsburg/Princes Town. The fort was to be the headquarters of the Brandenburgers in Africa.

into the Shore traders and Frederick the Great Elector of Brandenburg sent out an expedition & setup to trading castle at Princes - from Fredericksburg and at Akwidaa Fort Dorothea. I had good photos of Princes but now I have photos of Akwidaa & am writing an article for the Geographic Magazine for I have made an archaeological discovery! The chief at Akwidaa was drunk (palm wine) when I arrived & eventually after a lot of palaver he is seeing that I was bothering him a lot about the ruins nearby and took me to a filthy hut where covered over with sheepskins was a carved stone - a relief of the Arms of Brandenburg in good condition. At the cost of 5/- I had it out in the sun and photographed it. You will imagine how excited I am about my find & my joy on going to P.C's office yesterday to find that it was not known of and quite uninvestigated. There is lots of interesting popular history about the times & I have found a translation of German documents so I have great hopes of the article.

Oh Beloved I'll send you the photos but they will only hint at the beauty of that walk along the coast. I must have wished you were there every 100 yards the 14 miles. I love you, Alan

18th Oct 1944, Sheila, Wakefield to Alan

Dearest on Earth,

I dreamed a lot of you last night all very confused, but so pleasant I struggled to stop waking up. The Whitaker's came round to spend the evening last night & old Charlie is really most amusing. Your testimonial from Timmy has arrived as follows -

"Lt. Col. A.C. Stevenson D.P.H. R.A.M.C. has asked me for a testimonial, & I am very glad to have the opportunity of doing so. From Sept. 1939 to June 1940, when I was a D.M.S. to the 3rd Division in France he was my adviser in Hygiene & Sanitation & commanded the Field Hygiene Section. I always placed great confidence in his judgement & opinion & particularly admired the way he adapted himself to unaccustomed duties & new conditions. In addition he is possessed of a charming personality & it was a pleasure to work with him". - Well that's that. I'll send you on the note he enclosed with them. He enclosed three copies.

I have a note from W. Heaton today asking for payment for a filter they are sending to you & mentioning that you asked for other goods which they are unable to supply. I'll send the filter money right away.

I've planted 300 chrysanthes (wallflowers to you!) & am distinctly stiff. There is an amazing lot of spadework involved in our "garden"! Also I have a gumboil so you won't be getting more than this one letter tonight!

I had a letter from Steven this week & he mentioned that he'd just had one from you. My latest ploy is to drive a hard bargain with old Sanderson & buy the house for Mr Whitaker! He is very keen to get it but doesn't want his name to get in & shoot the price up!

I've engaged a maid today to come on Monday week. I wasn't going to bother changing but Mrs G. sent her out & she seems keen to come so we can at least try. Her husband is a prisoner in Germany. She is 21 & has no teeth! Wants to be with children. Teeth coming in January!

The babes are blissfully asleep & thank the lord I can indulge my gum & not speak any more until tomorrow!

I had Priestley's "Daylight on Saturday" from the Reprint Society yesterday. It's just about my level these days & I'm enjoying it. I've just finished Linklater's "Men of Ness" & thought it excellent.

Oh! Husband it's a dreadful thing that you will never know how I love you. Sheila

20ᵗʰ Oct 1944, Alan, WAF, Accra, to Sheila

Air Mail

My Very Own Beloved,

I returned here today to find two letters from you dated 8ᵗʰ & 10ᵗʰ. I'll not complain any more about being out here for I should hate you to become tiresome. I'm not convinced you are capable of being tiresome but I'm taking no chances.

What again - rumours of Frankie being engaged? He will never bring himself to it. I'll see about curtain rails though I doubt whether they will be obtainable. It's funny about Robert being a pacifist & David an aggressive lad - takes after you I'm afraid. If you get tough with the blackout frames please save the wood!

I have not yet received Poems of Poets Greek Anthology but I'll send it back quick. When you get the trunks please say whether the sheets & towels are useful. They are terribly cheap.

You don't say what the boys thought of the coconuts! I am so interested in Robert at school and I'm longing to see them both.

How would you like a year or two out here post war? There is a job at £1,200 plus house light and so on (2/1 in £ income tax) in one of the Gold Mines. Six months leave each year, free passages. It would be great fun & the world for us is young.

Well my very own Dear One you never know what that variable man you married is going to suggest next. I'm making further enquiries but I think I could have it if I wanted it. Six months leave is not to be sneezed at is it. We could go home by car over Sahara & visit Greece! My Dear I need 20 lives not one.

I am getting excited about enlarging my latest negatives tonight. They look good to me. I sent you four lbs more jam today. Would you like me to send Anthony a canoe or would that break Roberts heart? Oh I wish you were here to write the European History side of my article for Geographic Magazine. We shall & I can't think of any greater pleasure in all the world. I admire you. Alan

22nd Oct 1944, Sheila, Wakefield, to Alan

My Very Dear.

Firstly Col Blake's testimonial -

"Dr Alan C Stevenson served as D.A.D.H. (In rank of Major) under me in Aldershot District for about a year 1941-42. I formed a high opinion of his knowledge & work. He was very keen & enthusiastic & put in very useful work during his time with me. Aldershot District provided scope for a specialist in Hygiene as in addition to the routine work many new schemes for buildings were initiated for which his special knowledge was most useful. He was cooperative, pleasant to work with & I was very sorry to lose him when he was promoted" - He enclosed a letter to you which I am sending on along with Roberts idea of a letter to you. I really must settle some time with him & help him to write a proper one, only he'd get bored very quickly! I'll be forced to go & see Cocker I'm afraid in the morning, my mouth isn't clearing up at all & I've had it for 10 days now. It's where I had the famous wisdom tooth out & I had the same thing in July but not nearly so badly. I suppose there must be a bit of tooth somewhere. If only it will settle down until you come home and I can have a day off & have it attended to!

I had a wonderful day on Friday - four letters from you. Two most beautiful bags & a bottle of perfume. Having sent me bags already I have a feeling you may mean these as presents for some of your family for Christmas but you aren't going to get them from me easily! I'd sooner part with something else! They were such nice letters too & made me feel all warm and happy inside. Oh! I nearly forgot to mention the shoes you sent for David, they are sweet but your David will never wear them - they will hardly go on his toes, he takes sevens! Shall I give them to Susan or keep them for the next unintentional error! Robert has had a letter & the photograph of the canoe. It looks beautiful, I hope to goodness it arrives.

Daddy has a meeting in London next Monday & there is a chance they may look in here at the weekend. He is going to "Ruthin Castle" a clinic in North Wales[1] in November for thorough overhaul & to have diets worked out. This has been talked of for some time. I have yet to hear anything against the place, which you may have heard of & perhaps they may do him some good.

We've been to McVicar's for tea. It's been a fine day for once & I gardened quite a bit in the morning. I always try to do as little as possible on Sundays & make them just a bit different from the other days. The boys caught worms & ladybirds & put them in wee boxes! Now for the news & bed.

Yours ever & long after that. Sheila

23rd Oct 1944, Alan, WAF, Accra, to Sheila

Air Mail

My Very Dear,

---

[1] 'Ruthin Castle still exists as a hotel & spa.

I'm looking forward to tomorrow for I hope for mail. I've just received the books. Thompson's Greek, Poets of Greek Anthologies & Sheridan. Thank you very much. I'll report impressions.

Will you think seriously of that job on Gold Coast for I understand from important persons here that it's more or less mine for the asking? The conditions are "Six months service on the mine and six months on leave as nearly as can be arranged". "Starting salary £1,200. Free mine & kit allowance, first-class passage out and home, free bungalow, lighting, water etc." The commencing salary of £1,200 at Gold Coast income tax is worth at least £2,000 at home & it would be rather fun. Yes I'm afraid you have hitched yourself to a *vapid* man I know - I know. The children? Well five months at home each year & you could go home early sometimes - or does that blast back on me in a way to make my ears burn?

24/10/44

Dearest on reading this over morning I was very tempted to tear it up but I felt that you knew me well enough to laugh at me or curse me as you wish. One point I did not make was of course that I would be released from present duties which would be about the only point acceptable to you as good.

My Prussian Forts article is taking shape & I have 12 of the best photos I've ever taken to illustrate it. This historical research is very hard work. So far I have consulted over 20 books & papers in the Achimota library. I love you much too much Beloved to do anything which you do not want so tell me you love me & then your opinion. Alan

24th Oct 1944, Alan, WAF, Accra, to Sheila

Sea Mail

Dear,

I'm in bed - it's 9.30 - I should be working on these incredible doings of the Prussians in Akwidaa in.1688 - I am trying to read the Rhesus of Euripides but as I cannot think of Rhesus without thinking of the Rhesus Monkey and I can't see any connection - I'm writing to you. I'm sober. I'm now going to listen to the news.

Later:

My writing is horrible - I know it, I can't read it myself often - I shall never be able to improve it - I see it getting worse & worse & my mind flying so far ahead of my hand that I shall be escriptionate, if there is such a word & does it matter - if you cannot spell it. You know I hate to think of your reaction to the Mines at Aboni. Beloved I'm <u>bad</u> to you. Oh I had almost forgotten about being <u>bad</u> to you. It's nice having a wife like you to be bad to.

I should call on Mr Angus Taylor on Saturday when I go there. Mrs A Taylor has I believe gone home. I'm going to stay not at HQ but with Gilbray an Australian who I have mentioned before & whom I like very much because he loves his wife very much.

Gilbray - little - Dubh, the red bearded lad. Yes I read my place names of Scotland a lot & even if with my Gaelic grammar shortcomings but I'm an inconstant scholar.

Do you know anything about children's toys & why I should find myself speaking to a bunch of dusky brothers on the subject over the wireless. I know nothing my dear but I gather the drill is to speak SLOWLY and DISTINCTLY as if to a born imbecile who has had the misfortune of being dropped on his head in piccaninnity followed by the misfortune of cerebral deterioration which begins in all Africans at the age of 14.

Beloved if you come to Africa I can positively guarantee a servant, nay four servants, <u>all</u> with teeth. I joking said to Jeremiah today if I stay here and while mining come you be my houseboy? He thought a bit & then said "no Sah, Missus trouble me, they do humbug me too much". So you are snubbed "one time".

Poor old Jeremiah I suppose I don't humbug him enough. He says good morning master when he brings my morning tea about 12.30. He always comes even if I'm in my office or the mess & says "I go for chop - I come back for tea". He comes after my bath & says "good night master" but he never says anything else unless I speak to him. He smells "small small" but it's not his fault, he baths every day & and has never heard of de - o - do - ro.

No doubt in the heat I am not too immaculate myself! Perhaps he goes back to his wives each night & says "my master he do smell too much". This Dear as you will know is a daft letter - consider the author and excuse all. Alan[1]

24th Oct 1944, Alan, WAF, Accra, to Sheila

Air Mail

My Own Sheila,

Dear person - it's Alan who loves you writing to you. Can you feel how much I love & long for you. I have not changed one iota Sheila in how I feel about you. I never shall Dear so remember that.

Tonight I had three letters - oh you have been good in writing to me so much. What it means to go up to the Mess & find three letters. You can't know but it just makes the next four days different altogether.

Dearest Class 16 isn't too bad - they go up to 76 or so and I still have hopes that my class will get out after the European war. Failing that there is this business out here in the mines which would make your mind easier for a little. I'm afraid I was a little dumped myself until I realised and I've infected you. I'm sorry.

Your gumboil - oh I'm sorry about that & hope it is better. I shall wire to you tomorrow.

David sounds terribly attractive & I feel you have fallen in love with him. Yes we shall go to Athens Sheila you & I and even if we are not so erudite as to appreciate the details no one will ever enjoy it more than we shall.

I've been asked to broadcast here two talks, one on toys & children & one on Hobbies. It arose out of a discussion in the mess one night and I was saying how odd it was that the African children never had toys. Someone told someone & now I am asked to give two broadcasts. It's a funny world & I'm bit chary of the business. I'll send you the script.

I'm so glad you are getting a maid, even an edentulous[2] damsel. Do see that she has her teeth for her husband coming home.

---

[1] This extraordinary letter baffled Sheila too. See later.
[2] 'edentulous' from Latin meaning without teeth.

The idea of buying the house for Whitaker is excellent. So go to it. Old Finney has let himself go - must be whiskey left <u>somewhere</u> in the UK. I'd be glad if you would pay Wallace Heaton.

Article to M C M[1] went off last night & my very bowels are going into the struggle adequately to depict the lot of a band of long dead Brandenburgers on the Gold Coast in the 17th Century.

I feel for you as a mother. No delivery was accompanied by such pains as mine! So glad you enjoyed "Men of Ness". I thoroughly agree.

I adore you & I love you & I kiss you in print.

Alan[2]

25th Oct 1944, Sheila, Wakefield, to Alan

My Dear One,

I have mentioned this before but as I feel it will gladden you to hear it I will say again how glad I am that I came back here. It has been & is a labour of love putting things in order here. Repairing, renewing, cleaning, all is fitting together now fascinatingly like a jigsaw. I am constantly occupied mentally & physically and everything I do is dedicated to your homecoming. The boys are very fit & I think David is looking better than I have ever seen him even at Nethybridge. I have had word tonight that the parents are coming on Friday afternoon & leaving on Monday morning for London. They are returning here on Tuesday evening & going to Glasgow on Thursday. This will make a break & pass a week even more swiftly than usual towards - you. I shall have to get the boys sleeping together & into the front bedroom before you return. Robert thinks he is with me for life & insist that we put you in the spare room! I am so pleasantly weary this evening that I can hardly hold the pen. I've had a busy constructive day & have been working in the garden all afternoon & have at last got part of it (the back) more like the place we live in should look. I suppose this seems

---

[1] M C M - Miniature Camera magazine
[2] I presume that this Letter Card was written <u>after</u> the extraordinary Sea Mail letter of the same date. It is perhaps an attempt to pre-empt reaction to the weird ramblings in his first letter.

dreadfully unimportant to you, but the place was a jungle & I just cannot live with that sort of neglect. The boys assisted (?) all the time with their wee red barrows. Their great joy is collecting worms & putting them into wee boxes & they will bring them into the house! Robert was most hurt when I refused to eat my dinner with a box of worms on the table & David goes about with a blue tin saying "see my pretty worms"

I am told that Robert is learning a poem to say at the Xmas concert so evidently he is reconciled to the idea.

I've sent Brunnings a cheque for your stuff so you will be getting it some of these days. I am expecting to have some Nethybridge snaps to send you soon.

What a sweet box the coconuts arrived in. I'm using it for a work basket. Oh! Beloved I love you so very very dearly.

In case you are wondering my mouth seems to be gradually getting better so I haven't been to Cocker. More love. Sheila

28ᵗʰ Oct 1944, Alan, WAF, Accra, to Sheila

Air Mail

My Beloved,

I shall be off today before the mail comes in - and indeed I hardly expect any after your three letters last time, but I shall be back on Monday and then I shall be here for Tuesday's mail. Last night I had dinner with Carradale of the Forestry Department and his wife. He is a great naturalist and an authority on Gold Coast mammals.

It was a very pleasant evening they were both interesting & charming people and as always when I dine out I so much enjoy a well-served, leisurely meal in a house after being so much in messes. He has a lot of tame squirrels who are very friendly.

Today I go to stay with Gilbray and he has arranged for me to get some sailing which I appreciate very much. At the end of the next week I shall be at my old experiments & at the end of the month I shall be up to see Wilfred and then where Ray Waddel once went & back for Christmas. Then I must get cracking at the Mess for I am the new Mess President.

I hope to get my historical article off before I go to see Wilfred.

When that's all over I shall be packing. Duff & I are going to make a strenuous effort to get back in April.

I could not compete with 'Poets of Greek Anthologies' but I enjoyed Thompson's The Greek Tradition. I've just worked through Carlisle's Frederick the Great which I consulted for my article & became engrossed.

Oh I adore you and I need you badly. Kiss my boys. Alan

30th Oct 1944, Alan, WAF, Accra to Sheila

9.30 pm, Sea Mail

My Dear,

I'm just back this morning after a few very pleasant days away. It was a great treat really to arrive & find three very good chaps waiting for me on the airport - all with parties arranged for my stay - Gilbray the Australian microbiologist whom I have mentioned before as a man I like very much, Chwatt the Czech and Major James - I spent the first evening chatting with Col Alexander. Next morning I worked and had lunch at a Hospital.

In the afternoon (Saturday) we went by canoe to an island, where Gilbray had been working, to attend a celebration given by his labourers on his return from leave in South Africa. Then we paddled back. I went & bathed & changed & then we all went to a Dr Carling's house for a drink. He is a Maltese.

Then we went to a hotel & had a good dinner on the balcony & talked until 1 AM. Yesterday (Sunday) I again worked in the morning then to a "Palm Oil Chop" the great West African equivalent of curry. I got away at 4 & sailed in a 16 foot boat with Col Alexander until 7 PM. I have seldom enjoyed company so much. They were such worldly travelled & interesting people and it was so good of them to arrange such a program for me. Oh how I wish you could meet some of the people I know like Gilbray & MacDonald & James & Chwatt & the Carradale & Dr & Mrs Reid.

My Dear I make no attempt to say I did not enjoy myself. I did, hugely, but I know that you won't think I was not thinking of you & the boys. In the canoe, in the boat, sitting having lunch on an old balcony, everywhere Sheila my mind kept wandering to you &

wishing, aching, you could be there.

You can do so many things out here that are impossible at home.

I suppose I have been fabulously lucky in travelling about so much but oh I want to travel more.

I'll write an air letter after mail tomorrow. I love you. Alan

30th Oct 1944, Sheila, Wakefield, to Alan

Dearest One.

Firstly Robert requests me to tell you that he is a good boy, because as he says he doesn't want you to know he is a bad one!

Major Schofield phoned on Friday evening & is coming over to see me someday.

I've had the parents since Friday until this morning when they went to London & they are coming back tomorrow evening. Now for your letters of the 17th & 20th inst. which came in on Saturday. I am very thrilled about your discovery & the Geographical Mag article. So often I have been pleased about your *learnings* large & small simply because of what they mean to you but they have perhaps left me unmoved because they were of small interest to me or outside my comprehension. But this latest effort trivial beside the others is giving me a terrific kick! I am looking forward so much to the photos.

About a year or two in W. Africa after the war. Really Beloved you should have the sense not to unsettle me by asking such things. I would love it & since your letters came I've sailed hundred times for Africa & lived there more than here. You have however taken care not to mention the boys & I will be interested to hear what is your post-war planning for them! I long with all my heart for a break of that kind, but at the age the boys are I couldn't abandon them to enjoy myself. Can't you find the same kind of job somewhere they can go. The pay is good but why six months leave in the year? That makes one think the pay possibly ought to be double.

Just had your daft letter of the 24th. I'll need another card to answer it, the half I can make out anyhow! I've no time just now because the toothless one has just arrived. It's a very peculiar letter this latest one of yours beloved. I think you should be very careful about keeping your head covered!

I love you & I want to do daft things with you. Sheila

31ˢᵗ Oct 1944, Alan, WAF, Accra, to Sheila

Air Mail

My Dear,

I just had two letters from my very own girlfriend. Oh I hope your mouth is better now. You had better see about it though even if it has died down. An X-Ray would show up a cyst which could easily be removed when the gum was not inflamed.

The bags I sent are for you, no-one else. I sent a couple to Mummy but yours are nicer. Is the perfume nice. I have more - a litre in fact. Sorry about the shoes. Give me lengths in inches of Roberts & David's feet and your size & I'll see what I can do. Give the shoes to Susan with my love. Ruthin Castle is good. They have first-class physios there and are very good with tummy cases.

I'm so glad you're people are coming down. It will be a break for you. My Dear it means more than I can tell you to have you write about the house, and how you look on all you do as for my homecoming.

I love you so much and all my future is bound up in loving you. Tonight it's 9 PM & I'm back from mess feeling pretty sleepy after a long hot day.

As I write a film is developing of photos of the old Prince of Brandenburg Castles in an old German book I unearthed in the Secretarial Library. I am fearfully excited about this article.

I now have to do 10 talks on the Gold Coast Radio, 8 on health, one on children & one on hobbies. I have a great worry that I won't be able to spin out these eight talks.

A year tomorrow on the coast. I'm driving with Duff to celebrate in his mess. A year, & six months to go. Oh Sheila how wasteful it is to be away from you. Kiss my boys and tell them I love you all.

Alan

31st Oct 1944, Sheila, Wakefield, to Alan

My Dear I've been re-reading your very queer letter of the 24th & it's come to me that perhaps the secret of my love for you is that you can be so varied! I'm sorry Jeremiah doesn't want me, it's quite quite spoiled my day. I have never in my life heard of "de - o alo - ro" you've mistaken the name but given me a good laugh. Please send on your talk on toys. The nightmare of a wartime Christmas is again confronting me & although I'm not counting on any aid from your talk it will at least be seasonable

I don't quite know what to make of the toothless one. She is odd but will possibly grow on me. She is so self-conscious about her mouth that she really ties herself in knots & having been married at 18 & husband four years P.O.W. has a somewhat gloomy outlook, but I think will be quite useful over the winter months. I am sitting waiting on the parents arriving from London. Their train arrives at 10.30 p.m.

Bill Stephens went overseas, tropical kit, the other day. Hugh Fulton went to France a few weeks ago, having narrowly escaped being blown up in London. He lost all his things. Why did Mrs Taylor go home so soon? I am expecting your mother to stay with me in the next few weeks. Mother was meeting Doreen in London yesterday afternoon. The boys are fine, appallingly noisy & wicked, what a godsend schools are! Great minds think alike, I've saved the blackout frames & am storing them in the cellar stop

Just finished re-reading Jew Süss & enjoyed it very much. My brain won't work tonight & I can't think of anything more to tell you, except that I am very deeply in love with you, which, as I have always told you, is very different from just loving you.

Daddy is coming back here today because tomorrow is his birthday. Sweet! & so unlike him. He looks so ill I do hope Ruthin Castle helps him a bit.

I must go & lift the boys now and kiss them for you. Sheila

2nd Nov 1944, Sheila, Wakefield, to Alan

Dearest on Earth,

Other two letters yesterday. About the G. Coast job. Well firstly

I don't feel at all like laughing at or cursing you. You have unsettled me very badly, for after the boredom & repression of the last few years it sounds just wonderful to me. The snag of course is the children & for me at any rate it's a snag which I see no way of getting untangled from. Our people are quite incapable of having them & I just can't see myself farming them out as Mrs Taylor did. A sense of guilt would follow me always and would take the edge of any enjoyment and if anything went wrong I'd never get above it as long as I lived.

I have defended Mrs Taylor quite hotly against a lot of criticism & will continue to do so because for one thing I don't suppose she or they had any choice in the matter, it was his job when the children came, it wasn't like deciding in cold blood afterwards. If they were near boarding school age it would be quite different. It's easier for you, because for a long time you have had no near responsibility for them. it's well over two years since you even lived with us apart from leave. That being so it may be that my responsibility (you will never know how heavy I have felt it) has become an obsession, but the fact remains I just can't see any way out while they are so small. Funny how much more you wanted children than I & yet it I can't get away. Well that's that, now the point is I think you should take the job! I've been parted from you so much that six months or a year or two when (& this is all-important) I knew you were not in the Army & was relieved from dread of the future, would not be insupportable. If they should send you East I feel it would nearly finish me & years of desolation lie ahead.

Go to the mine by all means & who knows I might manage a very short trip out. Oh! Beloved if only the boys were a little older. I do so long for you & happiness & excitement too. I was in a daze all day yesterday & wouldn't admit to myself the impossibility of it for me, but now I am calm & there's no way out. Your release from present duties just makes this all-important to me as far as you are concerned. As for me the release would be so wonderful. Oh! How good it would be to talk to you & how much easier. I'm too full of longing to go & love for the children (& their father!) To write any more just now. Love Sheila

3rd Nov 1944, Sheila, Wakefield, to Alan

My Very Dear,

I am shaken to the core today. I had the new snapshot of you this morning & Oh! It's so very good. I had forgotten how much I love you Beloved. Of course I loved you dreadfully & you alone in all the world, but I had forgotten the uncanny fascination of your presence has always had over me. When I saw that photo I could have walked out on everything & come straight to you. It's a cold dark wet day & I long for hot sunshine & life. I thought after Wednesday's battle I had finally, or for the time being, exchanged vision for reality but now as usual I am weak & torn. Why Oh! Why did you unsettle me like this! Up to last Wednesday I was contented or reasonably so & quietly preparing for your homecoming & now nothing seems worthwhile & I'm as cross as two sticks with the children because I can't get my mind on them at all. Perhaps tomorrow I'll be able to think clearly again, today I am stone deaf in one ear & partially so in the other, which makes me feel extra dense. Dr Mac D. Smith is coming armed with syringe tomorrow. It's nearly 6 years since I last was troubled with this & the Doctor then said I'd have to have them done every six months! I'll be glad when tomorrow comes as apart from the deafness it's dreadfully uncomfortable.

Glad you liked your testimonial I must get on with typing them out. I am all right as long as I take my time & it's easy copying something.

You go ahead & take that job on the mine, if it's not too bad a part it's in. When do you have to decide? Why the very long, or rather very frequent, leaves? Oh! It would be good to know definitely what you were doing after April (or May!). The war is by no means over & I'm very alarmed about the future, the world seems mighty sick. Oh! But this abstract fear of mine is a wearisome thing. Dearest one I love you madly & you must do as you think best but if no demobilisation then the miner's my choice.
Sheila

4th Nov 1944, Alan, WAF, Accra, to Sheila

My Very Dear,

There was no letter yesterday so I've no questions to answer and have not a bit of news. I am very busy getting my Broadcast talks ready. I give my first on Thursday next. I shall be glad to have it behind me. It's very difficult not to be too oily and to be sufficiently honest in the opinions that I give on civilian medical matters here without raising a controversy which would split Army, Civil & African opinion.

I am so anxious to make use of the chance to boost the Army but to do so unduly is to show up the pre-war conditions in very sharp relief.

I came back from the last of my experiments yesterday & oh I am very glad to have it over. I'll tell you all about that project one day.

It is an extraordinary thing how dishonest are the higher scientists as regards the information they are given. As for altruism in this human activity - well I have not found it yet! Very cynical - very petty, still there it is.

Now my dear I'm getting on in the 13th month. I'll soon be able to talk of coming home to you. Oh how wonderful it is to allow myself to daydream & think of that. Alan

7th Nov 1944, Alan, WAF, Accra, to Sheila

2nd Letter of that Date

My Dearest One,

I received your letter of 20th last night. The new times for your postings are Wednesdays and Sundays I think. I don't believe Robert is bad & I don't think he is bad for he is my very own boy so you can tell him so. I'm glad you've heard from your parents.

My article for the Geographic Magazine is finished but it will take a little time to get the photographs, maps etc. properly prepared & arranged.

Yes Beloved I didn't mention the boys & West Africa did I? I don't follow your logic about the salary should be double because the leave is six months. We could keep a house going at home and

I would have to work at home also on such long leaves.

Beloved I'm very naughty & I know it but I do understand how you feel & I know too that equally you will know me. I enjoy living more than most people. I think possibly because I have a well-hidden romantic streak I have been able to satisfy a few schoolboy urges out here. I like West Africa and its only natural beloved that even your very old man should pass through a second childhood.

But Sheila I know about the boys. Oh Dearest I want so many lives as long as I meet & marry you in all of them.

My Tribe is my very own and I love them. But if as was inevitable I came abroad away from you then I'm lucky for you have had less worry about me than if I had gone elsewhere & I have had a very rich experience which I shall always remember.

Oh Dearest another week has gone. I love you. Alan

P.S. first broadcast is on Thursday. I'll send you the script.

7th Nov 1944, Alan, WAF, Accra, to Sheila

1St Letter of that Date

My Beloved,

Another week of the last month of the first year gone. I'm in good heart and shall I say again - longing, aching to come home to my very own Twibe.

Beloved I've got wanderlust badly. I want to go dozens of places and see thousands of things with you. I'm all for Reiff & Camusglashlan but we must go places too.

Now finance is a problem (- isn't it always?) But we must set our souls to work hard at a system of journalism. It will have to be worked at. Planning of what would sell deciding on what journal will buy, then going to the places & drafting outlines of the articles on the spot so that we shall not miss anything.

It will mean preliminary reading before we set off on our tours. We might well make a start with our journey to Greece but extended slightly by going on to Turkey. What say you?

Then I think a visit to Sweden would be a paying proposition, if I could get really good photographs. I must improve though for this one just missing being good enough. It seems to me that colour photography will be essential post-war but there will be a big rush to cash in on that.

Beloved I want you to see tropical countries. There is a very great fascination for the way of life is always striving to be like that at home, but it never is never can be. Then next we must go to Switzerland and Czechoslovakia and there is a lot of good country round the Caspian Sea. In fact Beloved we could solve the housing problem by staying away!

Oh Sheila these things can be done and we must try. You and I will never get old and stuffy and "it's Friday so we go to the pictures". Tell me how you feel.

If you can find it send me the small folding camera (black leather covered) which is somewhere in the house.

I adore you especially behind the ears I like. Alan

8ᵗʰ Nov 1944, Sheila, Wakefield, to Alan

My Dear Beloved,

Winter is upon us! Gales, hailstones, thunder & lightning have been going on for days & it's beastly cold. I daresay you could do with some of it, but it doesn't suit me at all. I've had so many letters from you recently dear & they do make me feel near to you. Today I had one of the 31ˢᵗ October. Yes I'll send you the length of the boy's feet at the end of this letter. Yes the perfume is delightful. I'm sorry if I forgot to say so. I am intensely interested in your "Brandenburg" article. I think the sooner I learn shorthand the better if you are going develop into a writer. My typing improves daily (I think!) & I'm well through the testimonials.

I phoned your people tonight to thank your father for the cheque he sent me for the bags you sent. Shall I credit it to Glyn Mills or buy the boys Saving Certificates?

I had Andre Maurois' "Call No Man Happy" from the Reprint Society yesterday & I'm enjoying it very much.

The "Toothless One" seems to have settled down. She comes in before blackout on her days out as she is afraid to be out in the dark!

Your mother talks of coming to see us about the end of the month which will be another break for Christmas. I nearly forgot to mention that yesterday I had your letter telling me of your good times with Gilbray etc. Sailing & so on. Beloved, I wouldn't have expected you not to enjoy yourself & you don't need to apologise! Oh! How dearly I love you & how glad I am that you can enjoy such things so much. The boys are very fit & full of life. When the doctor (Mac D. Smith) came to do my ears on Sunday, he looked at them & said "what a picture of robust good health, just how children should look". I was sorry for him, for his boy has T.B. & his wife is far from well & home with her mother. This seems to mean he goes home & cooks his own supper & so on!

Well now I'm going to bed & with my latest snapshot of you on the table beside me.

Robert has not been late for school yet which is a marvel considering what a sleepy head his mother is. This morning however I dozed off after the clock had gone off & had a frantic rush. I have to hammer up the "domestic" who sleeps like the dead! The most lovesick woman in the world bids you good night. Sheila

9th Nov 1944, Alan, WAF, Accra, to Sheila

Air Mail 1 (2 Air Mails, same date)

Dear Woman,

I'm so glad to have your letter tonight before I go off early in the morning by train to the Ashanti country. My big trip is off meanwhile & I hope to be back on Monday or Tuesday.

I'm so sorry about your ear. I hope it's all right after the syringing.

Surely no man ever had a nicer letter from the woman he loved than the one I had today. I don't pretend to know why you liked the photograph of the straggle haired large nosed jovial looking chap who was sitting on the rock.

I going up to the mines a week on Monday to have a look see. No, it's not an unhealthy place but salaries are big out here and all the commercial firms are reducing their leave to 9 months as they say people get "coasting" if they don't get long leaves. The coasting is in my opinion usually drink. The miners are rough & tough citizens from the four corners of the globe and the Africans are Dagombas who are amusing rascals either in a devil of a temper or laughing themselves silly. But the senior people have magnificent quarters complete with refrigerators & fans and all the gadgets which make living comfortable. They take so much money out each year that they don't know what to do with the money.

I gave my Broadcast tonight & was I frightened. Beloved it was awful sitting at the table with crickets whistling outside and a feeling that my voice was playing arpeggios on the scale & what I was saying was nonsense and that everyone was saying - My Lord Why do they put chaps like this on. I have not been so shaken for many a day. The people in the mess said it was fine but then they are polite people. I'll send you the script & the newspaper cuttings which may say anything from "The scoundrel should be sent out of the country on the next boat" to "he should be knighted".

Beloved I'll continue in another letter card. But I love you.

Air Mail 2

To continue.

I sent you two big tins of pears today - South African & I shall send you more when I come home. What I really want is potatoes. Yams and Cassava & tinned potatoes have no taste at all. I also want Brussel Sprouts & turnip and the kiss before my meal. Can you just please arrange. In fact beloved give me the kiss & I won't bother with the rest.

And so I'm "bad to you" am I by unsettling you. Well I don't want to be "bad to you". I'll stall on this job until seen the place & tried to bump up the terms.

Then I shall see what prospects of demobilisation are at that time & if things look bad I'll have a shot at it, but insist on first needing three months leave. The Secretary of the Chamber has asked me to spend a night with him & I probably shall. Ankola River, the Portuguese name. The River of the smoke how grim it must have been in the old days but now - well we could have tennis & golf - no riding I'm afraid due to Tsetse but you could have your own canoe & six strong smiling paddlers, and the cook (+ small boy) and a chauffeur (+ small boy). Those in brackets would do all the work but those first mentioned would be the only ones paid. The three of them would cost about £10 a month & would find all their own food. Beloved I am ("bad to you") but I love you and long so much for you to share the things I have enjoyed out here. Remember that though I am so very variable in what I like & don't like & what I want & don't want & so on, as regards loving you I'm certain.

Sheila my Dear my relief demand is in, the first step back to you. Kiss my boys, I love them too. Alan

12th Nov 1944, Sheila, 6 Crown Mansions, to Alan
This, Beloved, has been a real November day, torrents of rain, gloom and cold. The boys fought incessantly from waking until at 3.30 we went to McVicar's for tea! Yesterday afternoon I had Major Schofield & his small girl to tea (wife prostrate with headache). The children had a fine romp & we bellowed at each other above the din. I enjoyed meeting him very much but gather he has by no means left his heart in W. Africa! He brought the photographs which are marvellous & the perfume for which many many thanks. Your boxes (two) arrived safely on Friday & have disgorged books, sheets, towels, junk etc. Also tinned butter which gives great pleasure & dried milk, also most useful as we can only get two pints per day & the National Dried Milk is skimmed. Major S. seems very anxious to get out & return to his practice.

He suggested (naturally without prompting from me) that you would be pretty sure of demobilisation if the local Authority applied for your release. Jim funnily enough was speaking on the same subject this afternoon & suggested that you should get them to apply for you a month or two before you were due home. However I have no great faith in the infallibility of these measures & meanwhile I have advised you go to the mine, so I shall await your reply with interest. Major S. seemed to think you (& he) stood a good chance being posted East, which has of course been in my mind all along. He (Major S.) is still beautifully sunburnt but not (or I may be wrong) very full of the joys of life. He is impressed he says with how much more weary everyone is of the war since he went away. Oh! Beloved - the books! I had just the other day coped more or less successfully with my "headache" & got them all more or less stowed away. I lined the tops of wardrobes with them with brown paper on top & resorted to various other dodges to get them where they wouldn't get harmed & then I am overwhelmed again by the contents of your boxes! Never mind I love em! I am reading & greatly fascinated with the life of William Morris. I shall of course follow up with "The Eastern Paradise" - or some of it! I have finished Andre Maurois' "Call No Man Happy" it is most interesting, but for some reason I don't feel Andre would appeal to me at all. In the first place I don't agree with him that you can "call no man happy until he is dead" it seems stupid sort of creed & he is just too obviously fond of himself. Dearest one it will be fun to be together again. I'll write again very soon. Love Sheila

13th Nov 1944, Sheila, Wakefield, to Alan

My Dearest Man. Today, or rather tomorrow, I shall post at the same time as this letter three photographs which Nonie took at Nethybridge. I hope you won't be too startled at the sight of your family & that you will like us a little. My film should be ready this week & Oh! I do hope something turns out! The towels & sheets are fine beloved. Are there any pillow slips? The children thank you for the balls. One simply terrific treat is that tin of butter. I in particular have a dreadful craving for butter & could almost grab the boy's rations from under their noses. Twenty years of war would never reconcile me to margarine.

I've been hard at it in the garden all afternoon & am dead tired, but pleasantly so. When we came home from McVicar's last night it was dark & the boys got a terrific thrill, neither having been out in the dark within memory, unless in a car. Also it was pouring rain & David kept saying "dark night Mummy, David can't see anything" it wasn't until we were halfway home I discovered the poor child's sou-wester was right over his eyes! Robert has produced two large new molars. I forgot to tell you that he says the shoes you sent to David have "furniture soles".

My alarm clock has conked out & I just have to wake by willpower now, which is very trying!

16th November

Dear One. Sorry I've been so slow in getting this off. The cold weather seems to make me slower all round. I haven't had a letter from you for nine days or so, which having been so fortunate lately, seems quite a long time. However I know you are off on your wanderings again so I won't expect any for a while yet. I'm longing to know what you decided about the "mines" but am also much cheered to read that doctors are to be demobilised in the same way as others.

Robert has taken a great fancy to Belinda Sweeting at school. I have asked Mrs S.to bring her to tea next week. We are going to the Maternity Hospital for tea on Saturday week, it should be quite amusing!

I have developed a dreadful desire for stacks of new clothes! I love you dearly. Sheila

14th Nov 1944, Alan, WAF, Accra, to Sheila

Dear Wife,

I came back last night after a hot sticky journey on the train. I had a lot of accumulated sea-mail waiting. I'm glad you did not settle Lewis's account as it is all wrong. I'll send them a cheque for correct amount.

I've sent script of my first Broadcast, & a note from Medical Research Council saying they liked my article with Findlay to Mummy, for perusal & sending on to you. I give my next talk on Thursday. Try tuning in on Thursday night at 7.25 at home to Station ZOY on 15.94 or 60.5 m and you might hear me. Short waves are odd things and sometimes travel extraordinary distances.

I am going for the last time to the old experiment grounds on Friday to bring back my jeep & I shall see the Secretary for Mines. I have a great wheeze to put myself over big as Hygiene Adviser and a huge salary - enough to fly out and back as the spirit moves us.

Beloved you are surely the nicest woman in all the world! No amount of being 'sex-starved' makes any other woman seem any better to me. I'm just longing for you and being with you. I'm thinking of drawing up rules for you when I get back be sure you're not "bad to me". For example you are not to knit for I shall so often want to come & put my head on your knees & I hate getting pins in my hair.

Then you are to shut me up if I tell you about West Africa (I won't ever talk in company in any case so you will be saved that). Then you must not get agitated if your hair gets ruffled when you are kissed. Then when we go to dances you must dance nearly all the dances with me. Then you must never agree with me for the sake of peace for that's "bad for me".

I love you & the tribe & I'll be a very very happy man when I see you. Alan

15th Nov 1944, Alan, WAF, Accra, to Sheila

My Dear,

An extra letter which will I hope catch the post. Its beginning was suggested to me by my new 4/9p N.A.A.F.I.[1] pen. It has a fine nib & suits me very well. I thought I was finished with my article but the Editor says he only wants 3000 words so I'm trying to compress 6500 into 3000 words. It's such a pity for it restricts my flowing English! Even more serious I have to leave out so many interesting bits & pieces of information which I had dug out at great trouble from a large number of books. It seems to me that one must learn to be unscrupulous about checking data & just pinch stuff from someone else's summary if one wants to be successful in journalism for it's not economic to have to put so much work into it. Probably I shall learn a technique by experience. Beloved tell me more (if he tells you) about Robert at school & about the boys in general. I'm a very proud father you know.

It seems likely that I shall get away in April but it all depends on War Office providing a replacement at the correct time. I wonder

---

[1] N.A.A.F.I - Navy, Army and Air Force Institute. Set up in 1921 to sell goods & services needed by the Armed Forces, and to run recreational establishments.

what is going to happen in Europe. The policy judging by the news is to keep up relentless pressure by moderate attacks here & there until a big effort can be made.

Brig Wigmore goes home in January or February. He wants to stay until February for some reason or other. I shall be sorry when he goes for I know him pretty well by now.

Well beloved I'm off to have a squash before lunch. I need two pints to refresh sweat by midday!

I love you. Alan

17th Nov 1944, Alan, WAF, Accra, to Sheila

Beloved

It's 2 P.M. & the mail did not come yesterday but is expected today. So as I have not had a letter for a week I was glad to be able to delay my departure until tomorrow. I shall answer any letter I get before I post this.

I gave my second talk last night & have sent you a copy. I still felt very scared, unfortunately I gave you the wrong wavelength, the correct one is 83.21 metres - not that I think the set would get it unless by a freak.

Oh Beloved I'm longing to be home. I'm missing so much of you. I shall never get enough of you Sheila & I am worried about you if I have to go away again when I get back.

8.30. p.m.

Well the mail is yet another day late so I shall not get anything until Wednesday. Still I'll have that to look forward to. Oh my dear I wish you would suddenly materialise just here tonight for I want you to talk to so very badly.

I'm getting packed to be off and I'm very used to that by now. I'm so wondering if Roberts's canoe has arrived at last & Oh Dear I'm wondering how you will look & whether my very own boys will be very jealous of me when I get back and oh so many things about my own wee twibe. I'm very sleepy & tired tonight. The temperature was 94°F even at 4 o'clock today and I can assure you that that means plenty of sweat.

I'm off this time to bring my jeep back and hand it over. I shall miss it badly.

Good Night Dearest one - time is slipping by & I'll soon be home. I love you. Alan

18th Nov 1944, Sheila, Wakefield, to Alan

This is 3 Air Mails written as one on 18th & 20th.

Dearly Beloved,

I am already mighty weary of the winter & it's only beginning! This dismal dripping ugly part of Yorkshire is enough in itself to depress anyone who reacts to that kind of thing. It's all right as long as I stay in the house or garden but this afternoon I took the boys a walk to the farm as they were pathetically anxious to feed some hens & they don't have a lot of amusement poor lambs. It was a dismal enough November afternoon to start with & got worse as we progressed. Everything was ugly & decayed & diseased looking. The hideous gaunt factory chimneys belching black smoke stood out overpoweringly way on a background of slatey nothingness. When we got to the farm it stank to high heaven & was a sea of black mud & puddles surrounded by gloom. Some white ducks with filthy shirt fronts appeared and partook of the bread the children had brought. Wallowing at intervals in a puddle of slime and mud & defecating copiously & noisily thereof.

This amused the children & nauseated me! Then it started to rain & we got soaked coming back. David wanted to be carried for a bit as his shoes weren't visible for mud & I (as always too affected by external things) in a bad temper & informed him that he would get left behind if he didn't step out. Tonight I feel a brute & it's saddening because I feel that way so often nowadays and have so little patience. I have never been any good at playing with children & although I feel uncomfortable & guilty about it, have never had any great interest in them. But I do love my two very dreadfully & wish I had not these shortcomings. I always comfort myself that when the war is over & I am less preoccupied (in other words when you are with us) & my heart is light again I shall be better. I have never had children in these circumstances so I can still hope. Also the lack of toys is very wearing. They can appreciate toys (decent ones that work) so much & would spend hours with them & now Christmas again & nothing but the dreary old things that have been in the shop year in year out & would be a swindle at any price.

Mother sends Robert as many parcels as she can knowing how he enjoys receiving them. I shall however have to tell her to stop because he sat and wept over the last parcel of chocolate biscuits, because he had so hoped for the impossible toy. How I ache & long for these boys of mine to know the joy of having their father living with them. How much they are missing I don't know if you fully appreciate, but I know & it's bad for them. Don't laugh at this beloved I am so sincere that there are tears in my eyes as I write. My prayer is that you could be demobilised when the German business is over & I could straighten my shoulders from the weight of these years. If only I could be sure of this I would beg you not to think of that mine (at any money), for the boys sake because they have not had a fair deal in being without you for so long & in me they have an abnormal person to live with when I am separated from you. Any prolonged wanderings of ours must by the most elementary calls of duty be postponed for a few years. And yet you very well know the conditions under which I think the "mines" would be as light beside darkness (mine of course) & you must decide for us. I'm sorry if this is a depressing letter but I suppose I must get it off my chest some time & as you know very well I am seldom as dull as I seem to be tonight. It may be reaction to my visions of renewed youth pleasure & excitement conjured up by your suggestions of Africa & my gradual realisation of the utter hopelessness of it so far as I was concerned. I love you so much & I love my boys so much & dammit I think I love myself too much. What would I not give even to have an hours talk with you.

Anthony has "chicken pox" so the chances are Susan and David will have it too!

The latest gossip which is unfortunately a fact is that Macdonald Smith & his wife have separated. That bare fact is true, the sordid details I will not give as I know nothing of their truth & they are uninteresting I think to write of anyway. I would know nothing of it yet but for the gross indiscretion of a lawyer to Jim.

The negotiations over the buying of this house will have me white haired soon. I have now made a hard offer of £1150 which is several hundred less than Sanderson wants. I shall have to restrain Charlie to play for time for it has become apparent to me that he is determined to have the house at almost any money!

It sounds a bit of double-dealing to me & if Sanderson hadn't proved so damn mean & Mr W. hadn't been such a staunch friend I wouldn't have touched it.

However I'll carry it through. Mr W. is brim-full of all the repairs & alterations he will at once put in hand & is like a child with a new toy!

Robert has now four new molars & his new front tooth has quite filled up the gap.

Monday 20th November

Dear One. A letter from you of the 9th inst. written in two parts but only one has arrived so I'm left somewhat in the air. As I gather the second one would have dealt with what you call my "reactions" to the mine, I feel I may have missed something important & can only hope it will turn up.

We are all fine, truth to tell our livers were all disordered for a few days by an excess of Canadian butter. Tummies inured to margarine cannot it seems cope with a sudden supply of butter!

I have just finished "The Story of The Glittering Plain", did you read it & what did you make of it if you did.

I suppose with the approach of Christmas the mails will slow up a bit. Beloved if you don't get any Christmassy Greetings from us at the right time forgive me please. I've done no shopping so far. However you well know you will be constantly in my thoughts & well as the children say "Daddy is coming in the spring"!

All love, Sheila

19th Nov 1944, Alan, WAF, Accra, to Sheila

My Very Dear,[1]

I missed the mail as you will know from my last letter but I shall be back in Accra on Wednesday. I have very little more to do here in my final clear up - in some ways I shall be sorry not to be coming back here for I have had such a wonderful chance of getting about in the Bush & seeing the real Africa.

Don't be surprised when a cheque for £44 is coming off my bank balance. I paid it to an officer for a very good camera plus exposure meter - both out of order. I think I can repair them and sell them at a good profit.

Oh Dearest One I shall be glad when the New Year comes for then I shall feel that the time is really short until I see you. Tell the boys I love them.

Bless you my Dear. Alan

22nd Nov 1944, Alan, WAF, Accra, to Sheila

1st Air Mail

Beloved,

I came back in my jeep today to find your letter but first some news which will cheer you up I think. We are given to understand that when the war in Europe is over in six months or so only those who are not likely to be released for more than a year after that will be sent to Far East so that improves our chances there.

Now for your letter. I'm so glad you had a spate (of letters) from me. You forgot to give the lengths of all your feet. Buy yourself savings certificates with the £5.

You are good about me having a good time. I was up at the mine yesterday. There are two mines & two Doctors are always on leave & the other there. There is a 40 bed hospital & a hundred Europeans & 6000 Africans to look after. The district is just a cut in enormous forest but is hilly & seemed quite pleasant. I have planned to go & stay with the Main Reef Manager next month just to see how I like the place. I like the atmosphere about the place & the mine

---

[1] Addressed to North Gardner St

managers are as nice a set of chaps as I have met. The present M D tells me he is making about £1650. In other mines the M D makes more but do a year & then have three months leave.

Oh it's good Dear to hear of Dr Mc Smith's remark. I'm very sorry to hear of the ructions in his family. I'm longing to hear what you think of the sheets & towels in my boxes. If you like them I'll lay in a store for they are very cheap.

I hear the weather is very bad in U K & think it is delaying our mails.

My Broadcast tomorrow is off as the station is not functioning properly & meanwhile they can only relay, home programs - I love you. Alan

22nd Nov 1944, Alan, WAF, Accra, to Sheila

2nd Air Mail

Beloved,

This is my second letter to you today - to answer your second which came in tonight. I'm so glad Schofield came to see you. Don't worry about what he thinks. He is a confirmed pessimist - never went out of distance of the place he was staying (why should he if he did not want to but it's the people who don't get out into the bush who least like West Africa). He is a good chap & we miss him as his successor is so wet that he drips.

Regarding boxes presumably there was one medium-size & one small one of books. There is also on the way a large crated trunk like box. Full of books. No Beloved it's not & I'm bad to you.

I'm glad you liked the life of William Morris. I cannot remember the author's name but Mr Privy told me it was the standard & best life of Morris. It's very good for giving an insight into the pre-Raphaelite characters. They did a very good job & their own work will be forgotten when their influence is still strong. I'm very fond of Gabrielle Rossetti's (and Christine Rossetti's) poetry. Morris's stuff is terribly profane & I got too tired & but interested very quickly in his epic poems. I'll have to go pony riding in Iceland one summer & see the valleys mentioned in Burnt Njall & the Hrafnkels Saga.

By the way Schofield had a bad go of Amoebic Dysentery which probably accounts for his looking so tired.

"Call No Man Happy Until He Is Dead"? Sheila sometimes I'm frightened at how fortunate & happy we have been. Look at me in robust health - last night they threw a party at the Hospital in Takoradi because it was my last night. We got to bed at 2 AM. I had breakfast at 7 AM & left in the Jeep at 7.30 & drove it for 166 miles in the heat to get here at 12 noon. I did some work, had lunch, wrote to you & worked from 2.15 until 5 clearing up stuff. Had tea in my room & then typed until 6.45. Bathed, had dinner - typed more & now at 9.30 I'm in bed & sleepy but very well.

Hope the boys are sound in their senses as well as their bodies. You as far as I know are well. We all have each other and we all love living. If I died tomorrow I would have had my share & more.

I had a letter from Daddy tonight. Mummy seems to be pretty fit these days and Moira is fairly well and has gained seven pounds in weight. Mummy is terribly excited at the chance of seeing you and the boys - so am I and it's 20th November & time goes on.

Jeremiah has I regret to say retired to hospital with a particularly virulent attack of venereal disease. These Africans are amazing they are always having, have just had or are about to have some form of V.D. The latest variation on the theme of black bodies is "advice makes the blacks go blacker".

It is astonishing how many Europeans have casual or regular "Mummies". Apparently the best way is to get a girl of 14 guaranteed virgin cost about £15 plus 10/- per week keep! Sounds fantastic but it's true. It's an odd world & there are odd people in't. They were talking last night about an officer in a V.D. ward out here contracted from a black woman. He kept a photograph of his wife & child on his bed side table! Can you account for that?

It's so odd to think of you with fog & ice - ugh - horrid. I'd just put up with it though to be transported!

Good night Dear Woman.

23/11

Enclosed letter & photograph arrived this morning. It will amuse you to see O'Toole in my jeep. Bless you sweetheart of mine. Alan

22nd Nov 1944, Sheila, Wakefield, to Alan

Dearest on Earth.

Only another week left in November. It won't be so very long now until I can start counting the time between us in weeks.

It's funny to think of the last time I was here & the few weeks between your frequent leaves seemed such a dreadful age! Beloved I hope I don't seem very hoary when you get back. I feel as young as ever I did, but I suppose I am getting middle-aged! Your other letter (the continuation of the one that arrived) hasn't turned up so I suppose we can count it as lost. I hate to think I've missed it.

I am just finishing Balzac's "Wild Ass's Skin" the first of his that I've read. I find it a terrible long winded, but in bits a positive treasure trove & must read more of him. He had an extraordinarily descriptive pen. The sheets & towels you sent home have come out of the wash with flying colours & are excellent. The weather is still pretty dreary but has turned warm again. The boys are fine & David when he went to bed last night said "Daddy love me?" Anything either of them break they set aside for you to mend on your immediate return!

Dear One it's been so long that I cannot quite picture the relief it will be to have you with us again.

Beloved I can imagine as we grow older a tremendous intimacy & dependence growing between you & I, who have known so much of each other's youth & who almost as far back as we remember things clearly have been everything to each other. I do not mean that we are not, as it is, dependent but I think we shall get a bonus so to speak of understanding as the years go by.

Meanwhile & for ever I love you with all my heart. Sheila

24th Nov 1944, Alan, WAF, Accra to Sheila

My Very Dear,

Another letter yesterday! Thank you & Oh Sheila I'm missing you more badly all the time, it does not get easier. I'm looking forward to the Nethybridge photographs. My enlarger lamp &

condenser arrived safely and are a great delight as I've been in some trouble with my enlarger for want of a lamp.

I'm so glad you want new clothes. Buy yourselves a lot & I shall have another big issue of coupons when I get back & am laying in stocks of stuff here. Oh Beloved I want to go places with you.

I'm hoping that Roberts long delayed canoe will be with you soon. It was sent off two months ago. I have your letter enclosing those of Ian Finney & Col Blake. I shall write to them.

I must write to Robert too. It's long time since I did so but I feel so out of touch with him now & don't know very well how to interest him.

I shall send off the copy of the Brandenburg Fort article tomorrow - I'll send my original & the version as condensed to 3000 words.

I'm having a complete day off today setting my enlarger to rights & generally playing about. I hope you see Mummy & Daddy soon and oh I really hope you see me in April not May for I need you so much. Alan

26th Nov 1944, Sheila, Wakefield, to Alan

My Dear One.

A letter from you yesterday posted on the 15th inst. It was mostly in pencil and gave directions for the chance of picking your voice up on the short waves! The instructions were partly obscured and I should think the chance is pretty slender but I'll try. We are all very well. Roberts's neck is getting too big for the neck bands of his shirts and his kilt is noticeably shorter so he must be expanding & stretching! Yesterday we had tea with Miss Perkins, anyway I did. She had had a wooden slide affair brought in from the clinic & the boys were so entranced with it that they refused point-blank to have any tea! It was raining cats & dogs when it was time to come home & of course quite dark so I had a taxi & that gave them a fine thrill to finish up with. I really must go into Leeds this week & try to find some Christmas toys. Jim is going to get tickets for the Pantomime for some Saturday afternoon & Monica and I will join forces & have a taxi there & back & take Anthony & Robert. Jim will stay behind & look after Susan & David! From what I have heard of the bookings it will probably be February or March before we go but it will be fun when it comes. Funny to think David is just the age Robert was when we took him to "Peter Pan"!

Your parents propose to spend a weekend here in about a fortnight's time, so that will make a break before Christmas. It seems unlikely now that we shall go north at Christmas time as Daddy is still waiting on word to start for Ruthin Castle & he will be there about four weeks they expect. Mother is going to stay in a hotel nearby.

David trod on my instep with his outdoor shoes on yesterday. It hurt horribly at the time & I'm lame today. It's queer to think that there is enough of David to do that, but he's a hefty lad now.

I'm enjoying this months "Reprint" book very much. It's "The Three Bamboos" by Robert Standish & is I think very clever.

Thanks for the first few "rules for when you get back". I am knitting all the wool in the house into socks for the boys & then I shall clear all my pins into the "[Illegible]". I don't think I'm the knitting type anyway! I do love your worries about "talking about W. Africa"! It will be hard to realise I suppose that there are few mightily interested in the topic, but you can count on me, I'll drink it in!

Beloved I'm "sex starved" too, but fortunately we are affected in the same way by it!

Dear, time is getting on, do you realise it's hardly worthwhile sending you any more books?

All the twibe's love goes out to you but mine most of all, because without you I am an unreal shell.

I love you. Sheila

27th Nov 1944, Alan, WAF, Accra to Sheila

Sea Mail

My Very Dear,

I don't quite know why I'm writing to you but I was sitting here in my office day dreaming of you and I thought I would just as well be employed writing to you and that you might get an extra letter as result which would make you happy & therefore make me happy.

For Beloved I was thinking how nice you are, how attractive & sweet & lovable and how I look forward to years & years of your company, and how you are the only woman I have ever known by whom I would willingly have had children. it's odd how I saw you and liked you a lot and thought of you many times but I think I must have lost my heart irrevocably when I saw you that funny time at Seamill when I had been playing golf with Daddy & you came up from bathing. I was certainly dreadfully upset emotionally for I was "filthy" to the family & when Mother said "there are few girls would look as pretty as that girl after a bath" I gave her to understand that I could not see it even if it mattered.

But I must obviously have been inoculated with you for I know I knew you were at Seamill & I was on the lookout for you. Or was it at a University Dance where you were with Nonie & I half thinking aloud, half just being rude, asked Anne Benjie "do you want to see a really lovely girl?"

I'll tell you a secret which I have always concealed from you before Sheila. After I left you, when I told you first I loved you - I cursed myself for a fool & felt that I had tied myself down & spoiled all the interesting selfish things I wanted to do. And I felt terrible for the few days until I saw you again. Immediately I saw you & spoke to you again that feeling disappeared forever.

I suppose most people - not excluding you - felt like that but it was very odd.

Oh Beloved suppose I had not met you or had, because of an indiscretion before, felt that I could never ask you - there would have been no love as we know it there would have been no Robert and no David. It's odd - very commonplace but absolutely unique.

While I was writing this this morning in came two air letters from you which had been delayed in a strayed mail bag. A very pleasant surprise especially as there may be another mail tonight.

They are dated October 31 & November 2 and they are nice letters Sheila.

I'd better answer the letters as there are various questions.

Sorry for Nancy & Bill Stephen's wife (can't remember her

name). Mrs Taylor went home with her husband on leave at the end of his tour of 18 months. He was obviously well through his tour when she arrived.

I hope your Mother & Father are well. I'm a bit confused, is he on his way to Ruthin Castle or did he just think of it.

Now Dearest about the question of the job. There is no question ever of me taking a job when I could not have you with me for at least 10 months in the year. That's the first thing. Therefore, for the present at least, while the boys are young it's impossible I know & I agree with you absolutely & entirely.

That does not mean I think you will agree that in the future we shall have become too old in the spirit and sluggish in the body to entertain the idea of working abroad for a year or two if a good opportunity offers. If, for example, one of these five year professorships in Singapore, or Jerusalem, or Cairo etc offered itself and the leave was good I would see no objection to going as a family.

For if the boys are so dull of intellect that such a change in their educational program set them back, well that's too bad but indicating that they would be better in jobs requiring brawn rather than brain.

Again we shall make our holidays real "adventures", every one. I have no fear that you (or I or rather and I") will ever become a vegetable - what fun to marry a man on the high road to transmutation into a vegetable & so to infuse life into him that the idea is not even offensive but - well just fun!

As regards the immediate future I shall stall & stall until I see ahead a little better & if when the time comes it seems advisable to do one tour on the mines before the war ends I shall try to do so for I do want you free from worry. Oddly enough I gather from Wiggy that he has been approached unofficially by the Civil Medical People to find whether I'm interested in a Hygiene job here post war.

So Beloved you see that I think on these matters very much as you do - not in a submission of either of us to the other's opinion for we must agree to differ certain things if we feel strongly - but because the overriding factors are the same for both of us. We have each other and we have our sons.

If I could develop the knack of writing articles round photographs, it would simplify the expense side of our holidays so I must work hard at it, here, and when I'm back home. It is a knack and an attitude of mind to catch the sellable idea, but like other knacks it is not necessarily inborn but can be planted & cultivated.

This is a long letter the longest I've written to you for some time but the burden of it is that I love you. Alan

27ᵗʰ Nov 1944, Alan, WAF, Accra, to Sheila

Dear Dear Sheila,

I've just had your three letters of 18/11. I'm so glad I wrote you a long sea mail today before I received them. Beloved the war will not take long now. I shall be back to stay with you and our boys and I shall not leave you now, not for the mines of El Dorado.

Oh Sheila I know the depression & grime of Wakefield - because I love you I know how you feel.

Sorry about the sad effects of butter. I could make nothing of the "Glittering Plain"! Beloved I'll not write more tonight. I am lying naked in bed sweating & even the effort of writing is sufficient to make me sweat more. I love & think of you waiting & I'll pray for you all & thank God for you all.

Tuesday 28ᵗʰ

I shall set to today to see if I can make any toys for the boys. The easiest thing to make is a boat but that leads to messes in the bathroom! But I shall see what I can devise. I'll have a shot at the Fort. Sheila you know, don't you, how I feel about you all and I do know the squalor of the grime & mud Wakefield.

We shall not stay there long though. I'm very interested in this sale of the house palaver. He is a shocking old twerp to demand these sums for a house which he would have sold to me in 1937 for £750. I think you should have a 5% fee from Whitaker for acting as his agent. Well I'll write often and am always thinking of you. Love Alan

28th Nov 1944, Alan, WAF, Accra, to Sheila

Sea Mail

My Beloved,

Since receiving your letter about toys I have started work on a Fort for Robert but I doubt whether he will get it by Christmas.

I'll also make a boat which goes by elastic & see what can be done with other things.

Dearest the boys no doubt would benefit by having their Daddy if only because there would be someone else in the house but you forget that I get irritable with them too - quicker than you - unlike you I only hope it was because I was always on edge knowing I was going away again.

I know beloved that you do not love children in the abstract or in the mass or as individuals - except Robert and David. I like children in the mass possibly more but I love my own because they are ours.

I've just had Robert's drawing of the car which came from Achiltibuie getting petrol and a letter from Miss Burton who is a "Robert fan".

She says Miss Eales is bullying everyone & taking advantage of Dr Allardine being afraid she will go away!

No Dear, Wakefield is no place for us. We liked it because we made the most we could of it and we were happy together - we . . .
. . . . . . ¹

28th Nov 1944, Sheila, Wakefield, to Alan

Dear One.

A letter yesterday of the 15th & today of the 17th inst. I'm very sorry about your having to cut your article, you should have told them you'll send it elsewhere!

Beloved, this morning's letters disquieted me considerably by yet another allusion to "going away again when I get back". Schofield and then Jim separately advise me that should the "Local Authority" apply for your release after the German war there was no doubt in reason that it would be granted. They are possibly

---

¹ Letter, addressed to North Gardner St, ends here, obviously a page missing

wrong, you will know best, but if they are I have begged you to go to the mine. Yet now I hear nothing of the mine & only those hints that your return home will only be prelude to a much longer absence. It is a very widespread dread (here at home) of people that their sons or husbands will be sent east for it obviously means several years. Right or wrong as this may be it is & has been a very obvious worry of mine which I have tried very hard not to dwell on. However from your persistent reference to it I am bound to gather that you are of the opinion that the worry will become a fact & therefore I await news of the mine with very great anxiety. It is more than possible that the missing letter contained replies to my questions & feelings on the mine question but in case it didn't, I would very much like to know when you have to decide - when you would be expected to take up duties & what length of contract they require of you.

The money is of secondary importance besides the larger issue the importance of which is everything to me. No doubt it's very selfish, no doubt one should simply be thankful to be alive & to have no insupportable sorrow these days, but the fact remains that a few months after you get home you will as you well know have been away six years. No matter how I dislike the look of it the fact remains that I shall not have many years left of youth (or should one say comparative youth!) & though as patriotic as anyone, & considerably more than some, I feel with all my strength that the "gaps" should be dealt with -

New Air Mail
- by other than you. The boys are growing quickly, if another few years separation is to be added to the already large total - but no it's not really possible to contemplate. If I am making a mountain of a molehill beloved forgive me & remember how demoralising is inaction & solitude & everlasting waiting. The 101 pinpricks of life these days get on top of one sometimes & several hours blank depression can, one suddenly remembers, be traced back to - will coal ever last out & how to make 2 pints of milk a day keeps the boys even half satisfied - trivial I know but life is like that at home.

As to happier things Roberts's canoe arrived yesterday & he is simply delighted.

He took it to school today & the teacher let them all draw it & she sent Robert home early in case the other boys might break it!

Robert's magnificent canoe

Of course the bath had to be filled & it launched shortly after arrival & I shall have to settle down seriously to rigging it one evening as I can't get it to balance with the masts up. The maid's brother (a petty officer in the Navy), home on leave, came up to see her on Sunday evening. I'd have doubted it was her brother but they are as like as two peas! Anyhow Robert took complete possession of him and had him drawing ships for about an hour. He is reputed to be making a boat for Robert! The canoe really is a very pretty bit of work & positively ornamental.

David had a nightmare last night & woke roaring that Robert was taking his pudding! He is developing so very quickly these days. Indeed I sometimes have an uncanny feeling that there is someone missing & realise it is David as he was. The dream child of Dell Farm first emerging from babyhood has vanished for ever & to be called the baby is to him an insult as it never was to Robert.

Monica is coming to spend the evening, & Mrs Morton is coming on Thursday evening. She (Mrs. M.) is just a bundle of jerks & nerves poor sole & lives quite alone now.

Robert is watching ardently for birds' nests & lambs & longing for you. You would have loved to see his joy & pride in the canoe. Yours always. Sheila

1st Dec 1944, Alan, WAF, Accra, to Sheila

Dear Dear Sheila,

13 months gone! Last night I had your letter posted on November 23rd and oh it was a good letter to have. I'm glad you liked Balzac - life is so short in comparison with the number of things one wants to know - books to read & so on. I'm glad the sheets & towels work well, more are on the way. I'm laying in a store of shoes & underclothes & all useful things for myself, then you can have my coupon.

It makes me nearly weep to hear of David asking "Daddy love me?" - yes tell him I love him & the two putting away things to be mended when I get back - what pleasure it will be to do just that for them.

Yes - I agree Beloved that is why being married to you is such fun - there is a past there is a present & there is a future which in our mutual interdependence for our happiness will as you say give a "bonus".

Dear you talk of being old but not feeling old. Age matters less to us than most for we to each other are Sheila and Alan eternally.

You have the delusion that women age more quickly. Well many men who always like to have a girl in the offing go through a long strange sort of kitten behaviour in which they persuade themselves that they are young in the heart, so to speak. You don't think do you that I shall be like that? I love you and am doubly linked to you by the boys. I have never had to wonder how to occupy my spare time to be dependent on any society male or female for my amusement. So Beloved I think you have me for life.

The article is badly held up by the map which Survey provided not being ready but it will be ready soon.

The Fort is giving me tremendous fun & should be ready to post early next week. I love you very very much, Alan

1st Dec 1944, Sheila, Wakefield, to Alan

My Dear One.

Your letter of the 19th November arrived today, In it you speak of being so glad when the New Year comes & now there is only 30 days to go! I hope you make a good profit off the camera. Also arrived the copy of your second broadcast. Very interesting & excellent beloved, I do wish I could have heard you. My only observation is that in speaking of the money spent by the Brazilian Government on the extermination of the "*gambiare*". I think you should have used dollars instead of pounds. I have recently read the cost was approximately $2 million. This last makes me feel so smart I just couldn't resist it! Oh! Beloved you are so dear to me & I do so long to hear all the stories of your doings.

3rd December

Two more letters yesterday one air & one sea both posted on the 22nd November! Thank you for the photo, it's nice to see you looking so frisky. Your demobilisation news with regard to the Far East has simply made a new woman of me. I'd been feeling dreadfully fed up for a week or so & didn't quite realise that fear of the future was the whole cause of it. Since getting your letter yesterday I feel a different person altogether. Robert is in bed today with a streaming cold, but he is very full of beans & will I think be almost better tomorrow. David spent most of the day in the other bed insisting that he also had a cold & had to be forcibly removed to get him downstairs for dinner etc. They just hate being separated now-a-days.

I couldn't get anything at all on the shortwave on Thursday evening. The wireless is pretty poor these days. I must try to get Steven on to it if he comes again next month. I'll see if Jim can pick you up & if so I'll be there the next week. I too had thought how lovely it would be to go riding in Iceland. I must get down to the

"Burnt Njall" again. I tried it a few weeks ago but didn't get very far I'm reading Balzac's "Lost Illusions" just now.

Robert is fast learning figures these days trying to understand the clock & so on. Daddy is due at Ruthin Castle tomorrow, somehow I can't see him there a month but we'll see.

Oh! my Beloved thank you for these letters of yesterday, it's so easy to be absurdly cast down when one is alone & filled with longing & not living for the present at all. Thanks for the "absence makes the Blacks go blacker" et cetera. Yes it's a queer, very queer world. I suppose it's easy as to be "unfaithful" when one is not fastidious in oneself but what one is not tempted with is hard to understand.

10 PM

I've just had a fine hot bath & am lounging almost naked at the fire in Robert's room. If he wakes up I shall have to dive under the bed! Oh! It's nice to be warm all through in this foul climate. Also nice to have the excuse for a fire in the bedroom. I love you, Sheila

Dec 1944, Alan, WAF, Accra, to David

Dear David,

Yes, Daddy loves you. Daddy loves Sheila and David too. Daddy comes home to play with David & Robert & mend their toys.

Daddy has made toy for Robert now he make toy for David and send it home to him in a big ship. Love Daddy

3rd Dec 1944, Alan, WAF, Accra, to Sheila

Sea Mail

Beloved,

I have today finished the Fort and am in a fever of excitement to get it home for I'm very thrilled with the result but oh how long it will take to get to you.

I have a faint hope which you had better not communicate to Robert that I may get it home by plane in time for Christmas.

The Fort has four bastions. The "Robert", "David", "Sheila" & "Alan" bastions. The main Castle is "Fort Robert" and the small top tower is "Reiff Tower" so you will see that my heart was in the work. There is a drawbridge which when pulled up shows on the under-side

"NO ENTRY - TWIBE IN RESIDENCE"

There is a backdoor catch by which he can put things into the 'dungeon'. I cast a rock for the moat in plaster of Paris.

I'm now making a crane for Robert which will turn on a turn table and wind up & down by gears.

I'm a bit stumped for David but I shall think of something.

Beloved it's hard to express how much pleasure I have had from making this Fort.[1] The thought that it would please you & Robert was always with me as I worked & therefore I was happy.

Beloved you just don't know how I love you. Alan

Fort Robert

5th Dec 1944, Alan, WAF, Accra, to Sheila

Two Letter Cards

Beloved One,

Three letters again last night. It is good of you to write so & you

---

[1] I still have "Fort Robert" in a cupboard. It's an ingenious self assembly fort - Alan was very good with his hands. The paint is now very faded but it means a lot to me.

would be amazed to know what joy it gives me. Glad to think of you going to the pantomime. I hope your foot is better from David's trampling.

Now Beloved as regards my future when I get back. Firstly I have offered for the mine job but that is dependent on my being released of course & whether my release would be confirmed or not I don't know. What I do know is that I have definitely decided not to stay abroad after the war until at least I have been home & lived with you and talked, so that any question of going to the mine would only be until the end of the war.

Also no West Africa for me post-war as it is impossible to have you and the children.

Next as I said in the last letter it is commanded that we won't be sent East if likely to be released within a year of the end of the war with Germany, but Medicals are not automatically reduced as other people when their class is released because they are short of doctors.

So you see Beloved that we are still very much the playthings of the Fates. I'm inclined to see if Wakefield will offer for me.

I definitely won't be home in April as the letter of the law has been decided on, 18 months from November 1st 1943. Alan

Air Mail 2, 5th December

Dearest, to continue. Not coming home until May is probably better from the point of view of my release as it will be one month nearer the end the German war, but oh Beloved it's a long time.

I have sent the Fort off by ordinary post today. I could not persuade anyone to take it by air. So you should see it in two months or so. I have also finished the crane and will start on a motor car for David as soon as I can I'll write a sea letter explaining how Fort is assembled.

Beloved no one knows better than I do that neither of us are getting younger & that I soon shall have been away six years. I don't know how you feel but I personally cannot want more of a family than we have, for above all I want your company after the war and I want to be free to go places with you.

I'm very relieved to hear that the canoe arrived at last, it would give him a big thrill to take it to school. The Fort should be a success too - I don't suppose he has any soldiers poor lamb?

Well Beloved keep yourself "young in the heart" for me. I need you very much. Alan

6th Dec 1944, Alan, WAF, Accra, to Sheila

Sea Mail

Beloved,

I have today sent off Roberts's crane. To save weight I have had to send it without baseboard so will you put any wood I have at Mr Whitaker's disposal & ask him to prepare a board about 17" x 10" to which the crane can be screwed.

The crane, or rather derrick, looks like this from the side & the baseboard is dotted in. I have tucked in spare supply of cord to save tears if it breaks.

I love you, Alan

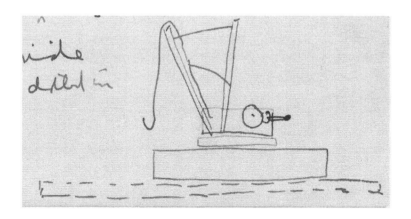

Sketch of the crane I had it till about 30 years ago
but fear it was thrown out.

7th Dec 1944, Sheila, Wakefield, to Alan

My Very Dear,

I've had a terrific mail today, six letters from you some of which had been on the way a very long time and account for the gap in my information on the mine! The dates are - 4th 7th 9th 24th 27th (two of the last) Nov. and include the missing continuation of the letter the 9th Nov. which I have referred to with some agitation! I'm sorry I wrote asking more information as if you had neglected to give it, but you will realise now how lost I felt and with other November letters coming in never dreaming there were others in between held up somewhere. It's never happened before, I wonder where they've been, beloved they are all such nice letters too. I wonder how I was clever enough to find you, for there's no one else in the world who would have suited! Do you really think you could land a professorship in Jerusalem? What a thrill that would be what a grand centre for my interest in your part of the world is very slight although if I had to go there I would become I expect deeply interested. On the other hand the Near East has my interest ready-made. Perhaps my disillusionment would be great but I'd risk that. I'm also glad your enlarger lamp et cetera arrived safely.

Daddy arrived at Ruthin Castle last Monday. I gather he is not exactly in love with it but if it does him some good it's worth a lot. Mother and Maggie Ross are in the hotel at Ruthin and they say it's like a nice house! I still have no definite word if your parents are going to manage down before Christmas. I had a letter from your father yesterday enclosing your first broadcast talk, and he said it was very difficult for him to get away just now.

I enjoyed your first broadcast even more than the second (which I read first) and am getting positively stuck up about my husband!

Beloved you wouldn't believe how long I feel I've been typing and I'm not halfway through yet. It's not a very good advertisement for my typing anyway. I can't seem to think and type at the same time. I'm getting quite speedy all the same and may be quite useful to you in the future. Do you think I should try to learn 'shorthand'? I have a feeling it takes a long long time to be anything like good and I doubt my staying power!

Robert's cold is all better and David has naturally taken it over! Nice they are getting it over before Christmas. The Mc Vic's are insisting on us going to them for Christmas Day and although I said no I feel it's a bit much these days, especially as I refused when we came back in Sept. as I thought we would be going away. I think they are going to be offended if we don't. It will be very nice to get the day passed in their company.

I just can't keep it up any longer, it takes too little space![1]

Dear on one some of our (prosaic!) Holidays we must go over the marches of Montrose & Claverhouse. There are so many things I want to do with you beloved & I think for the most part we like the same kind of things. It was funny, Monica when here the other evening said "you know I do so long to travel, but all Jim ever wants of a holiday is just to go straight to some seaside place & sit on the beach all day".

Again my dear let me say how lucky I feel to have found you! I am sitting looking at a map of South-West Asia, already imagining us in Jerusalem. My Dear I'm nearly as daft as you are, not quite of course - getting on! Oh! You must come home in April, I think I can just last that long I need you so much in such an assortment of different ways & I'm dreadfully starved for you. Looking back I don't know how I existed this time last year!

David's temp is up a few points tonight so we look like having a restless time. He is terribly sweet & chatty about his ills & so much less agitating than as an infant. He talks away about you coming home & it will be fun to introduce him.

I went into Leeds on Tuesday afternoon & got a few toys for Xmas. Awful rubbish & awful awful price but one has to do something.

Oh! Beloved if you just knew how much I loved you you would be ashamed of me! Sheila

9th Dec 1944, Alan, WAF, Accra, to Sheila

Sea Mail

Beloved,

I have sent you today two wooden trays (The third of the nest is bigger & I shall send separately).

I bought for us yesterday 19 ½.yards of white native woven cloth

---

[1] At this point Sheila abandons typing for longhand.

2'6" wide. It is very strong and will be valuable for chair covers or curtains or at worst for bath mats. It will be able to be dyed to any colour. It is a new cloth from Togoland and I am sure that you will like it. I enclose a sample. Will you let me know the maximum length of a curtain so that I can cut it into convenient lengths for 19 ½ yards is a very heavy parcel. It costs 3/9 per yard.

Which of the following are most likely to be useful, they are all in lovely native wood polished only with natural polish and not stained. (As are the trays & that is how to deal with them)

1.   Nests of 3 coffee tables - square longer size of top 1'6"
2.   Dining room table 3' x 6'
3.   Book rests
4.   Book cases
5.   Study chairs - wood with wicker panels.

I can get them home by using them & then storing until after the war and having them sent home crated. I know that we have no space but there must be some articles of furniture which you can foresee we shall require. The woods available are Adum (as in first heavy box[1]), Mahogany, self coloured, Cedar or Satinwood. I have made friends with the forestry man who makes these things & he will see that I get really good seasoned wood.

I plump for sectional book cases but I'm not certain of colours. What about a big chest cum hall seat?

I love you. Alan

10th Dec 1944, Alan, WAF, Accra, to Sheila

Sea Mail

Beloved,

I'm hoping for a letter tomorrow meanwhile I have little news.

My four Nigerian photographs were accepted for the Weekly Times and were reproduced in an October number. I have not seen them but Dr Reid tells me they are there.

I'm very pleased about this, as they are the first photographs I have had accepted as photographs alone. I expect I shall get £4-4-0

---

[1] Adum is an area of Kumasi in Gold Coast, Ghana.

for them. It is very pleasant to feel that at last I'm beginning to get somewhere with my writing and photographs.

Perhaps after the war I shall be able to keep writing & illustrating articles and so be able to augment our income and do & write things with you which would give great joy.

I was at a wedding yesterday of an officer here. The Minister in his address said to the couple that they must realise that they would, if they were blessed in a happy marriage, experience greater happiness than they ever expected to enjoy as individuals. I echoed that in my heart & thanked God for the truth of it.

Beloved think of the things we can do and the sort of historical geographical articles we can do. I have in mind such things as: "Montrose's March to Inveraray illustrated". "The Wester Ross Mountains illustrated". "McKenzie the writer of Ossian",[1] "The Norwegian Societies". "By Car to Athens" (three articles) & so on ad infinitum.

The pleasure of getting excited about the subject & looking it up & consulting references & so on would be most exciting apart from the interesting places our researches take us. Oh my beloved don't you agree?

Enclosed cuttings will amuse you. You might send for parents to see.

I love you. Alan

11ᵗʰ Dec 1944, Sheila, Wakefield, to Alan

Dearly Beloved,

I'm getting very excited at the way time is going - in only a fortnight it's Christmas! I discovered recently that Leonardo Da Vinci observed "Man always festively awaiting the new spring & the new summer, complains that the longed for things are slow in coming, and fails all the while to notice that he is longing for his own end" and for ages now I've been trying to get the days in as quickly as possible!

Still after the New Year comes I shall feel I am really getting near

---

[1]Alan means "*McPherson* the writer of Ossian".

to you again & when I get to you time may go slowly always, it will never be slow enough.

Robert has been complaining of toothache of late & indicating the back teeth Andy filled in the spring.

I had the feeling it was just his new molars pushing through as his mouth was very inflamed but took him to see Cocker on Friday. Owing to his pleasant experience with Andy he was delighted to go! Cocker said the fillings were perfectly all right & it was only the very painful state of his gums (ulcerated in places) he touched them with "blue store" whatever that is, which gave Robert great joy. I had just put Roberts's things on & had turned to speak to Cocker, who was asking for you or something, when there was a series of bumps, a yell & silence. I looked around - no Robert! Dentist nurse & I rush out of the room and find a sadder & wiser Robert coming up the stone stairs from the basement, very dusty. He had slipped out of the surgery & with his fatal curiosity had opened the first door he saw and was lucky not to break his neck & suffered from nothing but fright.

He had your letter about "The Fort" on Friday & is terribly thrilled. We have already bought some soldiers for it.

After suggesting a colour scheme of pink, purple & yellow he thinks you'd better go on as you suggest!

David also wants a Fort so you've got your hands full, there's no question of one of anything now. You can't think how grown-up your youngest son is getting! I have also had a cold, but am fast recovering. Our tickets for the pantomime are for the 31st of March!

We have had snow all this afternoon & it's lying, but wettish. The boys are delighted. The lengths of the boy's feet are - Robert 7½ inches. David 5½. I am sending an outline of their feet as a further help to you. Yours ever & longer if possible. Sheila

12th Dec 1944, Alan, WAF, Accra, to Sheila

Sea Mail

Beloved,

Will you look out cassettes for 35 mm film - they are the little fellows which are in aluminium boxes & which hold the film in

Leicas, they look like this and are blue or green or black.

(sketch of cassette)

As many as you can find up to 8 please send to:
Col the Viscount Downe, Wycombe Abbey, Scarborough & he will bring them to me. They are in a cardboard box & were in my wardrobe.

He is taking the camera I bought & a meter home for repair & they will be sent to you. Please keep them till I get back. Sorry to bother you. This is a hurried letter to catch the post.

I love you, Alan

P.S. Downe is taking Robert's Fort Flag & a few small books home.

12ᵗʰ Dec 1944, Alan, WAF, Accra, to Sheila

Air Mail

Beloved Wife,

Your letter posted on December 4th arrived last night. Sorry no Dollars for Brazil - will remember next time.

Sorry to hear that Robert has a cold. Has he thrown any books at you? It's sweet to hear of David pretending he has a cold and wanting to be with Robert. Oh I have always so wanted them to be fond of each other.

I agree Burnt Njall is very heavy going & I'm glad you read Men of Ness. I have a good little book here called Edda & Saga[1] in the Home Universal series which explains a lot. Your mention of "a fire in the bedroom" brought back such happy memories. I am lying in bed with a towel round my middle at 7 AM after a dreadful night of heat - the worst I remember in Accra. I lay absolutely naked for about two hours and mopped myself with a towel. The trouble is in the Army that fans are not provided and the big ceiling fans just make all the difference in the world in airless houses.

I'm busy just now trying to write a short biographical article on

---

[1] Edda & Saga - The *Poetic Edda* is a collection of Old Norse poems from the Icelandic medieval manuscript Codex Regius (Royal Book).

George Maclean[1] a very fine governor of Cape Coast Castle about 1840. He married an odd hysterical woman who died two months after she arrived out and he was suspected of having poisoned her.

You will probably get a note from L. Downe about Christmas time. He is back in U.K. to bring out the new General early in January.

I am off from 14th to 23rd this month on tour so I shall not have any more letters from you until the latter date.

In January I go on leave & then on a recruiting tour and then to Nigeria where I hope to do a photographic series of Zaria market for the Picture Post.

I'll write again later today. I love you, Alan

14th Dec 1944 Sheila, Wakefield, to Alan

Dearly Beloved,

I should have written to you last night as usual but I'm afraid this week you are a sacrifice to youth! Anthony is having a party on Saturday with "ice cream" (horrors!), a Mickey Mouse Cine & all the rest of it. The main problem after food is there are no decorations of any kind, no flowers, no crackers, holly almost too expensive to look at & nothing to make the table bright for them.

Result I spent last evening illustrating place name cards for them. You should have heard the swearing at Robert's utility paints & brushes! I enjoyed myself hugely & they are nearly finished & look very gay & nice. I even missed the news I was so absorbed!

Your cable arrived yesterday & was most welcome. Your family aren't coming up now until January.

It's bitterly cold and though thawing today seems even colder. My sinuses are giving their usual trouble after a heavy cold, what a blight they are.

David thanks you for your letter & is very relieved that you love him! He is wildly excited about the party (he is the only little one going) and goes about saying "this is Saterterday, I'm going party" then he provocatively turns to Robert & says "you staying home".

---

[1] George Maclean (1801-1847), Governor of Gold Coast from 1830 until 1844. Member of Royal African Colonial Corps.

In a few moments a full-scale fight is in progress.

As an indication of the stage of talking he looked out the window this morning first as it was getting light & saw two lighted windows on the other side of Pinfold Lane. He shouted "look, look two headlamps shining faraway Street". So very like Robert at that stage!

I'm dying to see the "Fort" you must have worked hard to have it finished so quickly. We've just had dinner & are now sitting by the fire. I can hardly keep awake. We had our meat ration today as mother has arranged for a goose from Inverness Shire to come to us at the weekend. The McVic's are coming up on Sunday to help us get started. I'm having my Dell Farm Turkey at New Year. I love you always. Sheila

17th Dec 1944, Alan, WAF, Accra, to Sheila

Air Mail

Beloved,

You will see from my address where I am. Unfortunately I missed Wilfred, he has just gone home. I have been here for three days and have had a most interesting time.

I flew in a small plane with the local Station Commander up to a small unit "away up bush" which takes two days to reach in the miniature train. The landing ground was very bush and our take off on the return trip was spectacular! I took many photographs but it remains to be seen whether they will come out.

I expect to be back from Gambia on 23rd in time for Christmas at my own mess. I'll send you a cable as soon as I can but there is a veto at Christmas.

I sent you six wooden bowls which I hope you think of use. They are making me a big one 12 inches across & 3 inches deep.

By the way have you had the key for the second box? You have not yet sent me shoe measurement of yours & boys.

I am enjoying my tour - had a good bathe yesterday and hope to have another today. Sierra Leone is though a bad place in that it's always overcast & you never see blue sky. I love the blue sky & fleecy clouds you see at the end of the rains in Gold Coast. It really is lovely then but too hot now. Well Beloved I'll write again tonight so meanwhile bless you and my boys for I love you. Alan

19th Dec 1944, Alan, WAF, Accra to Sheila

Air Mail

Dear,

Just another note to let you know I'm grand, enjoying my tour, & looking forward to getting back for my accumulated mail. I sent another cable today which will I hope be an extra surprise for Christmas.

I have had a very good time here and have been extremely well entertained. It has just been a case of everyone falling over each other to make sure I see all I want to see and to dine me in every possible mess. The snag is that I just cannot compete with the late nights. I am sorry to have missed Wilfred but I daresay he is not unduly worried!

The Harmattan[1] has commenced again and it's so strange to have the dry air and to have the dampness out of clothing.

Beloved soon it will be January and 1945 and the year I come back to you. I'm wondering if you have been getting any of my parcels of jam & if my big created trunk has arrived. I have another trunk about ready.

I gave a few books + the flag for Roberts Fort to Downe to take back for me but oh Beloved there is no Christmas Present for my Dear One.

I am not allowed to send the type of thing suitable for you as imported stuff is verboten while the native stuff is crude. I may manage to get some filigree ware in Gambia.

Bless you Sheila & remember how much I am always thinking of you and loving you. Alan

20th Dec 1944, Sheila, Wakefield to Alan

Dear One,

Let me say for a start I'm worried stiff over the German counter-

---

[1] Harmattan Winds, cold dry & dusty trade winds.

attack. Let me also say I seem to be quite alone in this as everyone is very smug about it - please God they're right. It's astonishing the feeling of lack of interest in the war all around one, somehow & most disheartening.

Robert got his holidays yesterday & they extend to Jan 17th! by which time I shall be off my head I imagine, but he thinks it's wonderful! His school report was sweet. I'll give extracts - Scriptures - Good. (He has actually asked me, in effect, why if God is good & omnipotent is there any evil!). Arithmetic - Robert has made excellent progress and works hard. Reading - Will soon be able to read small words. Writing - Good careful work. Nature Study - Is observant & interested. Elocution - Robert learns quickly & uses expression. Handiwork - Robert uses his hands well & thoroughly enjoys the subject. Drawing & Painting - Has a good idea of shape & colour. Literature - Is appreciative & enjoys stories. Singing & Band - Can almost sing in tune & has an excellent sense of time & rhythm. (He has no idea what ever of tune but loves music!) General Progress - Robert settled down quickly & is most anxious to learn. He shows promise. Conduct - Excellent.

Sweet isn't it? No doubt we'll look back to it with sighs! The concert is tomorrow & Robert plays a Tambourine in the band. I trust his excellent sense of time & rhythm stand him in good stead. I'm taking David too, all the little brothers & sisters go it seems & it's such tremendous relief to me that he is of an age to go places. I'm never happy unless I've them both with me.

I'm reading "A History of the Early World" just now & have become so fascinated with the civilisation of the Pharaohs that Cairo now ranks much higher in the list of good places for your professorship than it did a few weeks ago! It's so very annoying not to have a good second hand book shop handy where I can follow up interest like that.

I was speaking to Daddy on the phone tonight. He says he really does feel better (I've never heard him say that before) & he thinks it's a very good place (Ruthin). He leaves there on Jan & they may look in here on their way north. I must try to get Robert roller skates, he is quite skilful with a wooden engine on each foot! Two more tins of jam arrived yesterday. You are the best as well as dearest man in the world, Sheila

21st Dec 1944, Sheila, Wakefield, to Alan

Beloved. I can't settle to anything tonight - for worry about the war. By the time you get this no doubt things will be all right again & the Germans back where they belong, one hopes much mauled, but Oh! I'm worried about it.

The concert went off very well & all the children were very good. I was very proud of Robert. He did look nice (I'd never seen him on the stage before!) & astounded me by taking the stage alone & saying a poem & saying it jolly well too!

David was very good & thoroughly enjoyed it. Robert is tearful that there won't be another concert until next Christmas. We are going to a party at the Sweeting's on the 30th with a special request for Robert to wear his kilt? I just can't face a party alone, all the Daddies are so wonderful on these occasions!

Today arrived the "Forts" article & I just can't tell you the pleasure it is giving me. How I wish I could have been there when you were writing it. I could always have hunted up things & done some typing & I would have got such a kick out of it!

I have at last got the house for Charlie at his figure. I feel it's been quite hard work & I'll tell you of my final gesture in the matter when I see you. I think I'll go & have a bath before the 9 PM news. I'm dreading it & the bath will fill in time.

I wonder when you will hear the result of your application for the mine. I had understood from your first mention of it that you would definitely be released in the event of your taking the job.

22nd December

Thank you for news cuttings on your broadcasts. I am so glad about your photos getting into the Weekly Times. Thank you also very very much for your Christmas Cable which came in today. I thought it wasn't worth trying a cable from this end just now after my one last December taking two weeks!

I found and sent off the cassettes to Downe within half an hour of the arrival of your request so I feel quite virtuous! I could only find seven. David says "Daddy in Africa, coming home pring". Oh Beloved I wonder what on earth he expects! At the concert when the children first came on the stage there was a moment's silence, broken by David's yell "look, look there's Robert". He insists on calling himself "wee David" now. Yes I'm all for the historical geographic journeys you speak of. I love you. Sheila

24th Dec 1944, Alan, WAF, Accra, to Sheila

2 Air Mails

Beloved,

I returned last night after over 1400 miles of flying on my tour to find a whole lot of letters waiting for me there from you being dated 7th, 11th & 14th December. Firstly I sympathise with you re typing. I quite agree it is impossible to fill up a letter in type. I should not attempt to write shorthand or to be an expert typist - you can buy either at a very cheap rate. I agree that this part of the world is not so very interesting but I'd love to come across the Saharan Caravan routes. In Gambia one meets so many fascinating types, the veiled Tuareg in his blue robes all muffled up. The white skinned Fulani woman quietly padding along behind her husband, the wiry little Berbers having walked to Timbuktu and then down. The southern Saharan fringe in French Africa is very wild and fascinating but the place above all is Spanish Rio de Onor which is quite unknown! A little Arabic & a little Hausa will see you all over North and West Africa. There may be opportunities in Tripolitania after the war.

I met a very tough hard drinking Australian woman doctor in Freetown who has just come from the Police Colonial Medical Services. She speaks some Arabic and is a very well informed & interesting woman. She takes the poorest possible view of Ronald Storrs saying "why he even tried to seduce me"! If that is so I agree he does need a cold bath! Latest news of home seems to be about first week in May.

I like your quotation of Leonardo da Vinci. What about length of your feet? Another follows. Love Alan.

Card 2, 24.12.44

Beloved, To continue.

I'm immensely bucked at the two boys going to a party. Oh I'm longing to see them & share them with you is very odd Beloved & very common I know but I can never quite get the idea that they are because we love each other. David must have advanced hugely in talking. He was speechless when I left & the next four months will make a difference. Glad to know you are having Turkey & Goose at Christmas.

The G.O.C. in C. took home with him an official recommendation for an O.B.E.[1] for me but there is many a slip. It would be of help in getting jobs later on.

I've had all your Christmas cards & I hope you had mine do tell me when the crated box arrives. There are also about eight parcels in the post for you but they take a long time. I am afraid that the Fort and the crane will take ages. I've started David's car & will make him a "weeny" Fort. I'm so glad you got soldiers for they will be fine in the Fort.

Had another letter from Steven who says you are looking younger & prettier than ever which I well believe. Kevin O'Toole (the other chap in the photo with me) is coming to dinner tonight with me & I am bidden to Christianborg Castle to dine with the Gov on 29th.

6.30 p.m.

Developed my tour photos. Some quite good I think from the baby plane, one especially of nose down towards the landing strip.

I love you. Alan

25th Dec 1944, Sheila, Wakefield, to Alan

Dearly Beloved.

I have thought of you so many times today & I know you were thinking of us. The children have really enjoyed their Christmas greatly, bless them. Personally I am profoundly thankful is over.

---

[1] Poor Alan never got his OBE. It would have matched his father's 1944 OBE nicely!

We've been at McVicar's all day, at any rate since 12.30. Jim's sister is with them for Xmas & I think she is very charming. They were here for tea yesterday. We've been wrapped in fog for over 24 hours now & it's freezing hard. The maid went out Saturday & I haven't seen her since! She'll get the boot when she does show up! Your Mother sent us a lovely Christmas cake - all pre-war icing & is quite a sight. I wish you could have seen the children with their toys today. They really did very well considering how terribly difficult things are & so happy with all the new things. I got Mr Whitaker to have the key & keep the kitchen fire while we were out so we came into a warm house & boiling water. Too intensely cold just to do with radiators.

I am expecting the parents on their way home from Ruthin on Jan 4th & Steven on the 8th. I shall I trust get another maid quickly. I phoned Mrs G. a week ago and told her I'd take a young girl if nothing else turned up, meaning to hang onto this one until I got another.

Thanks for your Christmas card & I just can't remember if I thanked you for your Christmas Cable, but Oh! Beloved it did make a difference.

Excuse this scrappy letter, I haven't slept very well the last few nights & I'm a bit dead from the neck up tonight - not ill or anything, just can't think! I'm going to have something to eat now & read yesterday's Sunday Express which I collected from McVicar's, as I can't get it.

Oh! Dearest one, will we be together next Christmas I wonder. There's so much trouble piling up everywhere it seems we'll never get to the end of this war. Never mind, soon we will meet again & Oh! How I love you. Sheila

25th Dec 1944, Alan, WAF, Accra, to Sheila

Air Mail

Beloved,

It's 6:30 AM on Christmas Morning & I waken thinking of Sheila and boys. Oh to see David's excited face as he fiddles about with the parcels, and I suppose Roberts superior air - ill maintained - as being a boy who knows all about Christmas. You will know that I am thinking of you because you know that the part of me which is here is not likely to get out of touch with the part which is with you on Christmas Day.

I must confess that these Christmases on which I have been away have been about the saddest days of separation. I just cannot raise any enthusiasm for jollification when I'm not with the people whom I love.

More & more as the years go by Christmas means more. The carols sound sweeter, the celebration of the birth of a child who has influenced all our world so much by his teaching has come to have different symbolic meanings for many peoples but to all it spells goodwill to mankind and love and thankfulness for children. Six Christmases - Oh me the Powers that rule this world have mercy on the people and cease all this strife before another.

26/12 6.30 a.m.

Well Beloved I spent Christmas Day making David's lorry & it's all finished now bar the painting. As last year I just could not face the Christmas Dinner so I am hungry now looking forward to breakfast.

Oh Dearest if you knew how much I thought of my Twibe yesterday - I don't think you were ever out of my consciousness all day long. I love you. Alan

27th Dec 1944, Alan, WAF, Accra, to Sheila

[Illegible][1] you write & tell him I expect him to be fit for a walk to the Hill Lochs when he gets out & I am back.

I played for the mess in the Boxing Day 7 a side soccer tournament yesterday. I lost at least two gallons of sweat and am "small, small" stiff today.

I'm Broadcasting tomorrow night again & I just cannot get down to my biographies. I have a terrific urge to write but am very shy about writing about personal experience.

---

[1] This single sheet is page 3 & 4 and the first sheet is missing. The date is correct, calculated from it being written the day after Boxing day.

Tell the Boys I liked their photographs & that I shall write to them soon. Oh Dear wee one I still have palpitations when I look at your photographs. Do you think it's good for me to have been continually in love for 15 years. Alan.

28th Dec 1944, Sheila, Wakefield, to Alan

Beloved,

Only three more days left in this old year which is the only one since I was 17 that I have passed wholly without you.

I'm very glad to see it go & yet to give it its due it has to date dealt very kindly with me. The fog of Christmas day brought all our colds back again & the boys have been coughing like old men for the past three days & have had the most streaming noses & horrible discharge from same I've seen for a long time. They are very cheerful & I am just keeping them warm (being alarmingly extravagant with coal!) & coddling them until they are properly clear. I've cured myself by liberal doses of Anesthone cream which I haven't used for years. An unorthodox cure but it's been most effective!

I've dispensed with the maid and we are almost clean again after her departure. She left a filthy room (evacuees nothing to it, if you know what I mean!) & the rest of the house looks very different now she is gone. I have Mrs Goose back in the meanwhile and am really afraid to try another maid, but will see. The boys had the books & flag you sent by Downe this morning & were delighted. What nice books they are too. Mother has sent us some beautiful grapefruit & I am revelling in it. The boys don't like it at all! Monica & Susan have colds too. The weather is dreadfully cold with iron hard frost. The fog, thank the Lord, has gone meanwhile.

I like the material very much dear. The longest curtains we have are about 3½ yards & it seems unlikely that there would be any call ever for longer. I should think the material will end up as chair covers however as the arms of the armchair are quite worn through! By the way are there any spare bicycle pumps your way?

I can see plenty of articles of furniture which will be needful for us (including a bedroom suite for the boys!). But we don't need a dining room table! Bookcases are a crying need but as you know our furniture is of dark wood & dark & light wood do not mix well. Also bookcases must have glass doors. I'm not very keen on light wood except for bedrooms where I love it. A big chest cum hall seat would be lovely, but I'll have to leave it to you. But just bear in mind the snag of mixing light and dark wood. The trays sound lovely. Please no coffee tables!

Unfortunately I haven't another letter card so will have to stop. I adore you beloved – Sheila

29th Dec 1944, Alan, WAF, Accra, to Sheila

Air Mail

My Dear,

Your letter dated December 20th arrived last night. Yes, I have never mentioned the term push in my letters but it's the saddest thing which has happened since we were driven back to Egypt & lost Tobruck for the second time. It remains to be seen how the war is affected. It's so hard out here to hear what is really happening.[1]

It's such an interesting letter of yours beloved, especially Robert's report. The bit I like best is "can almost sing in tune". Poor Wob! I'm now looking forward to hearing how the concert went.

So it's "Ciro" (Cairo) now! Well I shall try to oblige. I'm reading the Hakluyt Edition of Leo Africanus who was a Moorish slave educated by the Pope in early 16th century. He travelled all over Africa, up the Nile to Mecca, then all over the Barbary Coast and over the desert to Catriona in Northern Nigeria. These Hakluyt Editions are very fully annotated and with lists of cross-references to sources.

If you can get hold of Alistair Forbes' "Black Lamb & Grey Falcon"[2] read it. I take off my hat to her book. It must have required incredible industry to get it together.

I'm so very delighted to hear that your father really is feeling

---

[1] This must refer to the Battle of the Bulge, 16th Dec 1944 to 25th Jan 1945.

[2] "Black Lamb & Grey Falcon". This was written by Rebecca West. Alistair Forbes was sued by her for a scathing and inaccurate criticism of the book, and she won. An error on Alan's part I think - but his writing!!

better and I hope that he gets to see you the way back.

I have been quite busy since I came back with writing my tour notes and trying to cope with the accumulated work but this afternoon I am going shopping for various things I require such as a comb (left in Gambia) some photographic paper & so

I love you very much, Alan

1945

Notes on 1945

Sheila with David & Robert (this is not at Camusglashlan)

Early 1945 was a frustrating and very worrying time. Germany was finished but still fighting grimly. For Sheila and many others, the awful prospect of the army and navy being shifted east to help finish off Japan loomed after Germany's final surrender. Alan had to consider the prospect of being sent east on a 5 year 'tour'. Sheila felt that would be the end, she could cope with no more.

The atom bombs dropped on Hiroshima and Nagasaki finally forced Japan to surrender and the nightmare of invading the Japanese mainland was avoided.

David has reminded me that in later years Sheila, a keen gardener who loved flowers, had a passionate hatred of chrysanthemums. She wouldn't have them in the house. It seems probable this was because they were the Japanese Emperor's imperial emblem. The hatreds aroused at this time have taken many years to fade and can only be understood by those who were there.

Germany surrendered in May 1945 and the Japanese in September. Thus the Second World War finally came to an end. Only America had prospered as a result. Most other combatants were exhausted and ruined. Britain was victorious but bankrupt.

Some five million servicemen had to be brought home from all over the world. They had to be given civilian clothes and found jobs.

Alan was brought back by plane and landed at Hurn Airport (now Bournemouth Airport) on 26th June. As far as I can tell he went straight home to Wakefield. I remember him arriving in the middle of the night. He must have had leave for we all went to Aviemore. There is a cable dated 19th July from Alan in London to Sheila in Aviemore so Alan must have gone down to London to get his next posting and, as he proudly announces, he was promoted full Colonel. The next letter is 27th July by which time he was in Chester.

He didn't finally get home until October. He was not formally released from military service until 27th December 1945 when he was transferred to the Regular Army Reserve of Officers. He ceased to belong to the Reserve in April 1951, narrowly missing the Korean War.

1st Jan 1945, Alan, WAF, Accra, to Sheila

Beloved,

A good New Year to you and may we all be together for good this year. I brought in the New Year in bed writing and I did not even notice its arrival. I'm flogging myself to write for beloved it is not natural to me, yet I must learn to write interestingly and read quickly. I am so backward and bound down by the stereotypical phrases. I find it very difficult to discriminate in quotations and I so keep wondering whether anyone but myself would be interested in the particular subject I am writing about that a dozen times in a page I become convinced I'm wasting my time. So Beloved pity a poor man in labour and don't laugh too much when you see his first efforts. I expect a letter tonight so I shall finish this then.

2. 1. 45.

Beloved - two letters last night of 24th and 27th. I knew you would be very worried about the war and my dearest I understand. But the future is not so bad in Europe and even more than all this post-war conditions worry me. It is going to be difficult to avoid having very reactionary political views!

I'm very interested in your getting the house for Charlie.

Beloved it's astounding to hear Robert says a poem. Do you mean that he never told you he was getting on a solo act? It sounds to me like a very sensible little school and that Robert has had a good start. He is becoming quite the socialite with all these parties!

It was good of you to phone Mummy so often at Christmas time. She was extremely thrilled and getting presents ready and the cake gave her a great deal of pleasure. I had a long letter from her which was just all about the children's Christmas.

More follows. Love Alan.

1st Jan 1945, Sheila, Wakefield, to Alan

Dearest One, A happy new year to you. I am annoyed with myself tonight for I have run out of letter cards and specially want to write to you. I'll write anyway and copy it out tomorrow. I haven't been out for a week as the boys have been rather much under the weather.

I got the doctor to David on Saturday as on Friday night his temperature shot up and he was wheezing like an old man. Doctor said it was nothing to worry about, left a bottle for him, pulled out one of Robert's teeth (which he couldn't get out & the new one well up behind) and departed. David's temp went up again on Saturday night and yesterday the poor lamb had earache. He lay down like a lamb and let me put Sedonan in and was heartrendingly sweet about it all but obviously very miserable, and looked it. I was a miserable too on his account and it was New Year's Eve and all and I was alone and the one bright spot was Robert who was full of beans. I went to bed and slept in 1945 expecting a bad night with David. He slept the night through and woke up a new man, saying "my ear all better, Mummy clever!" He has been just fine all day and his cough almost all gone too. I am so hoping we are all out of the wood now and get so absolutely worried when they are ill. Robert called me upstairs tonight to ask me if I was writing you to wish you a very Happy New Year from him. The earthquake the other night was a queer experience.[1] It's very odd to wake up and find the ornaments on the mantelpiece doing a jig! I'm extra lonely for you these days beloved, perhaps it's because we've been tied to the house this week, but this last lap seems to stretch a long way ahead. On the other hand the war will take ages yet. I have had your S. L. letters on 17th and 19th Dec. Wilfred must have got back on time! I'm expecting Steven on either next Monday or Tuesday. No I haven't the key for the second box. When I think of your "spectacular take off" my heart seems to stop beating, but it's bringing back memories of my spectacular landing so many years ago! I am looking forward to the wooden houses. The other day I found David lying huddled on the floor, very still. I said "what on earth's the matter" and a wee voice said "I'm dead, German bomb kill me." Oh Beloved it's a dreadful time to live in and one is so tired of this endless cruelty and distorted existence.

I've had the piano shifted to the extension in the sitting room. It doesn't look so nice, but I'll keep it there for the minute, it leaves

---

[1] Earthquake - felt throughout northern England, 30th December 1944.

the boys so much more room to play. Had a letter from the Lanny yesterday. Kenny is still in Catterick! Oh my Beloved I want you badly, can you feel it at all? Sheila

2nd Jan 1945, Alan, WAF, Accra, to Sheila

Beloved,

To continue. Am so glad the boys enjoyed their presents - I'm just sorry that I have not had the sense to start making my toys earlier so that they could have had them for Christmas. Yes poor old David I wonder what on earth he expects. I'm afraid I shall be a big shock to his system.

It will be nice for you to have the *Jarrets*, then Steven and then Mummy and Daddy - that ought to see January pretty well finished.

I have no news of the mine. They will have applied for my release and it just remains to be seen whether they will succeed. I'm sorry if I indicated that it was automatic. I just don't know what the chances are at all.

I'm going to order the shoes for Robert and David today. I wonder how long they will take to make them.

I have been making small bookshelves like this - shocking drawing but you know the type of thing. They will be useful in the maid's bedroom at worst - if we get the literary model maid. *I'd* like to beat your beauty.

Well beloved, there endeth letters. I'm afraid I'm without inspiration at the moment. I love you dearly though, Alan

5th Jan 1945, Sheila, Wakefield, to Alan

Dearest One. Three letters yesterday, two of a day or two before Christmas and one of Christmas day. Then this a.m. other two of 27th and 29th Dec which is good going. A crated wooden box arrived yesterday, open, and one side of the crate all broken away! I am sending on to you the 'consignees certificate' cos there may be some things you may wish to claim. There seemed very little in it for the size. There were six lovely towels, a pair of shoes, a new army McIntosh, pair white shorts, pair drill trousers, wooden lamp, one bottle (contents unknown!) one ebony stick and another stick which I find hard to describe, this kind of one if you get me! a tin of sardines and another unlabelled which will be the stew no doubt and a rare mixture of "junk" which was drifting about all through the other things and has knocked the ebony walking stick about somewhat. I shall have to look back through your letters to see if the Ebony one is for your mother and the one for your father, I can't remember offhand. Also arrived today three tins of pears and one of jam. I wish you could have seen the boys, especially Robert, enjoying the pears at dinner today, it would have done your heart good.

I'm sorry I hurt your feelings in my spelling of 'cairo', you too have been guilty of some howlers, but I left off pointing out such things with my childhood, years ago!

I'm not attempting to reply to your letters tonight as I am almost prostrated after a day's sneezing. Why do I get these days?

Beloved, you are so good to write so often it does helps so much. The boys are almost better but haven't been out yet as the weather is bitterly cold. They are getting very excited about you coming home and we are counting in weeks now. I can't imagine how I shall survive my excitement when the time gets really near. I love you always and for ever. Sheila

8th Jan 1945, Alan, WAF, Accra to Sheila

Beloved,

The mail is not coming in tonight so I must write this before getting your letter in order to catch tomorrow's mail. I have not much news. I have been very busy with my annual report and am rather dashed that my local leave has had to be postponed again. Somehow I must get local leave before I finish this tour.

A sea mail arrived today bringing among other things your family genealogy going back to R.L.S. it would be fun to see if we were related. It is an interesting trail but my, my I'm distressed about the Campbell![1] I also have a curious ghostly photograph of my

---

[1] Sheila had sent Alan details of her ancestors showing her links with Robert Louis Stevenson. They revealed that one of her great grandmothers was one

complete family from Moira. It was taken before you left Glasgow and is <u>very</u> funny.

It is a little cooler at night just now with the Harmattan but oh Beloved the weather sounds terrible in England and I'm afraid you must be having an awful time. It must be pretty grim not to have fires.

Beloved I love you very much and the more I see of other women the more particular and fussy I am. I've been nearly 15 months away from you, but I just feel exactly the same about you as when I left. What's more if I live to be Methuselah I should still feel the same.

I have so much to tell you, and share with you, and plan with you and <u>do</u> with you beloved. The aeroplane is going to let us get to Jerusalem in a very few days for example after the war. My photography if properly used is going to make some things possible that would not be possible otherwise. More follows – Alan

8th Jan 1945, Alan, WAF, Accra, to Sheila

Continuation Letter 8th Jan 1945

Beloved,

To continue - for example as I lay in bed this morning I thought of a simple little article for the Geographic Magazine. It is characteristic of place names in a simple society that they either follow people's names or are purely descriptive. Norse and Celtic names follow the latter and the meaning of a name distorted by age often becomes quite clear when the place is seen.

So a series of attractive photographs illustrating place names in Ross would be very interesting for example:- It would be possible from a high top on Coigach to get four of the five places beginning with 'Ach' in the photograph. A photograph of "An Sail" would illustrate clearly that it is distorted Gaelic for 'the heel' and so on. That would be a most amusing article to prepare and would make me walk, for as you know I cannot be enthusiastic about walks for walking sake but I'd go hundreds of miles for a definite object.

Bethia Campbell. Alan's comment reflects common Scottish prejudice against the name.

Beloved love me and laugh at me but always love me, for I blossom or shrivel as I feel I am in your opinion.

I'm trying to wangle a liaison visit to Soudan and East Africa but I very much doubt whether I shall manage it. I have been reading Speke and Burton recently and I really have become thrilled about E. Africa. I adore you. Kiss my boys and tell them I love them. Alan

9th Jan 1945, Alan, WAF, Accra, to Sheila

Beloved,

The mail came in unexpectedly this morning with two letters from you, so I can just catch the outgoing mail. I'm so sorry to hear about all the colds. I have just seen Downe who apologises for not writing to thank you for the cassettes, but he was rushed off to London and they just caught up with him before he left. You will get a camera and exposure metre from Wallace Heaton where he left them for repair. I suggest that you advertise them in The Times personal column as follows.

Camera. EXACTA MODEL B. f2.8 Tessor Lens. Sixtus photoelectric meter. Both perfect condition. And take the best offer over £50.00 for the two.

I am sending you the keys for the box, and for the next box I am sending (which is my tin trunk). I wrapped one lot of bowls in material and I shall cut the rest in 3½ yards lengths and send it to you. You may have to pay purchase tax on it.

I'll look out for a bicycle pump and send one in trunk if possible.

I shall remember - dark furniture but as the wood is smooth finish it can easily be mahogany stained dark. I shall get enough wood to make the glass doors for the bookcases.

I hate to think of my David with coughs. He sounds a very nice fellow does David.

Love to Steven if I'm not too late, and love to the Messrs' Lemas en mass.

Oh beloved the time is going on. I love you. Alan.

9 Jan 1945, Sheila, Wakefield, to Alan

My Dear One. I was thrown into turmoil on Saturday by a phone call from Mrs. Stott to say 'Frankie' had resigned (and I gather there has been no little unpleasantness!). They were meeting on Monday (yesterday) to accept his resignation, which they would not ask him to withdraw and she wanted to know if she could inform the committee that you would be willing to take the job in which case they would apply for your release. I said I was very doubtful if they would think of releasing you and that this particular possibility had not been discussed by us and I could give no real answer. I said however that I did think it would be well worth while to put the idea to the committee and a cable would in a few days settle what your views were. She said she would use all possible influence and let me know last night. So to make a long story short 'Frankie' true to form has withdrawn his resignation! They are having another meeting tomorrow, when as Fanny said "we are going to speak very plainly to him!" and they have agreed that they should apply for your release to return in your former capacity as they can get no one else and he (Frankie) is quite incapable of running the show. I know even if you were willing to come back (you'd never stick it) they wouldn't dream of releasing you, there might have been a chance under the first set of circumstances but certainly not the second. Fanny however seems to think it's plain sailing! Steven was here last night. He arrived all in and nearly frozen stiff having stood in the corridor all the way and it was snowing hard. However there was a roaring fire and a bottle of Sherry and he soon thawed. Jim came up and shared the sherry. We had about half the bottle and I've put the other half away for the night you come in case there's no more. I'll have to start another card.

Continuation 9 Jan

Oh beloved if only it would have been you last night and the house looked so welcoming and I get more and more impatient as time gets nearer and the last two weeks seem like months. I did enjoy Steven's Company for the evening very much. We talked our heads off until midnight. A great deal of our after dinner talk was on religious problems. He said he wanted my advice because he didn't see how he could, being an atheist, teach his child things he had no belief in and he had never had the courage to face the subject with May.

We got his atheism reduced to agnosticism after a while and while quite out of my depth I enjoyed the only profound discussion I've had since you went away. Oh Beloved, it is I think one of my greatest sins that I leap like a duck to water to such talk and succeed sometimes in giving an impression to people who don't know me well that I know what I'm talking about and I don't - I don't. I think I am quite incapable of deep thought at all. It seems rather odd that Steven couldn't talk to May on such things and please there must be nothing that we can't get out on each other.

Wilfred got home on December 31st so he must have been dreadfully long on the way. The boys are more adorable than ever. David can 'pretend' now and Robert tells him (for instance) he's a hen and David obediently becomes a hen and will remain so for ages. He will sit patiently in a corner Robert explaining his hen's broody and has to stay there until recovered! Then they play houses and shops and phone each other up and so on. It is still snowing off and on and I am weary of this coldness. When giving the contents of your box I forgot to mention the tea and pretty napkin rings - thank you dear. The boys have wolfed down two tins of pears already, so please no more jam but pears if possible! Please don't give another thought to my Christmas present and in any case you are always sending me lovely things and I never send you anything. Re; the Australian woman doc and Stores - from your description I should think the wise father to the thought in her case and not be too hard on Ronald!

Robert is wildly excited about his fort and looks for it every day no matter what I say! Excuse this awfulness of a letter but I've been up and down stairs to the boys several times while writing and seemed to lose my grip. Beloved I love you so much as you want me to love you and so are very much more.

Sheila

9th Jan 1945, Alan, WAF, Accra, to Sheila

Beloved,

I am in a quandary tonight for I am asked to come back here for a second tour. There will be a complete change over and they want me to carry on. Now the favourable side of such a scheme would be:-

1. I would get away promptly May 1st on leave.
2. I would get a minimum of six weeks leave.
3. When my release time comes after the defeat of Germany I am released no matter where I am.
4. What is likely to happen to me when I return just don't know. I think it is unlikely as I said before that I go East but it is a possibility. I would probably go to Europe after my leave.
5. Whether this paragraph is favourable or not I just don't know.

Against this is: -

6. I might get longer in England before I went away.
7. I might have a better chance of getting out for good if I were at home.
8. If the war in Europe lasts a long time I shall be away for a long time and Beloved I am tired tired of it.
9. If I'm in Europe I shall get leave every six months or so.

Dear will you let me know what you think. Of course the mine may upset the whole thing but with the recent man power lightening I'm getting very doubtful that I would be released for that.

I'm very fit, "in myself" as they say in Yorkshire so that the health aspect does not enter into it.

You will get other letters in the same mail as this. Oh Sheila I'm tired of all this. Alan

11th Jan 1945, Alan, WAF, Accra, to Sheila

Beloved,

I've been worried ever since I sent you yesterday's letter on a second tour. Dearest Sheila I just don't know what to think about anything these days. Downe has depressed me a lot by talking about how tired people looked at home and how difficult things have been.

You are so good beloved you write so often and you never tell me about the wet treks into Wakefield to get your shopping done and the shortages of all sorts of things.

Personally I do still feel that the war now has a hope of being over in late Spring in Europe and as you know I have never been of the 'short war' school. Downe brought recent papers and it's hard to forgive the Americans for some of the things they say just now.

I'm going to photograph myself today for your benefit. Downe brought me a filter and a lovely Leica portrait lens which latter he has put at my disposal while I am here. By the way - sorry to be so flighty - don't try to sell the camera or meter. I'll do it when I get back. The prices will be much better in the pre-summer period.

I am sending copies of all my photographs to an agency from now on. They submit them to newspaper and save endless trouble.

I'm just aching to hear that the fort, the crane, the motor car and my trunk have arrived. I sent the keys of both yesterday. I love you.

11th Jan 1945, Sheila, Wakefield, to Alan

My Very Dear.

We've been floundering about in snow for the last four days. I haven't seen anything like it for years. I took the boys out on the Castle Hill yesterday and Oh! Robert does badly want a sledge! It's thawing tonight however and it's just about time we had a warm spell, it doesn't seem to have stopped freezing since before Christmas. The night is alive with weird plops as the snow slides off the roof. I've been dipping into Morton's three books on the Near East while going on with "ancient history". I was so afraid I'd be dreadfully disappointed in them after all these years and the reading I've done between. They are however as fresh and much more interesting than before in the light of slightly more knowledge and I realise more fully the reading and work necessary to produce them and find no desire as I feared to sneer at them as 'popular travel books'. His style is very delightful.

Have had no further word from Fanny. I was momentarily bitterly disappointed at Frankie staying, but am trying to believe it was for the best. I don't want to stay here and I can't see you here, but I'd live in Wigan if I could have you and the thought that my loneliness was about to be ended was heady. However perhaps he'll show up again. I am informed by Miss Burton that he is convinced that his heart is very bad and he suddenly sat down in the clinic last week and started gasping and clutching his neck. She said that the thought of what she should do if he collapsed unnerved her completely. I don't suppose she knows anything of his resignation. I say nothing, but listen with great interest! Mrs Goose has come wallowing through the snow all these days and I take off my hat to her. Mrs. Morris had a little girl last week (only one!). But from what I hear is pretty poorly. Mrs. Goose wanted me to cycle over to see her yesterday but the snow made it impossible. She is at Walton Hall. Her parents aren't going to visit her on their way home. The cross country journey in the present conditions being too much of a thought.

I am expecting your family on the 26th inst. David is going through another spell of growing and changing. Robert is going back to school next Wednesday. And I am glad to say is thrilled at the idea. Love you, Sheila

14th Jan 1945, Alan, WAF, Accra, to Sheila

Beloved,

I have very little news as I have been fairly busy in the office and have not been out of G.H.Q for a week except to drive with a Mr. and Mrs *Slojbedon* on Friday last. I enjoy driving out so much because one gets good food. It sounds crazy and I'm not complaining for food is just no problem here but it lacks taste, somehow I miss potatoes very badly. Yam and Sweet Potatoes or Cassava are poor substitutes. It's odd too but I seldom bother with fruit although I have paw paw each morning.

There were no letters last night so I'm hoping for some tomorrow and I'm longing to be sure that these nasty colds are things of the past at 66.

I have been reading some grand books on the Trans Sahara

Caravan routes and I'm wishing I could go to Northern Nigeria on local leave.

My leave is off just now pending the arrival of my opposite number from East Africa who is coming over to liaise with me.

Poor Col Archer the A.D.P. had no relief sent out last time and we have just been notified no relief will be coming so he won't get away until next March which is very bad luck.

I must drop a hint to W.O. that I must have my relief on time.

Oh Sheila I'm sorry to be writing dull letters these days, it's a spell and I can't help it. I'll write a 'reg' letter later today. I find myself better in in evening.

I love you. Alan

14th January 1945, Sheila, Wakefield, to Alan

My Beloved, nearly half way through January and by the time you get this there won't be much more than three months between us. Yesterday a great event took place - the fort arrived!

Or part of it did. I expect the other pieces will arrive tomorrow. I would be alarmed, only for the parcel showed no signs of having been interfered with. We have the base, the inner walls and roof and two bastions. Robert is positively delirious about it and you have risen enormously in his estimation. He keeps saying "Daddy's a very clever man isn't he?" "You could have never made anything like that". He can hardly go to sleep tonight for the excitement at the thought of the postman bringing the missing parts tomorrow. Let's hope he does! Honestly though beloved it's a work of art, an amazingly good effort. David says he hopes he'll get a big one too! Robert will not let him get within touching distance of his. Also arrived two very nice trays. They are a most useful type and I'm most pleased with them and thank you very much. They are playing on the wireless just now "Love is the Sweetest Thing". I haven't heard it for years, we used to dance to it in the early thirties beloved. Strange how a tune can bring things back so clearly.

An interesting little book Blunt's "The Acts Of The Apostles" and especially to me just now with the other books I have been reading. Truly the ancient world is intensely interesting. I don't know why that should be but it is! Oh My Dear I do so want you to talk to.

The hankies that came with the fort have been a godsend sent to me. I was sneezing myself silly when the parcel came! I've had a wretched time these last few months with my nose and the odd thing is I was never bothered with it last winter.

We've been to tea at McVicars this afternoon and Robert distinguished himself by hitting Anthony a wallop in the eye after great provocation. Anthony at once collapsed and howled and Robert is so entranced with the result that I fear for him! Love from all tribe, Sheila

16th Jan 1945, Alan, WAF, Accra, to Sheila

Beloved,

I have still no letters to reply to as the mail is late and this must be posted today. It's 10 A.M. and I'm just in after walking round a local anti-malarial works since 8.00 AM - and I'm sweating "*small small*". Tonight I'm dining with A.D.M.S. Gold Coast and tomorrow I'm dining with Mr. and Mrs. Louis (Atty. General) so I'm having a very gay week! It seems a very long time until May beloved and so much may happen to the war before then. Things are much better in the last few days and I'm hoping they have been for you too.

Oh I'm longing for a letter and I hope it tells me things about Robert and David and how much you love me for these are the really interesting things. The world for me is very much a matter of you and me and Sheila I very badly need to know you and be myself again. I may be up in North Africa for a visit in a month's time and you can imagine my excitement about that. I've been reading more and more about the Sahara Caravan Routes and the big cities in the Sahara (Western) and the edge of the desert. Did you know that Djibouti is derived so - Jebel El Tarik - The Rock of El Tarik who was the commander of the Moorish - Berber Army which invaded Spain in the eighth century? It's a fascinating derivation. I'm hoping to write up Zaria as a typical northern Nigerian market town. I love you Sheila and I need you to share these things with me. Alan

17th Jan 1945, Alan, WAF, Accra, to Sheila

(1)

My Beloved,

Three letters last night and the outgoing mail delayed so that this will come in the same post as yesterday's letter.

Now first Beloved you did something which you tell me about in your letter which confirms to me if I ever had any doubt that you are the most wonderful woman to whom anybody was ever was married. I mean that when you were asked if I would accept the job in Wakefield, you said you would consult me. Feeling as I know about me being home you did that Beloved means you give me the wonderful dual position of being the most loved and needed man, at one with you mentally, and yet entitled to make a decision for himself without pressure where his own self-respect is involved. I shall never never forget this Beloved. Oh Sheila more and more you are loved and cherished for your very individual self. To sense my feelings, to love me with an emotion which must tend to distort reason and yet to accord to me the integrity of my own mind is to rise to a level of womanly wisdom and worldly wisdom which I have done nothing to merit having in the woman I have not for her wisdom but because she is my Dear Wife & the best companion I could ever desire.

Oh Sheila I see I have not even reached the question under discussion yet but I am so moved. I shall continue in another letter.

Alan

17th Jan 1945, Alan, WAF, Accra, to Sheila

(2)

Beloved,

To get down to the question. When an authority applies for a release it goes to Ministry of Health who if they approve apply to W.O. [War Office] who if they approve agree subject to the person being willing to be released. I do not think that the Min of Health or W.O. will agree at this time, but you never know. If I am eventually approached I shall say yes but I shall have to press for a decent salary as we could not manage on £700 per annum now.

I have no great desire to work under Frankie - indeed it would not work for long, but being out is the main thing. I agree that the chances of getting out as M.O.H. would be much better than for the Deputy's job. Frankie really is an incapable and stupid fellow and they should have got rid of him long ago. I could do his job - "on my ear" so to speak. But as you say I would not stay long in Wakefield. Mrs. Stott is an amazing find but she has tried to help me when she could.

Now to answer the other point in your letters. I'm so glad you had a visit from Steven and enjoyed his company. He is a good chap and we must see more of them after the war.

Re Sherry. I'll try to bring some home. I'd love to see David being a broody hen! More follows. Love Alan

17th Jan 1945, Alan, WAF, Accra, to Sheila

(3)

My Dear,

To continue - I'm glad to hear the box has arrived. The sticks are for parents. It was not very full but I wanted to get home to you (1) the box (2) the towels etc.

I don't think anything was missing. Is the bottle not eau de cologne? I have despatched more pears today belatedly.

I can only send 2 lbs of any one foodstuff so you will have to have one tin of jam with each tin of pears.

Sorry about my spelling - touché seeing we are being personal *pears*.

I'm sorry to hear about the sneezing day. I love you.

I expect the fort and other toys will be a little time yet judging by the other parcels.

I thought that crate would have stood anything, it was solid iroko wood and fastened by iron and brass screw nails.

I am sending you a bottle of lime oil. It is very very strong and burns the skin so be careful. A few drops in sugary water makes Rose's lime juice cordial (made in Rose's factory here) but the main use is to put a few drops in the bath water. It is very refreshing.

Beloved I have so much to tell you and discuss with you and ask you and debate with you. By the way I'll not ask for second tour until Wakefield clarifies itself. Kiss my boys. I love you. Alan

17th Jan 1945, Sheila, Wakefield, to Alan

(1)

Dear One. So our meeting is not to take place until May. Well so far as the international situation is concerned it is I think no bad thing that your return should be delayed for I take a very grave view of it. All the same I can't help hoping that you don't spend as many weeks on the journey as Maj Schofield did!

The party at McVicars yesterday went off very well. The games were a bit sticky and a bit of a palaver to start with and Robert at his first party was completely bemused and refused point blank to play. He and David retired to the sofa and sat whispering together and seemed to have some good jokes on their own! After tea however the Cine was a terrific success. David was simply delighted and good as gold. He sat in the front of the circle of children drumming his heels on the floor screaming with laughter at the funny bits, pointing and yelling "Oh, Look! Look!" There were two animal films and several Charlie Chaplin shorts and ice cream in the middle! When the lights went up Robert's face was the colour of a peony with excitement and he nearly wept because it was all over! The McVicars were here for dinner and tea today and we had a very happy time.

I am half dead tonight because the maid didn't come back after her night out last night. She played the same game last week and turned up in a taxi from Leeds just before dinner to say she was sorry but she had been to a party! Having had all the house to do including two fireplaces, potatoes and pudding (two!), a cake to ice, coal to haul up, the table to lay and goose to cook, not to mention the children to contend with, I was in a pretty fair state of rage when she blew in quite casually. I let her have it, to her considerable surprise so I imagine we will soon be parting company! I would hang on to her until the darkest days were over but I don't think I can stick it much longer. She is the biggest B.F. out and came home tight last week! Still she did wash up today! Getting angry and having to slate people like that upsets me considerably, I don't know why, one should take it in one's stride

By the way Maj Schofield has been posted somewhere near Durham, is now Capt Schofield, does nothing but inoculations all day long, is now fed up to the teeth and a lot further. His only bright spot is he is now Cat B.

Robert has produced another new tooth and is very proud of it! Your letter giving the plans of the fort arrived the day before the letter telling me you were going to send it!

Daddy is to stay four weeks at Ruthin and they have great hopes of *getting him fit*. I'm just sending off some more Dell Farm photos to you. Dreadfully poor but you will like to have them. I love you always. Sheila

17th Jan 1945, Sheila, Wakefield, to Alan

(2)

Dearest. The whole fort has now arrived and the crane. The rejoicings are terrific! The fort was assembled with no difficulty thanks to your guidance and looks splendid. Robert now sees you as a potential toy factory and bids me tell you he'd like a tank next! The crane is most ingenious and if only you could see the pleasure both toys give you would, I know, feel well repaid for your labours. He broke the string on the crane in a few hours of getting it, so your forethought in enclosing a spare piece was a mercy, as he was nearly in hysterics over the tragedy.

Aren't the Russians amazing? It would have been dreadful if they haven't got to Berlin first, we'd have messed it up beautifully. However they've still a long way to go, but there won't be any time wasted in considerations and discussions.

I am most interested and delighted with the "Golden Bough." I am much surprised to find it so easy to read and have sent to Smith's for "Adonis, Attis, Osiris" which should be good. I am still ploughing through ancient history. Ploughing isn't the right word really for I'm enjoying it immensely. All the same even though it's an old school book (never read) there's a lot in it and with constant reference to maps I find I can only concentrate on it in bed and don't stay awake terribly long there! It's dreadful to be constantly finding out ones ignorance of so many things.

We are going to tea with Miss Burton on Saturday. Perhaps I'll hear some more "Frankie" gossip there! What between the gold mine, the Russians, Frankie's heart, Carlisle and so on I don't know whether I am on my head on my heels!

Now I'm going to make some toasted cheese and cocoa (enough milk to spare, great treat!): and read some more Fraser while I eat. Robert started school again today and I gather had a good time. It's such a joy to see the evenings lengthen, not to mention the mornings. My Darwin tulips are coming up; they ought to be hit on the head, far too early. Love Sheila

18th Jan 1945, Alan, WAF, Accra, to Sheila

My Very Dear,

I wrote a note to Fanny yesterday to Fanny, says in effect that the W.O. even if they agreed to my release would consult me and that while I would be very willing as M.O.H., but that I would only come as deputy on one of the following conditions.

1. £800 pounds per annum.
2. Old salary with definite permission to seek another job within a year.

I hope you agree with that. You know I would be very content are as M.O.H. in Wakefield for a few years. It would be a fine stepping stone to a county job and on which to build up a reputation of having pulled the place together. We should have choice of present house or of House at Hospital which is more roomy and very well kept.

Dear Sheila how very many times have we considered possibilities like this!

Last night I had dinner at Louis's house with Mr. and Mrs. Louis and the Colonial Secretary. It was a delightful, restful evening and they were all such very pleasant people. Mrs. Louis is an absolute dear. She has a boy of 16 at Wellington and she is terribly enthusiastic about the prep school he was at. It is a favourite *Hard* Prep school and I must say she made it sound most attractive. Mrs.

Louis reminds me of you in some ways she is smaller than you but much the same figure and is very charming.

She is giving me full particulars and hopes to find a prospectus. Beloved I badly want to talk to you about our marvellous sons. Alan

19th Jan 1945, Alan, WAF, Accra, to Sheila

(1)

My Very Dear,

I have this morning your letter posted on Jan 12th. I'm so sorry to hear about all this foul weather and to know you are all over your colds.

I am so glad that you enjoyed H. V. Morton again. Funnily enough I came across an abridged Penguin addition of "In The Steps of the Master" and felt much as you did. It's odd that his weekly broadcast to overseas forces "Things At Home" is very poor.

I have ordered for you from a perfectly lovely Leopard skin. A belt - narrow for outside of coat. A cap round slightly higher at the front (or back) than back (or front) - very smart and sufficient is left of the skin for backing of gauntlet gloves. The gloves they make here are not nice. The skin is a beauty -with lovely spots and I'm now in my usual desperate excitement to get it to you.

As the cost is much above that allowed for duty free parcels and as a non-duty free parcel the luxury purchase tax is 100% plus 30% Customs Duty, I don't quite know how I shall get the things to you!

As I said in yesterday's letter I have written to Mrs. Stott. I'm beginning to dislike Frankie exceedingly. He appears such a stupid man to earn what he does. The trouble is, as he well knows, he will not easily get another job. Phone him and suggest U.N.R.R.A.[1] - just about his level. More. Alan

---

[1] U.N.R.R.A. United Nations Relief and Rehabilitation Agency, founded in 1943. Alan was clearly contemptuous of those who worked for the agency.

19th Jan 1945, Alan, Accra, to Sheila

Beloved,

To continue. It's very disappointing that your parents cannot visit you. I do so hope that your father really feels better. I'm glad mine are coming on 26th. Mother is positively feverishly excited about it. It so odd that she was so pathetically and tremendously pleased that you told her that Robert "gets a lot of pleasure out of the picture making set we sent him".

These boys have a very big set of admirers!

Tell Robert that when I get back I shall make him a sledge before next winter. I'm not sure that there is not one of mine in Kingsborough Gardens.

So David is growing and changing again. Please put him in cold storage until I get back for I was quite satisfied with him as he was.

Poor Duff got an internal obstruction yesterday obviously from an old appendix operation. He was operated on last night and is apparently doing very well this morning. It's very bad luck though and he will be invalided home for you don't 'pick up' after operations out here.

Well my very Dear One tell the boys I love them and that I love you.

Kiss them both for me. Love Alan

21st Jan 1945, Sheila, Wakefield, to Alan

I have had your letter asking my opinion of you going back on another tour. I have thought of little else since but of course it's quite impossible to know what to say far less advise. All I will venture is this - if it were anyone else asking my opinion I would say take a chance and come home. But I can't think straight about you at all, the stakes are too high. I have always been told and understood that in any case one was not posted overseas for three months after service abroad, is this not so?

It is hard not to be unduly elated by the Russians new drive: but my opinion is that this offence will not carry them to the end, but that they will pause for a final build up. Even so I cannot think the war will last longer than the summer, say Aug. For although the Americans looked like sitting by the Rhine 'till the cows come home' the Russians have no use for that kind of thing. And am I glad they're going to get there first - they'll give them hell and some more and here's strength to their elbow. In any case six weeks is an absurdly short time away from W. A. before starting another year and a half. You didn't say when you have to decide. It seems a silly idea to me just now but I know at the back of my mind it's because I'm so bucked at the news.

We are more than ever in the grip of winter now. I've never known a more severe frost and plenty more snow too, it has been a hard winter. Downe, I think, must be a bit of an ass. Of course people are tired, but I don't think it hits you in the eye.

For myself I could go on this way for a long long time if I had you, but on my own it's not easy. All the same the people have so little to put up with compared with other countries, except in the flying bomb area and that is pretty dreadful.

I'll write again tomorrow when I get more cards. I rather wish this new problem which confronts us had never arisen, life is quite complicated enough as it is. Love from the tribe. Sheila

22nd Jan 1945, Alan, WAF, Accra, to Sheila

My Beloved,

I've just had the photographs of the boys and am delighted with them. They are a very good series and I see such a difference in my chaps. I had to look for quite a time at the big 'head' until I decided whether it was Robert or David!

I like the way their ears stick out!

Then the picnic one is just grand. In the background is My Dear One, looking eminently cool and collected and kissable.

The three at the fence showing the boys hand in hand are very sweet and I just adore Robert in his kilt. You keep and dress my boys so sensibly and well Beloved.

Robert in his school hat is just a scream. He has that that grin of his which really is from ear to ear.

Can David ride the bicycle or only sit on it? David is a little knock kneed as you said but he will grow out of that. It's just that he is big and heavy. If you are worried about him arrange with Miss Burton for Dr. Crockett, the orthopaedist, to see him at his monthly visit.

I'm very fed up at not getting my local leave but I shall just have to wait and hope.

Duff is, I am glad to say, getting on well. He may even be able to complete his tour. This is Monday and on Friday you will probably be having Daddy and Mummy. How I wish I could join the party. Your loving husband always. Alan

22ⁿᵈ Jan 1945, Sheila, Wakefield, to Alan

My very dear. Thanks for the keys. Still living in arctic conditions. I have so many clothes on and I can hardly write! Many have no coal but we are fortunate so don't worry about that. The blinking pipes are freezing and don't I envy you have the heat! David's cold and cough came back last week and I was so miserable about him and wondering what on earth I was doing wrong and if I was coddling him too much that I got the doctor Sunday (yesterday). I may as well add that Robert's nose has run for about five weeks! McD.S was very sweet about it and said I needn't worry about my shortcomings in the matter as he had never known the child population so afflicted with colds and bronchitis which simply would not clear up. He maintains it's due to a nutritional deficiency but everything gets that dropped in these days and although it exonerates me I can't feel it applies to the boys at any rate. David has a new bottle with belladonna in it (I haven't the faintest idea why!) and gulps it down like a man and he is full of beans in spite of everything and doesn't cough much through the day now. Robert is enjoying school and is going to a party on his own on Friday. Up to now he has refused to go anywhere without me. It's funny but a few weeks ago David started asking for the first time to have his bedroom door open and "let the land light shine in". Looking back Robert started objecting to his being shut in the dark bedroom at exactly the same age. I had one of Robert's school mistresses and her sister in the other evening and they told me how much Robert talks of you at school and were amazed at how he loves making things and using his hands.

I feel Frankie won't last long somehow. *Blagden* buttonholed me today and started running him down right and left!

Eileen (Bill's wife) has asked me if she can come and stay for a bit. Bill is in Egypt and of course she has no home. I expect she and young Bill will arrive sometime next week.

I heard a talk by Gilbert Murray on the wireless tonight. He speaks very well and I enjoyed it.

Oh! Beloved aren't the Russians grand. The news is just starting. News over - better and better.

It's a bright moonlit night and the planes are roaring over. I have dreadful palpitations! I just can't read or settle to anything these days and live for the evening news. Oh! If only we could get a decent push going from our side. Now for hot water bottles and bed with half my clothes on! I love you dearly. Sheila

23rd Jan 1945, Alan, WAF, Accra, to Sheila

Beloved,

A most odd air mail arrived today with many Sea mail letters but only one bag of air mail. So I have a surface letter of Jan 7th enclosing Mrs. Morris's letter etc. but no air mail.

Mrs. M's letter is sweet. I go all dopey about charladies or anyone who appreciates you. I wrote to her, sent her some photographs, and I shall send her some jam. I am prepared to fall for anyone who is good to you and I like Mrs. Morris. It shocks me a bit to compare the chances of their 'poor wee sprats' and ours.

I'm still in the stage of carrying around the boys photographs and keeking at them from time to time. You know I don't know which is more attractive. They are both so very handsome in their own way.

I am definitely off to North Africa in a month or so and I shall try to get you some raisins. I have not permission yet to go to Cairo but as you will understand I shall leave no stone unturned!

If I get as far as that I shall of course return by the *Southern & Cargo*. The more I can see of Africa the better. What about settling in Kenya after the war? Splendid climate, trout fishing, skiing (yes I cannot spell - yes I'll look up dictionary "ski-ing") and no servant problems!

Leopard skin coat etc. not ready today but should be ready early in the week.

I'm trying to get things straight for coming home. Please fill in:-

Size stockings -

    Colour -

    Type face cream -

    Lipstick -

    Powder -

Do you prefer lisle stockings fully purchased at 4/6 in dozens or £1.1 silks in half dozens.

I'll write another letter later tonight but remember I love you till you get that. Alan

25th Jan 1945, Sheila, Wakefield, to Alan

Dearest Man. Still we shiver! The tiny twigs on the trees are as thick as the *icicles* with layers of frost. This is the seventh day of it. The windows are sheets of ice. In the kitchen yesterday, a roaring fire, the oven on the full for the dinner, the boiler boiling clothes and still the windows were covered with ice! I haven't sent Robert to school today. He came home blue yesterday and said he'd never been warm all morning and the backs of his legs were raw where his Wellington's had rubbed and I hadn't the heart to send him out today. David is very sweet and quaint. His funniest mix up in speaking is the word 'mistake', he has always pronounced it 'my take', then if he thinks I made a mistake about anything he says 'you're take' for my mistake! Last night he called me up to his room and with great excitement and with a finger on each of his eyelashes said 'I got two wee fevvers' and then with an air of discovery 'and you've got two the big fevvers'. After all if you feel your eyelashes it is just like a feather!

The length of my feet is 9 ½ inches but as you know they are a queer skinny shape so don't attempt anything but sandals which would be grand. The little wooden houses arrived the other day, all smashed bar one! They do great violence to things on the way. You should see how some of the jam tins are buckled.

Still the Russians sweep on, can they do it I wonder, I suppose it's because we got so hopelessly stuck in Sept we think they are bound to do the same. Still as I said before, even if they do pause they will finish it off in May or June, even if we never move from where we are. Is this wishful thinking? Somehow I don't think so this time. I'm in a dither wondering if you've decided to go back to West Africa. Somehow I don't think you will. I've been having an intensive practice of games with the boys this afternoon, Spin the Plate, Musical Bumps, Nuts in May and so on to prepare Robert for tomorrow's party when he'll be on his own. He is quite all right now he knows how to do them.

You'll never guess where I was on Tuesday afternoon, at the pictures. Mrs. Goose said there was a good picture on and she thought it would do me good to get out on my own and she would wait later than usual. So off I went and saw 'Wuthering Heights' and when I got back she had my tea all laid out by the fire and so I thoroughly enjoyed my afternoon and am grateful to her for pushing me out! David is losing his baby dimples and getting knuckles. No room for more except once more how we all love you. Sheila.

27th Jan 1945, Alan, WAF, Accra, to Sheila

Beloved One,

I have your two letters of 14th and 17th. I'm enormously pleased to hear that the Fort and the Crane have arrived so quickly. I just hope that David's motor arrives home soon now. I'm 36 years old today Beloved but I don't notice any difference so let's forget it!

I'm so delighted that Robert "hauled off and bust" Anthony one. Tell him I strongly approve. I'm sorry to hear that you have been having more bad nose running days. I'll pack everything with handkerchiefs. I hope you like the toys. I am so glad you are enjoying the Golden Bough. I agree in small doses it's not heavy. It is so incredibly stimulating and thought provoking and illuminates so many obscure things which are already in the Bible and Koran and other ancient literature. You can imagine how often I have passages recalled out here where society in bush is so primitive. Well Beloved I just ache to talk with you about these things.

Doesn't reading make other reading so terribly interesting? To come on things in books which tie up with other reading with which the other is not familiar is a great thrill to me. I am reading side by side just now:

1. The book you sent, Antiquities Northern Europe.
2. [*Illegible*], Edda and Saga.
3. Snorre's Heimskringla Saga

And I just want to weep that I have not you to enthuse with.

Last night I had a dinner party at the Club for Lt Col Bobby Bogart-Wilson from the second Africa. Boy Wilson, Archie (ADP), Downe, Boin (Judge Advocate) and Gilbray. We had a good dinner and the conversation was really interesting.

I hope to stay with B. W. in Nairobi. Beloved his home is there and he lives with his wife and children.

Oh Sheila I do love you and am so glad to be nearing the end of our separation. Alan

29th Jan 1945, Alan, WAF, Accra, to Sheila

(1)

Beloved, I have your letter so 21st and 22nd tonight. Now about a second tour - that is practically certainly off. The position is completely changed by a war office letter. I am group 16 for demobilisation. The instruction now is that groups under 24 are not to be sent to the Far East.

Now there is a quibble about Medical Officer demobilisation as you know and we have been told that we just will not be allowed to go with our age group but I think we shall go shortly after and I'm convinced that they will try to avoid sending us to Far East. So I am far better to come home for good in May and see what happens. I'm very sorry I mentioned it to you now but Beloved I am like you just lost and don't know what to do or think.

I am so pleased at the thought of Bill, Eileen and young Bill coming to stay with you. It will be good company and she seemed such a very nice girl. Get Bill's address for me and I shall try to look him up if, as I hope, I shall be in Egypt in the next two months.

Beloved I am convinced that if Frankie went and I returned in May that they would release me. There will be a difficulty in fitting me in if not in Far East especially as I have just had a record recommendation for promotion - very complimentary one sent to War Office, and I'm sure they would let me go rather than give me a command at home with so many old Full Colonels about.

I'm off to *Tokadills* to meet my E. African pal who left me for Freetown this morning. I go on Wednesday and take him up to Kumasi by road and back again. More in second letter.

Love Alan

P.S. Wireless just says 90 miles to Berlin. Yippee!

29th Jan 1945, Alan, WAF, Accra, to Sheila

(2)

Beloved,

To continue. It makes me feel very mollycoddled to hear of you with all this terrible cold. Oh I hope the pipes do not burst. Poor wee boys with colds. You don't complain and dear I do know that it must be miserable. I can hardly bear to think of the Russian palaver myself. I cannot see Germany lasting out another summer and the Good God alone knows what the manner of the end will be in Japan.

I cannot tell you how moved I was to read that Robert talks about me at school. What fun we shall have making things. You would have laughed to see me making notes for concrete strengths for Rieff and how I hoard wee bits for the boat. (My bed is full of ants and I must stop to spray them).

Ants and sand flies - I don't know which are more irritating. By the way to see if I had any suppressed malaria I stopped taking tablets for a month and have been as right as a trivet so I am very pleased.

Glad you enjoyed Gilbert Murray. I'm just reading up Burton's "First Footsteps in East Africa".

Well it's 11 pm. I must get to sleep. I worked from 8 - 1, 1.30, - 4.30, 5 - 6.30 and 8-10 at my office stuff today to get cleared up for getting away on Wednesday. I get very tired because it is terribly hot just now.

I shall try to write to Robert tomorrow. David's Motor Car must have missed the mail and will probably be another month.

I love you dearly beloved and I want to talk to you more than anything in all the world. Alan

31ˢᵗ Jan 1945, Sheila, Wakefield, to Alan

Dearest one. At last the thaw has come and today is quite mild. You can't imagine the relief. I'm so sorry about Duff, Tell him I was asking for him. I think you have dealt very well with Stott episode, but I can't make out whether you have had any direct communication from her. She promised to let me know what happened at the second meeting, but has not bothered to do so and I will not approach her on the matter although I am consumed with interest!

The news continues unbelievable good although for all the interest people seem to take the Russians might not exist. I just can't get over this apathy of "the masses". The pears have arrived which is quick work and all in the process of being eaten up. The Leopard Skin things sound very very exciting, there never was such a husband. Beloved, how on earth do you manage to be exactly what I want?

I am expecting Eileen and Bill on Sunday and don't know how we'll fit in together but we can but try. It will be good for me in that it will impel me to be better tempered. Oh! Beloved, my need for you seems to be rising to a crescendo these days and I have so little patience left. I wonder often how you will stand the constant din (I never could bear noise!) of home life!

Meals are dreadful. David looks over at Robert says sweetly, but with demons in his eyes "you're a drain pipe", or "you're a church hall" or something equally daft and Robert never fails to swallow the bait and makes a wild jab, with whatever implement he happens to be using, across the table and roars out "I'm not" then, as an afterthought "you are" which elicits yell of rage from David and the argument rises to full force David positively yelling "Mummy Mummy Roberts says I drainpipe". It isn't always David to start it but constant repetition is exhausting in the extreme.

I am so glad your father is so much better, our disappointment at their non-arrival last weekend was only tempered by the fact that it was impossible travelling weather. He really ought to take things more easily, nobody could go on the way he does. I may run up to Glasgow for two weeks at Easter and see everybody.

I love you dearly. Sheila

4th Feb 1945, Alan, WAF Accra, to Sheila

My Very Own Beloved,

It's 4.30 and just back from Kumasi - very hard and dry due to Harmattan. Your letter of January 25th was waiting for me. You will know by now of course that Daddy has had pneumonia and that he is getting on well, so you will not have seen them.

Oh I'm so grieved to think of you having to put up with all this cold and miserable weather. I'm glad Robert has a Mother who is good to him and keeps him at home and teaches him games so that the party will be good fun and not worry.

Tell David that Daddy has had a look, and he has "fevvers" over his eyes too. Beloved how on earth do they manage to make things so. I think it must be deliberate when these *brows* were *marked*.

Thank goodness Roberts Fort and crane were all right and Oh I do hope David's motor car does not get mislaid.

I could not agree more about the Russian show. It definitely means German war over this year. I'm so glad you got to the pictures.

Oh Beloved am I longing to take a girl to the pictures? My heart warms to Mrs Goose who had your tea ready at the fire. Tell David to keep one dimple for Daddy to kiss when he returns.

I had a very good trip all by road round Gold Coast and now some more of the country. Believe me I do enjoy seeing country and my boys Robert and David must do plenty of that even if I have to give up photography!

Duff will go home shortly and Wiggy is off to Nigeria for a spell so I shall be here for a bit.

I am promised by Bogarde-Wilson a real trip in East Africa and hope to see Mombasa, Dar es Salaam, Zanzibar and goodness knows where else.

I'll write another letter tonight for I'm still a bit dazed with the dry heat at the moment. Love Alan

4th Feb 1945, Sheila, Wakefield, to Alan

My Dear One,

Two things about the boys before I forget - Robert wants to know why are we here, and what use are we? Perhaps you can help him. I can't!

The other day they were having bacon and eggs. I started them on theirs and went back to the kitchen to cook my egg. When I returned to the dining room after several minutes Robert was well on with his and David, who adores bacon, was staring at his untouched plate with tears in his eyes. I told him to get on and he said "I can't Mummy. I can't it's pig, Robert says so". Robert eating away demurely his eyes on his plate - you can just see it!

We've been down having tea with Miss Perkins and Miss Burton this afternoon. Robert had his kilt and tweed jacket on and a small girl followed all the way and never took her eyes off him!

I am glad you have the Nethy Br photos at last. They are pretty poor but nice to have when there's nothing better.

My Dear, at last I fear the coast is getting you down. David is not knock kneed, never has been and isn't going to be. His legs have never given me a moment's worry and if there has been any suggestion that he's knock kneed, bow legged or splay footed, it didn't come from me!

Dear if the Russians get to Berlin there won't be any Sherry left when you come! I wonder what will happen in the next month or two. Such a lot could, and Oh! it <u>must</u>.

I had some eggs from Lannie this week, they are all well. Beloved only two months after this one and you should be leaving for home. David so often comes to me and says "I love you and I love my

Daddy". It's so odd he talks as if he knows you well. A scrappy letter I'm afraid but Oh! How I love you. Sheila

5th Feb 1945, Alan, WAF, Accra, to Sheila

Beloved,

Your letter of 31st January posted on 1st of Feb came in tonight - the best time yet!

I'm delighted to hear about the thaw. No, I've had no direct communication from Mrs Stott. I only write to her as I told you. More pears are on the way.

My love to Aileen and Bill. I hope that the boys are good to wee Bill. Tell them I said they were to be good to him. Your description of a meal with David and Robert in good form is awful. Tell them no more or I won't come home!

I am tired tonight for I had so much to square up in my office and Wiggy went off on tour this morning. Did I tell you that he was a grandfather. The daughter whom we met has had a baby.

Dad seems to have been pretty dicky but Moira assures me that he is getting on well now. Your mother has twice sent grapes the substance and thought of which has been very much appreciated. You have not said recently how your Dad is getting on after his rest and treatment.

I just cannot see the German war lasting for more than six months beloved, and in spite of all palaver about refugees I have hopes that I may get out. Oh Sheila I don't want to settle down to vegetative life any more than you do, but I do want to live quietly with you for a little until we can get settled between ourselves what we wish to do to enjoy ourselves. Be good to our boys, and be useful people in this appalling world.

My few photographs of my trip in Ashanti are not very good as I expected for that the Harmattan makes everything so dull and obscure with the rain. I'll send you some to amuse you.

Love to my boys. Tell them just to be themselves and not to be good but tell them to love you and me and each other. Alan

7th Feb 1945, Sheila, Wakefield, to Alan

Dearest of Men

A week out of Feb already. Oh! Beloved it will be simply astonishing to have your home. I have got to the stage when being alone seems the reality and life with you an impossible dream. I have a victory to record - I have been much better tempered this week. I just wakened up one morning and discovered nothing seemed to irritate me any more - I'm wondering how long it will last!

This morning I had four letters - 23^{rd,} 27^{th,} and two of 29th. Now how you can manage to embark on a Grand Tour of office at this stage I just don't pretend to understand. I love the speciousness of "I shall of course return by the Soudan and Congo" - of course! Then farther on you lightly remark that you have to stay with B. W. In Nairobi! I will have questions asked in Parliament about you if you're not careful! Beloved, I'm as jealous as a cat!

Your interest in my wishes as to face powder, creams and lipstick does you great credit and is positively pre-war!

Oh! My dear these days passed a long, long time ago. Do you know I couldn't tell you the name of the cosmetics I used when the war started. For five years now one has just scrounged what one could get, usually the chemists own concoctions. Face powder however still occasionally turns up with pre-war maker's names but these again one just takes what's going thankfully so that it's dreadfully hard for me to guide you. Particularity so as all the makers have, or did have, a host of shades and all called their colour range by different names! All I can say if you are determined to see it through is a rose shade of powder, a pale "rochelle" no use at all, and as to cream, nothing heavy (meaning greasy). Coty cream is useless for me but their powder is OK. Honestly tho this is out of your grasp all together! My stockings size is 9 or 9½. As to shade - the oddness of considering shades, far less trying to write them down is extraordinary! Pre-war the shade of ones stockings in relation to one's clothes, was, as I remember as though in a dream, a quite important thing. Now and for many a day past one is darned lucky to have a whole paint and shade. So that I can't even think of names of shades, but anything but black or nigger will do. Dash it you must have looked at my legs sometimes!

To be continued

(2)

Now all the foregoing about stockings is a waste of time because lisle makes my feet sore and I don't wish you to pay £1.1 for a pair of silk stockings. Let us keep our sense of proportion dear, it is quite absurd and I should be miserable wearing them. The ones we get there aren't bad and very soon they will start having them fully fashioned, so a "matron's" legs are not worth £1.1 stockings, and neither are anyone else's for that matter!

I've wasted a lot of space on these matters so that you won't think I am not appreciative of your thinking of getting these things.

You know I am frightfully sorry I forgot all about your birthday until I was dressing this morning and then your letters arrived to remind me! We always forget each other's birthdays beloved, I wonder why!

There has been a case of mumps at school so I suppose that's the next thing. Aileen isn't coming until Monday. I'll send you Bill's address.

I also forgot to thank you for the cable you sent at the time your people were supposed to be here. It was very welcome.

Frankie shows no signs of re-moving himself. What is Fanny playing at? Don't forget to tell me if you have had a letter from her. She is a stupid woman in some ways. I never said a word to anyone here about the 'Frankie' affair and Fanny told her daughter all about it and she lost no time in telling the McVicars and they, I should think, thought it odd I'd said nothing to them, but one should keep one's mouth shut at such times.

It would kill me to find my bed full of ants, positively I shall not live in W. A. But great heavens can't you put the bed legs in something ants don't like?

Glad about your lack of malaria, it's very great good fortune.

It may be my fond imagination but I'm very pleased with the way Robert is drawing things. He has made great strides in the last week or two. His red blazer is ready now. He looks sweet in it and it will be fine for the spring.

(3) Continuation

I wonder if we'll ever get our three months (minimum!) holiday when the war ends, I don't expect we will. One thing you could send or bring me which would be a great treat would be a tail comb. You know the kind I mean don't you? You can't get combs here at all and tail ones even more than not at all.

It was nice of you to send the jam to Mrs. Morris. She is still in hospital, got an abscess and was taken to 'White Rose'. I doubt strongly that she has any regard at all for me, that is a thing I shall never believe or expect again, but she is a hardworking, and as far as I know, deserving woman and there is something likeable about her. My attitude to those I employ has altered since you went away. Sister Brown's defection has left a bitterness in me that will be there for life. I shall always tend to be a softie in my dealings with these people and I shall always help where I can, but the difference is there all right.

My dear, take care of yourself on your impending journey. I must confess against my will that I will be relieved when I know it is over. I get used to the idea of you in one place and all travel these days worries me stiff. Do send me a cable when you get back, it will make all the difference to my days and nights. I know how much you must be looking forward to this trip. I would too, but it's so different to be doing all these grand things from sitting here waiting.

So forgive my fussing and love me all the same and send cables (on second thoughts) whenever you can even before you get back. Never mind the silk stockings, pour the money out on cables!

David is lengthening and getting knuckles on his hands instead of dimples! They are adorable boys and Oh I am so glad about David. How dreadful if our careful planning hadn't gone wrong and I'd never known him.

The electric clock ticks like a 'grandfather' these days, can you think why? Yours ever, Sheila

8th Feb 1945, Alan, G.HQ Accra, to Sheila

Beloved,

Today I obtained your hat and belt and fully half a leopard skin is left over for your gauntlets. I'm a wee bit disappointed in them. Perhaps I was looking forward too much. But the hat can be remodelled at home and the belt buckle can be replaced as it is not up to standard. When you get them say if you would like an ivory buckle for I could have one made and I have the breadth of the belt. Just had another look - perhaps it's not too bad. At any rate Beloved, there is plenty of sound skin left over for another hat if you don't like it.

The mail comes in tomorrow but I'm afraid that this must be posted first. I bought two sheets and pillow cases and two large and two small towels today. They should be useful

O dearest time is creeping on and one of these days there will be a terrific shouting at the corner of Many gates Lane and I shall be rushing up to hold you and kiss you and try to get rid of the taxi man as soon as possible in order to kiss you more. I rather hope that it's at night so that all small boys are in bed!

There is a lovely drawing in Punch this week of a man sitting reading in a chair. The door is half open and the face of a worried small boy peers round saying "I've driven Mummy Dotty". Beloved you have stood up well to two very alive small boys. But you are first and foremost mine. Oh you don't know how much I need you. Alan

9th Feb 1945, Alan, G.HQ Accra, to Sheila

My Very Own Beloved,

I'm very thrilled tonight for I have packed your hat and belt into a tin and have great hopes of getting it home by air, and I've just had an ivory carver up. He is going to make a buckle in ivory for your belt something like this with your initials carved on it. It is being made in Kumasi and will take three weeks so I'm sending hat and belt without it and you can fix on the new buckle when you get it. I'll send the rest of the leopard skin when I get an opportunity. I hope they don't open the parcel and query the price.

Oh I do so hope it is really what you expected.

I sent more pears and jam today (I have sent Mrs Morris hers). Had a note from four Fountain Press today telling me that they had sent to £7.10 and that they just had not enough paper for a second edition but were doing a reprint now and would bring out the new addition as soon as possible.

Beloved. I'm wondering how on earth I'm going to get all the stuff I have accumulated home. I have still many books and Oh Dear so many nuts and bolts!

By the way I received 200 cigarettes yesterday addressed to me personally from St Helens Parish Church. Does this ring a bell?

I wish I did not get so sleepy at nights. Is just 10 o'clock and I can hardly keep my eyes open. I finished my four yearly statistics today and that's a great load off my mind.

Another night less without you is over.

Bless you my Dear.

Alan

10th Feb 1945, Sheila, Wakefield, to Alan

My Dear,

Firstly I report another cheque from the Fountain Press. It is for £7.1.0. and represents royalty on 188 copies from July to December. Secondly Bill's address is - No 7, Base Workshop R.E.M.E. M.E. Forces. His rank is Lt Col. Aileen is due tomorrow. I had to phone her this morning and warn her about the "Mumps". John Wardley started it last night - the first in Robert's class. The school was closed for three days in hopes of checking it, but of course it's quite hopeless now John has started. Anyhow Aileen has evidently decided to risk it as she was going to phone before lunch if she decided not to come. It's a great life! A fearful thing has happened this last week. I have lost interest in food! That this is just awful because I get such a kick out of food although it might be an indelicate admission! I keep thinking of all the wonderful things I could eat and look with glassy eyes on what we can get. It would serve me right to be starved no doubt but how wonderful it will be to be able to choose what one will have again!

We have been to the McVicars this afternoon. It's been a dreadful day - sleet. Your letter to Mrs. Morris had an immediate effect. Mr. Morris and his son arrived and settled down for dinner, bearing the letter like a talisman! I'm dreadfully hard up for news tonight - Oh! My dear I nearly forgot. David's car has arrived and is a great success. It's just fine and so solid and they are so pleased it has seats inside it. Altho Robert can't understand why there should be a seat in the back when it says "no lifts"!

It was a scream the day it came, Robert kept trailing after David and saying "David you can have my *army weevy*".

"David you have had it for a long time" then in desperation "Oh! David you can have any of my things that you want if you just let me have your car for a wee while". David says "my Daddy loves me and sent me a parcel from Africa" and he thanks you very much.

Both send kisses.

Beloved I love you. Sheila

12th Feb 1945, Akan, G.HQ Accra, to Sheila

Beloved,

Three letters tonight dated fourth, seventh, and seventh Feb. Dearest answer all Roberts questions, as a mother should, before I get home! He seems a bit philosophically inclined to me. Poor wee David and his "pig".

I seems to have stirred up something when I suggested knock knees - all right, all right I take it all back.

I'd rather have the Russians in Berlin and miss my sherry! No sherry I'm sure.

I'll get a selection of lipsticks and things you might like.

Beloved you write very nicely. I wish I had a nice flowing hand like you, mine is just getting worse and worse. I too am very thrilled at the thought that Robert may draw well. I always wish you would start again.

I'm busy trying to get down to an M.D. Thesis on malaria in military forces in British West Africa. I'd like to prove to myself that I can concentrate to write an M.D. Thesis at the end of a tour as it seems to be accepted that you are semi-crackers at this time and I don't feel even quarter crackers.

Your hat and belt will not after all I think have gone by air but I managed to have it registered so the parcel should reach you. I'll hold on to the rest of the skin meanwhile.

Duff is going home soon and War Office say they cannot replace him so Lesley Sparks is coming back. Wiggy is giving up the unequal struggle and is getting very excited about going home. Yes I shall let you know if I hear anything from Fanny.

I'm glad to hear Robert wears his kilt. When he is bigger and won't - in England - but it's good to get him used to it. They sound awful nice boys my boys. How could they be otherwise brought up by you? Alan

14th Feb 1945, Sheila, Wakefield, to Alan

My Very Dear,

Two letters from you today. It's lovely to hear you so optimistic about the war. This will be a short letter as I've mislaid my pen and Aileen wants to write to Bill and I've got her pen. We are all fine.

Aileen is perfectly sweet to have in the house but I shall be glad to be on my own again. It's finding food for a bigger family that is an awful grind and having to cook two different kinds of dinners because there isn't enough of one kind and supper is a headache.

However one thing is there isn't a spare moment now in the day so the three weeks will go like a flash and I shall be so much nearer to you quickly. The boys after being new fangled with young Bill for a few hours now hardly notice him and play together as usual! He (young Bill) is perfectly happy pottering around on his own, so it's probably just as well that way for anyway they don't fight!

Robert sends you six kisses and wants you to know how much he loves you.

There are 22 off school with Mumps today which leaves only 11. I had a talk with McD. Smith and he says it seems a mild infection and in his opinion they are much better to get it over young. He said it was useless to keep Robert away from school which was my own impression. Odd mothers seem to be taking it too, so I shall probably join the happy throng, not having had it!

Glad to hear about Wiggy's daughter - they are nice things families (!!!) in moderation!

Excuse this scrappy note I'll find my pen tomorrow. Oh! Dear One I love you. Sheila.

17th Feb 1945, Alan, G.HQ Accra, to Sheila

My Beloved,

Last night no 3 of the series of letters written on Feb 7th arrived, and also letters from Moira and from Dad himself.

I was getting worried about not hearing from Alan and cabled a few days ago. Talking of cables, I have fixed to leave about March 7th and everywhere I go you will have cables. Don't worry beloved. It's very much a routine business these days travelling by air.

Combs will be sought and obtained somehow with rat tail handles even if I have to modify ordinary combs.

Don't let the Sister Brown palaver change your attitude beloved she was so psychophobic that while not certifiable she was just as cracked as people in asylums and you would not be upset by what a loony did. You see loonies are not just difficult people. They are people who have at one or more stages reacted abnormally to some difficulty and have thereafter proceeded quite logically on false premises. When the results don't *conform* with reality, as inevitably they don't sooner or later, they are so far astray that the only refuge is to delude themselves that what is obvious and clear to other people is not existent. So arises their behaviour which makes them such outcasts. I should imagine that Sister Brown was in her youth a nymphomaniac and probably her upbringing was a strict one. When her physical need was greater than could be controlled by the self-deception imparted by her upbringing she had either to acknowledge that according to the code of morality of her circle she was vicious or to resort to some self-gratification which was

(2)

not based on fact (that is - a delusion). Undoubtedly one of the delusions which she had in self-justification was that everyone else was really "immoral" although they had managed to conceal it.

Another related delusion was that she was the object of persecution. This arose (a) From being found out while other people (who her delusion said were the same) were not. (b) From being unhappy and financially insecure (again others were not) and (c) In our case, from the perfectly infuriating complacency of you and me.

In such a person unstable, paranoiac (deluded) it is quite possible, and to her poor mind the incongruity is not apparent, genuinely to be fond of people as she was I believe of you and the children, and at the same time to spread slander about them.

I don't know if that helps at all but I feel that one must pity her deeply and forgive her, recognising that at the same time she is a social menace to a degree short of requiring legal restraint.

There are few people like her though all of us show her illogical thinking in mild degree on occasion.

To draw a false conclusion i.e. that no one is worthy of trust is to fall into her mistake in small degree.

Beloved how awful it must be to have a sermonising husband!

Roberts's letter to Alan made an enormous impression. Thank you for phoning so often. Tell the boys that I'm getting very excited about coming home. Kiss them both.

I love you, I love you more than you will ever know. Alan

17th Feb 1945, Alan, G.HQ Accra, to Sheila

Beloved,

I have note of Jan 12th enclosing the Geographical Magazine rejection of my article. I'm disappointed of course but not very much for your nice wee note - almost in a tragic vein - takes all the sting away.

What can you expect from people who head their letters "January the tenth" instead of "Jan 10." As ordinary people?

I'm not very surprised for I realised the whole thing was a bit heavy. When I get back I shall have a shot at American Geographic after I have if necessary rewritten it.

The more I see of this sort of thing the more I realise how much easier it is to deal through an agency and leave them to "place" the article.

Beloved it's Saturday night and I'm getting down to my MD. Thesis so I shall have to stop ere my resolution fails.

Oh how I love you. Alan

18th Feb 1945, Sheila, Wakefield, to Alan

My Dear,

This letter long overdue but you must forgive me if they are not so numerous for the next week or two. I've had an appalling days sneezing today and the McVicars to tea into the bargain. Whenever I bend my head I just drip! Anyway you'll know it's not tears on the letter. Today has really been a scream. Bill[1] has nearly driven Aileen crazy. She has spent a considerable time rubbing out scribbles on the dining room wall, breakfast and dinner were a battle to make him eat anything and Aileen trying very hard to be tough did get some down, now his tummy is upset and she has been rushing round in frantic circles with pieces of washing! This afternoon he covered his face with her lipstick and also all the windows in the bedroom. He put a dirty spade in his mouth and she rushed him upstairs to wash his mouth with Dettol and evidently made it too strong for the howls were sad and prolonged.

If you see Bill and report any of the things I tell you of his son I will never forgive you! Aileen is the sweetest person to have about the house and I think Bill is a very fortunate man.

The weather is glorious and today has been like summer. The boys were playing in the garden all morning. Robert has been looking particularly nice today in his kilt. David looks awful. He fell down the steps yesterday and those weathered front ones and has a dreadful bruise on his forehead, a nose like a cherry with a cut (a wee one) in one nostril and chin all scraped and lumps on his knees and elbows. He is amazingly tough about bumps and never even changed *colour* yesterday and insisted on starting out for the walk, which we were embarking on when he fell, just as soon as he was cleaned.

Oh! Beloved my mind is a blank tonight. Jim asks me if by any

---

[1] Young Bill

chance you can get him a sponge! If you can will you think of me too! I know one gets them on the coast of "Cyrenaica" but I don't know about where you are.

Robert again asks me to send you three kisses. Joan (Moyes) has arrived home with her boys and Mrs Moyes is very thrilled.

I believe your father is up again, he must have been in bed about four weeks. Oh! How I ache for you to come beloved. Sheila

21st Feb 1945, Sheila, Wakefield to Alan

My Dearest,

Firstly the boys thanks for their letter and photos which they were very thrilled about. Robert took his to school. Now about the ones you sent me - I think your African girlfriend is sweet. How clever of you to find her! The ones of yourself are priceless - dear, do you notice how your tummy hangs over the towel? You look as if you needed me to take care of you or, as you loathe "being taken care of" shall we say "love you"? Oh! My dear how I do long to have you to love and spoil. Letters get more difficult to write I find as time draws nearer to your coming. I get such waves of excitement and in the few moments of laziness before getting up in the morning and falling asleep at night a marvellous sense of bliss flows over me when I think how near you are getting and I discover there is a wide smile on my face. Yes it would be wonderful if you came in the evening for us, but I feel selfish when I think how the boys are looking forward to seeing you arrive. David says "I'll take my 'darling down' and show him to Daddy and will he love him too?" His 'darling' you will remember is his teddy bear.

Beloved, what do you want to do with your leave? It's so dreadfully difficult not knowing what is in front of us and four weeks is really terribly short.

The weather is almost like summer now which is wonderfully enjoyable but is bringing things out too quickly.

The boys are looking so much the better of being out so much more and enjoying knocking about the garden again.

Robert is so sweetly careful of my plants and is teaching David to be the same. They like flowers and David nearly had hysterics when he accidentally trod on the beginnings of a Darwin tulip.

Oh! My Dear, how I love my boys and how I love you. Sheila

22nd Feb 1945, Alan, G.HQ Accra, to Sheila

Beloved Woman,

After some delay of mail your letters of 10th and 14th today. Sorry to hear of the mumps and hope that you escape though we have been extremely lucky so far. I do so hope that you are on your food again. What is really wrong is that you need kissing very badly.

The arrival of David's car has given me more of a kick that I can tell you. I so wanted it not to go astray for I felt that it would be practical and visible proof to my David that he really had a Daddy who loved him. My heart bleeds though for Robert, but I suppose it's good for him to get the sense of "mine" and "thine" properly incalculated.

I just guffawed out loud with sheer joy when I read that after three days "Aileen is perfectly sweet to have in the home but I shall be glad to be on my own again". Oh Beloved don't get me wrong. I understand absolutely and I'm exactly the same myself when my friends from the other colonies come up to consult with me and I have them for a few days, but it is funny isn't it.

You are certain now that after say five days I should not be one of these whose presence is not strictly essential!

Now my trip - it begins March 7th and is divided in two as I have to be back to meet the new D.D.M.S. in Sierra Leone. Then I go off to East Africa, probably in early April. Cables you shall have in plenty. I sent you yesterday a cigarette tin for the side of your bed and a piece of Ashanti cloth. More Alan

(2)To continue Beloved.

Today I sent an African carving and some more Togoland (chair cover) cloth. The carving is in soft white wood blacked and polished by me, and I like it. I don't know how it will strike you.

I also sent a book rest and I am also getting rid by post of my heavy books as I should be stuck for space, or rather weight, in my boxes.

Please let me know if you have to pay duty on any of these parcels.

Before I forget my regards to Aileen and kiss wee Bill for me.

Down has lent me a telescopic lens and the viewfinder for my trip so I should get some decent photographs.

My M. D. Thesis proceeds slowly. It's an effort to steel myself to get down to it at night. When I get back from dinner my shirt is just a black soggy mass and my whole chest is covered with drops of sweat standing out of it.

Daddy seems to be making steady progress judging by the letters from Mummy and Moira.

My dear you can't imagine how excited I get when I realise that in six days I shall have completed 18 months.

I expect if my relief is provided according to plan to get away in the latter half of May. I shall try to get raisins when in North Africa.

I am trying to persuade the carver of the figure to make one of an Ashanti woman sitting on the Elephant Stool. Your ivory buckle for the Leopard Skin has not arrived yet but it should be done any time and I shall try to get it by letter. I'll also write more later.

I love you. Alan

(3)

Beloved One,

I've now had dinner and the mail goes off in the morning. It's terribly hot and I regret to say that defying all mosquitoes I'm clad only in a pair of underpants. These are only to prevent me sticking to the chair.

Beloved all through dinner I was talking to people and so on - thank heavens the storm has broken and now the rain pouring down it will be cooler soon - but Beloved all through dinner I was thinking of you and the boys and turning over in my mind again and again the things which you say in your letter.

I am grateful to you Sheila for writing so often and so interestingly to me. Anything that you do or the boys do or say is of vital interest to me. I'm very much dependent on my family. It's part of me and without them your Alan is just not a whole man.

After all when I love you as I do and we have two wee boys whom I know and whom you clearly love more and more, it would be strange if I could be self-sufficient. Now my dear I must get down to the Thesis writing. I'm very lazy and very sleepy now that there is a cool breeze.

Tell Robert that I love him and that I hope he does not get mumps. Tell David that I'm very glad he likes his motorcar and that I love him.

Tell them both I love you. Tell yourself I want to love you and cherish you always. Alan

25th Feb 1945, Sheila, Wakefield, to Alan

My Dear,

Your letters of 9th, 12th and 17th Feb have come in. I wonder how long the hat and belt will take to arrive. How good of you to go to all that trouble over the *[Illegible]*, it sounds fine.

Before I forget I paid Whitaker my life insurance last week by G.Mills cheque £33 odd. St Helens Church must be the local church. Robert's school mistress phoned me at Christmas time in a great state because they couldn't find your regimental number. Evidentially the whole church was going to be put off its beat if they couldn't find you. I promptly forgot all about it! Good luck to the M.D. thesis, the only thing is you are probably so completely "crackers" you don't ever notice it. Schofield said he felt very "crackers" before he left.

Bill had a slight cold last week and Robert developed one yesterday and I kept him in bed. He sneezed all day but seems almost clear today and says he is going to school tomorrow. He has a top tooth loose now.

Thank you for saying you'll cable me of your tour. One knows air travel is routine these days but there have been so many happenings of late not at all routine.

Thanks for notes on Sister B. but you mistake me beloved. I have not come to the conclusion that no-one is worthy of trust at all. But it is a sharp reminder to me that any familiarity with those one employs is to say the least of it unwise. As to pitying her delusion, as I see it, one might as well deeply pity and forgive Hitler. I'll explain why when I see you!

Dear, dear one your old wife is very much in love. I suppose I must be going to feel like this all my life! I could happily live with you feeling so much less than I do. But there's this terrific attraction that is going to keep me always hopelessly in love. Oh! Dear, I'm silly with sleep I must go to bed. Always, Sheila

27th Feb 1945, Alan, WAF Accra, to Sheila

Beloved, I have your letter posted on Feb 18th. I'm so sorry to hear of you having more sneezes. Oh My Beloved, what a curse the thing is. It is very regrettable that wee Bill should be badly behaved. It's just one of these things about wee boys.

Sorry to hear of David's tumble. He seems to be the tough member of the family.

I shall see if anything can be done about sponges. Tell Robert I send back four kisses and that I'm sorry I have not written recently but I have been truly very busy for all the hours I was awake.

Sparks has arrived to take over from Duff and Wiggy is hopping about waiting for his relief who is two months overdue.

I'm pounding into my M.D. Thesis and wondering in odd moments why I bother!

By the way I can get Loofahs if I can't get sponges. They grow on all the balconies.

I'm glad to hear that Joan Moyes is home. It will be good company for Mrs Moyes. What a changed house Joan must have found it.

I am dining with the Americans tonight - a waste of time and tomorrow morning I go off to Lagos for a couple of days.

My Dear I'm getting very home sick and I do wish the European war would finish.

They seem to be so terribly short of Medical Officers. No word from Fanny.

Well my Dear I seem to have very little to say today. My love to my very own dear boys and kiss them from me. Love to wee Bill and Regards to Aileen. Your Loving Husband. Alan

27th Feb 1945, Alan, WAF Accra to Sheila

Beloved,

Since I wrote the first letter today I have had further confirmation of what I was hinting at when I talked of shortage of Medical Officers. Apparently Medical Officers, due to the shortage, cannot be promised release when their age groups come up. Nor do things like not being sent East if due for release within a year apply. Two of my Malariologists were asked for by the Colonial Office and a very strong negative reply was sent from W.O. saying no; immediately they finish their tour here they are required for India.

I therefore am wondering again about another tour, for which to be absolutely frank I would like to see real service. As far as I can see I shall never get out of Hygiene and I don't fancy sitting for the tour in India for five years at some Base Area. After all if releases do apply they apply equally if I was here. Now no decision on this can be made quickly or before the new D. D. M. S. arrives but I would like you to write about it to me.

I'm absolutely foxed as to what to do. To go away for five years is just to go away for the rest of the best years of our life.

Oh My Own Sheila I want to live with you and never to be far away from you. To share with you all the things we enjoy and to watch the boys grow with you. I don't want ever to be away from you again. It's awful to have to write like this to you and I know how you will be when you get it. But oh Beloved - I just don't know what to do and I'm a bit lost. Pray for us to be together Sheila. I love you. Alan

1st Mar 1945, Sheila, Wakefield, to Alan

My Dear,

Do you realise that next month we'll be able to say - next month!

This has been a sort of hectic week. I had another dreadful sneezing fit on Tuesday the second in just one week. When you get home I really must take drastic steps to cure or find something to check it. These last two days have been just about the worst ever and now I get a hang over on the second day and my ribs ache like anything through the frantic exercise they have been through!

Anyway about 10 p.m. on Tuesday I really felt if I sneezed much more I'd go completely off my head and was getting ready to go up to bed when I heard screams from Aileen and on going to the rescue found she'd scalded all the fingers of her left hand with the kettle. She was very miserable and never having been burned before very amazed at how it hurts.

I dressed it and offered to help her to take her rings off but she not surprisingly refused point blank. (you can only see them, the rings, now). She was well blistered yesterday and, as we were at the hospital in the afternoon collecting some eggs Miss. P. had for us, I asked her to look at it and she has taken the blisters in hand and Aileen travels down each day to have it dressed. Of course it's a dreadful drawback having a bad hand in one's primitive kind of work, but it's wonderful how she manages.

Tonight I stuck three boys in the bath, you should have seen the water! Anthony developed Measles yesterday. Fortunately we didn't see them on Sunday. I'm keeping Robert off school for three days as a new batch is about to start off now. Measles is raging altho not at our school so far. Ah! me I suppose it's just a matter of time! I don't expect I'll get my trip to Glasgow at all. I was thinking of going the first two weeks of April.

Beloved are you coming home? I don't seem to be able to wholly take it in now it's getting near. Yes it's a "howling wilderness" all right without you and I am unable to believe the dawn is really coming. But it is beloved isn't it?

Everyone seems so scared of the Russians now. I can't make myself - am I stupid?

2nd

This is the second impression of this letter! Bill tore up the one I wrote last night and I could have wrung his darling little neck!

Got your letter of 17th Feb today. I'm glad to know you've survived the row about the article. I thought it was just dreadful (the news dear, not the article!). I adore you. Sheila

(1)

Beloved,

Sixteen months completed, Sunday afternoon and a letter from you after a gap of 10 days. I'm glad that you like the photographs. Yes yes Beloved, I did notice the tummy in my own photographs - trust you to mention it! I'm still here you see. The planes were held up and I could not get to Lagos but I'm off north on the 9th.

I'm very sorry about the letter about recent tours and the cable. You see I just get so bothered as to what is best and I get nightmares about you being left again and so on.

Re my leave to talk of pleasanter things. I get 28 days which is not much and I think we shall have to go North. What about Achiltibuie?

I'm so glad that the boys are getting out and looking well. I'm glad to note - no Mumps so far. I'm still grinding away at my M. D. Thesis for I'm determined to finish it here and not have anything to do with it at home.

I am at the stage now that I think it's <u>awful.</u>

By the way - do tell me if you have custom duty to pay on parcels and what amounts. Also, have you had receipt from Wallis Heaton of my camera and light meter which Col Downe left for repair?

I'm being pestered by the Income Tax people in Wakefield to pay royalties income tax but I am taking no action as I just can't square it out here so if you have the Bailiffs send them to Accra! I'll now go on to number 2. but I love you in this one. Alan

(2)

To Continue Beloved,

I shall not present my Thesis through the usual channels as I don't want to be labelled a "Malariologist", though if I had to start medicine again that is what I should be!

I've sent you an odd selection of junk recently and I'm longing to hear how you like the cloth and above all how you like the Leopard. The buckle has not turned up yet but I have hopes of it early next week.

Thinking of things to take home to Robert and David is not easy and I <u>really</u> have not time to make more toys.

Oh Sheila I am fair to modestly enthusiastic about work still (from time to time) and I do so look forward to being in a job on my very own with no "chief" or DDMS above me.

I'll write more later tonight.

Well Beloved, as you say in your letter, the longer the separation goes on the less one has to say. But Sheila you written so regularly and have always been so interesting in your letters especially about the children. I wish they could write and tell me about you. I am annoyed that I have not been able to get leave and I did so hope to get away but time is drawing in now and I see no chance of it.

Oh Beloved I'm very weary for you. Weary to heart and longing to see you and share with you with the boys and the boys with you. They have been constant work and trouble and you must've felt terribly tied by them so often. I wonder if they will appreciate this. Well beloved it doesn't matter much for they have their own lives, but you and I are all important.

Alan

4th Mar 1945, Sheila, Wakefield, to Alan

My Dear,

I'm glad you don't arrive home today because the end of my nose is like a cherry! For ages now I've had sore bits inside my nose which flare up during a cold or after sneezing and for the last two days I've had a revolting 'gathering' at the end of my nose. Don't think but that I have spared you the knowledge, only I've just hit it a whack with my hand by a mistake making it throb like hell and I feel it's one of the most important things in the world!

Robert is convinced he is taking Mumps tonight because he has a pain in his toe!

I suppose I'd better mention "evening activity" last night because I know Eileen[1] wrote to Bill of it today and he might speak of it to you. Anyhow it wasn't very alarming and no F.Bs but we didn't get

---

[1] Eileen was spelt Aileen in previous letters.

any sleep until about 3 this morning. Anyhow we didn't wake the children which was a blessing. I'll tell you now we had a miserable hour with Flying Bombs going over on Christmas Eve. I had to get the boys up and poor old Robert was simply scared out of his wits. I was alone in the house and believe me I prefer the good old fashioned kind of bomb! It was a scream last night because every time I heard anything coming above I rushed out of the door to keep an eye on if it was an F.B.[1] and each time I came back and said, beaming all over "thank the Lord it's a plane". Now it turns out it was only planes that came over! The more I think of it the funnier it is.

Eileen's hand is slowly improving and she will soon have more use of it. She is staying until the 12th, a few days longer than she first thought. I've enjoyed having her here but in many ways will be glad to be on my own again. I never seem to have time for anything just now and never get any reading done at all.

Anthony is getting along all right. The latest "Mummy" to take it is Mrs Wardley!

I've just had a phone call from parents. They are very keen for me to go up north and give me a fortnight's holiday in a hotel before you return "for your anniversary" as Daddy puts it!

I don't know quite what to do for in a way I feel I'd just like to sit here and think of your coming. However probably a fortnight's sprucing up would do me no harm. It would be a joy not to bother about food for a week or two, but we'll see. I love you. Sheila.

7th Mar 1945, Alan, WAF Accra, to Sheila

My Beloved,

I was glad to have another letter last night and sorry to hear that Robert has another cold. You certainly have had your share this winter. I'm not looking forward to my first!

I'm off on the 9th and just clearing things up before I go. I am progressing reasonably well with my Thesis though it really is a very big job and a tremendous sweat out here.

---

[1] F.B. = Flying Bombs or V1s. See Appendix 9

I shall cable you whenever I have an opportunity while I am away and write too.

Oh Beloved another week gone. How glad I am to have the opportunity to write and know this will get to you in 10 days. It must have been frightful out here in the early days of the war when letters took at least two months. Beloved I'm so very anxious to work on my own after the war and not have a chief as I said in my last letter. I just don't work really well unless I am on my own. I hear that the new DDMS is an interfering chap who knows everything. I'm glad I'm going in that case.

Tell Robert I'm sorry about his cold and that he and David are to have all their toys ready for repair when I come home.

Bless you beloved and bless my very own Dear Boys. I love you.
Alan

8th Mar 1945, Sheila, Wakefield, to Alan

My Dear,

I am filled with curiosity and a certain amount of trepidation for yesterday I received your cable about not taking any notice of letter of Feb 27th. I haven't received the aforesaid letter yet and am frantic to get it!

Beloved I have now got the wooden table mats and I think they are lovely. Also the first instalment of the cloth. Thirdly thanks for the tinned pears, they are very good.

I'm glad you understand my attitude to Eileen's stay. Honestly tho to have people staying, with help only a few hours in the day, and children to look after is killing. You however will be welcome permanently.

You will be away on the first part of your trip beloved and enjoying it as much as you expected I hope.

It must be frightful having to work on the Thesis under described circumstances. There is a bit in the series of three letters dated 22nd Feb which is beyond me! Firstly you say that in 6 days you will have completed 18 months. Also you go on to say you hope to get away in latter half of May. I was under the impression it would be the first half, please clarify!

I am finding difficulty in writing these days, for, if you are away so much in the next month, by the time you get letters it will be nearly time for you to be packing.

Beloved what can be in that letter of the 27th? Something nasty I'll be bound or you wouldn't have cabled so quickly. I hope it comes soon.

The boys are in great form and send you their love. They are very sweet our boys.

The news is fine tonight. So we are across the Rhine at last. It's queer to be able to visualise the Rhine and Cologne and Dusseldorf and so on. Robert's favourite song at the moment is "Onward Christian Soldiers" and he has almost got the tune.

Dear one, I need you so very badly, you just can have no idea at all. Do let me know quickly if you were quite sane when you said second half of May! Sheila

12th Mar 1945, Sheila, Wakefield, to Alan

My Very Dear,

Your letter of 27th has arrived and thank heaven I had your cable first. But Oh! Dear, what can the "other circumstances" be? It will be ages before I know and I just can't fathom it at all. It was bad enough getting the letter even after the cable and there is a bit at the back of my mind which has absorbed the letter more than the cable. I wonder where you are now. Aileen and Bill went off this morning. You'll laugh when I tell you about Bill - he would turn a place into ruins in no time! I have now decided I'm not such a bad bringer up of children after all!

We all went into the Stafford Arms for dinner again yesterday and took Miss Perkins along with us. She seemed to enjoy herself hugely.

The weather is simply glorious. I have decided to go off for the aforementioned break next month as I have a feeling you won't be home until about August! I'll let you know soon where we are going. I'll have a week's shopping in Glasgow and then a fortnight somewhere probably north. Aviemore would have been ideal but unfortunately they don't open until June. You must believe me when I say I do like Eileen, but it is nice to be peaceful again. It just seemed to be one constant rush all the time.

I'm in such a queer state of suspended animation wondering about these "other circumstances". Five years on top of the last 5 ½ would just break me. The last 18 months has been a long long time altho it has gone well in many ways. I love you dearly. Sheila

14th Mar 1945, Sheila, Wakefield, to Alan

My Dear One,

No letters to reply to, but I'm expecting a cable from N.A. any day. There is nothing new here. The boys are fine and looking forward very much to their Easter Holiday. I'm longing for a letter. I had a weird series of nightmares last night to the effect that your soothing cable only meant that it was India for three years instead of five! You had come home to tell me so and were completely unconcerned about the whole affair!

Robert likes school more than ever I think. He tells me he usually gets 'excellent' for arithmetic which I venture to doubt, but he is very taken up with 'takings away' as he calls subtraction. David's hair is even more difficult than Roberts, it's so dreadfully thick and is all over the place in no time. Bill had curls which never altered all day. Which was hard to live up to! In development I should say he was about 8 months behind David which is rather interesting and not at all exaggeration.

Robert was very distressed about Aileen going away, they had become quite fond of each other. However he was completely comforted by her promise that she would bring Uncle Bill up to Achiltibuie after the war. Uncle Willie has been very ill but seems better again.

Beloved I just can't write decent letters these days. Everything is so frightfully uncertain and I don't even feel now that I can count on your being home in the Spring. If you are anything like Wiggy it will be the end of the Summer. I wish I knew.

David's great exclamation these days is 'gosh' and I regret to say when overwhelmed by Robert's superior strength he has taken to spitting!

When I insist on Robert doing something he can't be bothered doing I often surprise him sticking his tongue out at me secretly! Yes it's big changes you'll find when you do come home.

Oh! Beloved. You must be weary of hearing how hopeless a person I am without you. I've had plenty of time to try but I'm just no good at it and never will be.

The news is pretty good isn't it? But it sort of takes the edge off when the future seems so black. Still there may be a letter soon to clear up the mystery. You'd swoon if you knew how much I loved you. Sheila

16th Mar 1945, Alan, WAF, Freetown, Sierra Leone, to Sheila

Beloved,

I'm back in Freetown after a very good trip indeed. Unfortunately I did not get to Algiers as the ADMS from there came over and met me in Casablanca, but I've been in Casablanca and various places up there and Oh My Own Dear One I never wanted so much to have you with me. Do you remember that, but for the shipwreck, we should have gone to Casablanca on our honeymoon?

It was cold with bright sun in the mornings, warm in the middle of the day and afternoon and cold at nights - just like Madeira.

I have bought you a Morocco leather pocket book and some wee animals for the boys made of sandalwood. In addition, at long last, I have got a little purse for you which will slip into your bag. I have also a small silver trinket box for you.

Oh Beloved it's all so odd, the Arab farmers, the camels, the sandy desert coming right down to the sea. The market women, the mosques, the odd half Arab half French people - they are all what you would like to see and would enjoy. Oh My Beloved I must go travelling with you after the war.

I am very fit although the long flying is tiring. We lived with the Americans and I am grossly over-fed. Still flapjacks, syrup and coffee are no substitute for a decent breakfast!

I love you. Sent you cable today. Alan

17th Mar 1945, Sheila, Wakefield, to Alan

My Dear,

I had your letter of 7th on Thursday and the two of the 4th yesterday. I got an awful *drop* when in your brief reference to your letter of the 27th Feb and cable, you do not mention any 'other circumstances' at all. Must I then look upon the 27th letter as still standing for what to expect of the future and the cable as meaning nothing? I really wish your tour extended until the end of the summer when at least one war might be over.

However it probably will be getting on that way by the time you getaway. However as you haven't indicated this, we will go on the presumption that you leave W.A. in the second half of May as you said.

You know I love Achiltibuie as much as you do, but the only possibility there is the hotel and I (and I'm sure you) don't think we should spend your leave in a hotel. Also the hotel is eight miles from where we most want to be and with the boys and no transport other than bicycles we would be completely tied.

I have a suggestion, and it's only a suggestion (in fact the idea only was born yesterday) to make and it's this - that I try to get a small farmhouse at Nethy Bridge where I know the ropes and would not have to waste any time settling in, and try to get Mrs Whitelaw who was with me last summer to come up for the month, which would mean we could go out in the evenings and have a days without the boys if we wished and could even take them on a flying visit to Achiltibuie if we felt inclined.

The little place I have in mind is a sweet farm called 'Rothiemoon' (of all delightful names!) it isn't usually let out but last year they said they might let it this year. To cover the uncertainty of your time of arrival I would take a place for June, July and even Aug. for it's the easiest thing in the world to sub-let for July and Aug. If by any chance you didn't get home until late summer, well we'd go there just the same and wait for you. Just let me know what you think of this.

28 days is dreadfully short, six weeks would just make all the difference. I had a parcel of cloth yesterday and had 8/1 to pay. it's

grand cloth, I only wish it was possible to have it dyed, but that's off while the war lasts. I've no more letter cards so will have to stop. Love, Sheila

18th Mar 1945, Alan, WAF Accra, to Alan

(1)

My Very Own Beloved,

I'm back here to find three letters from you, March 1st, 4th and 8th. First I'm very sorry to hear of your nose. Both the sore bit and the sneezes. Oh Beloved I'm sorry to hear to about the flying bombs and things. It's so odd to be here in peace and you having all that. Sorry to hear too of Aileen's burn. Give her my condolences.

I should have loved to see you with three boys in a bath.

I hope the boys don't get Mumps, or selfishly that they get all these things over before I get back. Tell Robert that I've never heard of Mumps starting in the toe!

My Dear it would do you good to get up north and I hope that you manage. So sorry that I worried you about your cable. No it was not nothing beloved. As a matter of fact I've had plenty of time out here to think of my sulkiness and bad temper and that's <u>finished.</u>

Regarding end of my tour all I can tell you (or know) is that it's likely to be sometime in May that I get away from here. The system is that the relief must arrive and take over so you can imagine how I'm sweating on the top line over that notification of my relief.

Sorry for the slip of my pen, for <u>six days</u> read "9 weeks. I shall have completed my tour". I of course shall have been here 18 months on May 1st. Thereafter a relief has to arrive and I have to find a boat. I've had a very good trip but I shall tell you all about it in the continuation of this letter. Meanwhile beloved I <u>love</u> you such a lot. Alan

18th Mar 1945, Alan, WAF Accra, to Sheila

(2)

Beloved,

About my trip. Firstly it's on the next half that I hope to see Bill. I have been in Casablanca and that area but <u>most</u> unfortunately the

ADMS from North Africa came across to see me, and after many twinges of conscience I decided that I had done my business with him and had no excuse to go up to Mediterranean to see him at his place. I was very angry for I was just enthralled with North Africa. I got in late this afternoon and I've added another 6500 miles to my air travel total. As usual I had a good time in Sierra Leone, the white man's grave is a haunt of good cheer when I get there! I was at civil houses for dinner two of the three nights. Andy McKee's friend in Gambia was on leave. I just put on 6 lbs weight on French and American food!

By the way do you want me to buy you a watch? If so draw the approximate size on your next letter.

I have really enjoyed myself Beloved and I'm saving up so much to tell you when I get back.

I am sending you tomorrow two combs with handles, Morocco leather pocketbook and purse and some wee animals for the boys made of sandal wood. They are "a present from Morocco". I also bought some rather fine books from the American library.

<u>Oh</u> Beloved you just have no idea how excited I am getting. I can't think of work or anything else but your brown eyes smiling at me and your arms around my neck. You will never know how I've missed you beloved. Alan

22nd Mar 1945, Sheila, Wakefield, to Alan

My Dear,

I had your first cable on Tuesday and another yesterday and it's just made all the difference in the world to me having them. I have no letters to reply to. Yes, I now have both your parcels from Wallace Heaton and they have received cheques.

I hope to go to Glasgow about April 3rd and we are going to Nethy Bridge Hotel on the 12th and stay until the 26th. I thrive on changes and it will do us good. I've had another frightful days sneezing and now have a horrible sty in my eye. You wouldn't love me a bit if you saw me today!

David is having his afternoon nap and Robert is helping to wake him altho it is not really time. Such a change from the old days before they were able to play together and Robert's face used to fall when I said I was going up for David.

The other night when they were in bed Robert was calling softly from his room. "David, call Mummy and tell her you want a drink of water". David "no". Robert "go on". David "no" and so on!

The painters are coming on Saturday to start distempering the spare room, which the boys are going into as soon as it's done. I expect I'll have some hectic nights to start with! I shall miss Robert out of my room, he has been with me a long time now.

Robert is now about the only child in school who hasn't had mumps. I'm hoping he is immune as he must have been in contact with them in the last eight weeks. Anthony has now recovered and we go to the pantomime on the 31st. perhaps you'll remember and be thinking of us. I love you, Sheila

24th Mar 1945, Alan, WAF Accra, to Sheila

(1)

My Very Own Beloved,

Your two letters of March 14th and 17th arrived yesterday. I really am sorry to have upset you regarding the cable and letter and so on. My Dear you must know how much thought I give to what will happen when I get back and how it will affect our separation. There are of course no "other circumstances" it's just that I changed my mind. I'm not very sane or sensible on such matters and therefore I wrote that letter. Nearly everyone who goes back from here has gone to the Far East and I had just heard of a few more who had been sent there. If one is at home for more than six months then one loses one's past overseas service as counting towards the next spell. For example, the tour in India is four years. If a man is sent there within six months of return from West Africa, his tour is only 2 ½ years. If he has a full six months at home his tour will be 4 years. I was thinking that if I came back here I would avoid that but frankly Beloved I don't want to volunteer (or accede to the request) for West Africa again for it really would be against my *conscience*.

Oh Beloved how hard it is to write these things instead of to talk of them with you. I think that all we can do is wait and see. Oh My

Dear I hate to think of Robert putting out his tongue at you. You will have to restrain me if I see him do it.

About my leave, I told you of the expectations in my last letter and I still hope to be back at the time I said. More in next letter.

Love Alan

24th Mar 1945, Alan, WAF Accra, to Sheila

(2)

Beloved,

I just cannot see what is best for my leave. I shall have to go to Bridge of Allan for a few days. It may well be that I shall have to go to the War Office to try to find out about my future and try to get General Richardson to listen to my requests. Then I want some days in Wakefield to get Miss Goldthorpe to start the first typing on my Thesis. (I may at the last moment have to get an odd reference from the B.M.A. library).

As regards living in a hotel - well beloved, I feel that you would be much more free in that way than if we were in a house and you need a rest from housekeeping. On the other hand I do see that we must make plans or we shall neither have a house nor accommodation in hotel. So I think that is best for you to fix up at Nethy Bridge if you can. As you say we can always cancel the arrangement. I suppose that June and July are the months. Glad you like the cloth. I hope that you feel the duty worthwhile. Please let me know what duty you have to pay on the things and the price I put outside.

I purchased eight more yards yesterday but I cannot get as thick stuff as the first lot.

I'm still going all out on my Thesis and I shall with luck have completed it. It is shaping quite well and I might manage to get slightly more than an ordinary degree. I love you. Alan

25th Mar 1945, Anniversary, Cable sent 23rd March

"HERE'S HOPING LAST ANNIVERSARY APART. AM VERY
FIT. LOVE YOU AND BOYS WHAS LIKE US?
                    ALAN STEVENSON"

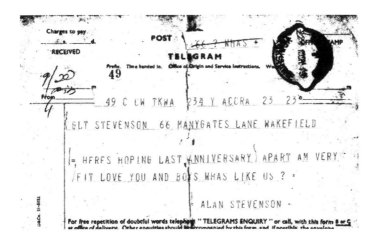

26th Mar 1945, Sheila, Wakefield, to Alan

My Dear One,

How lovely to get your anniversary cable on Saturday. I wasn't expecting one. Also arrived the hat and belt, what perfectly lovely skin. I shall have the hat re-modelled as it doesn't suit yours truly as it is, but it will be perfect in a softer style. This will have to be done in Glasgow of course and I shall wait until the rest of the skin arrives. Thank you very much beloved for being so thoughtful. It's fun having a husband like you. We have also had more pears and jam in the last few days. The pears are in process of being eaten! Also the book rest has arrived, all whole! The large wooden bowls came last week, one being cracked. The wood is very lovely.

We all in the throes of painters and Spring cleaning, so I'm sure you are glad you aren't present! The weather is glorious and the news is grand. I feel perhaps the war is going to end some day after all.

Robert and Anthony were wildly excited about the pantomime.

27th March

Dearest it's the neglectful wife you have for this letter should have been posted yesterday.

I had your letter, written on your return to Accra, from Casablanca, today. Yes, someday we will go places together.

I'm tied up in knots with getting ready to go away and the cleaning. Believe me I'm no longer Spring cleaning! All the boys clothes seem to need mending all at once, and buttons are flying off in all directions just to please me. I get so hungry in the evenings and it's dammed difficult to find something for supper sometimes!

The news is so splendid I really can't take it in properly. I feel there must be a catch somewhere.

Don't worry about writing to changed address's in the next few weeks, all my mail will be sent on. I love you always, S

30th Mar 1945, Alan, WAF Accra, to Sheila

My Very Dear,

I had your letter of the 17th waiting for me after a two-day trip to Nigeria and this morning I had one of the 22nd.

Poor Beloved I'm terribly sorry about your sneezing again. I wonder what on earth it is which starts you off like that. It's so trying and wearying and one day of it is enough to spoil the effects of a holiday. I would love you though stye or no stye.

It is perfectly sweet to hear of Robert and David being so fond of each other. Yes, I can remember the look of horror of which used to appear Robert's face when it was suggested that David should be brought in. Do you remember how he used to dash about and gather up his toys like an old hen chasing after her chickens.

Had a Letter from Dad and one from Moira. He seems to be coming along quite well and he is very cheerful. He has been elected President of the Institute of Engineers and Shipbuilders for the next year. Beloved we must go to their dance for old time's sake.

Keep your fingers crossed for Robert to escape Mumps. The spring will soon be here and that sort of thing be over for another year.

Yes, I'll be thinking of you all at the pantomime tomorrow. I'm sorry the David cannot go. Do you remember Robert at Peter Pan in 1942?

My Thesis is coming along. I am almost certain now of finishing it before I get home. I have photographed all my charts and diagrams and I shall have it all ready to be typed. I shall lend Miss Goldthorpe my typewriter and she will do it well and quickly. I have written to the University asking for exemption from the clinical examination on the grounds of war service preventing me being able to do any clinical medicine. I think it will come off. I think that the Thesis is reasonably good and am beginning to wonder whether I shall manage to scrape a commendation out of it. That really would be a thrill.

I had a pleasant surprise today in getting a cheque for £4.4.0 from the Miniature Camera Magazine for my article on Miniature Camera work in the tropics. That was more than I expected and if I am paid pro-rata for the article which they have accepted on the home-made camera, I should get quite a fat cheque for that.

I'm longing to see the new D.D.M.S tomorrow to see whether he has any information from the War Office about my relief. I have discovered that, after three years in the rank of Lt Col. I can claim 4/6 extra pay per day. This will go back to Dec 8th 1944 and will be very acceptable. I should not be surprised if there is just no job for me at home. If that is so I shall drop my temporary rank for a bit which would be a bit of a blow financially. Perhaps they will try to avoid that when I am recommended for promotion to full Colonel.

At long last the Mepacrine Article has appeared. It is in the Annals of Tropical Medicine and Parasitology and I shall send you a copy. I'm very thrilled to see myself in print for the first time on medical matters.

You will be cursing me for sending home all these parcels of books. I just have no room in my trunks. Oh my very own Beloved when shall we live together again (not just on leave) and enjoy all our books together. Thank Robert very much for his drawings of the toys. They really are good efforts to have done from memory. It is an immense help to be able to visualise things accurately. My Dear I wonder if he will be a problem as to what he wants to do when he grows up or will have definite ideas.

Very soon now I shall be able to say 'next month' (with luck). Oh it's such a long time since I left you at Fleet. Well My Dear this is quite a long letter and my fingers are getting blistered.

Love me and love me when I get home Beloved. I love you. Alan

31st Mar 1945, Sheila, Wakefield, to Alan

Dearly Beloved,

I've had four letters from you today, two of the 18th and two of the 24th. I'm so sorry your tour didn't go exactly to plan! Still you don't seem to have done too badly you know! No dear, I don't think I want a watch I have an excellent one that looks like surviving the war. Looking forward to "a present from Morocco".

Beloved, you are mistaken, I never thought your famous cable was to take the sting out of a bad tempered letter. I just expected the kind of thing it turned out to be. Beloved the future is just beyond me altogether. I must say that the workings of your conscience is also beyond me, but that is I suppose your own affair. Anyhow, I shall try not to get disconsolate about things, it wouldn't do me any good anyhow. It's awfully difficult to know what to do about your leave. It's nice of you to think of a hotel for my sake so to speak, but I do so want to be peaceful with you (relatively!) and I imagined you would rather be in a house, unless you've changed. However with London and the B.M.A. library. B. of A. and so on we would have very little left of the four weeks by the time we got there. Of course if I went there first it would help, but on the other hand do you mean you'd want to come here first? It just doesn't seem possible as far as I can see to make any plans at all. Perhaps I'll think differently when I get up there and perhaps I'll have a more definite idea when you will be home.

We've been to the pantomime today and you have missed one of the great and good things of life not having seen Robert at the pantomime! I'll try to find another letter card but in case I don't, know that I love you. Sheila

3rd Apr 1945, Alan, G.HQ Accra, to Sheila

Beloved,

I have today your letter of March 26. I'm so glad that the lot has arrived. I have today sent 1) the rest of the skin, 2) 2 buckles of ivory for the belt one with initials and one without 3) ivory salad servers 4) a butter knife 5) a paper knife (very coarse) and dashed to me by the carver. More jam and pears are en route. I'm longing to hear of the pantomime and that you are safely in Scotland enjoying your holiday. With luck I should know in a fortnight if my relief is coming.

We are talking here of what form the celebrations of the end of the war in Europe will take!

Oh my love I hope the hat can be remodelled. There is plenty of lovely skin for a complete new one and I could get you another skin. I'm concentrating on bringing home silk stockings when I come myself. I can't think of anything for the boys.

My Thesis is really getting on splendidly. I certainly shall finish it here now, unless I have some unexpected setback.

It has been a terrific Labour but I suppose an M.D. will often impress lay committees who don't understand M.R.C.P and thus it might make the difference some time in the future in getting a job which I really want for you and the boys.

Well Dearest of Women I shall only write (I Hope) half a dozen more times and then I shall feast my eyes on your dear face. Alan

5th Apr 1945, Sheila, Glasgow, to Alan

My Dear,

We had a good journey up here on Monday except that a cold I had been fighting for three days caught up with me on the train and by the time we got to Glasgow I was feeling pretty well all in. Then when I saw Mother and Daddy on the platform I got a shock, they both looked so dreadfully ill and frail. However we got here, had a good meal and the boys went straight off to sleep. I was very feverish and didn't sleep a wink all night and next day I could hardly stand and simply had to lie in bed cursing myself and tortured by the thought of all the work I was causing. The boys were very sweet and good all the same and behaved like lambs. I went out today and must really get busy tomorrow. I've lost three whole days but I really couldn't cope until now. I'm going to see your people on Saturday. I hope the boys won't be too noisy for your father.

I've had a very interesting conversation with an R. A. M. C. Surgeon who has been with Bobby Tenant in Italy. I'll tell you details when I see you. However the point is he was fresh from meeting with the W. O. on his future and his version of graft and wire pulling there was hair raising. He says there is no hope of a job in this country but if one is perfectly clear in one's own mind what one wants and they realise you don't want anything out of them, and if a W.O. authority applies for one it's almost a cert one will get out. Even taking into consideration the shortage of M.O.s etc. etc. I won't enlarge any farther but have no illusions about what you will find in this country and for god's sake advise the 'local authority' in good time. I saw Steven at Carlisle. He and May can't go on holiday together because of the garden! Will we ever be that daft? Love. Sheila

8th Apr 1945, Sheila, Crown Mansions, to Alan

My Dear One,

No letters for over a week so nothing to reply to. The boys are in grand form and enjoying their change so much. David is as tough as they make them. Mother checked him for something the other day and he promptly picked up a bit of bread and flung it at her, he was going to follow up with a bottle of milk if he hadn't been restrained!

I took them to Bridge of Allan yesterday and we had a very successful day. Your father is of course very thin and frail but not really looking as bad as I had been prepared to see him look, and he does seem to be making slow progress. Your mother seemed very fit and she and the boys and I had lunch in the hotel. Then just an hour before I left Mother and Daddy appeared. I had no idea they were coming but Daddy wanted to get a glimpse of your father and I think they (your people) were very glad to see them. We were packed like sardines in the corridor of the train from Stirling to Glasgow and David was very sleepy having been up early and no afternoon nap. About halfway to Glasgow I just caught him as he was falling down in a wee heap on the floor and had to shake him awake. He is an ideal traveller all the same and never complains about anything.

I think I forgot to tell you that for the past two weeks the boys have been sleeping in the same room and how they love it!

I had dinner with Andy and Muriel on Friday night and going there to tea to meet Joan and her boys.

I am slowly recovering from my cold and I'm having awful sinus trouble, just about the worst ever, so I'm pinning my faith on this week's change to Nethy Bridge.

I do hope I have a letter from you tomorrow, although if you are moving around there may be a bit of a gap. When will we meet I wonder, I don't know how I shall contain myself when it gets really near.

Your loving wife. Sheila

11th Apr 1945, Alan, WAF Accra, to Sheila

My Very Own Beloved,

Time is standing still about getting home. I hope to know before I go to E Africa whether I have relief on the next convoy. I expect to make a start for Nairobi at the end of the week.

Oh Sheila it's been such a long time and I need you so much and now that the time draws near I just can't think straight at all for the longing to see you. I hope that I shall be there to go to next year's pantomime with Robert and David. I'm looking forward to your next letter telling me how Robert enjoyed himself. It is a good thing Our Marriage Beloved, it has made much love and affection and respect and beauty. How sorry I am for people whose marriages are not a success and for the asses who botch their own and their wives lives while out here. I'm too much in love with you am tied much too closely to you by personal love and the material joy in our boys ever to jeopardise all that happiness.

I wonder if you will think I have changed at all. You may for a day so until I have been thawed from this retreat into self which comes of living alone in a crowd, but I'm the very same Alan who loves you always.

I'll let you know when I set off and will send cables as on my last trip. This one should last three weeks or so. It will cost me a packet of money I'm afraid but it will cost the army about £500 in fares. Had notes from Miss Burton and Miss Perkins. They are definitely Robert and David fans so my heart warms to them.

I love you. Alan

13th Apr 1945, Alan, G.HQ Accra, to Sheila

Dear Woman,

I have your letter from Glasgow today. I am sorry about your cold. You need me to look after you when you get a cold. As you see I'm not off on my travels yet but hope to go on Friday or Saturday. I have not heard of the relief yet and probably will not now until I get back from East Africa but as you will hear from Wiggy, I expect to be home sometime next month. Oh Beloved it is a weary and troubling business this waiting at the end.

I hope you found them cheerful at Bridge of Allen. I'm sorry that you felt that Mamie and Jimmy were looking frail. It has not been any fun for the older folks either this war.

The death of Roosevelt is a hard blow at this time. It seems to me that as a statesman who has striven with skill and patience for the best for the whole world and the individual there never has been his like in all History.

As I write the news is so good that I cannot see why the war in Europe is going on at all. It will be over before I get back as we once said, but just.

Tell Robert and David how I'm longing to see them. I'm just sick for the sight of them and family times. Oh My Beloved I must finish in a hurry to catch the post.

I love you I love you I love you. Alan

14th Apr 1945, Sheila, Nethybridge, to Alan

My Dear,

As you know we have arrived! We had quite a good journey up and the boys are entranced with being in the wide open spaces again and also entranced with hotel life. If it were not that I'm a bit anxious not having heard of you for a fortnight I would relax joyfully doing nothing at all for two weeks. I had forgotten the bliss of having no care of what my household will eat and the joy of rising from the table with no further interest in the destination of the dishes.

Yesterday was a most lovely day, as warm as summer in the afternoon and the children were playing barefooted at the river. Today is almost as cold as winter but we have a charming private sitting room with a lovely big fire. The boys and I share a room together and have a nice warm private bathroom off it. I was still having wretched sinus trouble when I came up and was dreadfully stuffed up and keeping myself going with "*Colgatone*" and willpower. Then yesterday to crown everything I had one of my days sneezing and it was hell. Today instead of being much worse as I feared, my head is completely clear and the relief is terrific.

I wonder why I haven't been hearing from you of late and I wonder Oh! I wonder when you'll get home. I keep trying to imagine what it would feel like if you just suddenly walked in. You never mentioned whether Willie had got away in the end.

Oh! Beloved, I just can't write. I keep staring into space and wondering where you are and going limp when I fully realise that I may feel the touch of your hand quite soon.

They have German measles in school now (Easter holidays don't start until the 17th) so if Roberts been infected they will start next week!

I don't really think I have the energy to take a house up here things being so indefinite. Aviemore is opening in June so if we are desperate I'm sure Mrs Ross would fit us in somehow for a week or so. My Dear, I love you far too much. Sheila

17th Apr 1945, Alan, G.HQ Accra, to Sheila

My Beloved,

I was very glad this morning to have your letter of April 8th. I'm so sorry to hear of your sinusitis. Oh Beloved how I want to hold you in my arms and banish all headaches.

I am still here as you see. I shall not be away now (if I get at all) until around 26th. I rather think it's going to be early June or mid-June rather than late May before I'm with you but I cannot tell yet.

I'm delighted to know both from you and Mummy and Daddy how nice the boys seem to have been when visiting Alan. Their letters are just full of them. I'm so glad that Alan was not looking so bad. He is very cheery in his letters.

Had dinner last night with the *Leaveys*. They really are a charming pair and their dinners are magnificent. They are coming to dinner with me on Saturday. I am so very excited at the prospect of getting home that I can't settle to do any work or any serious business at all! In other words I've gone "bush". I'm so irritable with my boy that he thinks I'm mad!

Oh Sheila I shall be helpless with excitement as I near Wakefield. I'm so terribly keen to get back to you and not have you worrying about me while I'm on the way. Oh Sheila it will be strange to have a wife again.

I shall feel a bit embarrassed after being a Bachelor so long, but I've only got to see you and know you and two years will be gone and forgotten. Alan

18th Apr 1945, Sheila, Crown Mansions, to Alan

My Dear,

Two letters from you today and Oh! I am so glad to have them, the first since I left Wakefield. I'm so glad that the thesis is going so well, it's a splendid effort, you seem to have a genius for doing things under adverse conditions.

We are having wonderful summer weather here and are getting quite brown. After my heavy cold I looked like something from under a stone when we came up last week and now you could see my face coming in the distance! The boys are in terribly great form.

I must prepare you however that David is just about the cheekiest wee boy in Britain. He is simply a horrible little Imp. There is however something so robust in his naughtiness that I can't feel angry with him ever, although I have to beat him up at intervals. He told me brightly last night that he'd knock my head off, and this morning the worst thing he could think of saying was that we put me down a rabbit hole! - I adore him!

I hear your father has been out for several walks so that's a wonderful step in the right direction.

10:15 PM

I've just been sitting at my window watching the last light of a perfect day fading on the hills and thinking with distaste of returning to Wakefield! You are near enough to returning for me not to drive at keeping myself occupied to get the time over quickly, and I am simply revelling in doing nothing at all except walking and lying about in some sun. My tiredness is falling from me like an old skin and in a week or so I'd be impatient to be on the hills instead of looking at them. But for the moment the *animal* is uppermost and I haven't yet got over the thrill of attractive meals to hand without any effort on my part!

The boys are so easy out of doors and find endless joy at the riverside or playing amongst some pine trees on a carpet of cones and needles or on heathery slopes and short turf. I can lean back against a tree or stone and leave them to it.

19th

Weather still wonderful. You'd be amazed if you knew how much I'm thinking of you. The boys send love and David says he will biff you! My love is always. S.

22nd Apr 1945, Alan, G.HQ Accra, to his sons

My Very Own Dear Boys,

I am getting so excited about coming home to you. Very soon now I shall be packing my bags, saying goodbye to the black people and coming home in a big ship to you and Sheila. It takes a long time in a ship for it is so far away here but it really won't be long now. I'm very glad to hear that you went to see my Daddy. He tells me that he loved you both more than ever and Grandma says that you were both very good boys.

Kiss my Sheila for me. You have no idea how sad I get sometimes and how I miss you all but all what fun we shall have together when I get back.

I love you very much. Daddy

22nd Apr 1945, Alan, G.HQ Accra, to Sheila

My Very Beloved,

No letters from you yesterday but I hardly expected one with you moving about. I hope you are enjoying your holiday and that your sinuses have not given further trouble.

I have been quite busy clearing up of bits and pieces and I have found a good African Clerk to type my thesis so that it should be finalised bar a few oddments when I come home. That will be, I'm sure you will agree, a great joy.

How are my boys? I'm just getting into a dazed state and am unable to concentrate on anything for thinking of getting home to my Dear Ones. I'm off to Takoradi by road this morning until Monday. I'm going to spend Monday night in Elmina Castle[1] and take photographs. I hope this will be good for it will be my last chance the subject.

Well my Dear I really have surprisingly little news. I expect that you will have heard from Cols' Wig and Duff. I shall not be home quite as early as week would tell you but I hope not to be very much delayed. It all depends on whether W. O. has sent a relief. I love you Alan

---

[1] Elmina Castle was erected by the Portuguese in 1482.

Elmina Castle

23rd April 1945, Sheila, Nethybridge, to Alan

My Very Dear. Today your letter of the 11th inst. Also the other day a letter from Wiggy, a very nice one, warning me of a letter shortage in the next few weeks. I am writing this in a desultory way in the garden so excuse its shortcomings. I find the effort of writing getting heavier and heavier as the weeks draw in and the thought of seeing you is always with me. We have decided to stay on leave until Tuesday next (May 1st). Robert doesn't start school until May 9th so I am in no hurry to get back and will have a day or two in Glasgow before setting out for Wakefield.

I have to see dentist, attempt to get new health *appt* etc.

Sadie has arrived at Greenock and I'd like to see her but it will be difficult for her to move far from the baby and I think my two will have enough of trains without looking for more.

Robert has started this last month or so to turn his left foot in, which is agitating me considerably. I think I'll take him to a doctor in Aviemore or Grantown this week because I may be walking him too much and would like to know. David can walk four times the length Robert could at his age and he could walk Bill off his feet too.

I do wish I knew when you were going to be home, and what part of your leave we could call our own and go away for. I reckon we'll have about a fortnight away but will it be the first, middle or last do you think? Try to let me know which would be best for you. It's so difficult to book anywhere when I am so dreadfully vague. Willie said you hope to leave for home "by the end of May" but that might well mean any part of June for our holiday.

The weather, after reverting to winter for a day or two, is glorious again and I'm afraid I am enjoying doing nothing as much as ever!

I wonder how many more of these letters I'll write.

Beloved it's such a long time, I can't really clearly remember how happy I can be with you, not that I'm unhappy, but there's been no joy in life without you. Yours ever. Sheila

24th Apr 1945, Alan, G.HQ Accra, to Sheila

My Very Dear,

I am very sorry that you had a fortnight without letters. I have written twice a week as usual that there must have been some hold-up. Moira too had had no reply to several letters she wrote. Wiggy is gone and in good form and the new man is a real horror, very like Wade. I'm sitting on top of my temper all the time but I shall not let myself go. I shall tell you all about it when we meet.

I go to East Africa definitely this week at last. I shall be away for about three weeks and I hope to find a relief either here, or just about to arrive here, when I get back.

I cannot write to Nethy Bridge as you do not give address. Besides which you asked me to send all letters to 66. Have had a note from the University of Glasgow saying they cannot exempt me my clinical examination. It's a bit sticky considering that I've been away from clinical medicine, through no fault of my own, for six years. I'll go and see them when I get to Glasgow. I just cannot sit a clinical examination in my present state of knowledge. More following. I love you. Alan

26th Apr 1945, Sheila, Nethybridge, to Alan

My Very Dear, Firstly in case I forget - a tin trunk has arrived in Wakefield and they are keeping it for me at the station until I return. I was phoning your mother tonight and your father continues to make good progress.

Jim was released on the 18th and arrived in this country a few days ago. Sadie and babe arrived in Liverpool last week, so the lost sheep are beginning to come in! We have a P.O.W. in the hotel with his wife. He was only released 10 days ago and I must say he looks very fit indeed. He is a young artillery officer and was taken in Crete. He and his wife are simply bouncing with elation and it does my old heart good to see them!

Beloved, I have booked for us at Aviemore from June 7th to July 7th and have arranged with Mr Ross that I will let him know within the next two weeks which part of the period we will be able to come for and he will cancel the rest. It's a decent of them for they are well booked up, although they only open on June 1st.

The place is full of painters etc. just now. I hope you will approve this. It's been awfully difficult to know what to do. Places are getting well booked and should the German war end in the next few weeks there won't be a room anywhere. I will make enquiries to see if there is any chance of having the car brought up by rail although I don't suppose there's much chance.

28th

It's turned bitterly cold but bright and sunny. We went walking in the woods this morning (they are very lovely round here) and got caught in a heavy snowstorm. We built a big fire by the side of a stream and sat round it till it went out, it was most beautiful and turned the woods into fairyland. David was particularly thrilled!

Love Sheila

27th Apr 1945, Alan, Accra, Cable to David

David's 3rd birthday, 30th April 1945

28th Apr, Alan, G.HQ Accra, to Sheila

My Own Beloved,

I sent a telegram to Master David yesterday on his birthday. Three years old - and I hardly know him. Three years since my Dearest One had a really bad time and our wee mite was born. Oh Sheila it's no fun for you and you have all the hard work but I am so glad we have a family.

I suppose I'm a sentimentalist and that that is supposed to warp sober judgement. It may be, but all I know is that there is just no very adequate reason for my continuing to exist without you and our boys. I am so weary of being away. I don't get used to it, it just gets harder to bear and more intolerable to think of its prolongation.

I've written to Frankie asking him to put in a very strong request for my release at once. I'm perfectly willing to take my old salary for a short time & hope to get a better job later.

Well Beloved I'm off the day after tomorrow to Nairobi & I'll not get any letters until I get back in three weeks. I hope to find a relief nearly here by the time I get back.

Kiss my boys & tell them I love them. I love you Sheila. Alan

P.S. You might chance one note to me. c/o Lt Col Bogster Wilson, Medical Branch, HQ East Africa Command, Nairobi, Kenya

29ᵗʰ Apr 1945, Alan, G.HQ Accra, to Sheila

Beloved One,

The mail is delayed, so I shall not have an opportunity of replying to your letter before I set off in the morning. I'm very fit and looking forward to my trip but even more to being back and hoping to be on the way to you soon. I have been quite busy packing all I require into 44 lbs weight for air travel. I hope that my cable arrived in time for David's birthday. Oh how I long to see that lad.

Tell the Robert one that I shall be seeing Victoria Falls and plenty more black boys and then I shall be back.

I expect you will have heard from Duff by now. I shall be so glad to be away from here and I shall regard this trip as my long-delayed local leave.

Beloved I keep waking up dreaming I'm holding you in my arms these days and oh it's better to be asleep.

I love you. Alan

30ᵗʰ Apr 1945, Sheila, Nethybridge, to Alan

My Dear Man.

This will be another scribble I'm afraid. We go back to Glasgow tomorrow and I will go to Wakefield sometime in the next few days. We've had amazing weather in the last few days, heavy snow and howling winds, an appalling contrast from the first 10 days. I've no letters to reply to that there may be one waiting for me in Glasgow tomorrow.

David has had a very happy birthday and is very full of importance. We have had a very pleasant time here indeed and I feel a lot the better of it.

It's astonishing to see the country white with snow, the apple trees heavy with blossom and a cap of snow on top of it all. There will be a lot of damage done I'm afraid.

Robert wishes me to send you his love and 17 kisses and David also sends his love and I'm to be sure to tell you so!

9:30 PM.

It's snowing hard again! Let's hope it's a bit warmer when you come or you'll spend a lot of time trying to adjust yourself.

My dear, I'd love to know just how you're feeling about coming home. I'm so thrilled I am almost frightened, if you know what I mean. The news is pretty hot too, so perhaps we'll have some chance of a good break after all.

1st May.

Just having breakfast and your birthday card to David has come in, he is very bucked about it.

I wonder how you knew where to send it! Now to finish the last odds and ends of packing. I love you dearly. Sheila[1]

2nd May 1945, Alan, Grand Hotel, Khartoum, Sudan, to Sheila

(1)

Beloved,

When you see this address you will be <u>very</u> jealous. I arrived here this morning having left Lagos very early yesterday and I am sitting at my bedroom window looking out on the Blue Nile. Unfortunately (?).I cannot get a connection to Nairobi for a day or two so I am stuck here and thrilled to bits. It's so strange to be in terrific dry heat. Far hotter than West Africa (111° in shade today) but bone dry.

Everywhere signs are in Arabic and English, and the solemn Egyptian and Sudanese is so different from my cheery West African Negro.

The hotel is the last word in luxury, fans, iced gin, mango ices and so on, while across the road the feluccas and dhows glide up and down the river. It's so odd not to be able to talk to my room boy. He is a large Sudanese in spotless white turban and robes with red sandals.

I was lucky to find the local ADMS staying in the hotel. I was along at his office tonight and he is giving me his car for a tour around tomorrow.

---

[1] It was on this day, 30th April, that Hitler committed suicide. Sheila cannot have heard of it yet.

The crowd in the hotel is a joy. Old dried up chaps who just live here. Greeks, Americans, Egyptian, all sorts and sizes. Beloved you nearly lost me to an Egyptian lady. They are just too exotic like *perpetual* Hibiscus.

I'll have to start another letter I see. Love Alan

2nd May 1945, Alan, Grand Hotel, Khartoum, Sudan, to Sheila

(2)

Beloved,

There are a few white children here. It's a shame to keep them they are so skinny and fretful and precocious and hot.

I just cannot understand the news. First Hitler is dead,[1] then is not and so on.[2] I wish it was all over for I don't want to go away again.

I have not got the hang of the money yet. What a Piastre is I'm not sure. Everyone else seems to speak Arabic. There is some very good silver work of which I hope to buy some tomorrow.

Now I must go to bed for I'm dead sleepy. I'll add more in the morning.

6 AM

Reasonably cool morning after a very hot night. I'm just going to get dressed and go out for a walk along the Nile to see if I can get any photographs. I hope to send you a cable today. My dear I wonder if you are still at Nethy Bridge and if so when you are going back. There is no great hurry as you see for I shall not get away until the end of the month or so. I hope to find my relief waiting for me or just about to come when I get back to West Africa.

Beloved in a way, it's no bad thing if I'm a little later than I expected in getting back, for I suppose that I shall have more chance

---

[1] Hitler shot himself in his Berlin bunker on April 30th 1945. First he had poisoned his dog Blondie, then his wife of some hours, Eva Braun, took poison.
[2] Hitler was dead but the Russians, finding his burnt corpse in Berlin, had taken it away and then denied knowledge. It was years before they admitted this.

of getting out[1] the later I get back.

I'll write again later today.

I love you. Alan

5th May 1945, Sheila, Glasgow, to Alan

My Dear One.

I feel very wicked for I have missed a letter to you this week.

Since coming here on Tuesday I seem never to have had a moment. Your mother and mine came for tea on Thursday. Your mother was looking extra well I thought, and mine was having one of her good spells. Your mother is very pleased with your father's progress but Moira doesn't seem just so happy about him. Anyhow it's a great thing that he is getting out now. Sadie's husband got back from India two days ago so it's lucky she arrived when she did. Jim was here on Wednesday evening and he, Elspeth, Joan and I went to the pavilion on Thursday evening. It was a good show and Jim seemed to revel in it. He's looking wonderfully well but there is something vaguely pathetic about him

I am in a bit of muddle about my return to Wakefield next week as I'm sure I'm going to get involved in V.E. Day and I feel like waiting till it blows over as travelling will be impossible for a few days after, I should think. Also Glasgow is a forest of flagpoles and Robert is so anxious to see all the flags flying! I'll see how things look at the beginning of the week. There wouldn't be much for a child to remember in Wakefield in the flag and bunting line!

I am appalled by the news of Wiggy's successor! My tongue is hanging out for all the grisly details!

You should be in the midst of your trip now and enjoying it hugely I hope.

I've had letters from a Captain Tim Robinson from Helensborough and he says if you aren't home by the end of May you won't be home for another six weeks! Oh! Beloved the news is good, but the Russian - Polish business is worrying. Mother and I took the boys to see Donald Duck yesterday - they are confirmed

---

[1] 'getting out' - out of the Army, he means. Getting home didn't get you out of the Army.

cinema fans now!

Beloved I love you and I'm hoping for you all the time. Oh! My dear I wonder what lies before us. Also I wonder if you'll think me an awful old hag when you come!

Oh! I love you. Sheila

7th May 1945, Alan, G.HQ Nairobi, Kenya, to Sheila

Beloved,

A very hasty note. I'm setting off on tour by road for Tanganyika territory today. Had a good trip - 3 days in Khartoum, and 1/2 day at Kisumu on Lake Victoria. I'm very fit and am enjoying my trip immensely. It is delightfully cool and I'm staying in Col Bogster-Wilson's house. What a lovely place Nairobi is! I saw herds of Zebra, Buffalo, Giraffes and deer from the air within 20 miles of the town.

I am going to be back in Accra by about 23rd and I'm so desperately hoping that there will be a relief by that time.

Well my Dear I'd give a lot to have you with me. You would just revel in this country.

I hope to see Kilimanjaro today but it's the rainy season and rather clouded.

Well I must rush for the car is going off soon.

Kiss my boys. I love you always. Alan

10th May 1945, Alan, c/o 92 Malarial Unit, Dar-es-Salaam, Tanganyika, to Sheila

Friday

My Very Own Beloved,

I'm writing this in the plane between Mombasa and Dar es Salaam

I wrote yesterday from Mombasa but I don't know which you will get first.

I have no particular news to add except that I'm longing for letters and that I'm getting more mad and excited at the prospect of seeing you then you can ever imagine. Oh Sheila I do so love you and I'm so longing for that first kiss.

Nairobi May 14th

I'm so sorry for the long interval in completing this letter but life has been so hectic. I had 24 hours in Dar es Salaam and then back to Nairobi by plane. There I was met by some completely strange people wo told me that they were taking me to stay the night with people called Turnbull. I arrived there at 5 PM and by 6:30 PM was being whirled out to a farm 15 miles out of Nairobi where there was a very large party in a very small room. They danced eightsome reels, strip the Willow's and some petronellas[1] and drank lots. We got back at 2 AM. In the morning I dressed leaning against the door to keep out the Turnbull children whose acquaintance I have made the night before and who were apparently determined to renew it. I then was taken in hand by a Col *Adam* who took me to his office and to lunch at his house.

After lunch we went 20 miles out and 2000 more feet into the hills to his cottage and farm and had tea. More. Alan[2]

10th May 1945, Alan, c/o 91 Malaria Unit, Mombasa, Kenya, to Sheila

My Very Dear One,

So the war is finally over in Europe. I wonder how you celebrated. I can't quite grasp the significance at all for you and me. I have a feeling that a lot depends on Frankie now so do please phone him and chase him when you get to Wakefield.

I left Nairobi on Monday seventh and travelled over the Masai Reserve full of game to *Moshi* at the foot of Kilimanjaro.[3].On Tuesday we went over a very rough road to Taveta where we attended a party at the District Officer's house in celebration of V.E. Day.[4] It was an <u>astonishing</u> party and I shall tell you all about it some day when I get back.

Now I am at the Indian Ocean and am very thrilled at having

---

[1] A Scottish country dance
[2] Alan means more to say, so continues in next letter of same date.
[3] In 1881 Queen Victoria gave Mount Kilimanjaro to Crown Prince Wilhelm, later Kaiser II, as a birthday present, and it became part of German East Africa.
[4] V.E. Day (Victory Europe) is celebrated on 8th May so they were catching up!

travelled across Africa. It's a very big place. I'm glad to have slept in tents in East Africa and in a "banda", or mud house. I even know a few words of Swahili which is the easiest language in the world.

Tomorrow I go to Dar es Salaam and then start North on what I regard as the beginning of my trip home to you.

It's raining here today but I hope that it will clear up later for I want to see the anti-malaria work.

I'm just longing to hear that they have found Hitler dead or alive. He and Himmler[1] are the only two villains not in the bag.

Well my Dear you can imagine how I am longing for letters from you and I won't be back in Accra for nearly a fortnight. I'll try to send a cable today. Kiss my Boys. I love only you forever. Alan

11th May 1945, Sheila, Glasgow, to Alan

My Very Dear.

I'm still in Glasgow having been overtaken and left standing by the V.E. Day! Isn't it grand to think of one bit of the war being over anyway. Perhaps the other bit won't take so long as might be expected.

Glasgow has been amazingly bedecked with flags and the boys have been very thrilled with that all. We've had a terrific day today the boys and I. We've been to the zoo! We got the 9.50 train to Edinburgh, spent an hour in the gardens, met Kay (cousin) for lunch and then went on to the zoo. It's been a wonderful summer day and we did enjoy ourselves. It was a long long day for David but he has great staying power, doesn't get quarrelsome when weary, and he did love it so.

I just had your letter giving addresses in Kenya (Thursday) to write to but I really don't think at this date there is much point in sending this there, if you know what I mean.

David is now a confirmed gum sucker! Some Canadians on the train insisted on presenting him with a packet and he chews it

---

[1] Himmler was arrested by a British soldier on 23rd May 1945 as he fled towards Switzerland in disguise with a patch over one eye. When his identity was established he bit on a cyanide pill concealed in his teeth and died. There are, as always, other accounts.

indefinitely. Robert can't stick it more than a few minutes!

I am now going home on Monday! I really do promise to get there before you do!

I've had a nice chatty letter from Duff. He has never been able to get off on holiday as for some obscure reason the W.O. have kept him on call. I don't think he appreciates it much.

I just can't believe the German war is no more, it had become so appallingly part of one it doesn't seem real to be quit of it. Well beloved not long now surely. I do wish I knew how many weeks to count.

I love you dearly. Sheila

21st May 1945, Alan, Grand Hotel, Khartoum, Sudan, to Sheila

Monday

My Beloved,

Here I am with the prospect of not getting off until Thursday 24th due to mess up by movements over booking my plane passage. I last wrote from Nairobi and I'm going to send a wire from here this afternoon.

It's a frightful curse this, for I have no knowledge of what is happening in Accra and whether my relief has arrived and so on. I'm getting desperate to get home to you and every hour is an infuriating delay. I'd better calm down and tell you what I have been doing!

I left Nairobi by air on Thursday 17th and spent the night at Longido in Kenya Highlands. It was over 7500 feet up and pleasantly cold. The next day (Friday) I went to Kisumu on Lake Victoria and flew in flying boat to Pat Bell in Uganda, spending the night in the hotel at Kampala.

On Saturday I flew back and here I am. Did I tell you that Isabel Faulds is staying in Skye just now with the wife of the ADMS here a Col McLeod? He is a very decent chap and has been very good to me in letting me see about.

I am going to explore Omdurman tomorrow morning. I have bought for you some rather nice ivory candlesticks and a comb with a handle! And some other things which are expensive.

I'll write more later. I love you Sheila and I have never seen a woman is my type except you.

Alan

21ˢᵗ May 1945, Sheila, Wakefield, to Alan

Dear One,

We are home again and waiting for your coming. You will of course never know what it's like to be waiting for you so you can have no idea of my state of mind.

We had a comfortable journey down and all were very little the worse for wear. Robert went back to school on Thursday with great gusto but took ill on Saturday and has been "proper poorly". Violent pains in his tummy, sore throat and feeling very sick. McD Smith said yesterday it could turn into tonsillitis or scarlet fever so you can imagine my feelings. However his temperature has gone down today and the spots on his throat have vanished - my relief is extreme!

David is full of beans and great fun. He gives me great amusement trying to catch butterflies & spent about an hour this morning trying to put salt on birds tails!

I had the McVicars to supper last night to take my mind off Robert! It turned out to be Monica's birthday - fortunately, I'd brought a bottle of whisky back with me so we'd something to drink her health in. It was most successful evening so much so that Jim announced they'd come and visit me again this week but next time they'd bring their own whisky (they'll have to!). I wonder what our families would say to such innocent merriment! I feel that if some at least could have walked in last night & seen us sitting round the fire drinking our modest Tots we would have been all dammed for ever!

After the McVics had gone I went up to look at Robert for the umpteenth time in the evening and he proceeded to waken up & yell with pain in his tummy, knees drawn up and so on. That however is the last spasm & he is quite himself today and wanting to get up. Mc.D. speaks of the possibility of a grumbling appendix there behind a very slight hardness in that region, but that wouldn't have given him a sore throat!

Oh beloved can you imagine what heaven it will be for me to have you at home! I don't suppose I shall write again. I love you. Sheila.

23rd May 1945, Alan, Grand Hotel, Khartoum, to Sheila

Beloved,

Another note from the same address but I'm glad to say that I'm getting off tomorrow if present plans hold. I spent a fantastic morning in Omdurman. Firstly at the Mahdi's Tomb and then at the market. Very like Kano but with a higher standard of craftsmanship.

I bought you another present and if I had had any more money or air travel weight to spare I should have ruined myself. The Sudanese are a very dignified people and they greet you with some Arabic phrase which I cannot make out meaning "may Allah bless you".

At the moment I'm sitting on a balcony overlooking the Nile drinking iced coffee. In Sudan that means a pint glass and two large glass jugs of the milk and coffee. I'm dining in the Sudan Club tonight and then early to bed for I find air travelling very tiring and boring. Beloved somehow I feel tomorrow's journey is my first step towards you, even if I am held up for a little in West Africa.

Oh I so badly want to take you to Omdurman Market and Kano and Nairobi and Zanzibar and *Oretcha* and all the interesting places I have seen. We could do a tour of Africa on about £1000 for three months that include buying a car in Africa and doing about 10,000 miles, and then selling it on leaving. Beloved somehow we must save £1000!

Well my own dear Wife it won't be long now until you really have a husband to live with again. He'll be good to you. Alan

26th May 1945, Alan, 7 Malaria Fd. Laboratory, Lagos, to Sheila

My Beloved,

I am sitting waiting to see whether the rain will let up sufficiently to allow my plane to take me back to Accra. I arrived here yesterday from Khartoum and was met by Alan Bilbray who brought me to stay the night here as there was a guest night in the mess. It was a very good show though I, having been flying since 4:30 AM, was half asleep. I'm now just terribly keen to get back today to my mail and to see about my relief. I am getting dubious about the plane as it's thundering and pouring with rain.

6:30 PM

The plane did not go and so I have still a day to wait for news from you. It has been pouring solidly for six hours and as a result it is beautifully cool tonight. Oh my Sheila I don't like being so long as this without news of you and I keep having fears that all might not be well with my Dear Ones. Beloved I'm still very empty without you and if I was away for 10 years it would not get any better. It's bad for me to be alone and always aching like this. At least Beloved you can know that I come back to you your man and no one else's in any thought or deed. I know that I need not tell you that but I want you to know that I love and respect you too much to come back to you except as I left you.

I feel that when I get back to you I shall sort of thaw in some way inside and a whole part of me which has been frozen will be warm and happy again. Kiss my boys. I love you. Alan

27th May 1945, Alan, G.HQ Accra, to Sheila

My Dear,

Here I am safe back in Accra. AND my relief is coming. I don't know, and obviously could not for security reasons tell you even if I did know, when I shall get off but with luck I should be home before the end of June. I came back to about eight letters which I have just skimmed through but I have not time to reply now as this must catch the post in the morning.

It's 11:30 PM and I'm lying in bed trying to get used to the feeling of no need to pack tomorrow after so many moves.

Oh it's good to know that you have had a good holiday and that the boys are well, even if David is going to biff[1] me when he gets me back.

A note from Frankie says that he is going to ask for me to be released, but it's a bit dithering and vague and I wonder how strong he made it. I shall not be idle in my last week or two as I have plenty to do after my tour and to get packed up. I'm hoping that the ship will not be packed out on the way home. Well Beloved I'm just dropping off to sleep.

You will agree that this is the most important letter which I have written since I left you. It's an easy one to write and I'm a happy man. I love you. Alan

30th May 1945, Alan, Cable to Sheila

"BACK FROM. YOUR VERY FIT AND EXCITED HUSBAND. GOOD NEWS MY RETURN. LICENSE CAR. SUGGEST PHONE DAD ABOUT INSURANCE WITH MR WALLACE. LOVE TO ROBERT FOR BIRTHDAY MUCH LOVE = ALAN STEVENSON"

1st Jun 1945, Alan, G.HQ Accra, to Sheila

Dear Woman,

You will be getting a chit from Col Perrier when he gets back but I should be home a week earlier than you expected from his estimate. You will see too that last fortnight July will be too late for a holiday. Sorry about that but I just cannot tell you exactly for I don't know!

I'm packing furiously and I'm very excited - so excited beloved that I cannot write sensible letters!

The news about my release is excellent. They have started to release Medical Officers and the first 11 Groups have to be out by August unless they are specially held back. So that with luck I should not go overseas again but shall be released in the autumn.

Well Sheila I'll write again but I must get down to getting ready to hand over to my relief. I'll soon kiss you. Alan

---

[1] David had said (letter from Sheila 23rd April 1945), when Alan came he would 'biff' him!

4th Jun 1945, Alan, G.HQ Accra, to Sheila

Sea Mail

Beloved of Woman,

I'm sorry about the conflicting telegrams. The doubt and delay has been owing to the fact that I have to go to Gambia first and then I'll fly home. 1½ days from Gambia. So I should be home before the end of this month with any luck at all.

I'm off to *Truckee* tomorrow to pick up Mister Gregor (my relief) then and bring him back here, go to Gambia, do my job, and then come home to "Sheila" and the boys.

I'm just walking on air these days and hardly feel my feet touching the ground. Oh Sheila to think that in less than a month I should be kissing you. It gives me irregular heart *action* and makes me feel faint.

Tell the boys it won't be long now. Bless you, I love you Alan

15 Jun 1945, Alan, Cable to Sheila

"HOPE HOME BY AIR BETWEEN 24TH AND 27TH BLESS YOUR EYES LOVE = ALLEN STEVENSON"[1]

16th Jun 1945, Alan, General Hospital, Gambia, to Sheila

Beloved One,

It won't be long now. I hope to get off at the end of next week and to be home in three days. I'm very busy indeed on my Malaria Survey and am tramping about every day from 9 o'clock until dark and then writing it up after dinner.

I may have to go to the Air Ministry before I come up, in order to hand in my report. In that case I should call at the War Office and get that over and then try to fix that my leave only starts after I am finished in London.

I shall phone you just as soon as I get a chance.

Oh Sheila I'm so *dithery* at the thought of seeing you after all these long years that I'm not very sane these days. I hope that all is well with you for I have not had any word for a fortnight although

---

[1] Alan's name misspelt as 'Allen' in telegram

there may be letters still for me in Accra.

I cabled yesterday and you may have it today. If I am delayed at all (which is unlikely) I should of course cable again.

Well Beloved there is so much I can't say and won't be able to tell you until I hold you in my arms and kiss you.

Kiss my boys and tell them it <u>really</u> won't be long now.

I love you always and always. Alan.

19th Jul 1945, Alan, Knightsbridge, London, Cable to Sheila
From: Knightsbridge, London
To: Stevenson Aviemore – Inverness

"PROMOTED FULL COLONEL AND POSTED TO CHESTER. HOME THIS MORNING = ALAN"

27th Jul 1945, Alan, Medical Br. HQ Western Command, Chester, to Sheila

Beloved,

I'm lying in bed after a bath and it's 9 o'clock. I phoned the place with rooms at 6.30 PM and there was no reply. I phoned again at 8.20 just after dinner and the reply was "no, sorry but taken ten minutes ago". It's very disappointing but no doubt I shall get onto something else tomorrow.

Oh my dear, it's far worse being away from home in this country. I mean it's so hopeless to settle or to do anything when I know that you are near. There is no mess so the prospect is digs or a hotel and I really cannot see myself other than bored to tears in either.

Before I forget I cannot find the car licence book. I remember putting it in for Aviemore but I can't find it in the papers I have brought here. Will you have a look in the desk and desk drawer? I also put a few papers in the top of a black painted box which is on top of the blue trunks in the wee room next to ours. It might be in the envelope with testimonials which Moira is sending on. It might be in the inside pocket of my tweed jacket. I'm very sorry to trouble you beloved and I cannot remember what I did with it. However I shall need it here for petrol.

Oh my dearest I'm so depressed what with leaving you, and the tiff with the children this morning and the prospect of eight or nine months here which are either another move for you all and interruption of Robert's schooling or a dull time for me. I feel as if the bottom had suddenly dropped out of things. It's so odd beloved but having been with you again made me forget how to be sad or worried and made me so terribly dependent on you again.

I'll get off to sleep now if I can. I love you Sheila and there is no more to be said than that.

28th

Again in bed 8.30 PM. I'm much better today and I was so glad to get through on the phone to you tonight. I may have slipped the license book into any file or folder which I had at Aviemore or into the car registration and license file in the desktop drawer. The last time I remember seeing it was in the wee top drawer of the dressing table at Aviemore.

I saw General Blake today and he strikes me as being a decent old sod. He says he is willing to certify my not being able to get accommodation nearer and this to get petrol to travel for any distance up to ten miles. (Just remembered, the licence book could not be with the testimonials with Moira as I definitely saw it in Aviemore.)

I went to three house agents today and one said very mysteriously that he could fix me up and would phone me in a few days.

I can get priority for tyres as a result of using my car for military purposes here so that it will be a help.

Colonel Mansell has not had his posting order yet but expects them any day. It is a very big area, from Carlisle to Cardiff. I shall be in Carlisle quite often so I shall be able to see Steven.

This hotel is a dump and a grubby one too. It is a Trust House altogether not very attractive although the food is quite good. I'm going to see the manageress at Blossoms tomorrow to see if she will take me until I get settled. There is a "dames" school in the cathedral grounds which takes boys up to eight which Mansell says is very good. His boy was there until he became too old.

I found an old bookshop on the way home tonight selling 15 and

20 year old Amateur Photographers at one pence each so I'm well supplied with reading for tonight. Tomorrow is day off and I'm going to mend the puncture as I can't find anyone to do it.

I'll add more later but I must tell you first than I need you terribly Sheila. I can't tell you how lost I feel without you.

Sunday 12.30 AM

They can keep me one more day here, I. E. Monday night, but not thereafter and I've been searching for hotels with no luck at all this morning.

I took off the punctured cover this morning only to find that it was cut to pieces (I mean that the inner tube was cut to pieces!). So tomorrow I must get hunting for a new one for I cannot venture out without one.

I've been squaring up various papers this morning and am glad to find that the extra income tax amount is nonsense. I don't think I owe anything but may owe not more than £5 which is much better than the £38.9.0 which they asked.

I have written to Alvis asking for a new hub cap and I shall bore out the old one when I get it.

Am so hoping that I can land accommodation for you all soon for I need you all badly. Chester is very busy (partly with bank holidays I gather) and there are plenty of queues (doesn't look right) but the shops seemed very well supplied.

Well beloved I'll be phoning you and letting you have all my news. I love you Beloved and I need you dreadfully. Alan

P. S. I enclosed two accounts which I forgot to give you.

Oct 2nd 1945, 114 Convalescent Depot, Chester, to Sheila

Beloved,

I was very moved when I got your letter this morning. I like to think that we have retained our respect for each other in spite of all our intimacy and to have a love letter from my dearly beloved wife after all those years is remarkable evidence of that - if any were needed.

I'm glad it's your very last week end alone which has just past. Glad for you and glad for myself. I have long practised escapism in my leisure but I'm thankful that I won't have to walk up and down and wonder and get confused in my mind wondering and wondering when it would all be over and when I would get back to you.

I have such an anxiety about getting away from all this that every word I have to say to my relief to explain things to him is a real effort and I cannot think clearly at all. I am thinking like a very old man and I need to be back with you with no "until" so that I can recover and be myself again.

I don't suppose that in the past three years I have ever gone to sleep without thinking about you and me and the boys at Camusglashlan. I would be frightened of an anti-climax if I did not know that with you there is no anti-climax. With you my hopes take shape and my dreams become reality.

I believe you to be good - good as no other is good in this world - for Robert and David and I you are the standard - the pivot of our world. You will remain so for me even though they must change and rightly.

I love you more because I have tried you more and because I need you more and because you are Sheila.

Beloved to the future - unafraid together. Alan

EPILOGUE

I was doubtful about providing an Epilogue. I realised it could easily turn into an extended family history. I have done this brief sketch of the lives of Alan & Sheila after the war had ended. I mention my sister Gill (Aileen Gillian) for completeness, though she was not born until 1947 at 62 Sunningfields Road in London.

Alan was finally released from Military Service 27th December 1945 and transferred to the Regular Army Reserve of Officers in March 1949. He ceased to belong to the Regular Army Reserve of Officers in April 1951 (thus narrowly missing the Korean War) with the honorary rank of Lieutenant Colonel.

Alan returned briefly to his position of Asst Medical Officer of Health in Wakefield. Frank Allerdine, the Medical Officer of Health in Wakefield, advised him of a position that might make use of his experience, as a Reader at the London School of Tropical Medicine. Alan applied for and got the position.

Sheila had never liked Wakefield. It was a dirty industrial town far from her family in Glasgow. No doubt to her relief, we moved from Wakefield to 62 Sunningfields Road in Hendon, North London, presumably in 1946.

During our time in London we made the long journey to Rieff in the old Alvis, pulling a trailer, and work started on Camusglashlan. Gill was an infant, so Sheila not only laboured carrying materials across to the croft, but also look after our sister. We spent months up there squatting at Rieff in an abandoned wartime Nissen hut.[1]

In 1948 Alan applied for and got a position as Professor of Social & Preventive Medicine at Queens University, Northern Ireland. We moved house to 42 Green Road, Knock, Belfast. This was a happy period for Alan; he loved the work, threw himself into research, and became involved in genetics. Sheila however found the religious polarisation unpleasant and worried about the effect it might have on her children. She had no family there and made no friends. Alan loved the work and was successful. He served as an observer, and then a member, on the WHO (World Health Organisation)

---

[1] See Appendix 6

Committee on Nuclear and Allied Radiation.

In 1958 Alan was offered the position of Director of a new M.R.C. (Medical Research Council) Population Genetics Unit in Oxford. The unit was to be established in a new purpose-built office. Recruitment of staff and the organisation was up to Alan; it was to be his project.

So Alan and Sheila moved to The Haven, Eynsham, Oxfordshire, and there they stayed until he retired in 1974.

They moved to Inverness. The MRC did not want to lose him altogether and gave him a grant to enable him to carry on with some work he was doing. He rented laboratory space in a local hospital. He confided in Gill that he had completed enough research to carry on writing papers for years. He published a paper "Absence of chromosome damage in human lymphocytes exposed to allopurinol and oxipurinol". But then he had a stroke and ceased his work.

In 1985, feeling isolated and unable to deal with the cold and damp in Inverness, they moved to a bungalow at 17 Littledene Copse, Lymington, Hampshire. Sheila had always liked the south of England.

Sheila died in 1989 at their bungalow very suddenly, as she would have wished, from a massive brain haemorrhage. Alan died in 1996 in a nursing home in Lymington.

Alan and Sheila are buried together in the cemetery at Logie Kirk, nestling at the foot of the Ochil Hills near Stirling, where the Highlands meet the Lowlands. They lie beside their parents and Alan's sister Moira.

I (Robert) went on to work for IBM and made a career in computers, later setting up my own company. I now live in the New Forest, near Lymington.

David went to Trinity College, Dublin, where he began an academic career that was to lead to the universities of Glasgow, Aberdeen and St Andrews, specialising in the study of Scottish history. He now lives in Newport on Tay, Fife, Scotland.

Gill travelled widely and now lives in Sydney, Australia, with her family. She is an author.

APPENDICES

APPENDIX 1

Military Service of Alan Stevenson

MOD Reference 01/37372/DR2b1

Major (Honorary) Lieutenant Colonel Alan Carruth Stevenson P/38813 Royal Army Medical Corps

The military service of the above-named is as follows:

Appointment to a Territorial Army Commission as 2nd Lieutenant in the Highland Light Infantry and posted to 6th Battalion	04.10.27
Promoted Lieutenant	04.10.30
Transferred to the Territorial Reserve of Officers	16.05.34
Transferred from Territorial Army Reserve of Officers as Lieutenant in the Royal Army Medical Corps	19.07.39
Joined No 3 Field Hygiene on mobilization at Netley	01.09.39
Embarked for France	29.09.39
Granted rank of War Substantive Captain	01.10.39
Appointed Acting Major	09.05.40
Appointed Temporary Major	09.05.40
Returned to United Kingdom	01.06.40
Posted to Headquarters Aldershot Command	26.10.40
Posted to 5th Corp as Deputy Assistant Director of Hygiene	27.06.41
Appointed Acting Lieutenant Colonel	10.12.41
Posted to London District Transit Camp	09.01.42
Appointed Temporary Lieutenant Colonel & War Substantive Major	10.03.42
Posted to Headquarters Expeditionary Force	07.04.42
Posted to Headquarters First Army & Appointed Assistant Deputy Hygiene	13.08.42

Posted to Headquarters 12th Corp as Assistant Deputy Hygiene	13.08.42
Posted to No1 Depot Royal Army Medical Corps	23.09.43
Proceeded overseas	13.10.43
Embarked for service overseas Accra	14.10.43
Disembarked West Africa	01.11.43
Posted to General Headquarters West Africa assumed appointment Assistant Deputy Hygiene	03.11.43
Landed in United Kingdom	26.06.45
Posted to Headquarters Western Command	27.07.45
Appointed Deputy Director Hygiene & appointed Acting Colonel	07.08.45
Released from Military Service	27.12.45
Transferred to Regular Army Reserve of Officers	11.03.49
Ceases to belong to Regular Army Reserve of Officers and was granted the honorary rank of Lieutenant Colonel	28.04.51

Mentioned in Despatches:

Recorded London Gazette 20th December 1940. Brought to notice in recognition of distinguished service in connection with operations in the field March-June 1940.

The Oak Leaf was worn to indicate the wearer had been 'Mentioned in Despatches'.

APPENDIX 2

1940 AND DUNKIRK

From September 1939 until May 1940, the British and French waited for the Germans to make a move. They were confident that the French Army, supported by the BEF (British Expeditionary Force), could hold any German assault. The 'Phoney War' they called it.

On April 9th 1940 Germany invaded Denmark (neutral) and Norway (neutral), sweeping all before them. Still the Allies waited.

The German invasion of Belgium (neutral), Holland (neutral) & France, when it came in the early hours of May 10th 1940, and now known as Blitzkrieg (Lightning War), was shattering. They drove back the French and the British Expeditionary Force in confusion. The French on the British right wing collapsed and the British forces were outflanked. After a somewhat chaotic retreat the British Expeditionary Force was penned in on the north coast of France on the Belgium border at Dunkirk.

Alan later described being put in charge of a column of stragglers, drunks who had raided wine shops and been found asleep in ditches, and men separated in the confusion from their units. He was aided by a Roman Catholic padre. They made the men sing as they marched, to keep their spirits up. During the retreat they passed through many Belgian towns and villages where Belgian shops that sold guns, frightened of the Germans finding them with weapons, pressed their stocks on to the passing British troops. Alan acquired a small Browning automatic pistol, so although a doctor he was now armed. He led the column and the padre took up the rear.

We know from his war diaries that Alan arrived at Bray Dunes, Dunkirk, 29th May 1940, and was taken off the beaches between La Panne and Bray Dunes on 1st June 1940, along with 338,225 other British and French soldiers. All equipment including tanks, artillery and vehicles were destroyed. Alan described working at wrecking the trucks. You drained the cooling water out, ran the engine until it was red hot, then threw cold water over it thus cracking the cylinder block. He had two silver backed hair brushes, a wedding present. He hammered the silver backs and threw them into a duck pond. Nothing must be left for the Germans.

The men were made to line up in an orderly manner at the water's edge, waiting their turn to be taken out in small boats to the bigger ships lying offshore. They were being bombed and machine gunned by the German Luftwaffe, so Alan had to avoid panic and rushing for a place each time a boat arrived. He brandished his little pistol, threatening to shoot anyone who tried to jump the queue.

On getting back to Dover Alan was posted to G.HQ Aldershot in October 1940.

He may have got some leave on his return from Dunkirk and gone to Wakefield. However, invasion was expected imminently and he may not, which would explain why Sheila and Robert spent time down in Hampshire. We know that some time after May 1940 Sheila went down to be near him. They were happy times for her as shown in the pictures taken at the Malt House. Presumably that is why the next letter isn't until September 1941; if they were together there was no need to write.

The Battle of Britain had been fought and won in the air over the south of England in the summer of 1940.

German bombers continued to pound London. Sheila was in rented accommodation at The Malt House, at least some of the time, and had watched the Spitfires, Hurricanes and Messerschmitts fighting and dying in the clear summer sky.

She could see a great red glow in the night on the horizon as London burned. She had stood in the garden in the evening as British bombers droned overhead on their way to bomb Germany, punching the sky and shouting, "Give it back to them!".

APPENDIX 3

LARIG, MORLICH, TILDA & OTHER DOGS

Alan and Sheila had two Dalmatians in 1939. It is strange that neither Larig nor Morlich is mentioned at all in the war letters.

Larig & Morlich

Both dogs were called after places they had loved. Larig after the great pass through the Cairngorm Mountains, the Larig Grhu, and Morlich after Loch Morlich. Larig ('the pup') seems to have been a puppy in 1934/5 and was a big strong dog in 1936. He was Sheila's dog from before their marriage. Morlich was acquired after their marriage, I think, and there is somewhere a lovely picture of Larig and Morlich sitting in the fold-out 'dicky' seat of their two-seater Crossley with goggles on, noses pointed into the wind.

Larig stayed with Sheila when Alan sailed for France in September 1939 with Morlich. Morlich retreated through Belgium & France with him in 1940. They both rapidly learned that aircraft engines meant German Messerschmitt's & Stukas. On hearing the planes approaching Morlich, along with Alan and the men, headed for the nearest ditch and she piled in with them to avoid machine gun fire and bombs. She could not be taken off the Dunkirk beaches, so Alan's batman took her round the back of a sand dune and shot her.

But I don't know what happened to Larig. He did sometimes stay with Mamie. Was Sheila unable to cope with the chaos plus new baby and had him put down? Even in 1936 he was a difficult dog.

There was another Dalmatian called Matilda, Tidda, or in the letters 'Tilda'. It appears that Tilda lived, at least for some time, in Crawford Lodge, Ardrossan with Aunt Daisy (Margaret Crawford). In January 1944 Sheila says in a letter "Today I found him (Robert) clipping Tilda's whiskers with the big scissors, she lying peacefully asleep the while". On 3rd February 1944 Sheila says in a letter "determined to remain dogless until the end of the war".

In a photograph at the Malt House circa 1941 Sheila is holding a Black Labrador and I remember she told me she had had one. What happened to him or her? Gill suspects it was given away as Sheila found it a stupid dog.

APPENDIX 4

BRIGADIER WIGMORE'S TESTIMONIAL LETTER

10 Dorset House
Gloucester Place
N.W.1

18th July 1947

I have great pleasure in writing a testimonial
for Dr.A.C.Stevenson as I had him as my senior
hygiene officer for some twelve months in the
12th Corps and later for over 18 months in West
Africa where he has a very considerable
experience in preventative medicine, especially
in the control of all varieties of infectious
disease.

He carried out several valuable investigations
and was continuously interested in statistics.

Perhaps if I make a copy of the remarks I made
when I forwarded Stevenson's name for an award
of an OBE it may emphasise the fact that my
opinion of the officer is a very high one.

"This officer has shown marked energy and
initiative in any task he has been asked to take
up. He is always ready to accept all
responsibility for his actions, and is, in fact,
one of the most reliable and loyal officers I
have met during over 30 year service."

It is with confidence, therefore, that I
recommend him to the Senate of Queen's
University for the appointment to the Chair of
Social & Preventative Medicine in Queen's
University, Belfast.
    JBA Wigmore. M.D., D.T.M. & H.

APPENDIX 5

THE MACLENNAN FAMILY

The MacLennan family, as I knew them as a child, lived on Blairbuie Farm, close to Reiff in Ross & Cromarty, Scotland, not far from Achiltibuie. I played with their boys although, as I recollect it, the boys spoke Gaelic much of the time.

The Kenny (Kenneth) MacLennan, who Alan and Sheila knew, I shall refer to as Old Kenny to distinguish him from his eldest son who I refer to as young Kenny. Young Kenny is still there, crofting and running sheep over the adjacent land. Old Kenny's daughter, Christine Mullin, lives at Rieff.

Alan and Sheila were much closer to them than I had realised. Lannie was young Kenny's aunt, his father's sister, and appears in the letters helping out, as does her half sister Ina.

Old Kenny helped a lot with the croft at Camusglashlan. I remember him bringing bricks around by boat which he unloaded in Camusglashlan Bay, and appearing over the hill with others when the light was failing, carrying a metal framed double bed.

He was called up for the Army and at one stage was stationed at Catterick Camp in North Yorkshire. He suffered various ailments away from Blairbuie and never went abroad.

APPENDIX 6

REIFF AND CAMUSGLASHLAN

In August 1943 Alan noted in his diary "your mother and I have our dream house at Camusglashlan". Sheila and Alan both knew Ross & Cromarty in north-west Scotland well. Sheila had spent many holidays there with her parents, often at the Achiltibuie Hotel, before she got married (I plan to print the the1936 Letters which cover this period in 2017). She and Alan had camped, walked and climbed in the area. Reiff was reached by a dead-end single track dirt road from Achiltibuie. About ½ mile beyond the road end was a ruined croft marked on Ordnance Survey as 'Camas a' Ghlais lean' which they called Camusglashlan. Since 1936 they had dreamed of building up the croft and having a boat there.

I remember Sheila staggering back & forth between Camusglashlan & Rieff holding one end of a heavy wooden 'stretcher' with cement on it, or at the end of metal roof beams. During this rebuilding, in 1946 or 1947, I think, we all moved into an abandoned army Nissen Hut at Reiff, long since replaced by a holiday house. There was a tiny partitioned section at one end, the rest being an open storage area, in which we camped. No electricity or water of course.

Abandoned Nissen huts showing an interior

The following picture shows Camusglashlan before it was roofed. It never did get running water, electricity or a flush toilet.

Camusglashlan before work started

Camusglashlan 2010. Still used by the family for holidays

Appendix 7

AIR MAIL CARDS

Communication with Africa was slow. An ordinary 'Surface Mail' letter often took three weeks. An Air Mail card could take only a few days. However, the only address that Sheila had was G.HQ in Accra, which was also the only place from which Alan could collect and post letters. Consequently, Alan would arrive back from his travels to GHQ Accra (actually the suburb of Achimoto) to find multiple letters waiting for him. Then he could post the multiple letters he'd written in the jungle in one batch.

Air Mail cards were favourite, although the supply was rationed. There was not much room to write on them and Alan's awful scrawl took up a lot of space, twice as much as Sheila's neater writing, so it often became smaller and even more difficult to read as he approached the end. The reader will see many examples of cards marked 1, 2, and 3, written as one letter.

Appendix 8

BOMBS AND OTHER PERSONAL RECOLLECTIONS

66 Manygates Lane, Wakefield. Our rented semi-detached house

Like many others, I remember the bombers. Wakefield was lucky and not generally a target, but there were raids in August, September and December 1940 and six people were killed in March 1941. Certainly bombers coming over the North Sea on their way to Manchester passed over Wakefield, so we heard them quite a lot. We were alerted by the air raid warning sirens which gave out an up and down wailing note. At first we would go into the cupboard under the stairs. This was much like any cupboard under the stairs and had a triangular-shaped entrance. We squashed ourselves in, the theory being that it was the safest place. The first thing we did when the sirens wailed was to check that the curtains were drawn because flying glass was known to be a big hazard with a near miss.

All the windows of course were covered by heavy curtains or

black paper at night. There were severe penalties for allowing light to escape as it would indicate to enemy bomber pilots where the cities were. We would shut all the doors and creep into the cupboard. There we waited until the all-clear, which was just a steady tone; then you came out and carried on. Experience proved this was not such a good idea as people suffocated when trapped in the cupboard under debris if the house came down. It was then decided that you were best off sitting on the top landing with all the doors shut and all the curtains drawn. There was much less to fall on you. So we took to doing that.

My only personal recollection of the bombing is a particular incident which, for some reason, is crystal clear in my mind. We were sitting on the top landing and I now know it was on Christmas Eve, 1944, so I was 4½ (Letter 4th March 1945).

There we were, Sheila, David and myself, sitting on the top landing in the dark and we could hear the planes going over. At least I thought they were planes. David was crying and making a lot of noise. I became panicky as I thought the pilots would hear David and drop bombs on us. Sheila, presumably to reassure me and stop me strangling David, told me that they were not planes with pilots but flying bombs without pilots so there was nobody to hear David. This presumably did reassure me although I can't believe I was much happier! But I suppose it gave me something to think about.

The V1 Flying Bomb (nicknamed the Doodlebug), had a pulse jet engine which made a very distinctive stuttering sound and was easily distinguishable from the normal bomber. It also left a long burning tail of flame, easily seen at night. Most V1s felon London, fired from Launching sites across the channel in Belgium and France. It had not the range to reach Wakefield so in later years I wondered if I had imagined it all.

But it was true. The Germans had launched an amazing raid with 45 Heinkel HE-111 bombers across the North Sea and each carried a V1 Flying Bomb under its wing. Reaching the North Sea coast, they launched the 45 bombs towards Manchester of which 31 reached their target and 15 fell along the way on other towns or in

Flying Bomb: Official Picture

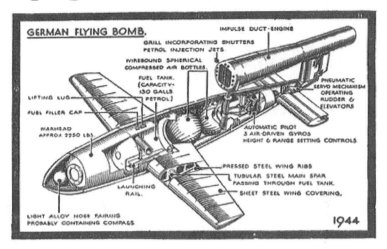

GERMAN FLYING BOMB.

IMPULSE DUCT-ENGINE

GRILL INCORPORATING SHUTTERS
PETROL INJECTION JETS.

WIRESOUND SPHERICAL
COMPRESSED AIR BOTTLES.

FUEL TANK.
(CAPACITY-
130 GALLS.
PETROL)

PNEUMATIC
SERVO MECHANISM
OPERATING
RUDDER &
ELEVATORS

LIFTING LUG

FUEL FILLER CAP

WARHEAD
APPROX 2250 LBS.

AUTOMATIC PILOT
3 AIR-DRIVEN GYROS
HEIGHT & RANGE SETTING CONTROLS

PRESSED STEEL WING RIBS
TUBULAR STEEL MAIN SPAR
PASSING THROUGH FUEL TANK.
SHEET STEEL WING COVERING.

LAUNCHING
RAIL.

LIGHT ALLOY NOSE FAIRING
PROBABLY CONTAINING COMPASS

1944

the countryside. 43 people were killed, many were injured badly and a lot of houses were destroyed.

The bombs would have passed over Wakefield from their launching point off the east coast of England on their way to Manchester. Sheila would have had no way of knowing at the time that it was a desperate last effort by the Germans. She didn't mention this to Alan in Africa for months in case it worried him.

The Cat on the Roof

Coming back from Dunkirk, Alan had brought with him a small Browning automatic pistol, .30 calibre, I think, and given it to Sheila. He instructed her how to use it and got her to fire a few shots so that she could defend herself against German paratroopers who were widely expected to land in the dark. One night there was a crash and scrambling on the roof. Sheila leapt out of bed, grabbed the pistol, and prowled around the house, peering up at the roof so she could shoot. But in the end it turned out it was only a cat which had missed its footing, tumbling down the roof and dislodging tiles. When I was a bit older and she told me about this I was rather disappointed. It would have been nice to have had a Mum who had shot a German, I thought.

Train Journeys

Sheila remembered well the very slow railway journeys (troop trains got priority) in dirty unheated trains where she would meet other displaced wives. One, she recollected, had a hot water bottle, an old stone one, I think, with brandy in it which they shared. Stone hot water bottles were  normal then (no central heating) and when filled with boiling water burnt your feet so usually had a knitted cover, or were wrapped in a towel. Rubber hot water bottles existed but were inclined to burst. You can still buy stone ones!

Machine Gun Attack

I remember Sheila telling me how once she was pushing the pram with David in it. She would walk up Manygates Lane, round the far side of the field behind the house to the old ruined Wakefield Castle and back to the house along the other side. The walk is still there, nothing has changed. This time as she got to the castle a German plane flew low overhead machine-gun blazing. It seemed to her a personal attack, but later she realised it was aiming at the searchlight position on the castle hill. She recounted running back to the house as fast as she could go with the pram bouncing along in front of her.

Alan Comes Home

In 1945 Germany surrendered. Alan came back from the war, landing in June at Hurn Airport, Bournemouth. I was used to the fact that 'Daddy' was somewhere in the background, but I had last seen him in October 1943 aged 4 years & 4 months, and during those first 4 years I had only seen him intermittently when he got leave. It was Sheila that we relied on. Now I was 6. David had no memory of him at all, being only 3.

He arrived in the middle of the night. We were woken up by this tall sunburned man, neither of us knowing at first who he was. The table between our beds was covered in presents, practically all carved wood, elephants, African figures and a marvelous canoe. It was obvious that our Mum knew this man. I was happy with this, delighted with the presents and soon grasped that he was my Daddy. David on the other hand wouldn't come out from under the bed-clothes and cried for ages, desperately alarmed at this new strange man intruding into our little world.

APPENDIX 9

The Boat

Sometime in 1941 Alan had bought a lifeboat in Scotland in the Achiltibuie area. It was a 26-foot open boat clinker built, designed to be rowed, and had been found washed up on the shore by a local man. Alan fitted it with a marinised Ford engine and kept it at anchor in Camusglashlan Bay or sometimes in Old Dorney Harbour. When we were not there it was beached in Rieff Loch, pulled through the entrance channel at a spring tide by willing helpers.

We had many adventures in it. It never got a name, just 'The Lifeboat'. We cruised widely in the Summer Isles, watching basking sharks and catching fish.

From what wrecked ship this boat had come we never discovered. There were no markings. General opinion was that it was Norwegian, but no evidence supports this.

In the above picture, taken around 2002, it is abandoned and rotting on the shore at Badentarbert near Achiltibuie. The engine, propeller and bilge pump have gone. Not long afterwards a great storm broke and scattered its timbers.

Printed by: Copytech (UK) Limited trading as Printondemand-worldwide,
9 Culley Court, Bakewell Road, Orton Southgate,
Peterborough, PE2 6XD